Rer

Renaissance Wisdom

How to Flourish in the Modern Day

Shane Sorensen

ISBN: 978-1-905633-33-3 (sc); 978-1-905633-34-0 (hc)

Printed and bound in the United States.

Contents

Introduction

Every epoch in mankind's history is defined by an idea. This book's aim is to identify a set of ideas and philosophies that sparked one of the greatest revolutions of human thought – the Renaissance. Perhaps more than anything else, the Renaissance was the rebirth of the classical world and of the individual; a new paradigm of the malleable and cultivated self-produced countless works of genius (across multiple disciplines), technological and political advances, economic flourishing, and a new emphasis on knowledge as a source of betterment for all humankind.

We'll spend some time galavanting through history to discover timeless principles that lead to a flourishing of art, architecture, philosophy, politics, and human accomplishment. Renaissance men like Giovanni Manetti, Leon Battista Alberti, Michel De Montaigne, Raphael, Galileo, Michelangelo, Shakespeare, Niccolò Machiavelli, Da Vinci, and a whole other host of great thinkers, from all fields of knowledge, were all products of this great time period called the Renaissance. These same ideas that helped produce polymaths like Da Vinci or Michelangelo are still accessible to us today in the modern world; this book will seek to revive these ideas so that anyone can apply them to their own life.

Despite the lore of the Renaissance, and much like today, the world faced many challenges. In the mid-1350s the black death (the plague) is estimated to have wiped out somewhere around 50% of the population of most of

Europe. Loved ones were lost, businesses and families were devastated, and entire bloodlines vanished into the mass graves and were lost to history. In Florence, the death was so widespread that decaying bodies literally lined the streets, and peasants, certain of their own impending doom, spent the little money that they had on lavish feasts of decadence.

City states and kingdoms saw multiple clashes, wars, and rebellions leading up to, and during, the Renaissance, so while populations were ravaged by famine and pestilence there were still wars to fight and the ever-present and ever-looming insecurity that comes from never feeling completely safe – even within your city walls. Peasants frequently revolted against aristocratic overlords and monarchs; civil wars ripped countries apart time and again; and let us not forget the ever-oppressive, ever-watchful eye of the Church. The Church was so oppressive to human thought that the years before the Renaissance are frequently referred to as the dark ages.

Why is any of this important today? Many great periods of crisis, oppression, and trial throughout our history have led us directly into equally vibrant and positively transformative periods. This duality of life – the cycles of life and death, and the periods of boom and bust – are almost always what leads to positive change as a society. Many times, the hardest times and the greatest pains lead to the greatest peaks of human potential. In the words of one my favorite philosophers, Friedrich Nietzsche: "To those human beings who are of any concern to me I wish suffering, desolation, sickness, ill-treatment, indignities – I wish that they should not remain unfamiliar with profound self-contempt, the torture of self-mistrust, the wretchedness of the vanquished: I have no pity for them, because I wish them the only thing that can prove today whether one is worth anything or not – that one endures."

The moral is this: if at any point during the reading of this book, you find yourself thinking, "Sure that must have been great back then, but there are just too many problems in today's day and age for something like the Renaissance to ever happen again", well that is precisely why it *is* possible. Every time period faces its own unique challenges; it is our collective choice to determine whether the trials of today will defeat or define us, immobilize or inspire us, turn us into ash or reforge us stronger from the flames.

Before we begin to discuss the Renaissance itself, though, it seems prudent to address what might be an elephant you find standing in the room at some point during the reading of this book; this book aims to dissect a very specific time period and people (specifically the city of Florence between the years of 1350 and 1500). In these years diversity was quite limited and, aside from the newly opened trade with the east, there was little connection of any of the men profiled in this work to any place in the world outside of Italy – and even fewer with connections to parts of the world outside of Europe. Philosophy shares a long tradition of heritage with many other cultures and places throughout the world. The pre-Socratic philosophers, Pythagoras, and Plato are just a few examples of philosophers from the ancient Greek world who probably learned from teachers in Egypt at some point within their lifetimes. Similarly great wisdom can be found in *many* cultures and time frames throughout the world; the author here has simply chosen to profile one special place in time to uncover its wisdom for the reader. Religion and culture from different parts of the world should not be seen as conflicting with the philosophical tradition found in this book and, in fact, are many times compatible with thinking to be found in many other places in the world. It is important to note also that many of the works of Plato and Aristotle (among other philosophers) that were able to survive during the Middle Ages were carried forward by Islamic wise men – this tradition of study directly preserved and carried on ancient wisdom back into the West during the years leading up to the Renaissance. Though this book focuses on the progression of the Western mind and its development during the Renaissance period, we should not limit ourselves as human beings to only one way of viewing the world in which we live. The powerful wisdom in this book can help transform the life of anyone who practices and applies its lessons, even someone from outside of the Western tradition.

The word "Renaissance" comes from the French word for rebirth. The people of the Renaissance, especially those of the Humanist movement, worked hard to revive ancient wisdom from Greece and Rome and used what they learned to revive their own society. Humanism focused on the importance and potential of the individual. The Humanists immersed themselves in the words of the great minds that came before them, and they sought to share that same wisdom with others. Any study of the Renaissance must include Humanism, because its focus on the potential of human beings puts humankind back in control of its own destiny. Humanism puts the power into the hands of the individual, it puts *you* in charge of *your* life, and it instills a belief in yourself. Simply put, if you don't believe in the power of the individual, and if you don't believe that you can or should make progress in your own life, then you probably won't ever accomplish much; the real danger is that if enough individuals don't believe in the power and potential of themselves then the entire system can crumble.

The overwhelming sense of apathy that comes from feeling helpless, small, and powerless is one of the largest threats to today's world. Groupthink, mediocrity, and moral decay can run rampant when the individual withers and dies. Talking heads, corporations, politicians, and dictators become our saviors when our own personal drives, desires, and virtues fail to spur us into action. Life loses all meaning and we seek out only immediate satisfaction, entertainment, and distraction when we don't define a meaning for ourselves. The ancient world, and the world of the Renaissance, put self-cultivation at the forefront of their cultures, it was strongly believed that one had a responsibility and a duty to better oneself. The Delphic maxim inscribed at the Temple of Delphi told Greek citizens to "know thyself", this call to improve oneself and to continuously seek virtue was deeply ingrained into the cultures of the ancient world.

In a new world where we no longer recognize the sovereignty and power of the self, where we focus more on the clothes on our bodies than we do on the thoughts in our minds, it is no wonder so many of us feel lost, helpless, and incomplete. Look around at today's day and age: celebrity idols and political actors take center stage and vie for our attention; corporations, social media entities, tv shows, sporting events, movies, politicians, and advertisers spend billions of dollars to influence the masses; people are encouraged to compete with their neighbors and consume more than others around them; shiny objects and technology constantly call to us to upgrade and once again join elite status. When the individual is weak, when one's own self-directed will becomes diminished or weak, when enough people choose comfort instead of seeking challenge and thinking for oneself, society becomes a walking mob of mindless consumers, i.e., the rabble. The mob is born when people are no longer strong enough (or wise enough) to think for themselves; when the individual dies, freedom of thought is stifled.

One of the most important components of Renaissance era Humanism was its emphasis on every individual's potential and well-being. For example, Italian architects focused on creating beauty not just in castles and countryside estates, but in city centers where peasants and traders gathered. Humanists sought to recover the lost wisdom of the ancients so that they could create a more enlightened, more eloquent, more moral, and more successful society. Republicanism was reborn as more people than ever became part of the political decisions of Florence and Venice. Leaders sought a fairer form of taxes and created social programs that were designed to help its citizens (and therefore the State) to flourish. Because the success experienced during the Renaissance was able to benefit a higher proportion of the population, the change was even more widespread and powerful. Meaningful movements are not often made up of a mob with pitchforks, they are made of a group of free-thinking and strong individuals united for a common cause.

Humanism focused on logic and rationality, it impowered the individual, and it led both directly and indirectly to the study and revival of ancient Greek and Roman philosophy, architecture, and art; It led the people of the late 1300s out of the depths of despair, and helped them rebuild a more beautiful, more democratic, and more enlightened world. Although it might have been the spark that started the transformation, Humanism wasn't the only transformative idea of the Renaissance. From the rebirth of ancient Greek and Roman culture sprung forth an abundance of ideas and thoughts that took root in the fertile minds of Humanist thinkers.

Aristotelianism, Stoicism, Platonism, and early forms of Empiricism all contributed to a mass social movement that transformed the Western world forever. We will expand on all these ideas and philosophies more in the coming chapters. The Renaissance was a very complex time, and the number of topics that could be covered could lead one to write hundreds of books; philosophy alone, one of my strongest loves in life, is a rabbit hole that one could easily climb down into, and emerge from only after many thousands of scattered pages had been written and read on the subject. The Renaissance is incredibly rich with history, and was not exclusive to Italy, However, in order to make a work as practical as possible, I have focused my efforts mainly on the city and people of Florence. No other city would experience such a profound blooming of the Renaissance spirit that was present in Florence between the mid-1350s through the end of the 1400s.

My intention with this book is to pick out some key ideas that made the Renaissance such a magical time, distill them down to their essence, and pass them on to a new epoch. We will discuss in more detail the history of the Renaissance and the characters of Florence that helped the culture of the Renaissance to flourish. We will study the Humanist movement, the revival of Plato's philosophy, and how Stoicism impacted the thinkers of the Renaissance. We will consider the effect of the ever-present threat of death and look at how an emphasis on personal growth fed the lore of the Renaissance and created the famed "Renaissance man" or polymath. Our study will be focused on how we can extract wisdom from these ideas and apply them to our lives today, all with the goal of reawakening the potential within us to create our own modern-day rebirth.

This book is not intended to be an academic treatise, but I have done my very best to research each topic and character presented here so that I can present an accurate portrayal of events. My hope is that these ideas will help transform your life and cause a rebirth of yourself. The

Renaissance was not born from revolution; it began with a few private and studious men who sought out wisdom from an ancient age in seclusion, and then through their own personal Renaissance they began to impart what they had learned and encourage the same study in others around them. These men were not fans of speculative philosophy, but instead sought practical wisdom that they could apply to their lives. While I appreciate the philosophy of thinkers like Hume or Kant, I have always had a special affinity for the philosophers who lived and died by their philosophies (Socrates, Cicero, and Seneca being just a few examples who literally died in the same fashion that they lived). Many of the philosophies and ideas that transformed the people of the Renaissance did so because they were practical – they were concerned with making people better. Epictetus told us, "Do not explain your philosophy, embody it."

I look around at the world as it is: people held back by their limiting beliefs, people seeking happiness at the bottom of a liquor bottle or behind the screen of a phone, society a thriving mass of consumers racing to choke down one more sandwich or buy the newest piece of tech. And it makes me sad, especially when I believe so much in the power of the individual. Until people take the reins and take responsibility for their own lives and philosophies, their thoughts and philosophies will continue to be built haphazardly by advertisers, authority figures, and mass media – in short, they will become another body in the mob. Philosophy can truly set you free, but only if you will focus your attention on the accumulation of wisdom and on challenging your own beliefs.

There was an ancient philosopher named Diogenes who used to be a sight of bewilderment to the people of Greece. He lived in a large ceramic jar on the streets, engaged in lewd behavior, and made poverty into a virtue (even going so far as to embrace the nickname that people game him, "the dog"). There is an old story of Alexander the Great as a young man coming to see Diogenes as he sat outside on a sunny day. Alexander was a young man but had just inherited a kingdom and a powerful army. He could have had anything that he desired, and, in fact, later he would nearly conquer all the known world. As Alexander met the mythical Diogenes he was impressed and offered that he would provide Diogenes with anything that he desired. Diogenes responded by asking Alexander to simply, "stop blocking his sun". There was nothing that Alexander (the man with "everything") could provide to Diogenes, because through philosophy Diogenes had already gained everything that he needed in the world.

Philosophy can truly set you free and, once you have conquered yourself, you are truly free to do anything in life. Philosophy is the key to a better world, that is filled with better and more free-thinking individuals. I hope to share with you this passion for philosophy; I hope to give you new excitement and energy; I hope that, through *you*, the world can become a more beautiful place. Let the wisdom of the Renaissance inspire you as it has inspired me. This book was written for the individual. This book of wisdom was written for you.

> "As a human being, you have no choice about the fact that you need a philosophy. Your only choice is whether you define your philosophy by a conscious, rational, disciplined process of thought and scrupulously logical deliberation – or let your subconscious accumulate a junk heap of unwarranted conclusions, false generalizations, undefined contradictions, undigested slogans, unidentified wishes, doubts and fears, thrown together by chance, but integrated by your subconscious into a kind of mongrel philosophy and

fused into a single, solid weight: self-doubt, like a ball and chain in the place where your mind's wings should have grown"

(Ayn Rand, *Philosophy: Who Needs It*)

Part I

A brief history of the Renaissance

"History is truly the witness of times past, the light of truth, the life of memory, the teacher of life, the messenger of antiquity"

(Cicero)

Chapter 1

The dark ages meet the first shimmer of Petrarch's light

In the year 1304 Petrarch was born in exile. This young boy would grow into the genius that led a powerful wave of change that we now call the Humanist movement. The Humanist movement, largely an extension of the ideas formed and crafted by Petrarch, came to be perhaps the most influential component of the Renaissance psyche that shaped our modern world. For this reason, Petrarch is considered by many to be the Father of the Renaissance. The Humanist movement is much like the Renaissance itself, hard to define and put into a box, but it did have some defining characteristics. The Humanists were lovers of antiquity and sought to revive ancient Roman and Greek ideas and writings, they adored the beauty of Latin and thought it was the ideal language to communicate ideas, and they believed that human life was meant to be embraced through learning and cultivation in one's own lifetime.

While it can be hard to pinpoint an exact beginning or end to the Renaissance (even historians disagree on this matter) Petrarch is a good starting point because of his focus on the revival of antiquity, because of his focus on self-knowledge and self-awareness, and because of his beliefs about humankind and our place in the universe. But, before we can begin to understand the true significance of Petrarch and of the Renaissance movement that followed him, we must first understand the context of the life that he was born into. For this, we must go back even further into the past. The largest empire in the world (Rome) had already been crumbling for many years and in 476CE the final Roman emperor Romulus Augustulus was overthrown. The Empire of Rome and its nearly 1000-year reign had finally come to an end.

Rome had been, at least for the citizens of Rome, a source of stability and peace throughout the world. As one large self-governed body, the Roman Empire was able to provide a vast structure that supported society in multiple ways. Roman roads connected most of the known world, allowing citizens to travel and goods to be brought throughout the land. This made trade and commerce rich and profitable. Additionally, the sheer power and reach of Rome provided a level of security to its citizens that would disappear soon after its collapse. For example, welfare programs provided food to Roman citizens but, as the citizenry became comfortable and grew fat off bread and circus, they also grew uninterested in the defense of Rome through military service (this is one of the contributing factors of Rome's downfall). Even as Rome ran out of enemies and its populace grew complacent, many probably felt Rome was untouchable and that peace would reign forever. People were fed, the empire and the spoils of trade were vast, human achievement and thought, it seemed, had reached a new pinnacle.

Towards the end of the Roman Empire though, as average citizens and elites enjoyed the fruits of Rome, it seems that the education of its citizens also began to decline. The citizenry had fully embraced the lavish lifestyle provided by the benefits of ruling the world; hedonism and luxury had begun to replace a personal desire for virtue or self-cultivation in the upper classes, and in the lower and middle classes a new religion made up of the followers of Christ had begun to reject the remnants of the culture of Ancient Rome and Greece still left in society. In the early 4th century Rome had 28 public libraries for its citizens, but by the end of the century Ammianus Marcellinus (a Roman soldier and historian) complained that the Roman citizens had all but abandoned reading and education. He tells us: "In place of the philosopher the singer is called in, and in place of the orator the teacher of stagecraft, and while the libraries are shut up forever like tombs, water organs are manufactured and lyres as large as carriages."

However, as economic and social problems began to take hold, and as the Germanic tribes fought back against Rome's seamlessly unending expansion, cracks began to appear on the surface of Rome's impenetrable exterior. Slave labor became scarcer as the empire ran out of new territory to acquire. The vast networks of roads became harder and more expensive to maintain. The mouths of citizens demanding to be fed began to drain empire stockpiles of wealth. Disloyal mercenaries were called in for Rome's defense, and even sometimes switched sides in the middle of battle. When Rome did finally reach its breaking point in 476CE, society as it was in the days of the empire completely crumbled with it.

Feudalism began to reign supreme over the land. Landowners swore loyalty to distant kings and would often vie for power with other landowners, and with the bands of thugs and barbarians that pillaged throughout country sides. Many people in desperate positions were forced to work as serfs for lords in exchange for basic protection and food to eat. Without the strong central command and government of the Roman Empire, people were forced to work much harder simply to have basic needs met. When one must spend the entirety of one's day just on food, shelter, and basic security, they have less time to think about philosophy or to enjoy the fruits of a higher education. When the decadent society of Rome broke down, and as people were forced into more dire positions, luxuries like books or education fell by the wayside. Most people simply spent their time working for food to eat and a modest place to call home. The cultivation of the human mind that was able to flourish in the glory years of Rome began to die out rapidly. Tutors and scholars went out of work, schools closed, and reading rates dropped. All the while "barbarians" ran free throughout the land.

Another factor that contributed to the decay of human education and advancement was a church that grew increasingly powerful in the vacuum created by the demise of the Roman Empire. Without powerful secular governments, the Church began to creep into public affairs, often vying for power and scheming amongst the other city states and kings of Europe. Despite the split of power between the Holy Roman Emperor and the Catholic Church that occurred starting in 800 and that culminated in a full break-up of the Church in 1054, the Church held great power and influence throughout the Middle Ages. As Church doctrine and dogma spread, what little knowledge of the greats of antiquity that had survived was often stamped out and called heresy.

The prevailing mindset of the Middle Ages, therefore, became very aligned with Church thought and doctrine. This mindset of the day was incredibly oppressive to human thought and knowledge, so much so that Petrarch later coined the term "dark ages" to describe the time that existed between the fall of Rome and his current age, he tells us: "Amidst the errors there shone forth men of genius; no less keen were their eyes, although they were surrounded by darkness and dense gloom."

Petrarch was perhaps the first great thinker of the Middle Ages to directly question the typical Church opinion that secular achievement and learning was akin to a spiritual darkness, although a case can be made that Dante paved the way for this to happen in his *Divine Comedy*. Petrarch believed that through the "dark ages" the light of secular learning had been extinguished; this is what he sought to revive: the wisdom of the ancients. Petrarch, born in 1304, believed that history could be divided up into the age of light, the ancient days of Greece and Rome, and the years of darkness, which he currently lived in. However, he believed that a new age of light lay just over the horizon, perhaps already shining in the distance. He later wrote:

> "My fate is to live among varied and confusing storms. But for you perhaps, if as I hope and wish you will live long after me, there will follow a better age. This sleep of forgetfulness will not last forever. When the darkness has been dispersed, our descendants can come again in the former pure radiance."

Petrarch believed strongly that once the oppressive darkness of the current age had been lifted, the wisdom of the past could again begin to shine. Fortunately, even though the Church had all but extinguished the spark of secular thought and achievement that had flourished during the years of ancient Greece and Rome, there was one hidden blessing amongst the Church-sponsored "dark ages": the monasteries of Europe that inadvertently preserved much of the wisdom of the ancient world's greatest minds.

Within the monasteries a seemingly banal and yet critical habit had helped preserve a host of texts that the Church would have probably rather had destroyed.

Monks engaged daily in menial tasks in order to cultivate discipline and keep them humble. One such activity happened to be the copying of manuscripts. Monks throughout Europe's monasteries directly preserved many texts through their many hours of text copying: Epictetus, Lucretius, Quintilian, and works by Cicero and Seneca are just a few of the many texts that these monks likely saved from extinction through their mindless hours of copying pagan scripts. Though these monks would have paid little attention to the meaning of the words that they copied, these many hours over a lifetime of writing were crucial in maintaining our slowly dwindling connection with the ancient worlds of Rome and Greece. Many other works – texts by Plato or Plotinus for example – may have been lost in the West, but Byzantine scholars in the East also played their part in preserving the thoughts and traditions of the ancient world.

Petrarch began a new tradition that later evolved into a large part of the Humanist movement. He sought out these lost texts and uncovered and translated several letters (the letters to Atticus) from one of his own heroes, a Roman statesman and philosopher named Cicero. In the case of Cicero, however, the reality of Cicero's life disappointed Petrarch; so much so in fact that Petrarch penned a letter to Cicero criticizing him for his activity in politics and in the affairs of the state. He explained to Cicero that this activity in the affairs of the state was a blemish on an otherwise pristine legacy. Up until Petrarch's discovery of these letters, his vision of Cicero was one of a quiet life of solitude and philosophy. But the letters that he discovered revealed him to be an actor in the politics of Rome, playing a big role in the affairs of governance. This critical letter that Petrarch wrote to Cicero was not the only meaningful work that Petrarch penned during his lifetime. Between the years 1345 and

1360 he also wrote letters to many other thinkers long since dead. Seneca received a reprimand not unlike the one that Cicero received (but Petrarch declared that Seneca was in fact an incomparable teacher of moral philosophy), and Homer received the most flattering of praise despite his preoccupation with the Greek gods.

In Petrarch's letter to Homer he laments his inability to read Greek and speaks excitedly of the day that the translation of Homer into Latin (the language familiar to Petrarch) would be complete. Greek was a language that had become somewhat of a dead language in the West during the Middle Ages. While Greek was still widely spoken and read in the Byzantine Empire of the East, it would be many decades before men proficient in Greek would become a mainstay in Florence. There is an old story told about Petrarch: he took his Greek copy of Homer that was given to him as a gift by Giovanni Boccaccio and he pressed it into his forehead and began to cry simply because of his pent-up desire to read Homer's works that were inaccessible to him. Petrarch, in his letter to Homer writes:

> "As for myself, although I may not be worthy to host such a guest, yet I have you at home in Greek, and I hope soon, if that Thessalian Greek of whom I have spoken completes what he has begun, to have you whole in Latin. Know, too, that to offer you a more private refuge, most lovingly and reverently I have prepared for you a special domicile in the core of my soul. In sum: my love for you is brighter and hotter than the sun, my esteem for you so great that it could not be greater."

Petrarch also makes a direct reference to the unforgiving nature of the masses, still blinded and brainwashed by Church doctrine to condemn the ancients:

> "This is all I have been able to offer thee, leader and father. Any attempt to free thee from the scorn of the rabble would result in detracting from thy singular and peculiar praise. Moreover, it is a task beyond my powers and those of any other, except perhaps of that man who will have sufficient strength to curb the passions of the mob. And although God has such power, He has not exerted it in the past, nor do I think He is likely to do so hereafter."

Petrarch was an avid reader of ancient books, so much so that in his letter to Augustine he describes his love of books as a spiritual sickness. As a voracious reader, and as a writer of letters to dead men, Petrarch ended up growing quite skilled in rhetoric and poetry as well. As an admirer of the ancient world, he modeled his writing and words after the great writers of the ancient world (men like Cicero, Seneca, and Quintilian). He tells us in a letter to his close friend Giovanni Boccaccio:

> "The ancient authors have become so absorbed into my being and implanted not only in my memory but in the marrow of my bones and have become one with my mind so that even if I were never to read them again in my life, they would inhere with me with their roots sunk in the depths of my soul."

Petrarch became so proficient at the use of words that he was eventually crowned Poet Laureate in 1341 in Rome. This was an honor that had not been bestowed on anyone else since the days of the ancient world. At the ceremony he delivered a speech, his "Coronation Oration", where he yearned again for the days of the ancient world and its boundless wisdom to return to Italy.

> "There was a time, there was an age, that was happier for poets, an age when they were held in the highest honor, first in Greece and then in Italy, and especially

> when Caesar Augustus held imperial sway, under whom there flourished excellent poets: Virgil, Varius, Ovid, Horace, and many others."

Petrarch shows us again and again in his works that he felt himself a man trapped in between two worlds. He was living in the age of darkness where the love of antiquity had been lost, but he did believe that a new age was coming. He sought actively in his life to restore works from great ancient thinkers and writers, and he worked hard throughout his life to revive old traditions and ways of living as well. Petrarch was not content to watch the ancients disappear into obscurity and he dedicated his life to helping them be reborn in his own age. Through his study of Latin, his dedication to the recovery and translation of lost works, and through his public stance on the poignancy of this forgotten ancient wisdom, Petrarch almost single-handedly gathered the kindling that would allow ancient fire to be reborn in the modern age.

Petrarch was highly interested in philosophy, specifically the moral philosophy of men like Cicero and Seneca. Petrarch preferred the moral philosophy of these men because it inspired men to become virtuous themselves. It seems that Petrarch had little appreciation for the Middle Age scholastic method of teaching the logic of Aristotle; it might show what virtue was on paper but didn't inspire men into action. Petrarch was also inspired by what seems to have been his favorite philosopher and theologian, Augustine of Hippo, a Neoplatonist theologian who did much to combine the philosophy of Plato with the teachings of Church doctrine.

In Petrarch's final great work *Letter to Posterity*, a work that was never completed, he wrote an open letter to the reader of a later age. The work is poignant, unique, and completely unlike anything written up until his time. Petrarch's focus on the lost works of antiquity must have led him to realize that history would preserve his works, and he must have known that he was engaged in a very important movement that would be remembered far into the future. The letter, written as a sort of autobiography, shows an incredibly potent self-awareness as Petrarch tells the reader about his humble life and intellect (this may have been a feigned humility). He also notes to the reader that the darkness that had become widespread in his age may have been suffocating, but that he had chosen instead to comb through the catacombs of history searching for ancient wisdom to live by. The illuminating wisdom of a brighter age was his guide for living. Though a master of language Petrarch tells the reader that his life matters much more to him than the words that he left on paper:

> "Among the many subjects that interested me, I dwelt especially upon antiquity, for our own age has always repelled me, so that had it not been for the love of those dear to me, I should have preferred to have been born in any other period than our own. In order to forget my own time, I have constantly striven to place myself in spirit in other ages, and consequently I delighted in history. The conflicting statements troubled me, but when in doubt I accepted what appeared most probable, or yielded to the authority of the writer...If only I have lived well, it matters little to me how I talked. Mere elegance of language can produce at best but an empty renown."

Through Petrarch's works and letters, it became clear that his was a mind that was formed and shaped by the ancient world, and his thoughts and work in return formed the concept of the Humanist movement. He was truly the Father of the Renaissance, even if Dante may have laid the groundwork.

Another important aspect of Petrarch's work was that he was able to start an argument for the fact that though secular works by great men like Cicero or Seneca may not lead one to salvation (only Jesus could do this in Petrarch and the Church's opinion), they could help one to become a better person in life. This was a critical turning point in humankind's view of itself, rather than life being a distraction from the glory of God, Petrarch started to make the case that life was a gift from God that should be cultivated. A person had a divine mission to reach their fullest potential. For years the Church had discouraged the study of ancient texts, not because they were secular and pagan, but because of their beauty and potency; the Church feared that the study of these ancient works would cause people to hold too much love for the world. This was a concern that Petrarch had expressed himself in his work *My Secret Book*.

The Renaissance age was not simply the rebirth of the ancient world, but also the rebirth of the individual and of individual worth and potential. The Renaissance gave power back to the individual to develop themselves, to seek out right action and wisdom, and to craft a legacy for themselves. The Middle Age view of man as a small insignificant part of the collective began to give way to the concept of man as a being created in God's image with the ability to shape their own character and legacy through study and right action. Though Petrarch still wrestled with the idea that perhaps knowledge was a tempting road designed to lead humankind astray, his lifelong obsession with the works of the ancient world certainly seems to indicate that he was able to reconcile any personal conflict of interest.

Petrarch dove into the study of any ancient writer whom he could access. But he tended to gravitate away from philosophy that focused on logical or metaphysical matters, and instead chose to focus on moral philosophy, poetry, and rhetoric, as these could help a person reach their potential and to become a good person in the process. While Petrarch remained a devout Christian throughout his life, even frequently carrying a cherished pocket-sized manuscript of Augustine's *Confessions* on his person, he still believed that secular study and human life had meaning in themselves. He made the first real defense of human achievement and erudition since the brilliance of antiquity had faded away into the past. Petrarch was a firm believer in individualism and believed that, through our lives, we could shape ourselves and our legacies through our studies and actions. His aim was to give power to the individual to again shape one's own destiny. In *My Secret Book* he tells us:

> "How is it you have forgotten all those wise precepts of Philosophy, which declare that no man can be made unhappy by those things you rattle off by name? Now if it is Virtue only that makes the happiness of man, which is demonstrated by Cicero and a whole multitude of weighty reasons, it follows of necessity that nothing is opposed to true happiness except what is also opposed to Virtue. This truth you can yourself call to mind."

The work that Petrarch began, reviving antiquity through a study of ancient poetry, history, rhetoric, and moral philosophy, did not end with Petrarch's death in 1374, but continued to live on through the lives of many of Petrarch's contemporaries and friends. But before the light of the Renaissance movement that Petrarch found buried in the past could truly begin to shine and illuminate Florence, Italy, and the rest of Europe, had to first conquer a series of catastrophes would threaten to drag the world back into darkness.

Disaster strikes: famine, pestilence, and economic hardship

The 1340s were not kind years to the citizens of Florence and the rest of Italy. A series of extreme events happened in unison and led Italy to the brink of collapse. A series of famines, a global banking collapse, and finally a wave of death so intense that the structure of society crumbled all hit Florence between the year 1340 and the year 1350. The first of the unfortunate events was a series of famines that began to batter Italy in 1339. With food supplies cut short, it became increasingly difficult to feed families and citizens. As food shortages spread throughout the region, food prices soared and wages dropped, adding an extra level of pain to the people of the age.

Next, a banking catastrophe wreaked havoc on Florence and the rest of Europe. The banking systems of the day and age were much different than the type of complex systems that we have in place today. There were no regulations, there was no coordinated central action, and there was no financial theory in place for governments to step in at early signs of trouble. So, when the wealthy Florentine banking families ended up holding the bag for the debt run up by England's wars, there was nothing to be done except to fail. To put the size of the default into context, the king of England defaulted on a debt of 1,365,000 florins, at a time when the entire combined yearly income of the city Florence was around 300,000. Such a vast sum was not simply able to be absorbed by lenders and it caused extreme hardship throughout Europe. As the banks faltered and failed it sent shockwaves throughout the region. Private and public deposits were lost, trade ground to a halt (the banks were the main financiers of trade), and governments had difficulty in financing new and existing ventures. The silver lining of the banking collapse was that it created a power vacuum in banking that allowed smaller players to enter the market, one of which was the Medici family (who we will talk about later).

The last of Florence's woes, and by far the worst of all, was the wave of plague (also known as the black death) that swept through Florence in 1348 and decimated its population. Estimates are that somewhere around half of the population of Florence was lost, and some estimates think it could have been as high as 70%. Giovanni Boccaccio (Petrarch's Humanist colleague and fellow writer) reports that when the leaders of Florence heard of the coming spread of the plague, they did their best to prepare the city. They passed orders to have its citizens stay indoors, worked to limit the arrival of travelers, and set rules for hygiene. Yet the plague arrived, and, despite their best efforts, it ravaged the city.

People who were infected with plague typically died within three days of symptom onset, and the disease spread rapidly. Dead bodies littered the streets, but people were too afraid to touch or move them for fear of contracting the disease themselves. And so, the bodies decayed there in public until some desperate peasant could be convinced to move bodies in exchange for a meal. The spread and intensity of the death was so severe that city functions and government meetings collapsed completely, leaving people to simply fend for themselves and pray for their own survival. It is likely that the plague was made even more severe by the fact that food shortages and economic woes had already been harassing Florence for almost ten years.

There was no treatment at the time for plague, and often any attempt to treat or care for a person that was afflicted would lead to the caretaker's death as well. Several accounts of plague by writers of the era can give us a better feeling of what the people of the time experienced. Agnolo di Tura tells us that "it is not possible to describe this horrible thing with human speech...father abandoned child, wife her husband, and one brother the other". Agnolo personally ended up burying all five of his sons before the plague came to an end and said that things seemed so bleak that people believed that the world was ending. Boccaccio tells us: "Were it not for the fact that I am one of the many who saw it with their own eyes, I would scarcely believe it."

With a huge portion of Florence's population wiped out and its populace still reeling from disaster after disaster it was finally ready to enter its golden age. Though death and destruction were widespread, it is thought that these catastrophes caused a type of reset in society, reconcentrating wealth into fewer hands so that society was better equipped to move forward and rebuild. The price of labor soared due to shortages of people able to work causing wages to increase for workers, and this new power placed into the hands of the working class helped to upset the longstanding traditions of serfdom and nobility in power (this would later promote the rise of the merchant class and ultimately would aid in better representation for the lower classes in the government of Florence). It was from the ashes of Florentine Middle Age society that the spark kindled by Petrarch would finally begin to grow into some of the finest years in the West's history. From the darkness of the Middle Ages, and the hopelessness of the 1340s, Florence was the phoenix that would soon rise from the ashes and bring the world into the new era of the Renaissance.

Chapter 2

Florence and antiquity reborn: the early Renaissance years, approx. 1350s–1400

The word Renaissance is the French word for rebirth. We commonly call this period after its French name because the historian who popularized the use of the word was French. However, the Italian version of the word (*Rinascita*) was used by Giorgio Vasari as early as 1550 in his famous work *The lives*. Some make the argument that for the term to be used in 1550 it must have already been widely understood and used in the current age to describe the time period. While we don't know for sure what the Florentines called the age that they lived in, we do know that at least a handful of people of the Humanist movement knew very well that the age they currently lived in was a special one. Petrarch and Leonardo Bruni are just two examples of Humanists who believed in a period of "darkness" in the Middle Ages that was coming to an end in their own age. It was nearly impossible as an Italian not to look back to the glory of the past: ancient Roman ruins still stood in Italy, the Italians still walked on the now crumbling Roman roads, and the Italians believed themselves to be directly descended from Roman antiquity.

The tradition and movement that Petrarch began was carried on by a string of contemporaries that is now known as the Humanist movement. The Humanists earned the name of their movement from their focus on the humanities (*studia humanitatis*). The humanities came to be defined as the study of classical texts in order to learn and perfect grammar, rhetoric, history, poetry, and moral philosophy. While Humanists differed in many areas of life and belief, they were united in these traits – a study of the humanities, and an appreciation for or a love of antiquity. And generally, they held a preference for the use of Latin. Some Humanists preferred Plato, others Aristotle. Some were students of moral philosophy; others were more interested in rhetoric and grammar for civic affairs. Some wrote important additions to philosophy or history; others simply absorbed wisdom from the past. All the Humanists, though, loved wisdom of some sort, and all the Humanists sought to revive the wisdom of the past and transplant it into the modern day. This, more than anything else, is the defining trait of the Renaissance: a love of wisdom (especially from the ancients) and a belief that through study we have the power to refine and improve the human mind and spirit. This was the true break of thought between the Humanist movement and the scholastic movement that preceded it: the Humanists were concerned not with learning philosophy so that they could conjecture and to classify everything in the world that they saw. Rather they sought to study philosophy to gain wisdom and to become better and more effective people.

The philosophy and writing that the Humanists studied and the wisdom that they sought to revive was not limited just to the literary world though. This new emphasis on antiquity spread throughout society, culture, and multiple disciplines. Artists drew inspiration from the rediscovered works of Rome, architects were inspired by the ancient ruins that they saw around them, Republicanism and a revival of Roman law and politics led the day's politics, and Roman and Greek myth and poems became a part of the cultural movement of the Renaissance as well. The Renaissance then was not simply an embracing of the ancient world in philosophy but in all aspects of life. The scholar Frederico Chabod coined the term "energizing myth" to describe Renaissance culture. This embrace of antiquity, and Italians' collective belief in the greatness of their (Roman) history became a self-fulfilling prophecy that defined, inspired, and strengthened the re-emergence of ancient culture and thought. Florentine citizens and Humanists then were not simply part of a movement; they understood the importance of their work, they believed in the power of the past to transform, and they promoted this "energizing myth" in their own lives and actions. The "myth" of Florence was self-fulfilling: the men in power believed in the uniqueness of their city and they worked diligently to manifest their beliefs into reality. Men like Leonardo Bruni and Coluccio Salutati believed that the Republic of Florence was descended from and directly linked to the Republic of Rome, and they sought to revive the once great city within the walls of their own.

Petrarch may have lit the pyre, but the Renaissance and the Humanist movement burned even more intensely after his death in 1374. During his life Petrarch formed relationships with and influenced other prominent men of the early Renaissance period, among them: Poggio Bracciolini (another important book hunter), Giovanni Boccaccio (another prominent Italian poet and politician), and Coluccio Salutati (Chancellor of Florence 1375–1406, and powerful promoter of Humanism and Republicanism). We will examine each of these men in more depth and consider how their teaching and influence set the stage for the full bloom of the Renaissance that occurred later in Florence in the mid-1400s.

Giovanni Boccaccio: writer, Humanist, diplomat

Giovanni Boccaccio (1313–1375) is best known as the author of *The Decameron,* a tale about three men and seven women who escape the death and destruction of the 1348 outbreak of plague in Florence in order to seek the safety and comfort of a country estate. *The Decameron* is considered a literary masterpiece and it is a unique look into the lives of the people living during the period. It also shows the recurring theme that knowledge, wisdom, and learning should be treasured and rewarded (a powerful belief of Petrarch and the Humanist movement that followed him):

> "You must read, you must persevere, you must sit up nights, you must inquire, and exert the utmost power of your mind. If one way does not lead to the desired meaning, take another; if obstacles arise, then still another; until, if your strength holds out, you will find that clear which at first looked dark."

Boccaccio first met Petrarch in 1350 and hosted Petrarch in his own home during Petrarch's stay in Florence. Petrarch was already a well-respected writer at the time, and surely this visit had a lasting impact on Boccaccio's writing and his beliefs. After Petrarch's stay with Boccaccio, they remained friends throughout their lives and wrote each other letters frequently; Boccaccio often referred to Petrarch as his teacher, and Petrarch helped to motivate Boccaccio to begin the study of Greek and Latin literature. Boccaccio was so moved by Petrarch's influence that he later states in his biography: "Indeed I was the one who first, at my own expense, made the books of Homer and of various other Greek authors return to Tuscany."

In fact, it was Boccaccio's effort to have a monk named Leonzio Pilata translate the works of Homer that Petrarch referenced in his fictional letter to Homer. This was the translation that Petrarch had waited for so longingly so that he could finally read the words of the great poet. Boccaccio later went on to write *Genealogia deorum gentilium* (an encyclopedia of sorts that covered the genealogy of the Greek and Roman gods). This work helped to revitalize the growing interest in classical works of Greece and Rome that Petrarch had begun in his lifetime. In Boccaccio's *Genealogica* he takes a firm stance in the defense of poetry and of the works of the ancient world; many in the Church believed poetry was heretical and would lead people to damnation through lies and deceptions, but Boccaccio defended the poets and their use of stories (not lies) as a way for poets to educate others and pass on wisdom, not to mislead. Just as philosophers use syllogisms and thought experiments to educate others, so the poets use stories to instruct. He tells us: "A story is a discourse which under the guise of fiction teaches or demonstrates something true, such that as the reader penetrates below the surface, the intention of the storyteller is revealed."

Boccaccio tells us that poetry came directly from the mind of God; the thoughts and emotions invoked by poetry come from the mind, and our minds come from and are connected directly to the spirit of God. In Boccaccio's opinion poetry was:

> "A venerable branch of knowledge, ripe with promise...it compels the mind to yearn to express itself; it devises strange and novel constructs of the imagination; it arranges these meditations in proper order, adorning what it has composed with a unique patterning of words and sentences, so clothing the truth in a tissue of lovely fictions."

Boccaccio worked as a diplomat to Rome, taught at the Academy of Florence, and frequently traveled throughout

Italy, likely spreading his work and the Humanist ideas of Petrarch further throughout the region. Boccaccio was not just instrumental in promoting and carrying on this new spirit of the Renaissance, but through his works he also assisted Petrarch in making a rational defense for this new type of study against the attacks of the Church, helping to ensure a safe space for the Humanists to continue to unlock the secrets and wisdom of the ancient world.

Coluccio Salutati: Chancellor of Florence, Humanist, writer, book collector

Coluccio Salutati (1331–1406) was perhaps the most important of the Humanists who directly followed Petrarch, not because of his personal contributions to the movement (though these were significant as well), but because he did so much to promote and spread the works of other Humanists that came after him. Salutati was instrumental in creating the next wave of Humanists who would lead Florence and Italy into the full bloom of the Renaissance period. In this way Salutati was the bridge that connected Petrarch's earliest inklings of Humanism to the powerful second wave of Humanism that transformed Florence into the picture of the Renaissance spirit in the 1400s.

Salutati became Chancellor of Florence in 1375 and, as Chancellor, successfully navigated Florence through several dangerous wars and was able to ensure that Florence maintained its republican roots even when faced by threats of destruction from the papacy or the Duke of Milan. Salutati, due to his Humanist beliefs on study and personal cultivation, came also to be known as a great orator and writer. Salutati achieved renown as an eloquent man of letters and was able to so powerfully rally the people of Florence against outside invaders that the Duke of Milan said that just one of Salutati's letters was worth 100 soldiers in the field. The skills he crafted through study of the classics and of the humanities also served him well as Chancellor and made him a successful and largely popular leader. Salutati was, like his friends Petrarch and Boccaccio, a promoter of individualism, and he seemed to believe that Republican Florence was in a unique position to become a modern-day revival of the Roman Republic. In his mind the reproduction of the same republican spirit that once lived in Rome would cause Florence to become the new and improved version of the ancient city: "I have always believed, I must imitate antiquity not simply to reproduce it, but in order to produce something new"

Salutati's love and appreciation for the classics, and for the wisdom of antiquity, was certainly fostered by his relationship and frequent correspondence with Petrarch throughout his life. Salutati was also, like Petrarch, a lover of books and was able to acquire and build an impressive library of ancient and rare manuscripts and letters. Salutati believed, much like Petrarch, that the peak of wisdom and eloquence had been achieved by the ancients and that serious efforts should be made in the modern age to revive the wisdom of men like Cicero, Seneca, Aristotle, and Plato. After his dear friend and mentor Petrarch's death in 1374, Boccaccio was also in poor health, but the next wave of Humanists to come were still too young to take up the torch of enlightenment. Thus, Salutati was instrumental in the movement's survival and growth during this period.

From 1374 (Petrarch's death), and until the next wave of Humanists were ready to take up the torch, Salutati actively worked to encourage the tutorship and education of young minds like Poggio Bracciolini, Niccolo Niccoli, and Leonardo Bruni. With Poggio and Leonardo, Salutati took an active role in their development and, by taking them under his wing, he was able to assist them in their education and provide them with powerful connections that helped them to: increase their knowledge, fund their studies, and further their lives. Salutati believed that through study and personal cultivation, people were able to elevate themselves in life, and some of his direct students and proteges would become some of the greatest men of the Renaissance age.

During Salutati's time as Chancellor he also arranged for the Byzantine scholar Manuel Chrysoloras to come to Florence and teach a course on Greek. This was important as few people in Italy read or spoke Greek at the time, which cut the Humanists and other scholars off from many of the important works of antiquity that survived only in Greek form. Few scholars at the time in the Italian states were able to work with texts outside of the Italian and Latin languages, and this visit from Chrysoloras also happened to be the first introduction of young Humanist Leonardo Bruni to the works of Plato and Aristotle in their original form. This introduction brought about by Salutati would inspire one of the great Humanist minds of the Renaissance (Bruni). Coluccio then, despite his many contributions to the growth and prosperity of Florence during his time of service, is perhaps best known as a bridge between two worlds. At the beginning of his life the light of antiquity just barely shimmered on the horizon. But Salutati would be the bridge that connected the most potent ideas of Florence's first Humanist wave to the even more powerful second wave of Humanism that would be made up directly of many of his students.

Chapter 3

Humanism's second wave: the beginning of Civic Humanism, approx. 1400–1450s

The second wave of the Humanist movement was composed of thinkers like Niccolò Niccoli, Leonardo Bruni, Poggio Bracciolini, and Cosimo de' Medici. These men, raised in Salutati's Florence, would continue the traditions started by Petrarch, Boccaccio, and Salutati, but would also expand on Humanist thoughts and study. Poggio made important discoveries in new texts and expanded the Humanist collection of manuscripts and knowledge, sharing his discoveries with Niccoli and Bruni. Bruni developed important historical records and biographies of great minds like Cicero, expanded the study of the humanities, and would develop new ideas on Civic Humanism. Niccoli would amass a library unrivaled in Florence and provide access to other Humanist minds to his impressive collection. Cosimo de' Medici would provide patronage and stability to the city of Florence and would also encourage the revival of the ancient world in multiple forms.

As the first dawning of light passed down from Petrarch to Salutati and then passed into the hands of men like Leonardo Bruni, the "dark ages" truly began to be washed away by the light of antiquity reborn in their modern day. Bruni built on the thoughts of Petrarch and believed that they lived in an age of darkness and claimed that the new age of light had already begun. The oppressive ideas of the Christian paradigm slowly began to shift during this time period, shifting away from an emphasis on personal meekness and a purposefully uneducated life, in favor of a life of personal achievement and cultivation. The life of civic duty and personal cultivation that was considered a sinful life of vanity during the Middle Ages, to men like Bruni, Poggio, and Cosimo de' Medici, became the new ideal way of living. The Roman Republic seemed to have been reborn in the city of Florence; it was a place, and simultaneously it was the crystallization of the Humanist belief in freedom, republicanism, and the individual. Many believed that Florence could be the new kingdom of man on earth, it could be more than a city; it could become a torch of light that would shine throughout the world.

Bruni told the world in his *History of Florence* that not only was the light of antiquity shining on Florence, but it seemed to have been reborn; it emanated out of the population. In the spirit of the times, the city of Florence was unmatched by any other city in the world. Along with Bruni's assertion that the love of philosophy and wisdom was strong among Florence's people, he also tells us that its population widely read and studied letters and books. Jacob Burkhardt (author of *The Civilization of the Renaissance in Italy)* tells us: "There was then, we are told, nobody in Florence who could not read; even the donkeymen sang the verses of Dante." This new thirst for knowledge that began with the Humanists had spread so widely that even the common citizen was literate.

During this second wave of Humanism, many new ideas were blooming, but Italy and Florence were still recovering from the devastating effects of a banking collapse along with famine and outbreaks of the plague. The power vacuum in the banking industry allowed the

Medici family to claim a meaningful foothold in the financial world, and the Medici would prove vital throughout the Florentine Renaissance by promoting education and the study of Humanist endeavors, while also providing classical educations to some of the greatest artists and architects of the region. The Medici, despite being manipulators of the Republic, seemed to care deeply for their city and took pride in its legacy, promoting the energizing myth that helped to shape the Renaissance epoch.

A source of strife that still existed during this period was the decades' old schism that had formed in the Church between the Byzantine Holy Roman Emperor and the Catholic Pope. This divide had worsened throughout the Middle Ages. But with the new shared enemy of the increasingly powerful Ottoman Empire, and to save the Christian world from destruction, the two divides of the Christian church saw a new need to heal the schism and reunite their efforts against a common enemy. This growing threat and the need for a united rule of the Church led to many Church meetings and councils through the years, one of which (the Council of Florence) ended up being hosted in Florence at the insistence of Cosimo de' Medici.

This Council of Florence brought a caravan of educated men, along with the emperor, and the royal party stayed at the Medici palace during their time in Florence. This provided Cosimo and the Humanists of the period with access to Greek scholars like Gemistus Pletho, who helped to reintroduce Plato to the Western world. The Byzantine scholars present in Florence during the council brought with them knowledge and texts that the Humanists of Florence had no previous access to, creating a new appreciation for and access to the ancient Greek world. Gemistus was invited to give lectures in Florence, and he spoke on the differences between the philosophy of Aristotle and the philosophy of Plato. Gemistus and his teaching influenced the Humanists and opened doors to the study of Plato and inspired Cosimo enough to have him commission Leonardo Bruni to translate the entirety of Plato's works into Latin, and to re-establish the Platonic Academy in Florence.

At the end of this glorious second wave of Humanism a lasting peace was also established throughout Italy. The Treaty of Lodi- and the Italic League that followed- was a formal agreement between the major territories of Italy to both maintain peace between them, and to pledge aid mutually to one another if any of the states should ever be attacked. This peace lasted almost uninterrupted until the 1490s when France began to set its sights on expansion into the Italian territories.

During this second wave of Humanism newly rediscovered works were uncovered and translated, Civic Humanism blossomed (including patronage of the arts and learning), the *studia humanitatis* was more clearly defined, the Italian economy began to recover and rebuild, and lasting peace was made between the Italian states. In many ways the second wave of Humanism was much more fruitful than the first. But Florence couldn't reach its fullest peak of Renaissance flourishing until the work of the second wave of Humanism had run its course. The golden years of Florence were still shimmering just over the horizon.

Niccolò de' Niccoli: Humanist, book collector, collector of all works of antiquity

Niccolò Niccoli (1364–1437) was a lifelong resident of the city of Florence and was an important player in the Humanist circles of the city. Known as a meticulous and well-kept man, Niccolò frequently corresponded with Poggio Bracciolini and they were friends throughout most of their lives; he also befriended Cosimo de' Medici (the eventual de facto leader of Florence, and an important patron of Humanism and the arts). Niccoli received and catalogued many of the texts that Poggio Bracciolini uncovered during his quests in monasteries-while looking for the lost wisdom of Rome and Greece.

Niccolo was a treasure collector as well, and he was able to amass a collection of ancient busts, coins, and other artifacts from the ancient world, in fact, one of the ancient Roman coins in his collection helped identify the equestrian statue of Marcus Aurelius in Rome that was mistakenly known as Emperor Constantine up until that time. Niccolò's favorite items were books and, working together with Cosimo and Poggio, he was able to amass over 800 manuscripts in one of the most impressive libraries in Europe. He made these texts easily accessible to anyone within the Humanist and elite circles of Florence, helping to further spread the ideas and wisdom of the ancient world throughout the city. Eventually, upon his death, this library became part of a collection that would later become a public library at San Marco.

Jacob Burkhardt gives us a beautiful story that illustrates the type of man that Niccolò was and what he believed in. In it, Niccolò approaches a young man named Piero de' Pazzi who was a son of a successful Florentine merchant. Piero was not only born into wealth but was also handsome. As a young, handsome, and well-to-do man in the city, Piero was focused not on wisdom or refinement, but more on enjoying the pleasures provided to a man of his position in life. One day in the street Niccolò called out to Piero and, because of the respect that the city held for Niccolò, Piero came to his call even though the two had never formally met. After Niccolò had learned that Piero was the son of a successful merchant, Niccolò said to him

> "As son of such a father, and so fair to look upon, it is a shame that thou knowest nothing of the Latin language, which would be so great an ornament to thee. If thou learnest it not, thou wilt be good for nothing, and as soon as the flower of youth is over, wilt be a man of no consequence [*virtu*]."

Niccolò's words struck a chord with Piero and he immediately replied that he would learn, but that first he needed a teacher. Niccolò found Piero a tutor and Piero saw to it that the teacher was provided with pay and housing so that Piero could study under him. It is said that Piero became so inspired by his studies that he studied day and night and soon became one of the most learned men in the city.

Niccolò was a believer in the wisdom that could be found in the ancient world. A strong believer in personal cultivation and potential, he helped to promote the ideas that respect and virtue were not to be acquired through birth but were earned through merit. This belief that acclaim and virtue could be had by all, regardless of one's position of birth, would go on to become a vital part of the Renaissance psyche of Florence. This idea would later crystalize in the life of his dear friend Poggio Bracciolini.

Leonardo Bruni: historian, Humanist, Chancellor of Florence, translator, philosopher

Leonardo Bruni (1370–1444) grew up under the tutelage of Salutati and carried on the Humanist tradition while also expanding the role of Humanists in government and public affairs through the development of Civic Humanism. While Petrarch preferred a quiet life of solitude centered on self-development, learning, and reflection; Bruni followed in Saluti's footsteps becoming both a philosopher and a statesman. This new focus on developing skills through the study of antiquity that would better prepare leaders to rule, while at the same time focusing on introspection and the moral betterment that came from philosophy, was instrumental in Florence becoming the Humanist stronghold that it grew into during the Renaissance. Bruni believed that people shouldn't study simply to find wisdom; they should direct their efforts towards making themselves into more effective and productive human beings as well: "The careful study of the past enlarges our foresight in contemporary affairs and affords to citizens and to monarchs lessons of incitement or warning in the ordering of public policy."

Bruni was an important Humanist author who wrote several works that would help to promote and define the movement. One of Bruni's important literary works was a biography of the Roman statesman Cicero (Cicero was also a personal favorite of Petrarch, who Bruni also wrote a biography on). In *New Cicero,* Bruni declared that Cicero "appeared to be the very light of education and of wisdom due to his vast erudition". He praised Cicero as both a man of wisdom and as a politician that pursued his civic duty to defend the liberty of Rome. Bruni declared that Cicero was almost "god-like" in his "greatness of character". His biography of Cicero seems to represent his personal ideal of the good life: a life filled with both civic duty and with the cultivation and improvement of one's character as well. Bruni seemed to believe that this spirit of Cicero (the spirit of eloquence and rhetoric) was now very much alive within the city of Florence. In addition to his biographies, he also wrote history. Perhaps his most important writing of all was his *Historiarum Florentini populi libri XII* (*History of the Florentine people*). In it he tells us:

> "Now what can I say about the oratorical skill and verbal elegance of the Florentines, who in these matters undoubtedly reign supreme? For it is agreed that, of all of Italy, in this city alone is found the purest and finest speech. All who wish to speak well and correctly, therefore, follow the pattern of this one city, where there are such experts in the common vernacular tongue that, compared to them, their rivals look like children."

In his *History* he followed the thoughts of Petrarch and outlined a clear divide in time, claiming that there was first a classical age of antiquity (a golden age of learning) followed by the middle age (or in Petrarch's words the "dark ages"), which was a period of decline, and then finally a new age (a "better age") which he believed that Florence had already entered into. Bruni believed that the recent revival of learning and culture encouraged and promoted by the Humanist movement had created a new and better age for Florence. He tells us that the appreciation of liberal arts (literally the study of arts suited for free and distinguished men) had reached new heights: "The study of letters, moreover-not the vulgar curriculum found in mercantile schools, but the liberal arts which are particularly suited for free men, which have always flourished among every great people, flourish vigorously in one city."

Bruni believed that the widespread study of the liberal arts in the city of Florence had created a new age. This is important because, while Petrarch lamented the age in which he was born, Bruni seemed to believe that a transformation had already begun and was taking place during his own lifetime. This was perhaps the first inklings of acknowledgement that these years would be remembered as golden years in Florence (perhaps this was the birth of the "energizing myth" of the Renaissance).

Bruni sang the praises of the city of Florence in his *History of the Florentine people* and described it as superior to all other cities. He claimed that the leadership was fair and promoted the freedom of its citizens, that the city was perfectly clean, and perfectly designed, and perfectly constructed, and that the citizens of Florence were a special kind of human being that used all their intelligence to become the best type of person that a human being could be. The city of Florence, founded on the principles of justice and liberty, was the standard that all cities should strive for:

> "Every provision is taken so that in this city justice is held to be sacred, without which a city cannot even exist; and secondly, that there may be liberty, without which the people of Florence could not live. To these two conjoined principles, as though to a guiding star or safe haven, all the institutions and laws of the republic are directed...to these magistracies, then, both worthy citizens and even men of the lower order must all obey and defer...Nor is there any place on earth where the law is more equitable to all; nowhere else does liberty thrive so vigorously, available equally to men of high and low station."

Bruni tells us that the city of Florence secures equality for its citizens and he makes a subtle reference to antiquity when he claims that a citizen of Florence may call the state to his aid simply with a call of "I, too, am a Florentine citizen", reminding one keen enough to notice the reference to a rallying cry of the ancient world, "*Cîvis rômânus sum*" (I am a Roman citizen). Cicero tells us in one of his orations that anyone traveling across the Roman empire was guaranteed safety simply by making this statement that he was a Roman citizen.

> "I, too, am a Florentine citizen. These words attest and clearly warn that no one may disregard him

> because he is weak, nor threaten to harm him because he is powerless. The condition of all men becomes equal, because the state promises to defend those of lowly station."

In Bruni's opinion, this city of excellence created a special kind of citizen, one educated in the liberal arts, a master of speech, and groomed for moral integrity. He tells us that the city of Florence is a revival of Rome in all the best ways, that greatness literally pulses through the veins of its citizens, and that Florence is unmatched by any other city in the world.

> "What ornament, then, does this city lack, and in what way does it fall short of the highest honor and greatness? In the greatness of its ancestors?-who are descended from the Romans! In glory?, when Florence has one and daily does such great deeds, both honorable and excellent, both at home and abroad! In the splendor of its buildings? In its adornment and elegance? In its wealth? In its bustling population? In its healthful and pleasant location? What more is there that any city could desire? Nothing whatsoever."

Bruni was more than just a statesman and historian. He also served as Chancellor of Florence from 1410 to 1411 and then again from 1427 to 1444; additionally, he spent time as secretary to four different popes. In his positions of power and as an author and philosopher Bruni further developed and spread the ideas of Humanism and philosophy throughout Italy. Bruni first used the phrase *studia humanitatis* to distinguish the study of the liberal arts (grammar, rhetoric, poetry, history, and moral philosophy), this term was inspired by Bruni's study of Cicero who called these types of studies the *humanitas.* The *studia humanitatis* were a vital part of the Humanist movement and defined exactly what knowledge

Humanists should seek to gain in order to become better humans and better leaders. Like Bruni's predecessor Salutati, Bruni believed in the unique opportunity of Florence to become the restored Roman Republic. He believed that the freedom of the individual that was protected in republicanism had to be defended at all costs, and that this spirit of Florence was present in all its populace.

Bruni also translated works by Aristotle from Greek into the more widely accessible Latin form, allowing other Humanists to access these important works. Through Bruni's study of philosophy, he came to believe that *eudaimonia* (more on this later in the book, but this Greek word essentially means flourishing or personal growth) was the highest goal of life, and that virtue alone was sufficient for happiness. In stoic fashion, he believed that neither imprisonment, nor torture, nor any pain could stand in the way of the happy life for a person of virtue.

Bruni is often considered one of the most important of all Renaissance Humanists; his writing and historical records were crucial in Florentine culture. But even more so his contributions to Humanism through the ideas of civic participation, a new "better age", and the *studia humanitatis,* all more clearly defined and united the Humanist movement. Bruni's defense of Florentine republicanism, and his assertions that wealthy and well-educated men were the foundation of a successful society all contributed greatly to the "golden age" of Florence that had already begun. If the oppression of the "dark ages" still lived in the culture of Florence, Bruni did much to eliminate this darkness through his emphasis on personal betterment and enlightenment. Perhaps Bruni's greatest contribution to the Renaissance was the creation and promotion of the "energizing myth" that came to define and inspire one of the greatest transformations of thought ever seen in the West.

Poggio Bracciolini: scholar, book hunter, papal secretary, Humanist

Poggio Bracciolini (1380–1459) was an important scholar and part of the second wave of Renaissance Humanists. A self-made man, born into a poor family, who raised himself to success and renown during his lifetime, Poggio had close ties with many of the prominent Humanists of Florence and was lifelong friends with Coluccio Salutati, Leonardo Bruni, Niccolò Niccoli, and both Cosimo and Lorenzo de' Medici.

Poggio's main contribution to the Humanist movement was an important one; as a talented book hunter, Poggio scoured old monasteries searching for lost treasures from antiquity. Throughout his life, some of it spent as a papal secretary (thanks to recommendations made by Salutati and Leonardo Bruni), Poggio had many chances to visit old monasteries and comb through their collections of books, searching for manuscripts that had been lost throughout the Middle Ages. On one outing during the Council of Constance, Poggio made a significant discovery that both inspired and saddened him. In one of his letters, he describes the various states of decay of the books that he found and he likens them to prisoners forgotten and neglected.

> "There amid a tremendous quantity of books, which it would take too long to describe, we found Quintilian still safe and sound, though filthy with mold and dust. For these books were not in the library as befitted their worth, but in a sort of foul and gloomy dungeon at the bottom of one of the

towers, where not even men who had been convicted of a capital offense would have been stuck away."

Poggio's love of books is clear as he expresses mourning over the sad state of their preservation and personifies the text not just as a *writing* of Quintilian, but as Quintilian himself. Poggio, following in the footsteps of Petrarch before him, believed that these lost texts were not simply a window into antiquity, but were representations of some of the greatest minds of the ancient world. As a book hunter, Poggio was prolific and uncovered many important works by authors including Lucretius (a student of Epicurus and Greek philosopher), Vitruvius (an important Roman architect), Cicero, and Quintilian (an important Roman teacher of Rhetoric). Poggio used his expert and beautiful handwriting to make copies of these works, which he then made accessible to men like Niccolò Niccoli, Leonardo Bruni, and the Medici family. Poggio was well known for both the beauty of his writing, and for his excellent grasp of the Latin language; his manuscripts were highly sought after by the Humanists of Florence in his age.

While Poggio spent much of his life under various popes and cardinals in the church, he still spent much of his free time engaged in reading, copying texts, or studying antiquity. Poggio believed that virtue was not something simply gained through salvation, but something that was earned through good actions and study. In his work *On Avarice,* he tells us that "the path of virtue is very full of toil and peril", showing directly that virtue is not inherited, but earned through sacrifice and hard work. In a letter to Andrea Alamanni, Poggio tells us about his feelings on the development of rhetoric: "we know that men become eloquent through the reading of orators, poets, historians, and philosophers, and by continuous practice" (echoing the words of Quintilian from his *Institutio Oratio*). Poggio clearly believed that great men became great not through accident, but through intentional study and effort. In a letter, he tells us about one of the men that he and the other Humanists modeled themselves after, Cicero:

> "At the age of twenty-five Cicero delivered the orations Pro Cuentio and again Pro Roscio so elegantly that none of his orations are more eloquent in their adornment of words or gravity of opinions. But we read that he had no teacher: rather, by the assiduous reading of eloquent men, by study, by diligence, and by practice, he reached the grade of speaking that no Latin has since approached. Afterward he crossed over into Greece – not for the sake of eloquence but for the sake of philosophy."

Poggio did his best to follow in the footsteps of the great men that he admired and studied, and he created his personal success in life through hard work and dedication; he realized full well what was possible to a person who dedicated themselves wholeheartedly to learning: "What is there... that could be more pleasing, more delightful, more welcome, than the knowledge of those things which make us more wise, and what is even more important, more elegant in our power of expression?"

Poggio was a believer in the idea that members of the nobility of Florence were not simply born into nobility; they had earned their nobility through virtue and accomplishment. Inspired by the other great minds of Florence – and inspired by the writings of men like Cicero, Quintilian, and Seneca – Poggio was always concerned with his own mind and self-cultivation and he followed in the footsteps laid down by the great men that came before him- always heeding their advice to study, read, and learn continuously.

> "Every man waits his destined hour; even the cities are doomed to their fate. Let us spend our leisure with our books, which will take our minds off these troubles, and will teach us to despise what many people desire.... sometimes I am free for reading, free from all care about public affairs...I live free as much as I can"

We see in Poggio Bracciolini the same feelings of Petrarch, a desire for a quiet life of solitude and reflection, even while actively engaged with the affairs of the Church and politics. Throughout his life he maintained close ties with the Humanists of Florence and often worked behind the scenes to ensure the survival and flourishing of Florence and the Florentine people. But it seems that right up until his death he remained a scholar, still finding and taking advantage of those quiet moments alone where he could transport himself into the wisdom of the ancient world through reading a book.

Cosimo de' Medici: banker, patron of the arts, Humanist, politician

Cosimo de' Medici (1389–1464) was the son of the prominent Florentine banker named Giovanni de' Medici. Giovanni, through good business and wise bets, was able to build the small family bank into a European powerhouse. Part of Giovanni's success surely rests in the fact that there was a vacuum left in the banking world after the Italian banking collapse of the 1340s. Giovanni took advantage of these opportunities with expert precision and was able to pass this same ability on to his son Cosimo. Cosimo continued the work that his father started and was able to build the bank into a highly profitable business, even securing the privilege to provide exclusive banking services for the pope. Between the years 1410 and 1415 Cosimo and his father Giovanni essentially bought the papal appointment for John XXII, only to lose influence after John XXII was unseated during the Council of Constance (the same council that allowed Poggio Bracciolini to make his biggest discovery of lost books). However, following in the prudent footsteps of his father, Cosimo was able to once again establish ties with Rome and secure exclusive banking rights, making the Medici family bank by far the most dominant of the Italian banks. In 1429 Giovanni passed away leaving the Medici household under the control of his son Cosimo. On his deathbed he gave advice to Cosimo to never linger around politicians, never to make a show in public, to keep out of the eyes of the public, and to never appear to go against the will of the people.

By the time of Giovanni's death, Cosimo was already a prominent man of Florence and was well respected in the city. Cosimo was able to exert extensive sway over the workings of government by using his wealth and influence to control a large portion of what passed through the Signoria (the governing body of Florence). Cosimo, ever a wise student, heeded the advice of his father Giovanni and acknowledged that the people of the city had great pride in their "republic of Florence"; tyranny or direct leadership would be vehemently opposed, and so he preferred to influence the outcome of things from behind the scenes, rather than out in the open. Cosimo used his money and influence to buy allegiances and to ensure that the government was filled with men who shared in his common interest and were loyal to the Medici family. Pope Pius II, said of Cosimo: "Political questions are settled in [Cosimo's] house. The man he chooses holds office... He it is who decides peace and war... He is king in all but name."

Cosimo took the words of his father to heart and lived by the law that the Medici clan should not appear in public with extravagant displays of wealth, should avoid walking through the streets under armed guard, should dress humbly, and should speak to the citizens of Florence by name whenever possible. The illusion of a humble wealth and life that Cosimo was able to cultivate was crucial in his ability to win over the support of the common people and working class, many of whom saw Cosimo as a working man who was able to create success for himself through hard work and intelligence, rather than viewing him as simply born into aristocracy or noble blood. This all contributed to Cosimo becoming an incredibly popular citizen of Florence, considered to be first among a common folk rather than a dictator.

But not *all* the citizens of Florence were thrilled by Cosimo and the growing power of the Medici clan. In fact, several rival families sought to bring about the downfall of Cosimo and some of them worked behind the scenes to ensure that it would happen. In 1433, a conspiracy created by the Albizzi, Strozzi, and other powerful families of Florence was able to undermine Cosimo while he was away at his country estate. While on vacation, Cosimo received a summons to appear before the Signoria to be tried for undermining the Republic – an accusation that Cosimo had exerted undue influence over the law and workings of the state for his own benefit. Rather than flee (this would have been easy to do for a man of Cosimo's standing) he appeared at court as requested. He was quickly imprisoned and the rival families sought to have Cosimo killed while in the dungeon. But Cosimo was able to use his influence, even behind the dungeon walls, to ensure his own survival. Legend has it that his jailer checked Cosimo's food for poison in order to keep him alive throughout his imprisonment. Eventually he was able to have his sentence reduced from death down to exile and rode off into his banishment downtrodden but not defeated.

During Cosimo's banishment he still exerted influence over the affairs of Florence and continued to build the family wealth. In his absence, matters in Florence began to deteriorate, and it was not long before the lower class began to lash out at the handful of wealthy families that now seemed to be running the affairs of Florence. Eventually the working class revolted and forced everyone associated with the banishment of Cosimo to flee the city – that or be faced with the justice of the mob. Facing sure destruction, the rival families and their henchmen fled, paving the way for Cosimo to return to the city triumphantly. Upon Cosimo's return he was welcomed like a successful Roman general as he paraded through the streets of Florence. His first act was to banish the families that revolted against him forever from the city. In the adoration and celebration that Cosimo experienced on his return from exile it was clear that Cosimo returned not just as a normal citizen, but as a sort of savior. But true to the advice of his father, and despite his adulatory welcome home, Cosimo did not attempt to take control of the city in an official capacity, choosing instead to allow the spirit of republicanism to live on – at least in appearance. Despite his obvious sway over the city, Cosimo continued to dress and act humbly and was seen as a champion of the common people, rather than as a prince or oligarch.

Cosimo contributed to the flourishing of Florence in many ways, one of which was his dedication to peace in Italy. Cosimo worked throughout his lifetime to promote the interests of Florence throughout the region, often working as an emissary with foreign powers in order to ensure the best outcomes for Florence. In 1454 Cosimo participated in the Treaty of Lodi, a major peace treaty between Florence, Naples, and Milan. This later evolved into the Italic League, a larger agreement between the papal states, Venice, Milan, Naples, and Florence. The

Italic league was more than just a non-aggression pact; it was a pledge of mutual support and cooperation between the Italian states. It declared that if any of the states were ever to be attacked by outside forces, the states would rally together in defense of the attacked territory. The Italic League set up deeper diplomatic relations in Italy and allowed the region to flourish in ways never seen in the region (these have come to be known as the golden years of Florence that Cosimo's grandson Lorenzo largely reigned over in his lifetime).

Cosimo, who received his Humanist (classical) education in a monastery school, believed that explorations of human potential were important. He contributed to the arts and to the spread of Humanism in Florence, thus starting a tradition of patronage that his grandson Lorenzo would continue to build upon during the golden years. Cosimo was a believer that art and cultural excellence could elevate society in the city that he loved and his support of the arts and of Humanist scholars continued to build upon the traditions of Civic Humanism that began with Salutati and continued with Leonardo Bruni. Cosimo clearly demonstrated that those who were blessed with wealth and success had an obligation to their city; he commissioned works by and secured work for Donatello, Brunelleschi (who completed the famous dome of Florence at the Santa Maria Del Fiore), and many other artists and architects in Florence.

In 1438 Cosimo was instrumental in convincing religious leaders to host their attempt to heal the schism in the Catholic Church in Florence. This brought Byzantine scholars and holy men to Florence who ultimately inspired the Humanists to dive even more deeply into ancient Greek culture and writings. This would later inspire the lives and works of men like Marsilio Ficino who would carry on the final wave of Humanism throughout Florence in the golden years. In fact, Cosimo himself commissioned Ficino to translate the complete works of Plato from Greek into Latin, as these texts had become inaccessible to the minds of Florence since few people could read Greek. Cosimo's own appreciation for the works of philosophers like Cicero and Plato would eventually inspire him to work with Marsilio Ficino to re-establish the Platonic Academy within the city of Florence as another beacon of light revived from the ancient world.

In 1444 Cosimo founded the first public library in Florence at San Marco. This collection of books and manuscripts was a goldmine for Humanist scholars and thinkers in Florence. The library was just another example of Cosimo's dedication to Civic Humanism, and of his desire to help the city of Florence to thrive. In order to build up Cosimo's growing collection of books, and in order to help his Humanist friends, he sponsored trips by Poggio Bracciolini to search for lost books throughout Europe, Syria, Egypt, and Greece. And after Niccolo Niccoli's death, Cosimo paid off Niccoli's debts in order to acquire his personal collection of around 800 manuscripts. Cosimo said in a letter,

> "All those things have given me the greatest satisfaction and contentment because they are not only for the honor of God but are likewise for my own remembrance. For fifty years, I have done nothing else but earn money and spend money; and it became clear that spending money gives me greater pleasure than earning it."

Towards the end of Cosimo's life, he wrote a letter to Ficino telling him "come to me quickly and explain to me Plato on the highest good, and do not forget to bring your orphic lyre". Ficino responded and told Cosimo that great possessions and virtues are worthless and can even be detrimental to a person who is not in possession of wisdom. Cosimo had touched the lives of many people in the city of Florence. He established some of the fairest tax laws ever seen in a republic, arranged grain distribution for the poor (an early form of assistance for the unfortunate), was a patron of the arts, encouraged the study and spread of philosophy and the humanities, and he helped nurture the works and minds of great thinkers like Marsilio Ficino, Poggio Bracciolini, and his grandson Lorenzo. Cosimo cared deeply for his city and (perhaps inspired by Ficino and his Platonic teachings) seemed to be a devout seeker of virtue as well. He passed away while listening to Ficino read him Plato, a fitting end to a man who had grown increasingly interested in philosophy throughout his lifetime.

Cosimo was a friend to many and was so popular that after his death he was awarded the title *Pater Patriae,* Father of the Fatherland, or Father of the Country. This was meant as a great honor towards his life and legacy. This same title had been given to one of Cosimo's personal heroes, Cicero (the Roman statesmen that was also a favorite of Leonardo Bruni and Petrarch), Julius Caesar, and Julius's nephew Augustus. This revival of the same term used to describe Cicero in the days of Roman antiquity was another ode to the light of antiquity that Petrarch had seen shimmering through the darkness of the Middle Ages during his own lifetime some 100 years before Cosimo's death. This light was growing ever brighter inside the now flourishing city of Florence.

Chapter 4

Full bloom: the third Humanist wave and the golden age of Florence

With the roots of Humanism firmly entrenched in the culture, artists, thinkers, and leaders of the city of Florence, the final wave of Florentine Humanism was ready to begin. This final wave of Humanism would be the full bloom of Renaissance culture that we typically imagine when we think of the Renaissance period. These were the years of great thinkers like Leon Alberti, Giannozzo Manetti, Marsilio Ficino, and Giovanni Pico della Mirandola. Lorenzo de' Medici oversaw the well-being of the city and provided patronage, jobs, and education for artists like Leonardo da Vinci, Sandro Botticelli, Domenico Ghirlandaio, and Michelangelo Buonarroti. In these same golden years, the economy flourished, in part due to regional peace and robust trade in the Italian states. Life was good for many. We can see the grandiosity of Florence's success and culture during this period as the result of a ruling class that had been raised learning the humanities, trained classically, and cultivated through the application of philosophy to their own lives. The citizens that held power in the city participated in and encouraged this culture that celebrated the potential and dignity of human beings to grow and thrive. Self-made scholars and merchants ascended into wealth and power, and many began to believe that, through mankind, all things were possible. The "energizing myth" of the Renaissance had finally come full circle, fulfilling its own prophecy.

The third wave of Humanism during the golden years was the strongest of all. The traditions and ideas laid out by men like Petrarch, Leonardo Bruni, and Poggio Bracciolini evolved into a new view of human life. This view claimed that humankind was not a slave to any universal fate or plan but had been given full liberty from God to determine its own place in the universe. This new view of human life on earth gave a new dignity to existence that was not previously present, and that was almost totally absent in the Middle Ages.

During these golden years, Marsilio Ficino (with help from Cosimo de' Medici) re-established the Platonic Academy (a loose gathering of Florence's greatest minds to discuss ideas such as Plato's newly translated texts, along with other ideas of philosophy and the humanities). This increased the sharing of ideas and thinking amongst the Humanists of Florence, strengthening its influence even further. As briefly mentioned in the section on the second wave of Humanism, Gemistus Pletho (the Byzantine scholar) came to Florence during the Council of Florence, bringing with him knowledge of Greek texts, which created a deep interest in the Humanists circle of Florence. Gemistus and his talks on Plato inspired Cosimo de' Medici to refound the Platonic Academy in his own day and age and, together with Marsilio Ficino, began to hold regular meetings of the academy where the highest minds of Florence would gather to discuss philosophy and other stimulating topics. The academy inspired men like Pico Della, Botticelli, Lorenzo de' Medici, and Michelangelo, helping to instill the ideas of Humanism and Platonism even more deeply into the culture of the elite in Florence. The Platonic Academy revived deep interest in the works of Plato and the Neoplatonist philosophers like Plotinus. Plato's teachings and beliefs differ greatly from his student Aristotle (who had become the dominant philosopher taught throughout the universities). The academy would regularly meet and share ideas up until the death of Cosimo's grandson, Lorenzo de' Medici, in 1492.

While the Council of Florence brought the Greek scholar Gemistus to Florence in 1438, there were events occurring in the East that brought even more Greek scholars and influence to Florence as well. In 1453 the city of Constantinople fell to the Ottoman Empire and the great Eastern capital of ancient Rome fell into the hands of the Turks. The fall of the city sent a wave of refugees out of the East that now looked for new homes and careers in the Western world. Many of these scholars wound up in Italy furthering the new obsession with Greek culture in the city of Florence and its Humanist circles. Marsilio Ficino tells us of the period when the "spirit of Plato", which had lived in Byzantium since the days of Athens, had "flown to Italy". While many in Florence already idealized the ancient city of Rome, it now seems that the spirit of Athens was reborn in Florence as well.

In 1456 John Argyropoulos (another Byzantine scholar) found his way back to Florence and assisted the Florentine Humanists with translating and reviving the lost works of ancient Greece. During this time, the study of philosophy would reach a peak in Florence. Wealthy men in Florence sought acclaim not simply for their own wealth, but for the level and depth of their knowledge. A Humanist education became a mark of a person that should be respected, almost a type of social currency among the elites: this led to a genuine thirst for knowledge throughout the city. Donato Acciaioli (a scholar and student under Argyropoulos) tell us of the period that "The study of letters never before so flourished in

Florence, many are so trained in Aristotelian and Platonic teaching that they seem to have been brought up in the academy."

A love for ancient Greek and Roman art, culture, and writings reached its pinnacle as the Florentines simultaneously celebrated human potential, freedom and republicanism, civic duty, personal cultivation, virtue, and individualism. The Medici and the many artists and philosophers that they supported were made up of self-made men, not (for the most part) families of nobility, but from humble backgrounds. They had earned their merit through effort and learning, not simply through the legacy of their ancestors. Florence in the 1450s was a place where individual achievement was celebrated, the wealthy gave back to their communities through public works and patronage, and the citizens took pride in the great beauty and culture of their city. The ancient ideals of Rome and Greece had been restored, the human mind was cultivated, and human achievement and knowledge soared to new heights. The spirit of the Renaissance, born in the mind and words of Petrarch 100 years earlier, was finally at its peak –fully alive and flourishing within this Italian city of Florence.

Giannozzo Manetti: Humanist, businessman, Renaissance/Universal man, philosopher

Giannozzo Manetti (1396–1459) was a Florentine Humanist who (along with his contemporary Leon Battista Alberti) embodied the term "Renaissance man" or "Universal man". Born the son of a wealthy merchant, Manetti distinguished himself as a philosopher, mathematician, businessman, author, politician, and an expert of Rhetoric. He also knew Latin, Greek, Hebrew, and Italian. According to Vespiano da Bisticci, Manetti's father wanted him to be a good and successful merchant and so he made sure to get him a proper Humanist education and training in reading and writing. Giannazzo became so proficient in mathematics that by the age of 10 he was able to handle the cash and receipts for family transactions. His public career in politics began in 1429 and he participated in various forms of government in the city of Florence. Of note is that during a diplomatic mission Manetti befriended Alfonso "The magnificent" (King of Aragon, Sicily, and Naples) and would eventually make Naples his home. His work would help to continue the spread of Humanist ideas and learning, even outside of his birth city of Florence.

Manetti was famously intense in his areas of focus and a hard worker. It is said that once he took up study in grammar, Latin, and philosophy he studied without rest for nine years straight. Apparently Manetti quite enjoyed his use of logic and study, and in his famous work *On the dignity and excellence of man* he tells us:

> "What shall I say about the other interior senses? How great is the pleasure obtained from observing and discerning attributes of material things provided by the sense which, in their sum, the philosophers call the 'common sense'? In sum, in understanding? When those things which we have apprehended by one particular sense, we then proceed to conceptualize, analyze, measure, remember, and understand, experiencing a pleasure that words cannot satisfactorily express or explain."

Manetti believed that God gave man time in the same way that a merchant gives over money to a cashier at the bank (something he was quite familiar with as a successful merchant). At the end of the day when the cash is counted, if the amount recorded doesn't match exactly what is turned back in, it is a disgrace. Manetti was said to have been a master of philosophy, and was far more knowledgeable than many of the other men he discussed it with. He frequently participated in debates among scholars of philosophy and theology. Through his studies he also became so well versed at Latin and rhetoric that he could give an impromptu speech better than most other men could give even when they had pre-prepared. He wrote several books including biographies of Dante, Boccaccio, Petrarch, Socrates, Seneca, and perhaps his most famous work, *On the dignity and excellence of man*. He had children and a wife, and took time to run the family business; He worked in government and was also very active in the Church. He was seen as a very pious man; it is said that he was never involved in lies, he never spoke badly of anyone, and he endured hardship without complaint. It seems Manetti was quite intent to use his time wisely and hand God back the proper accounting of his life.

In Manetti's great work *On the dignity and excellence of man*, he declares that man is not weak, sinful, and wretched – a direct response to Pope Innocent III, who wrote that man is filthy, sinful, wretched. Manetti declares that man is capable of virtue through discipline and practice, and that through rigorous study man can be reborn in the perfect image of God:

> "Do not in any way doubt what I have written here, but let virtue be your goal. Suppress and crush vice, but love virtue with all of the force of your mind and body; love it, follow it, reach for it, I entreat you, engage it, embrace it since by continual and determined acts of virtue we are not only made blessed and happy, but we are remade, as it were, in the image of the immortal God."

In Stoic fashion, Manetti also declared that a person with knowledge and understanding of the nature of things will dismiss the inconveniences of life and their own mortality as fleeting and ephemeral experiences that are superficial in nature. It seems that for Manetti the active pursuit of personal cultivation and learning-seeking to come closer to the divine image of God the creator, was the greatest goal that one could have in life. Little else mattered:

> "Accordingly, if in living their daily lives men experience more delights and pleasures that they are tormented by pains and trials, they should rejoice and celebrate rather than wail and lament...Especially since nature furnishes us abundantly and sufficiently with sure remedies...To sum up, then: all those who examine the nature of things with any diligence, and consider it with a modicum of care, will dismiss as frivolous, empty, and fatuous all these complaints and charges about frailty, chills, fevers, pains, hunger, and thirst, things that smell foul or taste bitter, visions and sensations, lassitude, sleeplessness and sloth, food and drink, and other similar inconveniences encountered in human existence"

Manetti had an important role in helping to spread the ideas of Humanism and classical learning to other areas of Italy and, through his personal works, also helped to profile important men like Socrates, Seneca, and earlier Humanists like Petrarch and Boccaccio. As a true example of the idea of a Universal man Manetti was able to excel in multiple areas of life, seeking always to draw himself closer to the perfect image of the God that he believed had created humanity.

Leon Battista Alberti: Civic Humanist, writer, artist, architect, philosopher

Leon Battista Alberti (1404–1472) was another example of what would be considered today as a perfect picture of the Renaissance man, Universal man, or polymath. Gifted with knowledge and talent in writing, speaking, art, architecture, philosophy, music, and mathematics, and apparently gifted as a physical specimen- in his autobiography he claims that he could jump over a standing man in a single jump, climb mountains, and tame wild horses. Alberti was popular in the Humanist circles of Florence for the impressive depth and breadth of his knowledge. Alberti (much like Manetti) believed that all people could achieve the heights of accomplishment if only they believed and applied themselves: "A man can do all things if he wills". He also believed that God had given humankind three precious resources that we could either choose to cultivate or to throw away through neglect: mind, body, and time. Alberti shared in a view of humanity held by many of the Humanists: humankind was not simply subservient to God but was created by God and imbued with the power of its creator. Human beings are given gifts that they can choose to cultivate or allow to wither. For Alberti, God was not simply perfection, but God's perfection also rested within us: "When I investigate and when I discover that the forces of the heavens and the planets are within ourselves, then truly I seem to be living among the gods."

Alberti worked as an architect in Rome and Florence and wrote books on both art and architecture that helped to define the Renaissance style; he also wrote plays and other literary works as well. Alberti was not much of a painter himself, but he did write books on and explored the use of perspective, color, and composition; he was a believer that all great artists needed an education in mathematics, geometry, and the classics; Alberti believed that art was another way in which humankind could tap into the divine reserves of potential given to us by God: "Painting is possessed of divine power, for not only does it make the absent present, but also makes the dead almost alive."

Alberti was a man of status and well connected with the great Humanist minds and leaders of Florence; he had close connections to many dukes and princes and held close ties with Roman nobility. As part of the inner circle of Florence Alberti was exposed to the growing interest in Neoplatonism and was a reader of both Aristotle and Plotinus. As a Humanist Alberti was a strong proponent of Civic Humanism; he believed that wealth was a powerful tool for creating a better society. Not only did wealth "assist him to great and noble deeds", but he also claimed that only the wealth of the rich could save a state in times of severe crisis, such times as were experienced during the outbreak of plague or the banking collapse in the mid-1300s.

Alberti is remembered mostly as a picture-perfect image of the Renaissance man: gifted in many disciplines, well-spoken and virtuous, and a man of character. Georgio Vasari who later wrote *Lives of the Most Excellent Painters, Sculptors, and Architects,* said of Alberti that he was "an admirable citizen, a man of culture.... a friend of talented men, open and courteous with everyone. He always lived honorably and like the gentleman he was."

Marsilio Ficino: Humanist, Neoplatonist, writer, priest, teacher

Marsilio Ficino (1433–1499) was born into the Humanist circle of Florence. His father was the personal physician of Cosimo de' Medici and, from a young age, Marisilio was brought into the Medici household and given an excellent Humanist education. Marisilio grew into a bright young man and developed a deep love for philosophy and learning in general. His thirst for knowledge seemed to begin when, as a youth, he gained access to read a newly rediscovered copy of Lucretius's epic poem *On the Nature of Things*, found recently by Poggio Bracciolini. Later Ficino would grow into a staunch supporter of Plato over all other philosophers. But, as he matured, he received a top-notch Humanist education, including studies of the men championed by the Humanist study of the humanities. In 1462 Cosimo gave Ficino a Greek copy of Plato's *Dialogues* and tasked him to translate the complete work of Plato into Latin; Cosimo also gave Ficino the proceeds of a farm to provide for Ficino while he worked on his task, so that he would be able to focus his efforts exclusively on his work.

Cosimo chose Marsilio for many other important tasks as well. Aside from translating the works of Plato, Marsilio was also chosen to head the new Platonic Academy of Florence (a loose gathering of Florence's greatest minds to discuss philosophy and other intellectual matters) and to translate the *Divine Pymander* (an ancient hermetic work). Marsilio was also made tutor to Cosimo's own grandson Lorenzo de' Medici (the soon to be master of Renaissance Florence). Ficino was also tutor to perhaps the greatest of all the Renaissance minds, Giovanni Pico della Mirandola. Through Marsilio's writings and mentorship he had a profound effect on the intellectual culture and life of Florence, influencing most of the top Humanist minds throughout his lifetime. Marsilio and his passion for the philosophy of Plato inspired a new interest in Plato's teachings, and this became an important and defining part of the Renaissance Humanist movement, as up until this time Aristotle was much more widely read and respected by scholars in the universities of Europe. Marsilio's translations of, and writings about, the works of Plato became so popular that they remained the dominant commentary on Plato all the way up until the 1800s.

Marsilio made the most of his personal and professional connections and became involved with the Catholic Church as a priest, starting in the year 1473. In the Church Marsilio played an important role in reintroducing secular teachings, like the philosophy of Plato, to the Church body. Marsilio believed that the mission of philosophy was to help people to improve so that they could draw nearer to God and divine wisdom. He believed that Socrates and Plato (among other philosophers) were non-Christian men who taught others how to improve morally and this moral improvement would lead even non-Christians closer to God. However, like most of the great minds of the Renaissance, Marislio's openness to the wisdom and teachings of pagan antiquity did earn him some ire from the Church, so much so that in 1489 he was accused of heresy. Lorenzo de' Medici came to his aid at this time to argue for his forgiveness, and eventually the charges were dropped. Marsilio, though active in the Church, maintained this love of antiquity and maintained his love for the wisdom that the ancient world contained. In 1492 he tells us in one of his letters: "This century, like a golden age, has restored to light the liberal arts, which were almost extinct: grammar, poetry, rhetoric, painting, sculpture, architecture, music...And it happened in Florence...where Platonic learning was recalled from darkness into light."

Ficino believed that Plato's philosophy was compatible with Christianity and Church doctrine and believed that philosophy helped people to live better and more moral lives. Ficino referenced the fondness of St Augustine (the favorite theologian of Petrarch) for Plato and claimed that philosophy was simply a tool to help rational minds reach the knowledge of God. Ficino's philosophy promoted the personal growth and betterment of individuals, and the attainment of this highest good Ficino believed was the goal of both philosophy and of religion. If the highest aim of life was truth and goodness, then surely the philosophy of men like Plato would assist human beings in reaching that place of divine understanding. In one of Ficino's works *Concerning the mind* he tells us: "We cannot reach the highest summits of things unless, first, taking less account of the inferior parts of the soul, we ascend to the highest part, the mind." In another one of his letters to Antonio Canigiani he states:

> "Of the first sort are those virtues which regulate action: to them it is proper to render the soul tranquil and free from every tumult of the passions...To the second sort clearly belong those virtues which have to do with contemplation. For in fact these virtues, through the understanding and pursuit of divine things, raise up and exalt the mind in some way above human nature, so that it seems to approach as closely as possible to the life of God, which consists in contemplation alone. But it is clear that the condition of pleasure is contrary to both."

Ficino believed that the human intellect would always seek to understand, and enough understanding would always lead the inquisitive mind to God. Following the law of cause and effect, the mind will eventually reach a place of the original cause, and this original cause can only be explained by God. God, the infinite mind of the universe that has ordered all things, is the uniter of all things and all things in existence share in this divine plan. Ficino believed that man was essentially condemned to be unhappy. Our souls, trapped in worldly bodies, either overcame their senses with the use of reason, causing life to become laborious and stale; or one would give into the senses and constantly seek more, never reaching true fulfillment. Reason, the very thing that unites and provides us with a pathway to God, is the very same thing that prevents us from ever finding true peace. We are condemned always to search, to inquire, and to seek truth. To Ficino, then, philosophy was a pathway leading to the divine, but divinity could never be reached fully within a mortal body. In a letter he tells his friend Antonio Serafico:

> "Frequently when I contemplate what I may call the necessity of our friendship, my Antonio, that kind of writing we first employed is wont to seem entirely strange and different. For the letters that pass between us are crammed with those prefatory statements, circumlocutions, and overly obliging phrases. I confess that it is I in particular who have hitherto busied myself with this sort of writing and have devoted much time and labor to words, especially in the case of relationships as close as ours. But we, I think, have no need of that persuasion through words, nor for those excessive praises and that belabored manner of elegant speaking that we would use if we were complete strangers seeking to generate some new favor. Therefore let us abandon that old style that those babbling lightweights use, I think you know the ones that I am talking about, so that we may speak in the manner of philosophers, despising everywhere words and bringing forth weighty utterances."

We can see in the life of Ficino, a man who truly loved philosophy and the search for wisdom through its use. Ficino was different from the Civic Humanists around him who studied philosophy for acclaim or respect from their peers. He did not read the greats before him simply to become a better speaker or to gain personal benefit but, following in the ways of a true philosopher (like Plato or Socrates), he sought wisdom alone. Ficino then was not a strong advocate of the active life of the Civic Humanists or of men like Seneca and Cicero, but of the contemplative life of men like Plato or Socrates. Only within our minds, and through the contemplation and understanding of wisdom, could we truly become free. In one of Ficino's many letters to Cosimo de' Medici he tells us about the nature of the "good":

> "All men want to act well, which is to live well. But they live well if they are endowed with as many good things as possible. Now these good things are said to be riches, health, beauty, strength, nobility of birth, honors, power, prudence, as well as justice, fortitude, and temperance, and above all else wisdom, which indeed comprehends the whole essence of happiness...Wisdom ensures that we rightly use riches, healthy, beauty, strength, and the other things which are called good. For this reason knowledge is the cause of good and successful action, in the possession, use, and working of every gift. The man who possesses many gifts and uses them without intelligence is injured the more, the more he possesses, since he has more to misuse...thus none of those qualities which above were called good are good in themselves, for if they are dominated by ignorance they are worse than their opposites, insofar as they can plentifully supply the means of crime to an evil leader...Clearly, from these things Plato placed as the highest good in the soul, not acting but contemplating the pure intelligence of truth."

Ficino was instrumental in the psychological shift that occurred during the golden years of Florence. Through his writings and translations, he not only inspired some of the greatest minds of the high Renaissance (artists like Michelangelo and Da Vinci among them), but he also revised the study of Plato and further integrated his teaching with the teaching of the bible. Ficino in his role at the Platonic Academy of Florence influenced and taught his new message of Platonic teachings to a new generation of Humanists and helped to revive a genuine curiosity for philosophy that reinvigorated the Renaissance movement within the city of Florence.

Lorenzo de' Medici: Humanist, Florentine leader and diplomat, banker, patron of the arts

Lorenzo de' Medici (1449–1492) was the grandson of Cosimo de' Medici and was the only Medici who rivaled, and perhaps even surpassed, the renown and respect that Cosimo received during his lifetime. Known as "The magnificent", Lorenzo received a first class Humanist education and was tutored and mentored by Marisilio Ficino through his childhood years. As a teen Lorenzo also attended the meetings of the Platonic Academy led by Ficino. Lorenzo learned the poetry of Ovid, rhetoric, and ethics from Cicero, and he learned Greek and Plato from Ficino. Ficino praised the young Lorenzo for his prudence and great character and believed that even from a young age Lorenzo had great things in store for him in the future. Lorenzo did grow into a bit of a Renaissance man, and excelled as a poet, diplomat, hunter, horseman, and as an athlete. Throughout his life he wrote poetry that focused on life's temporal nature, love, and the human condition, and as a young man he won a major jousting tournament. Machiavelli said of him that he won "not by way of favour, but by his own valour and skill in arms". Lorenzo's intellect and skills also involved him with diplomatic missions from a young age where he gained experience dealing with other powerful men of Italy.

Lorenzo assumed his position of prominence at the young age of 20 after his father's early death. Lorenzo, despite being a skilled leader and diplomat, had to contend with many obstacles during his lifetime. In fact, Lorenzo at least feigned misgivings about taking over after the death of his father Piero, stating that he preferred not to deal with the dangers and pressures of leadership.

> "Although I was very young, being just twenty years of age, they encouraged me to take it upon myself the care of the city and the state, as my father and grandfather had done. This proposal was naturally against my youthful instincts. Feeling that the burden and danger might be too much for me, I consented to it unwillingly."

The affairs of the Medici bank that Lorenzo inherited were not in the best of shape, and the large reserves that were once within the walls of their banks had begun to dwindle. Lorenzo's political ambitions and involvement in the affairs of the State, despite generally being quite popular with the citizenry, did also make him a target of anger for some of the other powerful and wealthy families of Florence. In April of 1478 an event known as the Pazzi Conspiracy was perpetrated by a group of dissidents under the blessing of Pope Sixtus IV. It was arranged that Lorenzo and his brother Giuliano would be killed within the walls of Santa Maria Del Fiore by men disguised as churchmen. But only Giuliano wound up dead, and Lorenzo, despite receiving a wound to the neck, fought away his attackers with the help of some of his closest friends.

After the failed attempt on Lorenzo's life, a series of events escalated the situation to the point that war almost broke out in Italy. News of the attempted assassination spread quickly through the city, and mobs of Medici supporters (most of the city) rallied under the Medici banner and in a violent wave of bloodshed they brought justice onto anyone who was part of, or even suspected to have been a part of, the plot. The mob lynched the Archbishop of Pisa (an important holy man involved in the plot) as well as several members of the Pazzi family, and anyone else who was suspected of involvement with the plot. These men were ultimately stripped naked, hanged, and chopped into pieces in the square in front of the Signoria and their bodies were left on display in the public square as a reminder of what would happen to anyone foolish enough to attempt to disrupt the rule of Florence's cherished Medici family.

While the backlash of the mob removed many of Lorenzo's enemies from the city, Pope Sixtus became even more enraged when he heard of the treatment of the archbishop. He formally excommunicated Lorenzo and the whole of the city of Florence and seized any Medici assets that he could get his hands on. When the people of Florence still chose to stand by Lorenzo, Pope Sixtus formed a dangerous military alliance with the King of Naples to invade and conquer the city. As the large force prepared to invade and most assuredly conquer the city, Lorenzo took a bold and desperate action that ended up paying off. He sailed directly into the hands of the King of Naples choosing to put his own life on the line rather than risk the well-being of the city that he loved. The king was impressed with Lorenzo's bravery and ended up calling off his forces and thus spared the city. He also released Lorenzo back to Florence where his brave actions prompted even broader support from its citizens, who now saw Lorenzo not just as the young head of the Medici clan, but as a brave, crafty, and powerful leader. After the threat of war had subsided and the ripples of disruption from the Pazzi conspiracy had calmed, Lorenzo was able to maintain and promote peace in Italy throughout the remainder of his life. This peace and prosperity allowed the golden years of Florence to continue and thrive. He tells us: "All citizens must place the common good before the private good."

Lorenzo also built upon the legacy of his grandfather as a patron of the arts. Lorenzo sponsored artists like Botticelli and Michelangelo (even bringing the young Michelangelo into his home and allowing him to receive tutorship from the same man who tutored his own children). Through commissioning a few personal works of art, and by securing jobs throughout Italy for many of the artists who he knew and supported, he encouraged artists to thrive during this golden age. Lorenzo provided education for the young Michelangelo, and other artists within the Humanist circles of Florence, many of whom also regularly attended and were influenced by the discussions and teachings of the Platonic Academy. Lorenzo also played a role in the life of Leonardo Da Vinci. After Da Vinci was charged as a homosexual (a serious, though seldom pursued charge in Renaissance Florence) Lorenzo interceded on Da Vinci's behalf to find him patronage and acceptance in Milan. Lorenzo was a bibliophile and continued building the collection of books that was started by his grandfather Cosimo. Lorenzo set up workshops where copyists worked tirelessly to copy books that could then be spread throughout Europe. In 1471 Lorenzo calculated that the Medici family had spent around 663,000 florins on charity, buildings, and taxes (close to about half a billion US dollars in today's money). He said of this expenditure,

> "I do not regret this for though many would consider it better to have a part of that sum in their purse, I consider it to have been a great honour to our state, and I think the money was well-expended and I am well-pleased."

Lorenzo passed away in April 1492 and the golden years of Florence largely passed with him. Though there were still a few good years left, a young and radically zealous preacher named Savonarola, who was already growing in popularity, was able to seize control of Florence, taking advantage of the power vacuum that occurred after Lorenzo's death. It is rumored in conflicting stories that Savonarola, despite gaining power in part due to Lorenzo's blessing, either pardoned Lorenzo of his sins at his death, or condemned him to hell (depending upon which account one believes). At the hour of Lorenzo's death many signs were said to have been seen throughout the city: the cathedral was struck by lightning, ghosts appeared, and the lions of Florence (a sort of mascot duo for the city) attacked one another. Savonarola opposed and wanted to destroy all parts of the Humanist culture that Lorenzo and the rest of the Humanists had worked so hard to revive. Perhaps these signs (if they really did occur) were omens not only of the death of Lorenzo, but also of the impending death of the Renaissance along with him.

After Lorenzo's death the Signoria declared:

> "Whereas the foremost man of all this city, the lately deceased Lorenzo de' Medici, did, during his whole life, neglect no opportunity of protecting, increasing, adorning and raising this city, but was always ready with counsel, authority and painstaking, in thought and deed; shrank from neither trouble nor danger for the good of the state and its freedom..... it has seemed good to the Senate and people of Florence.... to establish a public testimonial of gratitude to the memory of such a man, in order that virtue might not be unhonoured among Florentines, and that, in days to come, other citizens may be incited to serve the commonwealth with might and wisdom."

Giovanni Pico della Mirandola: philosopher, writer, Humanist

Giovanni Pico della Mirandola (1463–1494) was born in the middle of the Renaissance golden years of Florence and grew into a man just in time to see the death of his close friend Lorenzo de' Medici and the beginnings of the downfall of Florentine Humanism with the rise of the religious fervency of Savonarola. Pico was a precocious child and an incredibly gifted young man with an unrivaled genius. As a young child Pico was taught both Latin and Greek and, at the age of 10, he was sent to Bologna to study canon law. After his mother died, he switched his studies to focus on philosophy at the University of Ferrara, then after visiting Florence and making friends with several men of the Humanist circles of Florence, Pico went to the University of Padua to continue his studies, ultimately ending up at the University of Paris for even more learning. Pico was said to know over 20 languages by the age of 21 and was always voracious in his seeking of knowledge. Because of his broad schooling and travel he was exposed to many ways of thinking. He was not only a reader of Plato, but also studied Aristotle, Pythagoras, Kabbalah, canon law and the bible, and even Middle Age Islamic thinkers like Averroes and Avicenna.

Pico's diversity and breadth of learning inspired his philosophy, and his beliefs were dramatically more tolerant, open minded, and more advanced even than the other Humanists who came before him. Pico formed a new philosophy, a syncretistic collection of many different religions and philosophical teachings that sought to incorporate elements of many different ideas into one continuous lineage of truth and wisdom. Pico sought out to reconcile the differences in teaching between Aristotle and Plato (Plato was the philosopher of choice for the new Humanist movement, while Aristotle was a favorite of most scholars of the Middle Age inspired scholastic tradition of education), but he also sought to reconcile the differences of philosophy from the teaching of the Church. He even went so far as to claim that men like

Plato were divinely inspired and connected to the same ultimate truth preached in Judaism and the bible. Pico's friends coined a term of endearment for him, *Princeps Concordiae* or "Prince of Harmony". His philosophy of shared truth and harmony, not surprisingly, did ruffle some feathers, especially inviting ire from men of the Church and the pope in Rome.

Despite Pico's very different views on the teaching of pagan philosophers, and his insistence on a shared truth present in all philosophy and religion, Pico himself was a practicing Christian. In fact, he met Savonarola (the man who would later bring ruin to the Renaissance spirit of Florence) at a young age in Florence and they maintained a close friendship through their lives. In 1484 Pico met Lorenzo de' Medici and Marsilio Ficino. Despite their personal assertion of the superiority of Plato over Aristotle, Pico became close friends with the men, Lorenzo watching over Pico until Lorenzo's death in 1492. Shortly after Pico's visit to Florence he became involved in an affair with the wife of one of Lorenzo's cousins and, when he attempted to escape with his new love at his side; her husband caught both trying to escape. He wounded Pico and threw him into prison to rot but, despite Lorenzo's blood ties to the man whom Pico betrayed, Lorenzo interfered on Pico's behalf and was able to have him freed.

While Pico recovered from his injuries, he began to study books on the Kabbalah, the oracles of the magi, and on Hermetics and magic. Pico was tutored by a rabbi on the Kabbalah and was taught that the application of magic was the final step in his spiritual evolution. This new understanding of these concepts completed Pico's philosophical development as he formed a new vision of truth and enlightenment for the people of the Renaissance. This inspired Pico to write his magnum opus, *Oration on the Dignity of Man*, the pinnacle of Renaissance thought, and considered by many to be the manifesto of the Renaissance. His oration declared that humankind was not bound by fate or created with a place designated for us, but that we are free to choose our own destiny, to choose our own place within the universe. In his *Oration* God speaks to Adam in the garden of Eden:

> "Adam, we give you no fixed place to live, no form that is peculiar to you, nor any function that is yours alone. According to your desires and judgment, you will have and possess whatever place to live, whatever form, and whatever functions you yourself choose. All other things have a limited and fixed nature prescribed and bounded by our laws. You, with no limit or no bound, may choose for yourself the limits and bounds of your nature. We have placed you at the world's center so that you may survey everything else in the world. We have made you neither of heavenly nor of earthly stuff, neither mortal nor immortal, so that with free choice and dignity, you may fashion yourself into whatever form you choose. To you is granted the power of degrading yourself into the lower forms of life, the beasts, and to you is granted the power, contained in your intellect and judgment, to be reborn into the higher forms, the divine."

This new view of humanity was revolutionary. Though these ideas had been bubbling up through the undercurrents of the Humanist movements since the days of Petrarch, they finally crystalized in the words of Pico's *Oration*. The *studia humanitatis* that were promoted by the Humanists did not just lead to one's improvement for the civic and worldly life but were actually able to raise one to the heights of the angels! Pico declares that we are born with nothing but endless potential and the freedom to choose our place in the universe and our own destiny.

The person that we become is not a god-given right, but a product of our own labor and cultivation of the self:

> "Imagine! The great generosity of God! The happiness of man! To man it is allowed to be whatever he chooses to be! As soon as an animal is born, it brings out of its mother's womb all that it will ever possess. Spiritual beings from the beginning become what they are to be for all eternity. Man, when he entered life, the Father gave the seeds of every kind and every way of life possible. Whatever seeds each man sows and cultivates will grow and bear him their proper fruit. If these seeds are vegetative, he will be like a plant. If these seeds are sensitive, he will be like an animal. If these seeds are intellectual, he will be an angel and the son of God. And if, satisfied with no created thing, he removes himself to the center of his own unity, his spiritual soul, united with God, alone in the darkness of God, who is above all things, he will surpass every created thing. Who could not help but admire this great shape-shifter? In fact, how could one admire anything else?"

Pico tells us that there are levels to our enlightenment. The lowest form of mankind is ruled by their impulses and appetites. The next is ruled by their reliance on the empirical world that we can see and interact with. Then comes the philosopher that is ruled by reason and logic. And, finally, the divine is the person that has transcended all worldly desire and awareness and has reached a meditative state of oneness with the divine:

> "If you see a person totally subject to his appetites, crawling miserably on the ground, you are looking at a plant, not a man. If you see a person blinded by empty illusions and images, and made soft by their tender beguilements, completely subject to his

> senses, you are looking at an animal, not a man. If you see a philosopher judging things through his reason, admire and follow him: he is from heaven, not the earth. If you see a person living in deep contemplation, unaware of his body and dwelling in the inmost reaches of his mind, he is neither from heaven nor earth, he is divinity clothed in flesh."

Pico's *Oration* and its declaration that "we can become whatever we choose to become", was revolutionary, but it's not what got him into opposition with Rome. The *Oration* was written as a companion piece to introduce his even more revolutionary *900 Theses*. These *900 Theses* were essentially 900 declarations made by Pico dealing with matters of theology and philosophy. Pico invited any wise or religious man or scholar to come to Rome to debate him and claimed that all 900 of these statements were undeniable truths. But in 1487 Pope Innocent VIII forbid the debate from happening and established a council to review the theses to decide if these were compatible with Church doctrine. Unfortunately for Pico, 13 of the theses were declared heretical. So, in 1489 Pico wrote and published his *Apologia* defending his views, which only further inflamed tensions with Pope Innocent VIII. Pico's book (*900 Thesesh,:*) was ultimately banned by the Church and almost all the copies in circulation were confiscated and burned. Pope Innocent said of Pico's *900 Theses* that it was:

> "In part heretical, in part the flower of heresy; several are scandalous and offensive to pious ears; most do nothing but reproduce the errors of pagan philosophers... others are capable of inflaming the impertinence of the Jews; a number of them, finally, under the pretext of 'natural philosophy', favour arts that are enemies to the Catholic faith and to the human race."

Lorenzo de' Medici, friend, and protector of Pico was able to step in at the height of the tensions and arrange for Pico to stay with him in Florence under his protection and watchful eye to save him from Church reprobation. Pico stayed in Florence until the death of his protector Lorenzo, in 1492, and then he moved to Ferrara. However, he frequently visited Florence to meet with his close friend Savonarola. Savonarola, the austere and fervently zealous religious man, saw himself as a prophet of God and, in the power vacuum created after the death of Lorenzo, he increasingly gained power and influence in the city. Pico became closer to Savonarola after the death of Lorenzo and, while he never relinquished his syncretistic views fully, he was influenced enough by Savonarola to eventually destroy his collection of personal poetry and to give away most of his wealth. Pico and one of his closest friends Angelo Poliziano both died under suspicious circumstances at young ages. In 2007 their bodies were exhumed and found to contain high levels of arsenic, likely poisoned by Lorenzo's son Piero after Lorenzo's death due to their closeness to the increasingly influential Savonarola. After Pico's death Marsilio Ficino wrote of him:

> "Our dear Pico left us on the same day that Charles VIII was entering Florence, and the tears of men of letters compensated for the joy of the people. Without the light brought by the king of France, Florence might perhaps have never seen a more somber day than that which extinguished Mirandola's light."

Pico represents perhaps the best example of the crystallization of thought that occurred during the Renaissance years of Florence. Incredibly well versed in multiple disciplines and philosophies, fluent in multiple languages, and a full believer in the potentiality and power of mankind, Pico's *Oration on the Dignity of Man* was a final declaration that humankind was free to determine its own fate. Unfortunately, just beyond the brilliance of the shimmering golden years of Florence that culminated in the life of Pico, the darkness of the Middle Ages threatened to reawaken through the influence of Pico's close friend Savonarola.

Chapter 5

Darkness returns: the rule of Savonarola and the condemnation of human achievement

A young Dominican friar named Girolamo Savonarola (1452–1498) was born into a wealthy family in Ferarra in 1452. It is thought that Savonarola received a good classical education, studying the thoughts of great Humanist minds like Petrarch, these same minds he would later condemn for leading the people of the world astray. After Savonarola's early education and his brief foray into poetry he renounced his wealth, poetry, and worldly life and joined the Dominican order to follow the word of God and become a servant of Christ.

In 1482 Savonarola first came to Florence as a young preacher. But the energizing myth of the Renaissance was still strong in its people: the Platonic Academy met regularly, the Medici family still had a strong hold over the government and ruled fairly, and the light of antiquity illuminated the city with its warm glow. But, in 1491, after years of correspondence and friendship with Pico della Mirandola, Savonarola again came to Florence, this time under the welcome banner of Lorenzo de' Medici, and at the recommendation of Pico. Pico saw Savonarola as a man who had direct access to divine intelligence and had formed a deep connection with God. He thought there was no better man to lead the religious life of Florence.

Savonarola was a master speaker and his preaching garnered growing crowds that eventually grew so large that his sermons had to be delivered in the public square because the cathedral was not large enough to house the crowd. Savonarola and his fiery sermons gained traction among the lower classes and guildsmen. These men were hungry for change and had not been as heavily influenced by the Humanist ideals that had been provided to the wealthy and prominent men of Florence through their classical educations. Savonarola directly attacked Humanist ideals like the love of antiquity, the celebration of human intellect and individualism, and art. As Savonarola gained more influence in the city he began to directly and indirectly oppose the Humanist leaders and culture of the city. Even as he openly began to oppose Lorenzo de' Medici, Lorenzo did not attempt to stop or stifle Savonarola. It is unclear why Lorenzo allowed Savonarola so much freedom; perhaps he didn't wish to be seen in opposition to the word of God, or perhaps his respect for Pico simply prevented him from action against his close friend.

In 1492 Lorenzo passed away and several reports tell different stories of the time of his passing. In one account Lorenzo repented for his worldly sin and was forgiven; in another account he remained quiet and was not granted forgiveness by Savonarola before his death. After Lorenzo's passing, Savonarola continued to grow in power and influence. Lorenzo's son Piero was ill equipped as a leader and rose nowhere near the heights of leadership and achievement of his father. And so, the citizens of Florence, increasingly afraid and looking for leadership, looked towards the authority of Savonarola.

Savonarola's teaching was radical, austere, and incredibly stifling to the individual and to human achievement: His sermons were tirades of fire and brimstone. He declared that the vanity of the people of Florence would lead them to destruction and that the study and embrace of antiquity had led the multitude astray. He began to tell prophecies about the destruction of Florence. The prophecies of destruction preached by Savonarola gained even more weight with the people of Florence when King Charles VIII of France marched an army over the Alps and into Italy in 1494. While the French army marched ever closer to the city walls, Lorenzo's son Piero, seemingly paralyzed by the futility of the situation, did nothing to prepare for the coming army. The armies of Florence and the rest of Italy were no match for this well-equipped and battle-hardened French army. The French were equipped with new weapons like cannons and mobile artillery; it was a far larger force than anything the Italians could muster, and they were well-trained professional soldiers. The people of Florence saw their coming destruction at the hands of the French king as proof of the credibility of Savonarola's prophecy. Savonarola was eventually able to work out a deal with King Charles to spare the city of Florence and he preached that the city had been spared due to their acceptance of God's call to reform.

Savonarola, now seen as the savior of the city, established a government through the creation of the 500 (a supposedly new republic of Florence) and began to call for the city of Florence to continue to turn away from its wicked ways and embrace the true word of God. While claiming this new government would return Florence to its republican roots and provide true freedom for the common man, they imposed new laws against crimes like adultery, sodomy, and public drunkenness. The council ordered brothels closed, ramped up the persecution of homosexuality (homosexuality was looked down upon but generally left alone under the reigns of Cosimo and Lorenzo de' Medici), and Jews were expelled from the city. Bands of men also roamed the streets looking for people engaged in sinful or immoral acts. Savonarola increasingly made calls for the citizens of Florence to renounce their wealth, reject sinful paganist teachings and ideas, and to destroy anything that existed in vanity (art, poetry, writings, mirrors, ornate clothing, playing cards, and anything else deemed ungodly). The same bands of men that enforced the laws of Florence worked to make sure anyone who disagreed with the decrees of Savonarola would be tortured into reform or made to disappear completely.

Savonarola eventually drew ire from the pope in Rome as he declared that the Church had also fallen from the path of righteousness; the push back against him from the Church seemed to only hasten and embolden the intensity of his attempts to cleanse Florence of "evil". In addition to pressure from the pope that eventually led to Savonarola being excommunicated from the Church, the city of Florence also faced new trials and chaos during this time. Eleven straight months of rain destroyed the crops of Florence, leading to famine, and a new outbreak of plague began to spread in the city. Savonarola ordered the granaries to be opened to provide food for the starving population and it resulted in a riot where multiple women ended up trampled to death amidst the chaos. Medici supporters tried to take advantage of the strife and attempted to have Savonarola assassinated but, after the attempt failed, it simply deepened the unrest within the city. The chaos only emboldened Savonarola and gave a newly revived credence to his prophecies of destruction by the hands of God due to the people's sin.

The culmination of fear was when Savonarola organized mass burnings of priceless works of art in Florence, known as the Bonfires of the Vanities. In February of 1497 the largest of these took place in the main square of Florence, destroying what would amount to millions of dollars' worth of: art, writing, poetry, clothing, furniture, playing cards, and musical instruments. Savonarola's goal through these bonfires was to literally burn away anything that still dignified and represented the heights of Renaissance culture that had only recently ended. As Savonarola and his radical fanatics looked on through the smoke, they watched what had taken the Italian Renaissance over a century to build go up in flames. Eventually Savonarola become so fanatical that he believed he and his followers would be spared if they walked through flaming coals and a public demonstration was arranged where his followers would walk through coals to demonstrate the miracle of Christ's power working through them. The coals were set up and in an obvious move of doubt they delayed the event for hours. Eventually the delay went on so long that a downpour occurred and extinguished the flames. The people finally had enough of Savonarola and his austere rule, and a mob gathered and captured him and his followers to be tortured and put on trial. Under torture Savonarola confessed to making up his prophecies and in May of 1498 he and two of his closest followers were hanged and then burned by the people of Florence.

Chapter 6

The light still shines: how the Renaissance spirit survived and continued to spread

And so, with the death of Lorenzo de' Medici, Pico, and the austere rule of Savonarola the light that once shone so bright during the Renaissance years of Florence had grown so dim that only remnants seemed to remain of this wonderful golden age. The Renaissance in Florence would end in the opposite way to which it began. It began with a warm embrace of the ancient world, with great men seeking to emulate and revive the wisdom of antiquity. It would end with the condemnation of that same wisdom by a religious zealot who made even the dark ages seem enlightened. The revival of the light of the ancient world was almost extinguished by the same darkness that caused it to disappear so many centuries previously. The curious and wonderful potential of the individual (and of humankind) was slowly strangled by the oppressive grip of a collectivist ideology that disempowered human achievement and the sovereignty and dignity of the individual.

The Humanist movement and its focus on the individual, and its focus upon the republicanism that had provided freedom for individuals to thrive, was replaced by a condemnation of those same values under the guise of the "democracy" of Savonarola. The energizing myth of the Renaissance began to die in the same moment that the trials of the time began to stress the populace into a place of terror and fear. As the people grew more afraid, they began to be ever-more willing to sacrifice their freedom and sovereignty in preference for a leader who could lead them to safety. Under Savonarola the individual and the spirit of the Renaissance that had led to a flourishing in Florence not seen since the days of Rome, was sacrificed in preference of the security of a strong leader that could lead its people through the trials that lay ahead. Unfortunately, though, as happens far too often, the promises of Savonarola to lead Florence into a new utopia that sought to destroy its connection to the glory of its ancient heritage led only to its return to the darkness of the Middle Ages. Thankfully though, no matter how dark it gets, the individual can never be completely destroyed; there continues to exist within each one of us a pulsing human spirit that desires to actualize itself through creation, learning, and achievement; and so, the same spirit of the Renaissance still lives on today within our hearts, spirits, and minds.

Even as Humanist and Renaissance culture went into decline in Florence, scholars and artists continued to spread their ideas of personal enlightenment and of the dignity of the human being and human spirit throughout the rest of Italy and Europe. Michelangelo would still go on to paint the famed *Creation of Adam* (surely inspired by his upbringing in the Medici palace and his exposure to the wonderful study and celebration of philosophy that occurred in the revived Platonic Academy of Florence), and Raphael would go on to paint the famed *School of Athens*. The printing press that first arrived in Italy in the 1450s (by the end of the 1400s it had already produced over 30,000 books in Italy alone), the massive libraries of the Humanists, the infiltration of classical learning into universities throughout Italy and the rest of Europe, the expectation that wealthy families and rulers would have a solid grasp on the wisdom of ancient Roman and Greek culture, the emphasis on the restoration of the city of Rome by Humanists popes (up until the sack of Rome in 1527), and the Humanist focus on the *studia humanitatis* all ensured that these Humanist principles would survive to be long cherished in the Western psyche.

The study of antiquity and the celebration of human dignity that found its first light in the works of Petrarch and culminated in the words of Pico's *Oration on the Dignity of Man* survived through the traditions of the Humanists and was passed on down through the history of the Western world and mind. Today we are in a position much like that of the Italians of the Renaissance age. We may have lost the direct connection with the wisdom and light of the ancient world, but the same desire for wisdom that existed during the Renaissance still flows through our veins. Just as Petrarch believed that within the Italian breast the Roman heart was beating still, within our breasts still beats the heart of the Italian Renaissance.

Aside from many of the most striking similarities between the dawn of the Renaissance and today's age, among them a banking collapse and depression that were followed by a global pandemic, there are many other reasons why today's age is ripe for a *new* Renaissance. The Renaissance saw a group of Humanists that sought to revive the teachings and culture of an age that came long before them. These Humanists focused on and embraced the philosophy of the ancients and looked to men like Seneca and Cicero as examples of a better way of living and looked to men like Plato and Aristotle for knowledge and wisdom.

While the Humanists of the Renaissance period sought to reconcile the differences between secular philosophers and the teachings of the Church (so that they could be studied more freely), Florence and other cities of Europe began to experience a growing and ever-more global economy with new opportunities in trade and commerce. Banking, the printing press, and other advances increased economic prosperity throughout Europe while the profits of nobility and the elite funded artists, architects, philosophers, and writers to create new works and dissect the works of antiquity.

A large part of the Renaissance movement was the study of the ethical teachings of people like Cicero, Plato, Aristotle, and Seneca. The ideas of ancient Greek and Roman honor were revived, the long-standing Middle Age tradition of leadership from birthright was upended as new wealth was created, and men became respected not through bloodline alone but through merit. The new and booming economy of Florence also created a demand for trained professionals. Writers, lawyers, accountants and many other skilled professionals came to be in high demand. Educational focus then shifted to produce men who could read, write, and speak eloquently, and that could carry themselves with prudence to work successfully within society. Civic Humanism (the idea of becoming proficient in the humanities – poetry, rhetoric, moral philosophy, history, and grammar -- so that one could become a better and more active member of their community) contributed to a new class of men raised up with classical education and trained to become better leaders.

Philosophers of the period also placed a special focus on the attainment of virtue and upon living ethically, which encouraged individuals to strive to be better personally. Even the wealthy elite of Italy (people like Cosimo De' Medici) were encouraged to give back to those in need, spread ethical teachings, and better themselves through learning and practice. Wealth or birthright alone were insufficient to earn respect in Florence; one had also to be a good person. In many ways ancient Rome and Athens became reborn within the city walls of Florence; antiquity was a time where people were encouraged to look within for the answers to one's problems – following the Delphic maxim to "know thyself". The Renaissance saw a real rekindling of that impulse.

Much like today's world, the Renaissance world was complex. Many currents of social issues, political struggles, and individual desires directed the flow of events through time. The Renaissance was not a perfect age, and likely the version you have read about here in this book has been romanticized. But I have chosen in this book (as I always do in life) not to search for what was wrong during the Renaissance, but instead to look for wisdom that might be useful to us in today's world. Disclosure: during the Renaissance, women were mostly treated like objects, the poor and working class still struggled for representation, people born in the lowest of society were often not given access to education and other valuable resources, and issues like famine or disease plagued society due to a lack of progress in medicine and science. However, rather than throw out the past because of what it lacked, many people wiser than us throughout history have looked to the past not for things to condemn, but for wisdom worth reviving. I propose that today we do the same. There is so much wisdom and so much good that we may gain from this wonderful time period known as the Renaissance. Let us not throw out the wisdom of the past simply because it was not a perfect age. After all, despite social progress today, we are still far from perfect.

I believe that today's age is the perfect time for us to look back at the past, not at its shortcomings, but at the wisdom still waiting there to be revived. In a world that has become increasingly secular, and increasingly consumer driven, most people no longer focus on virtue or even consider what is right or wrong from an individual standpoint. Many of us simply defer tough choices and instead look to others around us for ideas on how we should live. We have become increasingly focused on collective norms and appeals to authority rather than doing the hard work of determining for ourselves what *we* believe is right or wrong. Groupthink has become the predominant law of the land and, just as the ancient philosophers like Socrates and Aristotle feared, democracy has in many ways devolved into a rule by the uneducated majority. Society has turned largely into a mob that is simply manipulated by competing sides. We can see the evidence for this in the fact that political polarization is today at an all-time high.

We live in a world where people put versions of themselves on display that are carefully curated for maximum acceptance. The images that the rich and famous put out of themselves can be likened to show houses that are beautiful on the outside but barren within. This leads to ever-increasing levels of depression, stress, and hopelessness as people continue to focus more of their energy on getting what others have. After all, they look happy so those things must make us happy too. We have fallen into a trap of seeking happiness not within ourselves, but as something that can be gained through the accumulation of possessions and achievement. We have been deceived into believing that if we just work hard, buy a house, and have 2.5 children we can all share the American dream. We have become a society full of broken and empty people looking towards somewhere outside of ourselves to find happiness and fulfillment when the key to the good life rests not within the window of a retail store or behind a high-def screen; it lies buried in the wisdom of the past, still preserved by the words of the philosophers of the ancient world.

What we need today are more individuals, more people willing to look within for the answer to theirs and the world's problems, more people willing to look within for the answer to what ails them, rather than pointing the finger elsewhere. The ancient world, even the collective societies of Greece and Rome, placed a massive emphasis on the use of reason and logic. They taught their citizens that they had a moral obligation to become good citizens and to cultivate themselves because better and more educated citizens would always make a better and more educated State. A strong society will always be composed of a group of individuals seeking to thrive and grow; founded on the principles of virtue and reason. This is how ancient societies came to thrive and to revolutionize the way that we see the world, even still today.

How does one tap into their own personal power and sovereignty like a true Renaissance man or woman? What mental tools and habits can we bring back into our lives today that will make us better people and therefore create a better world? Those are the questions that I seek to answer here in this book. We can use the same tools and ideas that were used in Rome and Athens, and that were used again to create a new flourishing in Renaissance Italy and Europe. We've already seen how powerfully transformative these ideas were through the effects that they had on the Renaissance period. But now we need to apply these lessons and this timeless wisdom in our lives in the modern world.

The Renaissance also saw an age where the individual once again found power. The Middle Ages (dark ages) saw an oppressive Church that stifled personal exploration and human achievement in favor of a pious and modest life. But as Renaissance Humanism spread, people like Petrarch argued that mankind had meaning and purpose and that, as human beings, we do have some control over our own destinies. We once again need stronger individuals – not individuals looking to others for approval, but individuals strong enough to stand on their own and forge themselves into better human beings through reflection and introspective journeys of growth. We must realize that while participation in the world and in society in large is necessary, it is not necessarily the most important part of our existence. The search for wisdom and personal growth, this ability within each of us to determine our own place in the universe, is perhaps our greatest asset. As Pico Della Mirandola told us, we are free to choose whether we devolve into a mob of beasts devoid of reason, or if we will raise ourselves through reason and contemplation to share in all the divine greatness that created us.

The new Renaissance won't be led by polarizing political movements or heated debate. It will come from people, like you and me, simply seeking to become better humans. We must recognize the potential that exists within every human being to be great, to do good, to make a better world through a better self. Rationality, prudence and patience, free thinking, a thirst for knowledge and self-improvement: these are the qualities of individuals that can make a better world. Revolution can begin with a few brave souls who are willing to stop moving when everyone else is running forward. It doesn't always take a majority to make a change; it can start with just a few examples of what is possible.

The Renaissance began with a small group of individuals; introspective men like Petrarch looked towards the wisdom and glory of the past and saw a blueprint that could help lead them to create better lives and a better world. Though they didn't agree with everything from the past – after all Romans and the Greeks were pagans, not good god-fearing Christians — but they still believed that these ideas of reason, self-cultivation, virtue, and courage could lift up the people of any age. Today we live in a unique moment. We too have been disconnected from the wisdom of our past. But it is still so close, still so accessible, still living in the words of these wise minds who came before us. Together we can revive this great spirit of the past, the spirit of the Renaissance. Ancient fire still lives within us waiting to be rediscovered, and so, let us begin… our new Renaissance awaits.

Part II

Renaissance Wisdom

"You cannot teach a man anything, you can only help him to find it for himself."

(Galileo Galilei)

Chapter 7

Humanism, the spark that lit the phoenix: Petrarch's ascent of Mont Ventoux

The Humanist movement that developed during the Renaissance was one of the most pivotal transformations in human thought in our species' history. While most of this period's thinkers were still influenced by religious dogma and politics of the day, Humanism was still a remarkable shift in perspective that changed the way that people in this era viewed life on earth. Though its highly debated and hard to pinpoint the exact birth of Humanism, many scholars agree that it started with Petrarch, and he is considered by many to be the Father of the Renaissance.

Early inklings of Humanist thought can be found in several of Petrarch's works, but perhaps the best illustration can be found in a letter he wrote somewhere around 1350. In the letter he describes his ascent of Mont Ventoux, a mountain top at about 6300 feet in elevation. Petrarch claims in his letter that he was the first person to climb the mountain in at least 50 years and that an elderly man from the area had warned Petrarch against attempting the feat. Petrarch writes that he climbed to the mountain top with his brother and experienced quite a bit of difficulty reaching the top, owing in part to Petrarche:'s inclination to take longer but "easier" appearing paths that were available instead of charging ahead into the harder but more direct paths as did his brother. He describes the climb as difficult and notes that he experienced quite a few moments of self-reflection on the way to the top. Eventually, though, Petrarch did finally reach the mountain top and had time to reflect on his journey. He pulled out a small volume of his favorite writer, St Augustine, and, as he opened the book, it fell open to this quote: "And men go about to wonder at the heights of the mountains, and the mighty waves of the sea, and the wide sweep of rivers, and the circuit of the ocean, and the revolution of the stars, but themselves they consider not."

The words hit Petrarch hard:

> "I closed the book, angry with myself that I should still be admiring earthly things who might long ago have learned from even the pagan philosophers that nothing is wonderful but the soul, which, when great itself, finds nothing great outside itself. Then, in truth, I was satisfied that I had seen enough of the mountain; I turned my inward eye upon myself, and from that time not a syllable fell from my lips until we reached the bottom again. ... We look about us for what is to be found only within. ... How many times, think you, did I turn back that day, to glance at the summit of the mountain which seemed scarcely a cubit high compared with the range of human contemplation."

The letter is striking for several reasons. First, this climb is possibly the first recorded instance of someone pursuing something like a mountain climb for purely aesthetic reasons, simply to gaze out at the horizon and appreciate the scenery. Second, the letter shows Petrarch's guilt as he considers the vanity in what he had done. He climbed this mountain to gaze at nature's beauty, but in doing so, perhaps lost sight of the truly important meaning of life:

to cultivate and improve oneself. In gazing out at all of God's glory that is nature, he was reminded of that same vast inner world of the human soul. Perhaps this moment was a turning point in the life of Petrarch that helped shape his worldview, eventually becoming passed down through his friends and writings.

The Humanists had a vast variety of beliefs and are very difficult to lump together as a homogenous group. Some Humanists were deeply religious and opposed the teachings of the ancients for practical value. Some were accepting of the writers of Rome and antiquity and sought to reconcile their differences with the Church. Some of the Humanists favored Plato and disliked Aristotle, while others did the reverse. Some others still sought to bring together the teaching of all great teachers and philosophers to form one ultimate truth.

While what really constitutes a Renaissance Humanist is hard to define (even among scholars and historians) one thing that most are in agreement on is that the Humanists had a keen interest in the works of antiquity. They sought to revive ancient texts through new or better Latin translations and, while some differed in their views of what texts or ideas held the most value, all worked together to bring antiquity back in their age in some form or other. Many of the texts that they studied and loved had been lost through time or shunned by the Church during the Middle Ages and the Renaissance was exactly this: a rebirth of these works and ideas.

The Middle Ages saw an incredibly oppressive form of Christianity take root in the world that snuffed out individual freedom, secular philosophy, and the scientific and logical progress of humanity. During the Middle Ages philosophical progress ground virtually to a halt and works of theology were the dominant questions and ideas of the day. In fact, the Middle Ages were so oppressive to thought and human progress that the term "dark ages" was coined to describe it. The prevailing mindset of the day went a little something like this:

God created the universe and all the living things within it; God is master and lord of all things. Do not question, do not seek to increase personal knowledge, do not do anything other than God's work because it is ultimately a distraction that leads you away from the path of God. The best way to live your life is to focus on piety and to reject the treasures and pleasures of the world.

This general line of thinking led to an understanding and to a belief that life had little meaning; that the real show started after you die. In fact, life was seen as a source of constant temptao:tion that a truly pious person would have to fight against every waking second in order to satisfy God. The purpose of a life that was generated from this way of thinking was to spread God's word, glorify God through worship and study, to reject all forms of: wealth, success, and power, and to focus all energies on God. Aside from some of the more sinister repercussions of this line of oppressive thinking, like the Crusades, one of the most nefarious effects was the death of reason, and ultimately of the individual. In the words of St Augustine: "He fashioned hell for the inquisitive." Many religious leaders and theologists of the dark ages believed that the quest for knowledge and understanding of the world and of life were sinful, and this kept humankind largely in the dark.

The dark ages did eventually end though, slowly illuminated with the twilight of antiquity that crept in through the teachings and progress of the Humanist movement that revived ancient Greek and Roman thinking as they scoured dusty monasteries for manuscripts from a golden age. The dark age's oppressive way of living and thinking slowly began to shift during the Renaissance as Humanists began to rediscover Greek and Roman works that emphasized the use of reason and logic in the pursuit of virtue. This wave of rediscovery eventually bloomed into a more modern way of viewing humans and their place in the universe. The Humanists saw humankind thrust into the world and thought that perhaps the meaning of life was to learn and thrive as a human being. This was often in direct opposition to the Middle Age idea of humankind as a worthless cog inside of a God-made machine.

Many of the Humanists thought that perhaps the best way to glorify God was to increase their knowledge, sharpen their wisdom and logic, and to use human accomplishment and achievement to glorify God. The Renaissance-era Humanists were not the same as Humanists are today though (modern Humanism is almost always secular). Most of the early Humanists were still devout and religious men. However, they still differed greatly in their world view from their dark age counterparts. The Humanists viewed life not as a distraction, but as an opportunity to grow, thrive, and better themselves through the cultivation of reason and thought. The Middle Ages taught people that the search for knowledge was the devil's work, but then the Humanist movement flipped this notion upside down and declared that the search for knowledge and the refinement of virtue might be the *purpose* of life.

The shift of perspective that came with the Humanist movement caused people to view themselves not as just meaningless cogs in a great machine, but as individual operators in a great system designed by God. Suddenly man was no longer just a passive character in God's story but, through a cultivation of his nature, he could become the hero. This liberation of humankind's destiny from the hand of God unleashed a new flourishing of human endeavors. People began to seek out new ways to better and improve themselves; they sought out knowledge and looked to increase their God-given talents through study. Humanist thinkers like Petrarch, Marisilio Ficino and Pico Della Mirandola devoured ancient Greek and Roman texts, used reasoning and logic to arrive at truth, and attempted to better their society by providing access to new sources of rediscovered information for everyone daring enough to study. Though these Humanists still taught and believed in the word of God, for the first time in many years these intellectuals promoted the belief that there was practical value to secular teachings and philosophies.

This renewed view of mankind, not as subservient to God, but rather the master of his own fate, started a wave of transformation that led to great progress throughout society – in science, mathematics, banking, astronomy, architecture, and art (to name just a few areas). A new type of human being was also born: The so-called "Renaissance man" or "Universal man" was a new type of human being who increased their proficiency across multiple disciplines in an attempt to reach their God-given potential. Along with all the other forms of progress, an informational revolution also began to occur as the printing press suddenly made books more available to people from all walks of life. Not only did we have rapid progress during the Renaissance, but the printing press now made it more possible for those ideas and innovations to spread throughout the rest of the world.

The legend of the phoenix tells us of a bird that ignites spontaneously and burns into ash, then regenerates from the ashes as a new being. New epochs are like that; old ways of thinking slowly smolder into ashes and, as one society dies, a new society eventually rises out of its ashes. Without the belief that this life has meaning and that human knowledge is something that should be nourished and fed, the Renaissance would likely never have occurred and the phoenix never would have risen. The revived belief that individual lives have meaning and that virtue could be cultivated in a person set the individual free from the shackles of Middle Age theology and suddenly opened new worlds to the people of the Renaissance. The Humanist movement thus liberated mankind from the oppressive ways of the dark ages and prepared the way for individual progress to finally resume the work started by the ancient philosophers of Greece and Rome. Men like Aristotle, Socrates, Plato, Cicero, Seneca, Quintilian, and many others became once again practical sources of personal betterment and knowledge. This focus on the individual and the belief that one can be refined and improved in life was the spark that ignited the phoenix of the Renaissance.

Believe in the individual: Pico's *Oration on the Dignity of Man*

> "To mankind it is granted to have whatever he chooses, to be whatever he wills."
>
> (Giovanni Pico della Mirandola)

Humanism took individual human beings, subservient slaves of God, and turned them into powerful and free beings that, through reason, could ascend to the heights of the divine. The Humanist believed that humans were free to determine their own worth and merit, and that through study and personal cultivation we could ascend to the heights of the angels. That isn't to say that the early Humanists weren't still deeply religious people (they almost exclusively still were – at least publicly), but suddenly humankind was re-empowered to make the most of its time here on earth rather than to totally reject the earthly life.

Though the Renaissance Humanists were not a totally congruent group, they did have some things in common, the most important among them was an intense appreciation for classical texts and works of antiquity. As the early Humanists translated and retranslated works from the likes of Aristotle, Plato, Seneca, and Cicero, the values of ancient Rome and Athens began to renew themselves in the minds of these Humanists and take on new form as these holy men sought to make the secular texts of the philosophers compatible with the teachings of the Church. In the ancient philosophies of Greece and Rome most people saw humans as trapped in the clutches of the gods and of fortune, but it was still believed that humans had a sense of control over their own lives. They could always seek to improve or to make decisions that would allow them to exercise and develop their personal virtue. The Humanists began to preach that virtue could be cultivated, that individual human lives had worth, and that individuals possessed untold hidden potential and power handed down to them directly from God. Suddenly the individual once again had meaning and purpose on earth, we once again had become the masters of our own fate.

Nowhere in the Renaissance can we find a better picture of this new position of humans in the universe than what we find in Giovanni Pico della Mirandola's *Oration on the Dignity of Man*. In the *Oration* Pico places humankind on a pedestal and declares the endless potential that lies latent within us as creatures created in God's image. He declares that humankind was created with no clear place in the universe, but this lack of an assigned hierarchy was not meant to be a burden to us, but rather it was intended to liberate us. God created human beings endowed with the free will of our creator. We can choose to elevate ourselves to the status of the angels through cultivation – study, reason, and personal improvement. Or we can choose to neglect our capabilities and vegetate, devolving into little more than beasts, only seeking out our immediate needs. The *Oration* did not beg permission for humankind to achieve greatness, but rather declared that all human beings have an untapped potential for greatness and that it is our responsibility to cultivate ourselves through the humanities into more logical and reasonable beings, thus becoming more like the angels and less like the beasts.

But somewhere throughout history we seem to have once again lost our faith in the individual and, while inspirational quotes on Instagram and motivational speakers have most of us repeating the mantra "anything is possible", we still seem to lack real faith in our own potential abilities. Most of us will say anything is possible if you put your mind to it, yet we don't feel the saying applies personally to ourselves. More and more people today suffer from low self-esteem and body image issues as social media bombards us with unrealistic expectations of what we should look like, how lavish our vacations should be, or how magnificent daily life should be. We now carry around a piece of technology that assails us constantly and tells us exactly who we should be and what we should look like. Advertisers, news agencies, and politicians now spend billions each year telling us exactly what we should look like, what we should wear, what we should watch on tv, and what we should believe in or what causes we should support.

Not only are individuals experiencing more pressure than ever to blend into the crowd thus changing our purchasing habits or influencing us into looking a certain way, but today's political movements have also become increasingly polarized. Left and right are more deeply divided today than ever before and many independents have been pushed or pulled over to one side or another. As we become more polarized it becomes harder to think freely or to debate differing views with others. Disagreements about policy that may have been considered small details thirty years ago have become hard boundary lines, with armed mobs on both sides. While it used to be acceptable that others hold beliefs that might be different from ours, many of us are now convinced that political choice can be boiled down as simply as right vs. wrong or good vs. evil. Many of us have forgotten that the person standing across that line that we disagree with is another human being with unique experiences and beliefs. But today we don't much celebrate the individual; in fact, most of us would rather be an accepted part of the mob. The mob is on the left and on the right, the individual claims their sovereignty and freedom of thought somewhere in the middle.

The same mob that scorns individual thought or dissent has made huge strides in social progress, however; and this leads to much its appeal. It seems like a mass of people can get much more done when they put their collective lives and voices together and, in some ways, it can – sometimes revolution *is* needed. But what we need today is not more followers. We need more powerful individuals. We need more free thinkers, more prudence, more people being genuine and embracing their unique viewpoints and differences. Individuals possess the power to create *real* change. You and I hold the keys to a better world; through seeking to become better humans, by seeking to treat others with respect and celebrate their differences and, by seeking to achieve our own potential, we encourage others to do the same.

Many wise people of many different cultures and ages agree: the key to change starts with the individual. Gandhi has a famous quote, "Be the change that you wish to see in the world". Matthew 7:5 from the Sermon on the Mount quotes Jesus, who said this: "You hypocrite! First, remove the beam out of your own eye, and then you can see clearly to remove the speck out of your brother's eye". Lao Tsu said: "He who controls others may be powerful, but he who controls himself is mightier still". Seneca said: "Most powerful is he who has himself in his own power." What these quotes say can be boiled down to a very simple idea: focus on yourself first and get your own life in order. Don't scold your neighbor for throwing his garbage on the street, worry about your own garbage. Don't scream about the injustice someone else committed but focus on being more just in your own life. Don't point fingers at others for the world's problems, but first look in the mirror and ask yourself how *you* can make a difference today.

Try this: don't try to change the world, don't try to change and correct your neighbor, don't focus on what others need to do to make the world better. Focus first and foremost on improving yourself. Focus on developing yourself, find your own truth (and try not to force it onto others). Focus on becoming a better person through virtuous actions and studying ethics. The interesting thing is that people can often make the biggest positive impact on the world once their own affairs are in order. Now that isn't to say that there isn't a place for encouraging others to be more virtuous and play their own part in making the world a better place (we will get to that more in the next chapter). It's just much better to lead by example than it is to scold others for their shortcomings. "It is not by muscle, speed, or physical dexterity that great things are achieved, but by reflection, force of character, and judgment" -Marcus Tullius Cicero.

So why is the individual the key to a better world? Because when you take enough individuals who are changing themselves for the better, eventually all those individuals will end up making up a big percentage of the world. Then change will come not through force or coercion, but through leading by example. One person focusing intently on cultivating themself is like one person standing still amongst a bustling New York City street – when everyone is moving in the same direction, one person standing still makes the loudest statement. If you want other people to be better, then first become better and lead by example yourself. I hate to keep coming back to this, but it's something that speaks to me deeply: in today's political climate people spend so much time pointing fingers and telling others what they should be doing. Maybe though the best way to effect a sweeping change isn't by telling others what they are doing wrong… maybe it's by leading by example and treating others with respect. Maybe if we all focused on being better, the world could be better. Maybe if we believed in ourselves, and maybe if we had a little more faith in humanity in general, the world might not seem so dark.

I know what some of you will ask, "What about progress? If everyone just focused on themselves, their own passions and pursuits without regard to making the world a better place, wouldn't progress just grind to a halt?" Well, during the Renaissance many of the great contributions to society, in art, literature, mathematics, architecture, and other fields, were brought on by shamelessly self-indulgent geniuses who were simply following their passions (some sarcasm intended here!). So many advances were made during the magic age of reason in the Renaissance and all of them by people focused on increasing their own personal knowledge, their own standing, or their own legacies. The thirst for knowledge and improvement that existed in these individuals led to countless advances in the world.

Contributions came from Michelangelo and Da Vinci in art and anatomy, Filippo Brunelleschi in architecture, Johannes Gutenberg with the printing press, Copernicus and Galileo in astronomy, Francis Bacon in scientific method. All these advances came from the liberation of the individual that began when early Humanists began to argue for the worth and power of humankind and took back some form of control over their own destinies.

This idea of self-cultivation is not new, nor is it one that was born in the Renaissance. Like the Renaissance, the idea of stronger individuals making up a better society had its origins within the ancient world of Greece. In the *polis* or the Greek city state, individuals were encouraged to elevate themselves through the use of reason to become better citizens. There was a profound sense of pride that existed within these states in its citizens, and one had a duty to be their best, not simply for themselves, but for their polis: this is why athletes were so celebrated in Athens. Athletes had achieved the peak of physical performance: not only did they inspire greatness in others by showing others what was possible, but these athletes who had spent their lives honing their bodies and skills would also make better and more effective soldiers. The citizen, much like the athlete, had an obligation to be their best: a *polis* made of citizens striving to be their best would always remain strong. But if the citizens of a *polis* would ever become weak, lazy, and uneducated, then the whole *polis* would be at risk.

So, is it selfish to follow your heart and dreams? Is it selfish to ignore the world around you while you better yourself or seek tirelessly to achieve a goal? It depends on who you ask, but I certainly wouldn't want to give up the contributions to the world that "selfish" individuals have made. I think we already have more than enough people who stand around pointing fingers at someone else and explaining why someone else is the root of all their problems. I'd rather take a few more of those crazies who have the courage to look inward at themselves when they want to see a better world. I'd rather have more of those restless geniuses who become obsessed with some goal and don't stop until they've achieved it. Focusing on your journey doesn't have to mean hurting or taking advantage of others to get there. There is nothing wrong or selfish with following your dreams or working on yourself. The better *you* are the better *your world* will be.

The key to a better world, the key to happiness, and the key to health or wealth doesn't belong in the hands of society or some corporation with something to gain by selling you a product: it belongs in your hands, it belongs in your mind, and it belongs to the individual. Stop waiting for society to conform to your standards and go out and become the change that you wish to see in the world. Through *you* anything is possible and if I didn't believe in you, then I wouldn't be writing this. Until you are ready to grow, learn, evolve, and change... Until you believe that every human being is capable of change and that every human being has swaths of unlocked potential hidden inside of them... until then, we are stuck in the same cycle. So, let's help break the cycle. Believe in yourself. Believe in others. Believe in the power of the individual.

Learn to love learning: antiquity revived, the Humanist emphasis on the humanities

> "For books are more than books, they are the life, the very heart and core of ages past, the reason why men worked and died, the essence and quintessence of their lives."
>
> (Cicero)

Petrarch is considered by many to be the Father of Renaissance Humanism. He revolutionized Western thinking by suggesting that mankind had a responsibility to learn and grow in life and he preached the value of secular teachings (like those of Cicero or Seneca) to help human beings become better. He (and the Humanist movement that followed him) placed a great emphasis on the humanities (*studia humanitatis*), specifically grammar, rhetoric, history, poetry, and moral philosophy. The Humanists believed that by reading and studying the classical works of Rome and Athens, by understanding their history and philosophical thought, and by learning classical poetry and literature, they could better themselves and create a better and more ethical society. Greek and Roman myths, poems, and philosophy placed special emphasis on virtue and personal adherence to a strong moral code. Rhetoric helped people deal more effectively with others and communicate ideas. Philosophy (specifically Aristotle, Socrates, Cicero, and Seneca), taught people to thirst for knowledge and to be more virtuous and rational human beings. Many of the Humanists had grown tired of the traditional scholastic teaching method of studying the arduous and poorly translated texts of Aristotle paired with theology and mathematics. Instead, many of them sought out the answers on the *how* of living, rather than speculating endlessly about the *why* of it. The Humanists began to look to writers from the past for guidance on how to live the best sort of life, how to achieve virtue, and how to become better humans.

One of the main ways that Renaissance Humanism affected the world was through reviving the emphasis on learning – not just reading the bible or the words of the saints, but even on learning from the secular authors of antiquity. Many of the pre-Renaissance thinkers saw worldly knowledge (and the quest to obtain it) as a foolish and prideful endeavor. In the religious paradigm of the Middle Ages, the quest for knowledge was nothing but a distraction from God. But Humanist thought looked at humankind, thrust into the world, and wondered if perhaps humans were meant to use their reason and faculties to become better. Though they still believed that humankind was placed here by God, Humanists believed that humans must decide what sort of position they would occupy in the hierarchy of the universe. Humans could live only for superficial pleasures and emotions and live like the beasts, or through the cultivation of virtue and on a continuous quest for wisdom they could elevate themselves to the height of the angels or the Gods.

The Humanist movement taught that people could focus on becoming better people and make a better world, while traditional theology said that men were all born sinners and could only be made better by the blood and forgiveness of Christ. These early Humanists certainly were not atheists. They just believed that they had some control over their destiny and that through learning and improving they could better themselves and the world. They believed that by creating a society where values and virtue were taught and prioritized as a subject of learning, society would create citizens that were morally better and better citizens. The Humanists didn't just focus on ethics or teaching people to become morally better; in fact, their focus was on the *studia humanitatis* and moral philosophy was only a small part of what the Humanists set their sights on.

The *studia humanitatis* was a set of practical skills found abundantly in the classical works of antiquity. The humanities of study consisted of grammar, rhetoric, poetry, history, moral philosophy – all found through the study of ancient Greek and Roman texts. The end-goal was to create a human being well versed in the arts of writing and influence. This would make students more effective in day-to-day life and in civic life and leadership roles. The Humanists didn't just read these ancient texts for fun. Rather they sought out practical wisdom and skills that they could use to better their lives. By the time that the golden age of Florence had arrived its ruling class was no longer defined by nobility of birthright, but by wealth, participation in the community (civics), and by a refinement of their intellect. In Renaissance Florence, in order to be respected one could not simply be born into their position, but they needed to be learned men as well. An excellent example of this idea can be found in Chapter 1 in the discussion of Niccolò Niccoli, when he encouraged the son of a prominent merchant to take up personal study.

Let's forget the Humanist movement and its civic duty for a second and get even more granular. On a very personal level, the individual level, how can learning help you? Well, let's first realize that every opportunity that presents itself to you, and every single fortunate or unfortunate thing that happens to you, must be responded to by *you* (regardless of whether it was in your control or not). If you are the judge that must navigate through your life and propel yourself through time with decisions and actions that you see fit, then the more wisdom you can bring into each day the better the outcome will wind up being for you.

Experiences can teach us practical knowledge that helps in day-to-day life and can even save our lives. But when reading the works of the greats that came before us, or when reading about their lives, we can often find poignant examples of how it might be best for us to live as well. Through the study of other great minds in history, we may act as sponges and soak up bits of wisdom that they gained through experience. We can make these lessons ours with little effort simply through study. These things that we learn, through study or through our own experiences, eventually form our worldview and become like the lenses through which we view our world. Refined tastes and a wide variety of things learned become like a pair of glasses that perfectly fit our eyes: they allow us to see the world more clearly and react to events in the most effective ways. Neglecting new learning, meanwhile, is like viewing the world through dirty lenses, where we struggle to understand or make sense of anything that we see. Functional intelligence, virtue, and effectiveness as a human being are not fixed traits. They are changeable and able to be cultivated through learning and practice. The more we learn the better we become. The better we become the better our lives become. The better our lives become the better the world will become.

When you focus on learning and expanding your wisdom, you increase the ability of your mind to access information when it's needed. The book you read on public speaking may teach you a skill that lands you a job at a high-paying new company. The course that you took in college in accounting may someday prove useful when you are presented with a great investment opportunity or when you decide to open your own business. The philosophy book that you read may show you some new important way of thinking (like learning to let go of the things that you cannot control and to focus your energy instead on the things that you can) that saves your marriage. There is no way to know what information you will need in the future to be successful. But every bit of information you can cram into your brain makes you more likely to have what you need in some future time when an opportunity presents itself. This was a huge part of why the Renaissance was such a magical age. This widespread emphasis on learning and personal betterment created a society of people who were versed in many different skills, ready to face each day with courage.

Some people say there is no such thing as luck. But luck, fate, fortune – or whatever you might like to call it – certainly plays a role in life. There are an infinite number of good or bad things that can occur to us at any moment in life. Many of them are completely outside of our control. One person is born in a dirt hut in Africa or a ghetto in Oakland, while another is born with a 15 million dollar trust fund and a billionaire dad. Skill, knowledge, and experience may play little role in many of the things that happen *to us* in life; but these qualities do absolutely play a role in what we make out of those occurrences. Committing to be a lifelong learner will help you learn the skills you need to make the most out of your good luck – and your bad luck.

How does one develop skill and expertise at anything in life? Through *learning*. You learn when you read, push yourself hard enough to fail, take classes, hire a coach, drill and repeat skills, watch people who are better than you (and take notes), or when you listen to lectures or interviews. A lot of people don't realize this, but learning is a *skill*, and the better you are at learning the quicker you will be able to pick up new skills and knowledge. The more you use your brain, the smarter it gets. I for one do *not* believe in lifelong fixed intelligence. I truly believe that from almost any starting point in life a person can learn to be effective, articulate, and achieve some sort of success in almost any field that they choose. Human beings are imbued with an amazing potential to grow, change, and evolve, but we must be conscious of this fact and choose to exercise our minds and we must continuously look for opportunities to learn.

Learning will make you better prepared to respond to luck or fortune. It will make you wiser and better able to deal with others. And learning can set you free from superficial cares about things that don't really matter. Whether it's good luck or bad, the more experience that you have, the more you have learned, the more knowledge and wisdom that you possess, the more prepared you are to respond in a productive way. When you prioritize self-growth and invest in yourself regularly, not only will you perform and feel better, but you will begin to *see* more opportunities in life.

Learn to love learning. Take advantage of every opportunity to grow or improve. Listen intently to people you know and respect, watch, and listen to interviews of your idols. Read books by experts, learn about new fields like philosophy or psychology that expand your mind and make you better at dealing with others, take classes, try new things, read the classics. Expand your mind in every way possible and learn to get excited to fail because failure leads to new growth. What is life except for a chance to live and learn? If you aren't learning, then you are either on autopilot or you aren't pushing yourself enough to truly live.

Help others achieve their potential: Michelangelo's *Faun*

> "Non nobis solum nati sumus." (Not for ourselves alone are we born.)
>
> (Cicero)

Even Florence's Pre-Renaissance history seemed to celebrate the achievement of the individual and allowed space for mankind to reach its fullest potential. The republic was founded in 1115 and later Florence's wealth came largely from a combination of banking, wool, and merchant activity. As merchants and workers began to accumulate new wealth, they also gained the power that came with it. Soon the merchant and working class sought representation in government. This did not lead to *perfect* equality, but it did lead to a republican government that was established to ensure that anyone who owned land would be eligible for government. Though this was still a small percentage of the population it allowed far greater participation in government then was usual during the time period. This allowed anyone who accumulated enough wealth and was able to purchase land to have a say in the governing of Florence. No longer was governance simply by nobility and birthright. In 1293, the Ordinances of Justice not only established guilds for the working class and gave them representation in government, but it also declared that no one would be above the law; even those of noble birth would be held accountable if they committed a crime. Florence's architecture reflected this new form of government as well, as large and ornately designed public squares encouraged the gathering of large numbers of citizens to discuss matters of governance, thereby inviting a participation in the workings of the state even to the lowest of its citizens.

With the Humanist paradigm shift that humankind had the power and the responsibility to make the most of life on earth, a new focus was placed on the individual to seek personal improvement. Through studying the humanities, the Humanists believed that we could become better and more effective humans, more like the God that created us. The Renaissance Humanists thought it was important to change the way people were taught and took part in a large movement to reform the traditional scholastic learning method. With a new focus on teaching students rhetoric, poetry, history, moral philosophy, and other literature of antiquity, the future leaders of Italy, and eventually all of Europe, were better equipped to use reason and logic to make the world a better place. Many of the most powerful and successful leaders, artists, architects, philosophers, and intellectuals of Renaissance Italy were classically trained and educated with a strong Humanist education.

A new mindset that focused on the bettering and transforming of individuals through a new form of education also led to general progress and abundance throughout society. As the leaders (and veiled leaders like the Medici) of the Renaissance received Humanist educations, life improved for general citizens as well. The Medici, for example, believed that commissioning new works of art by up and coming artists and architects created a more beautiful city that all citizens could enjoy and take pride in. The Medici were also keenly aware that the lower and middle classes (the *popolo minuto*) were a fickle bunch that would turn on their leaders quickly if they ever felt taken advantage of- this fact alone encouraged them to regularly help people on the streets that they saw in need. In fact, Salvestro de Medici rose to power partially thanks to an uprising of the working class that he helped to provoke. Though the Medici family escaped harm during the revolt, significant property damage and loss of life occurred to other wealthy families of Florence.

Cosimo Medici established regular grain distribution for the hungry poor and lowered taxes for the working class. The republican government of Florence established dowry funds that helped provide dowries for financially distressed families, education funds for the unfortunate, and funds to provide for protection of the state in times of war. Young men typically were taught Latin starting at the age of 5, and the literacy rates of Florence were far above other European states. The reading of the classics didn't simply produce a literate populace, but also passed on the wisdom of the ancients through the study of rhetoric and eloquence as well. This is why Leonardo Bruni in his history of Florence claimed that the city of Florence and its citizens were unlike any other state in the world.

A good example of the type of patronage not uncommon during the Renaissance period was the relationship between the Medici family and Michelangelo. At a young age Michelangelo began to show promise as an artist and poet and became a young apprentice to a well-known master artist. As a head pupil, Michelangelo was referred for a commission by Lorenzo to produce a mask of a mythical creature called a faun. Lorenzo was impressed as he watched the detail that Michelangelo put into the mouth and teeth of the mask, but poked fun by saying that such an old faun wouldn't have so many teeth. Legend has it that Michelangelo took note of the suggestion right there and immediately knocked out one of the front teeth on the mask to make it more lifelike. Lorenzo was impressed and took a liking to the young Michelangelo.

Michelangelo had his education paid for by Lorenzo and even lived in the Medici palace and dined with the Medici children (including Giovanni di Lorenzo de' Medici, who later became Pope Leo X). Michelangelo was raised by the Medici and, as a result, was exposed to the multitude of artists, writers, and philosophers that the Medici had in their close circle. This rich upbringing and Humanist education surely had a huge influence on Michelangelo and helped him to develop into the artist that would eventually paint the Sistine Chapel and carve the famous *David* out of that massive block of marble.

Cosimo and Lorenzo Medici (the de facto leaders of Florence in their respective times) and other leaders of Renaissance Italy funded the studies and works of many other geniuses: Da Vinci, Raphael, Bracciolini, Ficino, and a host of others. The sentiment of the age was that those with wealth and power had a civic duty to give back to their city and make it a better and more beautiful place. This allowed for rapid new advances in fields like mathematics, art, architecture, science, astronomy, and many others, that eventually revolutionized the world and Western thought. Some of these advances trickled down to the lowest levels of society; the printing press for example, revolutionized learning and allowed wider distribution of classical works so that people could have greater access to information. Thanks also to the patronage of leaders like the Medici there was an abundance of newly recovered and translated classical texts that also trickled down throughout society. At first the ownership of many of these texts was based in private libraries, but over time, and especially after the printing press began running, these texts became accessible to many, both in public libraries and through decreased cost. The leaders of the Italian city states like Venice and Florence also focused on commissioning and building beautifully ornate cityscapes that every citizen could enjoy and take pride in. A quick walk through Venice or Florence, even today, inspires travelers with some of the most beautiful art and architecture to be found anywhere on earth.

Not only did the Humanist movement create men like Leonardo Bruni and the Medici (proponents of Civic Humanism), but through the Platonic Academy and a trickle-down effect of the learning of the elites, even "normal" citizens apparently gained from the revival of ancient wisdom during the Renaissance. By the year 1464 Donato Acciaioli claimed that it was as if all the citizens of Florence had been brought up in the Academy.

This all leads us to our last major Humanist principle – to help others achieve their potential. Helping others doesn't have to be exclusive to only helping those in urgent or dire need. There are so many things that we can do to help others immediately around us in everyday life as well: listening to someone's problems and offering them words of encouragement, helping to push someone to chase a dream, offering to pass on your knowledge or expertise to help someone in need, or even just saying something nice to someone are all small ways that we can help others shine. Of course, we can also make monetary contributions or bigger investments as well. But it's important to realize that just even offering kindness or encouragement to others empowers them and helps make the world a better place.

Just like the masters of the Renaissance, the best way that we can give back and help others is to first achieve success and stability for ourselves. Those who help themselves first are best able to help others. Someone who is unhappy, negative, or just in an unstable place in life will not be poised to offer much encouragement or help to others. In fact, they are likely the ones who need help and encouragement themselves. When you focus on finding *eudaimonia* (more about this in our last chapter) and happiness in your life and when you focus on healing scars from your past and making your own internal environment more positive and healthier, you will start to have an abundance of energy that you can then start giving out to others around you. This is why it is so crucial to take care of yourself first.

One of the unintended benefits to looking out for yourself first and working hard to improve your own position in life is that you are also better able to help others once you get established. A person with 10 dollars in their checking account that must make that money last until Friday will have a hard time loaning money to a friend, even if they really want to. Someone who has a couple thousand, or a couple hundred thousand in their account is much more likely to be able to help. Wealth, having money, is not the evil that many seem to think it is. In fact, the more wealthy and powerful you are, the more potential that you have to do good in the world. But of course, there is always the choice to use it to help others and give back or to use it to hoard massive reserves of money and assets for yourself. A world where people become successful and then help others succeed is the ideal. The Humanists promoted this idea through their idea of Civic Humanism: one who attains personal success and wealth is best able to give back to society.

Have you ever been on a plane and read the emergency instructions? There is a section where it talks about putting oxygen masks on, and it states to put your own mask on first before helping others (like your children). Why as a parent would you ever prioritize your own safety over that of your child you might ask? Well, if you pass out from oxygen deprivation you won't be much help to anyone; in fact, you'll require saving. While someone is busy saving you, who knows if someone will be available to save your child or not. Life is like that – it is hard to give oxygen to others when we cannot breathe ourselves.

Cultivate and develop your own success, become mentally strong, follow your dreams, and gain as much success as possible in life. And then, when opportunities arise for you to use your success to give back to others, choose to give back. Give encouragement, advice, money, or mentorship, whatever you can. Helping those immediately around you can have a massive impact in the world and truly make the world a better place. Contrary to the belief of many, success in life isn't a zero-sum game; there is no reason why everyone can't succeed and excel. When you achieve knowledge, gain experience, or improve yourself, then you become capable of passing on those same traits onto others, this can happen directly through education or indirectly as leading by example.

Some people, some of us call them "haters", enjoy seeing others fail because it makes them feel better about themselves. Maybe they are overcompensating for their own insecurities. Maybe they like feeling powerful. Or maybe they are just assholes! Ultimately though, the people who like to see others fail, or who even work behind the scenes to make sure that failure happens, won't achieve lasting success or happiness for themselves. People who help lift others around them, people who mentor and pass knowledge onto others, and people who like to see other people successful and happy will have a much better chance at achieving success and happiness themselves. So don't be a hater. Be nice and try to help others around you. Surround yourself with positivity and be the sort of person who cheers for the underdog instead of rooting for the fall of the person on top. Trust me, the world is a much better place this way.

By bringing a belief of the individual into your own life and by helping others succeed, you can also help others become better and create lifelong connections that make a positive difference at the same time. People who fight and trample others to get to the top may achieve some temporary success, but eventually, when the people you are standing on to get to the top fail, you end up falling too. Living your life in a way where you mentor and encourage others around you will make the base that you stand on much more stable. And the people around you might even grow strong enough to give you a hand on your way up as well.

Successful people don't relish in other people's failures. They don't want to look good just because no one else around them is impressive. They seek to be better versions of themselves and encourage the people around them to grow too. The elite of Italy knew this during the Renaissance and they gave money and resources to artists, architects, scientists, and mathematicians to help develop and grow the beauty and success of their cities and surroundings. The greater the accomplishments of the state were, the greater the legacies of all involved would be. Humanism preached the idea that everyone should be better educated and that the proper use of a human life was to cultivate intellect and reason. A transformation like the Renaissance starts with individuals seeking to better themselves, and then seeking to better the world through improving others' lives as well. The better world that we all want to live in starts with us. But it can only come to fruition when everyone around us begins to excel and succeed as well.

Chapter 8
Platonism

Introduction: The Neoplatonists – Plato revived

"Human behavior flows from three main sources: desire, emotion, and knowledge."

(Plato)

In the mid-1450s a young man named Marsilio Ficino began learning Greek. This young man's classical education would have one of the most profound influences on Western philosophy out of all the philosophers of the Renaissance period. As mentioned before, the dark ages saw many great philosophers disappear into obscurity since the Church stifled most philosophical inquiry as heretical. One of the philosophers who was virtually lost in the West was Plato, who had all but disappeared due to a lack of accessible translations. Plato and Greek copies of his works did eventually come to Florence in the mid-century, carried by Greek scholars who were also able to teach select Florentines the Greek language after the fall of Constantinople in 1453. Despite Aristotle's dominance as the philosopher of choice throughout the Middle Ages, Plato was soon to re-emerge as the leading authority on wisdom.

During Marsilio's early education he was exposed to an important philosophical epic called *On the nature of things* by Lucretius (this work had been only recently recovered by Poggio Bracciolini). The poem left a lasting impression on Marsilio and may have been the catalyst that started a lifelong passion in him to become a philosopher instead of following in the footsteps of his father. Marsilio grew up in a wealthy family with strong connections and his father was a regular physician of the Medici. This direct connection of Ficino to the Medici would prove most auspicious for Ficino in his lifetime; because of Marsilio's connections and because of his passion for ancient poetry and philosophy, he wound up early in his life in a position where study, translation, and lecturing on these texts became his life's focus. Ficino would later go on to translate the entirety of a collection of works by Plato known as the *Socratic Dialogues*, all under the sponsorship of Cosimo de' Medici.

Cosimo de' Medici commissioned Ficino in 1462 to translate Plato's works from Greek into the more widely understood and read Latin form. Ficino would later read these exact same translations to Cosimo on his deathbed, providing his lifelong patron with consolation and comfort when near death. His work was widely influential during the Renaissance and greatly aided the spread of Humanistic and Platonistic ideas throughout Italy and Western Europe. In fact, Ficino's commentaries on the works of Plato remained the leading authority on Plato up until the 1800s. Marsilio was so well versed in Plato and his works that Cosimo also chose him to head the revived Platonic Academy in Florence, an informal meeting place where Florence's leading artists and intellectual giants met to discuss topics like philosophy, art, and life.

Plato was a direct student of Socrates, and Plato himself later went on to teach and mentor a famous student of his own named Aristotle (the philosopher who has been juxtaposed against Plato's philosophy even to this day).

Diogenes Laertius tells us that Plato was also a perfect picture of the Renaissance man (though the term "Renaissance" wouldn't come into play until many years later). He tells us that Plato was a fine physical specimen as well as a philosopher and artist; not only was Plato a skilled wrestler and the king of eloquence, but he was also apparently a poet and a painter.

Plato, though he was the star pupil of Socrates, held many beliefs of his own that differed from and delved more deeply into the teachings of Socrates. In Plato's *The Republic* he showed us his ideal state, with philosopher kings running the affairs of the country. Plato also elaborated on and further preached Socrates' ideas on the immortality of the soul. Plato declared that all things are caused by God. Matter may be the substance of the universe, but God is the mind and order of everything. Plato also taught that virtue alone is sufficient for the good life and though good health or good fortune may be preferable, a wise person can live a perfectly happy and good life without them. He believed in four virtues (they just so happen to be very similar to the same virtues adopted by the Stoics): justice, prudence, courage, and temperance.

Plato wrote the famous *Socratic Dialogues* that are one of our few links to the life and beliefs of his teacher Socrates. One of Socrates' beliefs about philosophy was that it was a living thing that existed within discourse and dialogue; the act of writing one's philosophy down would allow it to be taken out of context or misunderstood. This led him to not write down any of his thoughts or teachings. Today our only real ideas of what Socrates was like or how he discoursed survive due to the accounts of men like Plato, Diogenes Laertius, and Xenophon. Plato used the *Dialogues* that he wrote on the life and interactions of Socrates to both portray the great spirit of philosophy in his teacher and used these stories to insert many of his own views into the *Dialogues* as well.

Socrates was so influential to Western thought that most people today use his philosophy to break up and divide "the entire history of philosophy. Before Socrates we had the pre-Socratic philosophers, considered by many to be of an inferior quality and not particularly important to Western thought. Cicero, for example, tells us that Socrates "pulled philosophy down from the heavens and sent it into the cities and homes of men". Socrates is considered by many to be the father of modern philosophy and one of the first Western thinkers to question concepts like ethics, the meaning of existence, epistemology (basically the study of truth and what we think we know), and mortality/immortality of the soul.

Socrates often rejected the normal trappings of society. A few stories told in the *Lives of Eminent Philosophers* by Diogenes Laertius illustrate just how differently Socrates lived and acted when compared to other men. Upon walking through a market and seeing all the items for sale Socrates, rather than being impressed by the selection, simply replied incredulously with the statement "How many things there are which I do not want." Diogenes also told of how Socrates was frequently beaten by angry people in the streets but wrote that he always took the beatings in stride and good cheer, continuing with his work of philosophizing with the citizens of Athens. Socrates once, after a particularly rough beating, was asked why he did nothing to defend himself and replied: "Suppose an ass had kicked me, would you have had me bring action against him?" Socrates seems to have cared for few things in life. But one thing that he certainly pursued, even to his own peril, was the truth.

One of the most challenging things about Socrates (and part of why he was sentenced to death by poisoning by a court in Athens) was the way that he applied and practiced his philosophy. Because he believed that truth could only truly be arrived at by dissecting one's beliefs and preconceived notions through dialogue, he made a habit of going about Athens questioning others. Socrates pioneered what today is known as the Socratic method – basically a frustrating method of questioning someone's definitions of a concept to have them take a stand on a subject, and then using logic to contradict and pick apart that position. This earned Socrates the nickname "gadfly" and certainly played a large role in the death sentence that would end his philosophizing for good.

Socrates encouraged others to question their beliefs about things, to not accept common logic and definitions, and to live virtuous lives in harmony with nature, always seeking out knowledge and learning. This thirst for knowledge is one of the critical components that we talked about extensively in the chapter on Humanism. It is an irreplaceable part of the spirit of philosophy. One can't truly be considered a philosopher without this healthy level of doubt, and without a true desire to seek wisdom, even if it contradicts one's preconceived notions or beliefs.

Socrates' main student, Plato, had big shoes to fill. He contributed many major ideas of his own. The theory of forms, an abstract idea that for everything that exists (thoughts, ideas, objects, and even life forms), there exists a perfect example of that thing in another realm, was just one of his many contributions to the world of philosophy. Plato believed that it was only through the study of the "form" of something that we could discover a thing's true essence. And so, though Plato believed, just like his teacher, that humans must use reason to reach closer to ideals like truth and beauty, we could never attain this perfection of knowledge with reason alone. To reach perfect truth or understand perfect beauty abstraction was required. We would have to leave this physical body and enter the world of the forms. This belief that to truly understand something you needed to study its perfect form, something that did not exist in the physical world, forms a foundational idea in the tradition of the Western mind. Even today the idea of the human soul, an essence of being trapped within a physical body, continues in religion and spiritual practice.

Socrates, Plato, and Plato's student Aristotle all promoted self-introspection and the use of logic in our daily lives. While all three had differences in beliefs and the ways they applied their philosophy, through the work of these three men the true nature of philosophy was born – the quest for knowledge and truth. This tradition of questioning, reasoning, and seeking out truth and knowledge was central to the Humanist, Neoplatonist, and ultimately to the Renaissance movement as well.

Marsilio Ficino and the other members of the Humanist and Neoplatonist movements contributed greatly to a revival of these classical virtues. Along with the Humanist emphasis on continuous learning and the belief of the individual, the philosophy of Plato helped to expand the minds of the Renaissance world. The revival of the works of Plato in Florence ultimately led to teachings that encouraged independent thought, the cultivation of the virtues (honesty, courage, wisdom), and the development of humility in the face of an endless amount of possible new information to learn and new truths to uncover. As you read this chapter, please keep in mind the true spirit of philosophy – the love of wisdom. As you read on, I encourage you to be humble, to keep an open mind, and to question what you think you know.

Be humble: The wisest man in Athens

> "What a man knows, whosoever he may be, is nothing when compared with his own ignorance."
>
> (Petrarch)

After Socrates earned fame as a war hero for saving the general Alcibiades during the Peloponnesian war, he was free to pursue his passion in life – philosophy (the love of wisdom). Socrates was influenced early on by the Sophists, a group of "wise men" who often collected large payments to tutor the wealthy and important citizens of Athens by teaching them things like rhetoric, philosophy, and how to use knowledge practically for personal gain.

In Socrates's opinion, the Sophists were a great example of what was wrong with education. Sophists encouraged memorizing and creating the appearance of wisdom by citing texts or reciting quotes to impress others. But he felt that their knowledge was like a house built on a bad foundation; it might look nice but it is destined to fail. The Sophists were good at appearing to know the truth, but all they really knew was how to appear knowledgeable to others. While the Sophists repeated the connotations and quotes of their own teachers, Socrates set out to break the mold by using reason and logic to arrive at truth, rather than to accept the opinion of others. Perhaps the worst part about the Sophists and their focus on rhetoric was that they had no concern for what was true or good, only about making a point. An example of this might be using rhetoric and oration to save oneself from prosecution for a crime that one was guilty of. A thought like this surely would have repulsed the Socrates (the man who later accepted a death sentence even though he knew that he was not guilty of any crime).

Socrates' search for truth led him to earn respect, and sometimes disdain, from other prominent men of Athens.

As the legend goes, a friend of Socrates, Chaerephon, went to see the Oracle at Delphi, who informed him that Socrates was the wisest man in Athens. In true Socratic fashion, Socrates immediately set out to find the truth and presumably to prove the Oracle wrong. After all, Socrates knew that he knew very little. To find one of the many men in Athens that was surely wiser than him, he sought out many of the "wise" and most respected citizens of Athens.

First, he sought out the politicians, then the poets, and finally the skilled craftsmen. With each group he spoke with them in depth about their fields of expertise. But he found each group lacking in true wisdom. The politicians thought they were wise and appeared wise, but he found that upon questioning they didn't know much about anything. The poets, though skilled with words and able to create beautiful art, couldn't even explain their process or how their works even came about. The craftsmen were very skilled and knowledgeable in their crafts and could create amazing works, but also displayed their ignorance outside of their crafts. The worst part of all was that Socrates found that for each of these experts, their expertise in one small area of life led them to an arrogant belief that they knew much about many things, things that they were ignorant of.

Socrates was shocked at the ignorant arrogance of these wise men and, ultimately, he came to reason that the Oracle was right to deem him the wisest of all, not because of how much he knew, but because he seemed to be the only man who realized how little he did know. Socrates told this powerful story during his trial while defending himself against the charges of elevating himself above the gods and corrupting the youth of Athens. This experience seems to have had a powerful influence on Socrates as he made his life's work to go out and uncover the truth in all that he did. Socrates centered his philosophy on dialogues designed to destroy the firm positions of belief that people often based their lives on. Through the Socratic method, Socrates' goal was to show people how little that they really knew in order to ignite passion for a personal search for truth. This dedication to the truth earned him the nickname of the gadfly of Athens, his job was to go about "stinging" the citizens of Athens, shocking them out of their stubborn ignorance.

The lesson that we should take from this story of Socrates is perhaps the starting point of all new knowledge acquisition: we must realize that there is much for us to learn before our minds will ever be open enough to seek new information. A huge part of what made Socrates so great and so wise was that he was not blind to his own ignorance. This place of humility and genuine curiosity is the starting point of wisdom, it is the essence of philosophy, and it is the spirit of the philosopher.

Most of us are guilty of conflating our own experience in one area of life into a general wisdom that is applicable to all areas. In other words, we mistake expertise for wisdom. Even a master in one area of life – chess for example – may be totally ignorant of how to change a tire or of what the Higgs boson particle is. Success and acclaim in one area of life or endeavor leads many to the false belief that their authority spills over into all other areas of life. Specialized knowledge in today's society is a requirement for success. But always remember that it means little outside of the field in question. No matter how knowledgeable we may be at one thing, there is surely something else that we are totally ignorant of.

Another problem in society today is that people are generally expected to have an opinion about hot topics; to be drawn to other people of a higher status when they give their opinions, even if they are completely outside of their fields of expertise. This is called the appeal to authority. It happens each time we look at an authority figure and parrot something that they have said instead of thinking through and reasoning a stance of our own. In our modern and specialized society, we can often save time and make *better* decisions by deferring to someone more experienced than ourselves. For example: if we know nothing about health or medicine, we would do better to follow our doctor's advice than to follow our own natural feelings and inclinations about what medicines to take or what diseases we might have. The line gets blurred, however, when we start heeding the health advice of our financial adviser as well. Many times, we mistake someone's status as an expert in one field as a blanket that gives them knowledge of everything. It's very important for us to realize and acknowledge that someone being respected in one field does *not* automatically give them expertise in another.

It's easy to fall into the trap of feeling smart when you develop a sought-after skill or become a master in one field. We earn respect and praise in one area of knowledge through our expertise and suddenly people start looking to us for answers. It is ok, nay even better to claim ignorance and say that you don't know than it is to fall into the trap of always needing to give an answer or state an opinion. Something we'd do well to remember as a society is the saying by Socrates, "One thing only I know, and that is that I know nothing." How much better society would be if instead of all of us believing that we know what is right and wrong, we decided to work together to try and arrive at the truth. To truly be wise you must know how ignorant you are. The awareness of this ignorance should challenge you to study and learn in areas that you are ignorant. It should help foster that love of learning we mentioned in the last chapter and lead us through humility and doubt into a place of true wisdom.

There is priceless value in being able to withhold forming an opinion until you have put in time to research something yourself rather than giving in to authority or popular opinion. There is immense value in not trying to seem smart by saying something, and instead educating yourself more deeply on a topic or listening to the knowledge of others before you give an answer. If you are an expert in your field then please trust your instincts. After all you have probably put in a lot of time and you have earned the right to form an opinion that's based on experience, time, and often rigorous study...just don't mistake your expertise in sales as an indicator that you'd be a great surgeon. Be slow to form opinions, be humble, always be learning.

The learning and growth that we are capable of generally stops right about the time that we decide we have nothing left to learn. This is why this principle to remain humble is so important to the world today. We have enough experts and guest pundits; we have enough people who claim to have the solution to all the world's problems and ailments. What we need are more people willing to say the simple phrase "I don't know". If we all spent more time working together in the spirit of curiosity, of philosophy, then the world would be a much better place. We have the power to start changing the world right away by first changing ourselves. Realize how little you know and how complicated things truly are. Realize that you might not have the right answer even if you are 100% certain that you do. Realize that the starting point of wisdom is the admission that we are fools. After all, the wisest man in Athens knew that he knew nothing.

Question everything: Plato's allegory of the cave

> "How can you prove whether at this moment we are sleeping, and all our thoughts are a dream; or

whether we are awake, and talking to one another in the waking state?"

(Plato/Socrates)

In the *Socratic Dialogues* by Plato, Plato wrote out stories of interactions in the life of Socrates to give us examples of the way that he spoke and lived his life. In the last section we discussed the trial of Socrates and how he used the story of how the Oracle at Delphi declared him the wisest man in Athens in order to show that he did not elevate himself above the gods or other men. Nevertheless, Socrates was eventually put to death for "corrupting the youth of Athens". Most historians agree that his Socratic method, meant to make people question their own stances and beliefs, had a lot to do with this death sentence. Socrates however didn't repent of his ways. In fact, he stayed true to his nickname (gadfly) up until the very end of his life, choosing to defend his actions rather than repent. When asked what sentence he would recommend for himself after he was declared guilty, he said that he should be given free meals for life. Socrates gave his life because he believed that making people realize how ignorant that they really were would help spur people to seek truth for themselves and think more critically about their opinions and beliefs. To Socrates, finding the truth was far more important than his own life or anything else of this world.

A good example of Socrates and his Socratic method of questioning can be found in the dialogue called *Protagoras*. In the story, Socrates is awakened by his friend Hippocrates who informs him that a famous Sophist named Protagoras has arrived in Athens and that Hippocrates intends on becoming one of his disciples. In true Socratic fashion, Socrates questions Hippocrates until he comes to believe he would have nothing to gain by following Protagoras. They then set out together to go and question Protagoras on what exactly he can teach anyone.

The meeting starts with Socrates questioning Protagoras about his teaching methods and what he teaches his students. But the meeting quickly devolves into an argument where they bicker over how long each other's responses should be to one another's questions. Bystanders and onlookers eventually intervene and set up a sort of debate where Socrates and Protagoras will take turns questioning one another. Finally, the dialogue leads them in a huge circle where Socrates and Protagoras end up switching sides and arguing for the opposite point that they each began from. Apparently in this case Socrates had met his match. The dialogue doesn't come to much of a conclusion. And perhaps that is the lesson – just simply to exhibit what happens when two philosophers get together and talk through and debate a topic. The dialogue is an example of the way Socrates thought that truth and knowledge should be sought out, through ruthless and unceasing questioning. Through examining, dissecting, and breaking down one's own beliefs one can come closer to truth and virtue.

All this rigorous questioning that Socrates passed on to his pupil Plato is today also passed on to us in Plato's *The Republic*, in his famous allegory of the cave. The allegory of the cave is a type of thought experiment that's used to illustrate a philosophical idea. In the allegory there are prisoners chained to a cave wall, but there is an opening behind and above their heads. The light from outside the cave goes through the opening and shines in front of them onto the cave wall. Behind them are puppeteers that use shapes and puppets to project a shadow image on the wall in front of the prisoners. The images that the prisoners see before them are real to them but are nothing more than shadows of the real thing. The allegory of the cave was ultimately an illustration of the theory of the forms: the belief that everything that exists is merely an imitation or "shadow" on the cave wall of the perfect thing that exists in the world of forms.

The allegory of the cave shows us the healthy level of doubt that we should integrate into our thoughts and beliefs: our senses may deceive us, and human reason and logic can only take us so far. A prisoner that was born and raised in the cave would believe that the shadows that they saw on the wall were reality. But if the same prisoner was able to go outside and see the real world, they would experience a mind-bending paradigm shift. The shift in perspective that would occur in the prisoner who stepped out into the world could be so overwhelming that they may choose to return to the safety of the cave. Even if the prisoner embraced this new-found view of the world, how would they ever be able to explain this new-found experience to the other prisoners still chained up in the cave? Many times, in life we see things or believe things that we really think are true. However, we frequently mistake these "shadows of truth" for the real thing. The allegory of the cave is ultimately just another reminder for us to always question things, even the things that we see or believe to be true. It tells us that there are limits to human knowledge, and that perhaps there are things that we will never understand. This healthy level of skepticism, this desire to never rest until we have looked at a thing from every problem angle, can help us come nearer to *truth*.

This brings us to our next principle: question *everything*. The same way that people tend to defer making decisions to the recommendations of experts, people have a habit of just adopting the beliefs of others as well. Most people do this every day without even realizing it. Even worse, many people's entire philosophy and belief set in life has been formed piece by piece this way. Many times, we hear something that *sounds* good or *feels* good, and we mistake this superficial and emotional judgement for truth, much like the prisoners in the cave accept the shadows on the wall as reality.

I've put considerable effort into making sure that the quotes and references in this book are strictly from the Renaissance or would have been read in antiquity. But I just simply couldn't resist letting Ayn Rand chime in on this topic:

> "Your subconscious is like a computer – more complex a computer than men can build – and its main function is the integration of your ideas. Who programs it? Your conscious mind. If you default, if you don't reach any firm convictions, your subconscious is programmed by chance – and you deliver yourself into the power of ideas you do not know you have accepted. But one way or the other, your computer gives you print-outs, daily and hourly, in the form of emotions – which are lightning-like estimates of the things around you, calculated according to your values. If you programmed your computer by conscious thinking, you know the nature of your values and emotions. If you didn't, you don't."

What Ayn Rand is saying here is that if you don't question things, if you don't make a habit of engaging your mind to figure out what you believe, your beliefs will just form naturally based on emotion and chance and you'll end up just thinking you know things without *really* understanding them at all (like the "experts" that Socrates spoke with in Athens). Without the conscious effort of dissecting your beliefs, even those that you hold most dear, how can you ever know if you are right or if you are just a prisoner chained to a cave wall staring at shadows?

Let's consider a real-world example in real time together. For example, let's look at your own personal stance on the morality of war. Do you believe that it is justified to fight a war and kill people if it is needed to protect your way of life and freedoms? Yes, or no? And, if we dig a little deeper and then ask, "Why do you believe that?" you might have some well-thought-out reasons that support your belief. Or, if you are honest with yourself, you might realize that you've just repeated the stance of someone you love or respect (like parents, heroes, friends etc.). Or you might not be able to even articulate a real reason at all – you might just think some generic thought to yourself like "war is wrong', or "you have to defend your freedom". If your only reply is some generic emotional response like "freedom isn't free" or "it's always wrong to kill", then I can say with about 99% certainty that you have never *really* considered your stance at all and more than likely you have just assimilated the views that somebody, somewhere, sold you. This exercise isn't to poke fun or make you feel dumb. We are all guilty of this; at some level we all hold dogma no matter how hard we try not to. If we are truly honest with ourselves, we all have some strong beliefs that we can't back up with reason or logic. The world is very polarizing and people like to make it seem like things are either right or wrong. But many times, the world is not so black and white if we are honest. War or violence, for example, sometimes might be justifiable and sometimes might be wrong. A starting point for true wisdom is to acknowledge and realize that we must use reason to judge each *individual* situation. It's rare in life to find one way of doing things that works in every situation. The true philosopher realizes the inherent paradox and ambiguity in life.

True knowledge of something is based on facts. It's based on study, data, personal experience, and real deliberation. The more time spent studying and experiencing a topic the better equipped we are to form a rational opinion on it. But some things can never really be understood no matter how hard you study them unless you experience them first hand. Take a sunrise for example: you could read about sunrises, study the physics that makes it possible, watch videos and look at photos, listen to 1000 different people tell you about their favorite sunrise. But you still wouldn't understand a sunrise until you saw and experienced one for yourself. Likewise, you can't truly understand something until you have studied it and understand how and why it works. You could watch 1000 sunrises and never understand what was happening until you learned the science behind it. Much like the prisoner in the cave, until we open our minds to step outside of our own preconceived notions and beliefs, how can we ever know what lies outside the cave walls? If we are honest with ourselves then we must acknowledge that it's difficult to find the truth. In some things perhaps we will *never* know the truth.

Most people go through life accepting the things that they see at first glance; we listen to someone's claim to be an expert backed up by all their accomplishments and then we blindly accept what they say as truth because of their accomplishments or personal titles. We see or hear something that gives us a negative emotional response and declare it as bad without ever questioning why we had that response in the first place. We follow the crowd when determining whether something is right or wrong, without ever stopping to ask if perhaps the crowd was "wrong" to judge it so. There are so many issues that we need to work through as a society, and perhaps the first step is for us to put down our pitchforks and start conversing and treating each other like humans again. Let's all forget what we think we know and open our minds to learning and seeing things differently again. Let's be willing to question our own beliefs and stances and listen to another perspective.

If there is a simple phrase that totally encapsulates the essence of Socrates' teaching, I believe it would be this: Question everything! Question what works and what doesn't. Question and examine all results. Dissect experiences. Question what people say. Question the "facts". Question yourself and your beliefs. Question authority. And refuse to believe something just because it sounds good or easy...Question everything.

Know Thyself: give me the examined life or give me death

"The unexamined life is not worth living."

(Socrates)

Inscribed on the temple of Apollo at Delphi, where Socrates' friend was told by the famed Oracle of Delphi that Socrates was the wisest man in Athens, were the words: "Know Thyself". This theme of seeking out self-knowledge is also mentioned again in Plato's *Apology*, the same dialogue where Socrates defends himself against charges of impiety and corrupting the youth. After being deemed guilty, Socrates is asked to speak on his own behalf to help determine the punishment for his "crimes". The prosecutor recommends death, and a normal person would have argued for leniency...Socrates was not a normal man.

Socrates launched into a tirade where he admonished the court and declared that if he had simply had more time, then surely, they would see that he was guilty of no crime. In fact, he had provided a beneficial service to the people of Athens. He claimed a fine would not be suitable for his punishment, because he was too poor to pay a fine; in fact, he had no money at all because he had dedicated his life not to wealth but to the discovery of truth. He denied himself imprisonment and declared that he would not be able to do what he loved, philosophy and discourse, seeking truth, examining himself, and examining others through dialogue. He also denied himself exile as he would have been accepting guilt when he had really done nothing wrong. He tells the court:

> "And if I say again that the greatest good of man is daily to converse about virtue, and all that concerning which you hear me examining myself and others, and that the life which is unexamined is not worth living – that you are still less likely to believe. And yet what I say is true, although a thing of which it is hard for me to persuade you. Moreover, I am not accustomed to think that I deserve any punishment."

The court ended up settling on the death penalty for poor Socrates. But before Socrates was put to death, he chastised the court that convicted him and let them know that they would soon face their own day in court when they would surely answer for the ways that they lived their own lives. Socrates later had a chance to escape his sentence while in prison when one of his followers arranged his escape. But true to his word and his honor, Socrates decided to face his death with courage. After all, a life without the ability and freedom for Socrates to examine himself and others wasnc:'t much of a life anyway. He'd be far better off freeing his soul from his earthly body so that his spirit could escape the metaphorical cave. For Socrates, not only was a life unexamined not worth living, but he was ready to die and did end up dying to uphold the integrity of that belief. This fundamental command to "know thyself" was a driving force in the life of Socrates. It is one of the keys to opening the door of wisdom in one's life.

If you ever want to understand anything complex in life, then you must first understand yourself, at least within the context of what you are trying to learn. We all have individual traits and quirks, strengths and weaknesses, preferences and aversions; knowing what makes ourselves tick gives us more confidence, more chances for improvement, and more persistence when times are tough. Even beyond the tangible benefits of finding the awareness of how to be better, knowing yourself is crucial to living a good life and finding happiness. One must understand our human impulses and desires. We must consider what we believe is right and wrong and forge or adopt a moral code. We must consider what is truly important to us in order to become the force that directs our life towards a desired end.

Life is complicated and human beings are complicated. We have a special set of needs that come with being human – security, health, food and water, and the company of others. These are powerful driving forces that influence our behaviors and decisions. And yet, aside from our more basic needs, we also have a set of unique desires that lie behind our decisions and motivations as well. Some desires are more primal and simplistic – the desire for sex or power may motivate us strongly – sometimes even against our better judgement. And then to make things even more complicated, along with our needs and desires we also have outside influences that steer us as well. Advertising, the fear of what others might think, or the opinions of others can also have a strong influence on our decisions and actions. Finally, philosophies and personal beliefs can also affect us and mold our behavior. Our concepts of right and wrong (morality/ethics), or our belief in, or lack of a belief in, a god or higher power may also motivate us. Every potential decision brings with it consideration of all these factors (whether conscious or not) before we figure out what the "right decision" for us might be.

To put it quite simply, life is complicated. And making the right decisions can feel damn near impossible! Many of these factors influence our decisions unconsciously as well and make it even harder to figure out the "right" choice. Therefore, self-knowledge is a key to any kind of success or lasting happiness.

Here is a real-life example. You might have an aversion to switching careers that is so strong that you would never even consider changing jobs. But then after an economic downturn forces you to take a leap into a new industry, you end up finding that you aren't just better suited for the new career path, but that your entire aversion to it in the first place was solely based on fear of the loss of security that your old job provided. If we learn to know ourselves more deeply it becomes possible to see things more objectively, and to free ourselves from excessive influence of emotion and impulse.

When we experience a response towards something, whether positive or negative, we have a great opportunity to dig down deeper into our beliefs and motivations and ask ourselves "Why?". This allows us to know ourselves better. One of the first and most important steps in self-understanding is to realize the ambiguity in what a self even is (we head right back into that curious spirit of philosophy). We've already touched on some of the components of decision making. Consideration of emotion, belief in a god, ethical and moral beliefs, desires/wants, needs, and social and relationship considerations can all affect every decision that requires some sort of deliberation. When you add up enough of our decisions compounded over time we start to develop and form a rough concept of "who" we are.

The self is an ephemeral, always changing, and yet still static entity. Philosophers have argued for thousands of years about what exactly a self is. Aristotle claimed that though a boy may grow into a man there is a continuous entity that simply changes from childhood into adulthood. Heraclitus makes the claim that "No man steps into the same river twice, for it is not the same river, and he is not the same man." To Heraclitus with each new moment we change, becoming a new entity, just as the water in a stream always flows.

The self is the combination of past experiences that have affected and programmed one's beliefs and desires, one's current understanding of oneself, and one's future desires reflected in one's current actions as they seek the attainment of goals and a fulfillment of their desires and needs. The self is a combination of past and future, existing fully now in this moment, the perfect balance of past and future. In each decision we are given an opportunity to follow the trends of the past or to make a new type of decision that when duplicated over time will lead to a new concept of "self". The self is really nothing more than a concept, an entity created by the human mind in a desire to solidify our worldview.

Even if we put aside the ambiguous nature of the self in a metaphysical sense, there are still the complications of our physical existence as well. There is an old thought experiment that gets credited to Plutarch called the *Ship of Theseus*:

> "The ship wherein Theseus and the youth of Athens returned from Crete had thirty oars, and was preserved by the Athenians down even to the time of Demetrius Phalereus, for they took away the old

> planks as they decayed, putting in new and stronger timber in their places, insomuch that this ship became a standing example among the philosophers, for the logical question of things that grow; one side holding that the ship remained the same, and the other contending that it was not the same."

In the *Ship of Theseus* thought experiment, you have a large wooden ship made entirely of planks: every day you go into the ship, remove a plank, and replace it with a new plank. Typically, as each day passes, you would still say that the ship is the same ship even though a few planks have changed. But fast forward a few years into the future and eventually you will reach a point where every single board on that ship has been replaced with a new one. One might consider, is the ship still the same ship that we remembered from long ago? Although it has taken up the same space and still has the same form, literally every single piece of matter that now makes it up is different. How can the ship be the same if all of what makes it up is gone and replaced with something new? Now consider the way the body grows and heals, how its cells continuously die and are replaced repeatedly. So, what is the physical self after all...atoms, skin, cells, energy, or just empty space?

The point of all this ambiguity is not to make you unsure how to understand yourself, but to help you realize that the concept of "self" is complicated. I simply want to impart to you how difficult it is to even conceptualize what a "self" is. If it's hard to pin down what a self is, perhaps we should be more hesitant to put ourselves into a box and define who we are. You should be very careful with limiting beliefs or statements about yourself. People say things like "I'm bad at math", "I'm just not athletic", or "I just can't pay attention when I read". These limiting beliefs often define our views of ourselves and limit the paths we walk in life. These types of statements take a malleable and changeable identity that we have power to shape with each and every decision and action and changes it into a rigid and unchangeable concept. It's good to know one's strengths and weaknesses, but also remember the self is like the Ship of Theseus – you can rebuild the self piece by piece. In each moment we possess the power to rebuild and change.

Understanding of self takes painful self-work and discovery. It takes trying new things, pushing yourself. It takes being unafraid to fail and take risks when called for. And it takes spending some time at your highest highs and time at your lowest lows. The best way to get to know yourself is to simply live with intention and dedicate some time for introspection. Seek out new challenges and experiences, refuse to live comfortably, set goals for yourself, examine your past, and try to learn from your mistakes. When you live with intentionality and realize that you can grow into anyone or anything that you want to be, while continuing to grow and thrive, you will begin to flourish.

So, what sorts of activities lead one toward self-discovery? Learning new things, trying new experiences, debating people you disagree with but with an open mind, examining your past, setting difficult goals for yourself, forcing yourself to do things that you initially feel uncomfortable with, challenging your own beliefs by trying to prove them wrong, and asking what lies behind the walls of your feelings and impulses.

Ultimately the subject of how to know oneself could be a book on its own. You must choose to live life intentionally and not be afraid to look back at painful experiences or to put yourself into new challenges for the purpose of growth. It's important at times through life to examine one's own direction, to ask why, to question one's own beliefs and concepts of self. Only by shining a light onto oneself can one ever see what that self really looks like. In order to know yourself, you must be willing to step outside the comfort of your cave. You must unchain yourself and step outside into the light.

Chapter 9
Stoicism

Introduction: The prosperous shipwreck

> "I made a prosperous voyage when I was shipwrecked."
>
> (Zeno)

Stoicism was founded in Athens by a man named Zeno of Citium. The Stoics, originally called Zenonians, eventually earned the name of Stoics, named after the *stoa,* or covered walkway, in Athens where philosophers often gathered to teach and discuss philosophy with one another. While none of Zeno's works have survived through time, many of his followers and later generations of the Stoics' works did survive. Today we know about the life of Zeno from second-hand sources and biographies like the ones found in *Lives of Eminent Philosophers* by Diogene Laertius, or in *Parmenides* by Plato.

While Zeno's works may not have survived the test of time, those of the later Stoics, like Seneca, Epictetus, and Marcus Aurelius, did survive. Many of these works were rediscovered, retranslated, and made more accessible during the Renaissance period and had a pronounced effect on the hearts and minds of the people of the Renaissance. Marcus Aurelius and his *Meditations* were not available during the Florentine Renaissance, and Epictetus didn't become available until near the end of the golden age of Florence (although it does appear that his work had some impact on at least a few of the Humanists of Florence). But one Stoic author who had a tremendous effect on the Renaissance was Seneca. His works were widely read and available even in the earliest years of the Renaissance (he was favorite of the Father of the Renaissance Petrarch). Cicero, though not a practicing Stoic, was also widely read and quoted during the Renaissance period. Cicero. who traveled to study at Plato's Academy, was well versed in Stoicism and frequently quoted and extolled the teachings of the Stoics as a guide to a better and more virtuous life. Stoicism (at least its practical meditations on ethics and virtue) played a profound role in the development of the Humanists of Florence, as their primary sources of moral philosophy in the early years were men like Seneca, Cicero, Quintillian, and Aristotle.

Stoicism practiced now for thousands of years, has become an integral part of the Western mind, and legend has it that this important philosophical school was born from a shipwreck that would have likely caused significant financial damage to its founder, Zeno. While it would have been easy to throw up his hands or curse the gods for his misfortune, Zeno chose another path. He went down the road that destiny had paved for him and changed philosophy forever.

The legend told in Diogenes Laertius' *Lives of Eminent Philosophers* says that around the age of 22, while following in his father's footsteps as a merchant, a merchant ship that Zeno was aboard sank off the coast of Athens, leaving him stranded in the foreign city. Details of the event are sparse, but one could be forgiven for assuming that a good share of whatever fortune Zeno may have possessed went down into the water with the ship. Stranded, and probably quite a bit less fortunate financially, Zeno wandered through the streets of an unfamiliar city and eventually wound up in a bookshop where he found a copy of Xenophon's *Memorabilia* (a collection of Socratic dialogues). He was so impressed and enamored with the text that he wound up as a student of a prominent Athenian philosopher named Crates, one of the cynic philosophers. Crates was a harsh tutor to young Zeno and, at one point, is said to have noticed Zeno's shyness and obsession with what others thought about him. Crate's ordered Zeno to grab him a bowl of lentil soup (considered peasant food), and then knocked the bowl out of Zeno's hands covering him in soup in front of a gathering of others. He then called out to Zeno as he ran away in embarrassment, "Why run away, my little Phoenician? Nothing terrible has befallen you." Despite the abuse and the dramatic shift in Zeno's life, Zeno was later quoted as referencing the shipwreck that occurred and led him down the path that ignited what turned out to be his lifelong passion for philosophy: "I made a prosperous voyage when I was shipwrecked."

After a long period as one of Crates' students, Zeno eventually founded a school of his own that was later known as the Stoic school. Though Zeno's extensive catalogue of books and writings has been lost to time, it is revealed through Diogenes Laertius that Zeno had many works attributed to him throughout his lifetime. Zeno earned a good amount of respect and acclaim throughout his life and was even offered Athenian citizenship at one point during his lifetime. After his death he was celebrated as an important figure of Athenian history. While Zeno's works are left mostly as mysteries, we do know that his philosophy was founded on the Stoic principles of logic, physics (nature), and ethics. The goal of his philosophy was to reach *eudaimonia* (happiness/flourishing) by living a virtuous, simple, and ethical life – all the while remaining true to nature.

Some of the most prominent and most widely known Stoics are Epictetus, Seneca, and Marcus Aurelius, and their writings are still widely read today nearly 2000 years after their initial creation. Part of the reason for their popularity was due to the Humanist movement of the Renaissance, which recovered, translated, and made mass prints of their works with the newly invented printing press. The timeless wisdom possessed in Stoicism makes its influence strong even today. I often recommend that people looking to get into philosophy or looking to better themselves or their situation check out works by the Stoics. They are a potent source of practical wisdom to improve one's life. I have a deep respect for the Stoics. Their almost monk-like teachings have been a powerful source of inspiration and strength for me and many others in the world.

I hope to pass on some of these teachings to you in this chapter, one very dear to my own heart. My hope is that when the next shipwreck occurs in your life, you will remember the story of Zeno and how an unfortunate event in his life led to other events that changed his life and the future of the Western world for the better. When your metaphorical ship is sinking, don't stand on the shore and reminisce eternally on what went down with the ship. Search out new wisdom from the experience and try to better yourself. Remember, "It's not what happens to you, but how you react that matters." (Epictetus).

Believe in providence: Seneca's letter to Lucilius *On Providence*

> "You are a great man; but how am I to know it, if fortune gives you no opportunity of showing your virtue? You have entered the arena of the Olympic games, but no one else has done so: you have the crown, but not the victory: I do not congratulate you

as I would a brave man, but as one who has obtained a consulship or praetorship. You have gained dignity. I may say the same of a good man, if troublesome circumstances have never given him a single opportunity of displaying the strength of his mind. I think you unhappy because you never have been unhappy: you have passed through your life without meeting an antagonist: no one will know your powers, not even you yourself. For a man cannot know himself without a trial; no one ever learnt what he could do without putting himself to the test; for which reason many have of their own free will exposed themselves to misfortunes which no longer came in their way, and have sought for an opportunity of making their virtue, which otherwise would have been lost in darkness, shine before the world. Great men, I say, often rejoice at crosses of fortune just as brave soldiers do at wars."

(Seneca)

In this quote Seneca writes to his friend Lucilius (in the letter called *On Providence*) regarding a question about providence. Lucilius apparently has asked Seneca how, if providence –oversight and rule by God – exists, can it be explained when evils befall good people? Seneca replies with a short but poignant letter addressing the issue. The main conclusion of the letter is this: trial, suffering, and challenges are not curses, but are hidden blessings. These trials that we go through in life, if we face them with courage, are the universe's way of revealing our true potential. The Stoics believed that the challenges that we face not only strengthen us, but literally transform us into better human beings. The key in this process is not to wallow in our pain, to curse God, or to curl up in a ball and give up, but instead to choose to believe that these tests and challenges we have been given have been given to us for a reason. That reason is to help us grow. We must know and believe that our trials have been sent to us not to destroy us, but to strengthen us.

In the letter, Seneca discusses the strength of spirit and strength of mind that comes from providence and acceptance. In his own words:

> "Just as so many rivers, so many showers of rain from the clouds, such a number of medicinal springs, do not alter the taste of the sea, indeed, do not so much as soften it, so the pressure of adversity does not affect the mind of a brave man; for the mind of a brave man maintains its balance and throws its own complexion over all that takes place, because it is more powerful than any external circumstances. I do not say that he does not feel them, but he conquers them, and on occasion calmly and tranquilly rises superior to their attacks, holding all misfortunes to be trials of his own firmness."

Here Seneca speaks about the Stoic idea that we should not allow life to overwhelm us or beat us down. He acknowledges that while some things may occur that hurt or scar us, we can choose to not just suffer difficulties but to learn to thrive throughout them. The key is that this transformative and strengthening effect can only happen with some sort of faith attached. The Stoics had a firm belief in destiny and the natural order of the universe that gave them an almost supernatural power to persist and thrive even in the face of danger or adversity.

Epictetus was a slave before he became a teacher of philosophy and he said that "Circumstances don't make the man, they only reveal him to himself." He even went so far as to claim that, while a slave, he had complete freedom in life, because no master could control or influence his inner state: "Any person capable of angering you becomes your master; he can anger you only when you permit yourself to be disturbed by him." Some sources state that at one point Epictetus' master forcefully broke his leg in order to maintain control over him and left him crippled. Despite being a slave and crippled, Epictetus continued to practice and later to teach the Stoic philosophy of being unmoved by the circumstances of life.

Seneca was a wealthy Roman senator and was a well-respected Roman citizen. He was a teacher to the brutal dictator Nero when Nero was a young boy. Despite Seneca doing his best to pass on Stoic philosophy to Nero, Nero grew into a brutal, ruthless, and paranoid leader. Nero eventually became convinced of a plot to overthrow him within Rome. There didn't seem to be any concrete plans in place, and it is unlikely that Seneca was involved in any way, but Nero believed that Seneca, because of his adoration and respect in the city, would be a likely candidate for his replacement. In order to stop the plot, Nero ordered Seneca to commit suicide. In true Stoic fashion, Seneca accepted his fate without attempting to flee or put up a fight. Seneca, an old man at the time, opted to cut his wrists to cause death but, perhaps due to his age, his blood flow was too slow for death to come quickly. So next he drank poison and, when that too failed, he steeped himself in a hot bath to increase his circulation until he finally died from steam inhalation.

As we discussed in the introduction, Zeno lost a good deal of his fortune and had his life path altered when his merchant ship sank and left him stranded in Athens. Many years later he remarked on the positive changes that had occurred because of this calamitous event in his life. Marcus Aurelius the great Stoic emperor said:

> ""It is my bad luck that this has happened to me.' No, you should rather say: 'It is my good luck that, although this has happened to me, I can bear it

> without pain, neither crushed by the present nor fearful of the future.' Because such a thing could have happened to any man, but not every man could have borne it without pain. So why see more misfortune in the event than good fortune in your ability to bear it?"

Marcus here basically tells us to be grateful for unfortunate events because, as Stoics, we are strong enough to get through the tests that fate gives us.

One of the repeating concepts of Stoicism is the strength of the human mind and spirit. The Stoics, while from diverse backgrounds, all shared a belief that it was not circumstance that determines one's position in life, but their response to life that truly determines what type of person they become. They believed that nature tests us so that we can become greater. This faith in the natural order of the universe made them not only resilient against setbacks but made them embrace it. If we want to be courageous like the Stoics, we must first learn to have faith and believe as they did.

Providence is defined as "the protective care of God or of nature as a spiritual power", and while the Stoics weren't a monotheistic group, they were a pantheistic group. Pantheism in very simple terms is the belief that nature and the universe are God. The Stoics believed strongly in nature and destiny, and they believed that all things that happened (even "bad" things) were necessary for their destiny to be fulfilled. In fact, the Stoics went so far as to welcome adversity and difficulty as a tool to further increase their virtue and become stronger and better individuals. Even if you have no faith in anything, including yourself, you can still find comfort in the fact that while things that happen to you in life may be outside of your control, you still possess the power to choose how you respond. This ability to accept what life throws at us, and to either have faith in something beyond us or to simply choose to keep going despite of it is a pivotal skill in Stoicism and is foundational for a happy life.

Belief in providence does not require belief in one God. It doesn't require submission to a universal plan or a strong belief in destiny. It could even equate simply to a belief in one's own ability to thrive under pressure and grow from trial. The key takeaway is that we must have faith in something if we want to truly be strong like the Stoics. If we have no faith in anything then we will surely sway when the winds of fortune blow us in the storm. One can choose faith in God, destiny, nature, the universe, or faith in oneself. Whatever suits your current belief system works to produce the benefits of a faith in providence.

Nietzsche famously said that in today's age "God is dead". In a world where, like the Stoics, one doesn't believe in a preordained meaning to existence, it is up to you to find and create meaning through the way that you live your life. This is the essence of existentialism: the idea that existence precedes meaning and not vice versa. If your belief system doesn't support the idea of a higher power, destiny, or of a God or gods, then you must be your own god. You must create your own meaning. Otherwise, nihilism (the belief that life is meaningless) will undoubtedly settle in.

Believing in fate, having faith in God, or even simply believing that nature has a way of working things out and that we are strong enough to make it through can give us comfort and strength during trying times. When we can suffer difficulties with the hope and belief that what we are going through will shape us for the better, suddenly life becomes a lot less menacing. Having a strong belief in something – God, nature, destiny, or even the strength of ourselves – can help us find solace even during the most brutal sufferings that life has to offer. Belief in something gives meaning to our adversity. Without meaning we will often have nothing but pain.

At best there is a preordained design, via God, nature, or destiny, that has our best interests in mind and wants us to be the best we can be. At worst there is no plan for us and so we should accept the things outside of our control and forge meaning in our own lives through living our lives in a way most genuine and true to ourselves. This is essentially our choice: to believe in something or to believe in nothing. But even if you believe in nothing, I still have one final trick up my sleeve for you.

There is an old saying that I use all the time, probably to the dismay of many people that I am close to: "It is what it is" I frequently say. Not because I am hopeless and helpless, but because I choose to just accept things as they are without needing to assign a value or meaning to them on a personal level. Sometimes just thinking about how tough a situation is can overwhelm us and leave us downtrodden. If you aren't the type of person to believe that there is a god, destiny, or a divine nature — and even if you don't have much faith in yourself – you can still choose to just accept things as they are and move on.

Through the acceptance of things beyond our control, belief in ourselves, and through a commitment to maintain a positive mental state – searching all the while for opportunities of growth and improvement – we become like gods of our own: immovable, unbreakable, and antifragile. We can be indomitable if we choose to take control of the narrative of our lives and cast ourselves as courageous heroes instead of helpless victims. But the choice is yours. Courage and a belief in providence go hand in hand. It is faith that gives us the strength to be courageous.

Be courageous: Hercules and the hydra

> "The greater the difficulty, the more glory in surmounting it. Skillful pilots gain their reputation from storms and tempests."
>
> (Epictetus)

In the ancient Greek myth of Hercules, we are told of a young demi-god (half man and half god). He is compelled to complete a series of tasks now known as the *Twelve Labors of Hercules*. Among the tasks was a battle against the hydra of Lerna. The hydra was a mythical beast with nine heads, one of which was immortal and was incredibly difficult to defeat. And just to make it more dangerous, it also had deadly poison. Legend has it that each time Hercules cut off one head of the beast, two more would sprout back to take its place. The battle was a difficult one even for a demi-god like Hercules; and he ended up needing the help of a friend to finally defeat the beast. Eventually Hercules did defeat the hydra, and accomplished the other labors as well, cementing himself into history as a legend of epic proportions. The legends of Hercules are still told today as symbols for strength and courage.

Epictetus references the legend of Hercules in his discourse *The Enchiridion*:

> "What would have become of Hercules do you think if there had been no lion, hydra, stag or boar - and no savage criminals to rid the world of? What would he have done in the absence of such challenges? Obviously, he would have just rolled over in bed and gone back to sleep. So, by snoring his life away in luxury and comfort he never would have developed into the mighty Hercules. And even if he had, what good would it have done him? What would have been the use of those arms, that physique, and that

> noble soul, without crises or conditions to stir into him action?"

Epictetus is clear in his meaning: Hercules was great not because of his strength, but because of his courage to test himself through battle and difficulty. These trials that we face in life reveal our true mettle – just as the hydra was a necessary evil for Hercules to prove his greatness.

All the Stoics exuded courage in their lives as we discussed earlier. Epictetus faced slavery and remained unbroken. Seneca was exiled and compelled to commit suicide but kept his resolve. Zeno faced the loss of his ship and embraced the journey that led to his new-found love of philosophy. And Marcus Aurelius would have preferred a quiet life of introspection but was compelled by a sense of duty and honor to lead as Emperor of Rome. In one of my favorite quotes from the Stoics, Marcus Aurelius sums up perfectly what it means to be courageous:

> "Be like a rocky promontory against which the restless surf continuously pounds; it stands fast while the churning sea is lulled to sleep at its feet. I hear you say, 'How unlucky that this should happen to me!' Not at all! Say instead, 'How lucky I am that I am not broken by what has happened and am not afraid of what is about to happen. The same blow might have struck any one, but not many would have absorbed it without capitulation and complaint.'"

Courage isn't just pushing forward against adversity. It is thriving from it. It is choosing to face the difficult path instead of the easy one by choice – not just because of circumstance.

In an extension of the ideas discussed in the last section (belief in providence) we now move onto the traditional Stoic virtue of courage. Courage really amounts to the choice to face challenges despite difficulty or danger to ourselves. Courage is motivated by a belief in something more meaningful and powerful than the current trial. This is why the belief in something that we discussed in the last section is so important: without faith in yourself, or faith in a plan that is bigger than yourself, it becomes difficult to face trials and other difficulties. If, however, we choose to believe that our trials are really opportunities to reveal the greatest parts of ourselves then we can truly be courageous. To be clear: courage is not just withstanding the fire, it is running towards the flames when others run away.

Courage starts with the ability to accept and understand circumstances and to believe in your own power to overcome them. Because without a belief in fate, or without a belief in yourself to overcome, it will always be harder to endure hardship. Courage is something that can be cultivated through seeking out challenges purposefully to grow as a human being. It is much like a muscle that grows stronger from use. As we repeatedly face challenges and scary situations with courage and yet we live to fight again another day, we become stronger through battle. But we also gain more faith in ourselves for the next test.

Sometimes people make the mistake of thinking that the courageous don't feel fear. But as Aristotle taught, a lack of fear is not equivalent to courage; it is more akin to foolhardiness. The courageous have simply made a habit of seeking out forms of danger or difficulty to cultivate discipline and personal strength. The courageous welcome and thrive on fear because they know that glory lies just past the battle ahead. The courageous have disciplined themselves to walk towards trials with their heads held high, knowing that a better version of themselves will be revealed through difficulty.

Ultimately, courage comes from a strong emotional center, from discipline and practice, and from a choice to believe that you are stronger than whatever it is that you are currently facing. When you know that things will work out, or when you have found a strong belief in yourself and your ability to persevere over anything, then suddenly challenges that would make others squirm don't look half as daunting.

Courage is the ability to stand in front of whatever life throws at you and remain undeterred from your path. Courage is not freedom from fear or pain; it is the ability to persist and proceed despite them. Courage is the discipline to remain calm and resolved even amidst the most dangerous and difficult times. Anyone can be courageous. It is not limited to the strong or powerful but can exist in the weakest and most downtrodden of society. Like all the traits in this book, courage is a choice that anyone can embrace. One is not born with courage. Rather it is a trait that is honed and strengthened through practice and discipline. Just as Hercules revealed his courage through his battles, we can reveal our own courage through choosing to face our own trials with resolve. Difficulty is the hydra that helps us find our greater selves, face it with courage.

Be temperate: Seneca's letter to Lucilius
On self control

> "The question has often been raised whether it is better to have moderate emotions, or none at all. Philosophers of our school reject the emotions; the Peripatetics keep them in check. I, however, do not understand how any half-way disease can be either wholesome or helpful. Do not fear; I am not robbing you of any privileges which you are unwilling to lose! I shall be kindly and indulgent towards the objects

for which you strive – those which you hold to be necessary to our existence, or useful, or pleasant; I shall simply strip away the vice. For after I have issued my prohibition against the desires, I shall still allow you to wish that you may do the same things fearlessly and with greater accuracy of judgment, and to feel even the pleasures more than before; and how can these pleasures help coming more readily to your call, if you are their lord rather than their slave! [But], you object, [it is natural for me to suffer when I am bereaved of a friend; grant some privileges to tears which have the right to flow! It is also natural to be affected by men's opinions and to be cast down when they are unfavourable; so why should you not allow me such an honourable aversion to bad opinion?] There is no vice which lacks some plea; there is no vice that at the start is not modest and easily entreated; but afterwards the trouble spreads more widely. If you allow it to begin, you cannot make sure of its ceasing. Every emotion at the start is weak. Afterwards, it rouses itself and gains strength by progress; it is more easy to forestall it than to forgo it. Who does not admit that all the emotions flow as it were from a certain natural source? We are endowed by Nature with an interest in our own well-being; but this very interest, when overindulged, becomes a vice. Nature has intermingled pleasure with necessary things – not in order that we should seek pleasure, but in order that the addition of pleasure may make the indispensable means of existence attractive to our eyes. Should it claim rights of its own, it is luxury."

(Seneca)

In this letter to his friend Lucilius, Seneca gives us several pieces of poignant wisdom about temperance. First, he tells us that we should moderate our own emotions. Though they are natural, the emotions that we allow to take e :hold in us have a way of multiplying and strengthening past the point of their usefulness, if we allow them to do so. He condemns excessive desires and declares that when we release these desires, not only will we still find pleasure and contentment, but we will be able to more readily call upon pleasure and contentment in everyday life. Finally, Seneca tells us that pleasure is not something we should seek for its own reward. Rather, pleasure was given to us by nature so that we may enjoy the "good things" in life, things like virtue and personal growth.

Stoicism places a great emphasis on limiting one's desires in order to find contentment and happiness in life. Seneca, for example, was one of the wealthiest men in Rome, but would regularly eat only stale bread and sleep on stone floors as a reminder of how little was required for a good life. He tells us to

> "Let the pallet be a real one, and the coarse cloak; let the bread be hard and grimy. Endure all this for three or four days at a time, sometimes for more, so that it may be a test of yourself instead of a mere hobby."

He also tells us that "Our life should observe a happy medium between the ways of a sage and the ways of the world at large; all men should admire it, but they should understand it also."

Epictetus tells us to "Curb your desire – don't set your heart on so many things and you will get what you need." Also "If thou wilt make a man happy, add not unto his riches but take away from his desires." The Stoics all seemed to be in agreement: the key to a happy life of fulfillment was not in getting everything that you want, but in having and being content with the little that we truly *need*.

The Stoics considered things like wealth or power "preferred indifferents". One would always prefer to be wealthy and powerful rather than poor and powerless, if possible, but it shouldn't make much of a difference to our happiness one way or another. Seneca and Marcus Aurelius certainly enjoyed the benefits of wealth and fame during their lifetimes, but they didn't allow those things to define who they were. Instead, their focus was on being good men, being examples of virtue and self-control, and upon cultivating their powers of reason.

So, what exactly is temperance? Temperance is the middle path or the way of moderation. It is moderation of desires, actions, and emotions. It is the choice to maintain sovereignty over our mental states and not to allow emotions, impulses, passions, or desires to overtake our reason.

Let's look at desire for wealth accumulation as an example. If you desire a million dollars simply to earn the status of millionaire, you will soon find more desire and anxiety once you reach your goal. Now, not only will you be wracked with the fear of losing what you have, but soon you will probably desire to have 10 million, 100 million, 1 billion. Money should never be sought simply for its own sake, but to obtain something good. This is what the Stoics meant when they referred to preferred indifferents. Wealth can be a powerful tool to accomplish good things and improve yourself. But if you seek out wealth simply for its own sake, no amount of wealth will likely never be *enough*. The same is true for everything in life. The more that we seek to have and obtain, the further out ahead of us in the future we place our happiness :– searching always for what comes next, rather than being content with what we already possess.

Our desires often create attachments to things that we believe are integral to who we are, but our need for things

– especially material goods or physical wealth – weigh us down and make us rigid and breakable. Desire distracts us from the fulfillment to be found in the present moment and makes us more prone to anxiety and depression. We should strive to improve as human beings, seek out wealth and good fortune when possible, and generally seek to build a better life for ourselves and our loved ones. But it is important to remember that, while we push ourselves to grow personally and forge meaning in our lives, we should never lose sight of the fact that all that is required for the good life is already within us.

If your happiness lies in some accomplishment, possession, or experience, then you have allowed desire to rob you of your sovereignty. Being content is a choice to accept what we already have as enough, rather than deferring our satisfaction until something else comes along. But temperance doesn't just apply to our desires; it also applies to our emotions and how much power we allow them to have over our lives.

Our emotions can be valuable tools. Given to us by nature, our emotions can alert us to danger, show us our attachments, and help focus us on things that are most important in life. But emotions, if allowed to run unchecked, can also lead us to our own destruction. Pain can alert us to danger or loss, but it can also lead us down the road to torment and despair. Love can set us free, but it can also lead us to paranoia and anguish. Desire can awaken us to our potential, or it can devolve into greed and obsession. Anger can spur us into action, but it can also lead us to death or our own destruction. Fear can show us obstacles and help us plan, or it can paralyze us into inaction. Emotions are good if they are useful or beneficial – after that the emotions are more of a distraction from happiness than anything else.

Pain, for example, can lead us down a dark path of depression. There is a certain quality, call it the "starving artist syndrome", where one not only perversely enjoys pain, but allows trauma and pain to define oneself as a human being. We can all be guilty of this at times – over accentuating and romanticizing our sufferings to garner support or earn sympathy. Or sometimes we simply just hold onto pain as a reminder of the good things we once had but now have lost. To grieve the loss of something or someone important is natural and human. But to define ourselves by our pain, or to allow our loss to wreck us, is just overindulgence into our own suffering.

Temperance is the true essence of Stoicism. It is what makes the Stoics seem so inspiring and untouchable. It's why they seem like otherworldly beings or story book heroes at times. Normal human beings get stuck in loops of emotion. These are then followed by impulsive decisions and then by a course of dealing with the consequences and blowback from our hasty decisions. But there is another way – the way of temperance. Temperance does not mean the absence of emotion or passion in life, even though many people mistakenly think that it does. It simply requires that we temper impulsive desires and choose actions that promote long-term prosperity, virtue, and stability in place of short term gratification.

The practice of temperance starts with us first identifying the emotions that create responses and impulses within ourselves, and then next progressing into a reasoning process where we weigh the pros and cons of different responses to ultimately decide that we believe is right. It's complex but can easily be practiced and improved through a simple focus on self-awareness. The next time you feel your emotions well up inside you, pause, take a breath, and take a step outside of yourself to identify the emotion that you are feeling objectively.

Then pause again as you consider the best response. Do this consistently enough and people may soon begin to mistake you for one of the Stoic sages in this book!

All actions or reactions start with an emotional response or impulse. Temperance is the ability to feel the emotion, step outside of our own thoughts and view the anger from the outside perspective of the observer. Once we identify the emotion that is controlling us, it begins to lose control over us, then we can use reason to determine how best to proceed. I often tell people that my favorite type of person to be around is a prudent one; Temperate people rarely make large gambles or overreact, they rarely say things they later regret or make impulsive decisions. That's because temperance teaches us the art of separating ourselves from the emotions that run most people's lives. Temperate people become the "observer" of their thoughts and feelings, thus separating themselves from the emotions and allowing them to let go of the initial feeling so that they can then use logic to make the best decision on how to respond.

Perhaps one of the greatest dangers to society and our world today is this lack of temperance and self-control in people, which was once such a sought-after and cherished quality in ancient societies before us. Virtues like honor, justice, courage, and wisdom used to encourage people to be slow to anger, to think through decisions, and to seek the middle path between extremes. Today's world promotes impulsive decisions through sensationalism and attention. We are trained to chant our materialistic mantra to consume more and outdo our neighbors. We celebrate the loudest and most ignorant among us because of the entertainment they provide (just look at our collective obsession with celebrities). And we scream from the rooftops that everyone should pursue their passions with reckless abandon.

Human beings have many unique desires and needs. We want to be accepted. We want to feel in control and have stability. We want to feel powerful. And we want to live forever. These desires can often lead to paths of toil and pain where we desperately seek out fame, fortune, bigger houses, nicer cars, or the perfectly surgeon-crafted body or face. Advertisers play on our insecurities and desire to fit in by creating ads that make us feel we must buy a product, drive a certain type of car, or look a certain way to be loved and accepted by others. The simple truth is that our contentment and happiness doesn't lie in the accumulation of more, but in the desire and need for less.

Goals are great, and everyone should have some sort of direction for their own life in mind. But when the sole focus of one's life becomes the achievement of some goal, or when your self-worth becomes dependent upon what you have or what you want to achieve, then you have started down a dangerous road of chasing a moving target that will perpetually move away from you. The good life requires little. It doesn't require riches, luxurious vacations, ultimate power, or a perfect appearance. It requires simple things like enough food to eat, shelter, the freedom to live and choose, a few friends or loved ones to support one another... And even without these basic comforts, we can still always rely on providence or upon our own courage to carry us through to better times.

Remember that we need little to live a good life. Emotions are not necessary past their utility. Happiness is not some distant end point – it is a choice to embrace and be grateful for the current moment. Let us remember to be grateful for what we have, and not to obsess over what we want. We already possess all that we need for the good life within ourselves. The key to satisfaction is not in gaining everything in the world, but in requiring less.

Chapter 10
Remember your mortality

"Must not all things at the last be swallowed up in death?"

(Plato)

In the year 49 AD Seneca was recalled to Rome after an eight-year exile and became tutor to the young emperor to be, Nero. Thanks in large part to the good instruction and influence of Seneca in the emperor's early years, they are largely remembered as good years, with fair leadership. However, as Nero grew older, and as Seneca increasingly stepped away from civic life in favor of a quieter life of philosophy and solitude, Nero began to lash out at his enemies and grew increasingly paranoid about plots to overthrow him.

Eventually elements of a plot were uncovered that sought to overthrow Nero, and although likely not involved, Seneca was implicated as a potential participant or at very least stood to become a possible leader if Nero was killed. Nero, in a fit of desperation, ordered that Seneca was required to take his own life. Seneca followed the order with seemingly little debate or dispute. First, Seneca severed several large veins in his legs to bring about death. But when that failed, he chose poison as the best route to death. When the poison failed as well, Seneca had hot water drawn hoping that a warm bath would speed his blood loss and end his life. But it was suffocation by steam that finally caused Seneca to succumb.

Seneca had a successful life. He was married. He very much seemed to enjoy his life of civics and philosophy. And yet when death called him, he readily went toward it with little to no objection. Aside from the obvious courage of Seneca, how was he able to be so well prepared for death that when it called his name, he went willingly with so much dignity and with no visible fear? Seneca told us: "Before I became old I tried to live well; now that I am old, I shall try to die well; but dying well means dying gladly." Also

> "Let us prepare our minds as if we'd come to the very end of life. Let us postpone nothing. Let us balance life's books each day. The one who puts the finishing touches on their life each day is never short of time."

These quotes make it clear that Seneca meditated upon death. He reflected upon its inevitably and, through consideration, prepared himself for its arrival. This practice is known as *memento mori* (Latin for "remember that you must die").

Seneca was not the first, nor will he be the last, great thinker to meditate on their own mortality. Many cultures and time periods from throughout the world have ceremonies and days of remembrance to remind us about death's inevitability. The Greek myths, read extensively in Renaissance Florence, are filled with many stories of death and violence. Heroes are made through killing and defeating their foes and sometimes become immortal when they die courageously in the heat of battle. There is even a story that mentions the term *memento mori* from the Roman Empire. The story says that when a triumphant general would return to Rome and parade himself through the streets on a chariot, a slave would stay near him, constantly whispering "memento mori" into his ear, reminding him that neither his life nor his victory would last forever.

Many philosophers and other great thinkers throughout history have also maintained an awareness of death and have written about it. In fact, philosophy has a habit of focusing our attention onto our mortality through meditations on death. They seem to place importance on the fact that death is always near. Seneca was not the only philosopher to accept his death bravely either. Many philosophers have shown courage and walked calmly towards a death that they had already prepared themselves for mentally. Socrates bravely chose to accept his death penalty rather than flee, when he could easily have escaped. Boethius (a philosopher of the Middle Ages) accepted his fate and while in prison awaiting his death he wrote *Consolations of First Philosophy*, a major philosophical contribution to Western philosophy. And Cicero was beheaded for speaking out against tyranny throughout his lifetime. Socrates, the father of philosophy, is quoted as saying that "In truth, those who practice philosophy correctly practice dying."

Here is just a small sampling of many great philosophers from antiquity and the Renaissance and their personal thoughts on death:

> "To fear death, gentlemen, is no other than to think oneself wise when one is not, to think one knows what one does not know. No one knows whether death may not be the greatest of all blessings for a man, yet men fear it as if they knew that it is the greatest of evils."
>
> (Socrates)

> "Death is nothing to us. When we exist, death is not; and when death exists, we are not. All sensation and

consciousness ends with death and therefore in death there is neither pleasure nor pain. The fear of death arises from the belief that in death, there is awareness."

(Epicurus)

"I do not wish to die: but I care not if I were dead."

(Cicero)

"Do not act as if you were going to live ten thousand years. Death hangs over you. While you live, while it is in your power, be good."

(Marcus Aurelius)

"I cannot escape death, but at least I can escape the fear of it."

(Epictetus)

"All things are transient here below and frail. Death only standeth fast for evermore."

(Lorenzo de' Medici)

"Time is a vindictive bandit to steal the beauty of our former selves. We are left with sagging, rippled flesh and burning gums with empty sockets."

(Raphael)

"This is what I mean. Everyone knows, and the greatest philosophers are of the same opinion, that of all tremendous realities Death is the most tremendous. So true is this, that from ever of old its very name is terrible and dreadful to hear. Yet though so it is, it will not do that we hear that name but lightly or allow the remembrance of it to slip quickly from our mind. No, we must take time to realise it. We must meditate with attention thereon. We must picture to ourselves the effect of death on each several part of our bodily frame, the cold extremities, the breast in the sweat of fever, the side throbbing with pain, the vital spirits running slower and slower as death draws near, the eyes sunken and weeping, every look filled with tears, the forehead pale and drawn, the cheeks hanging and hollow, the teeth staring and discoloured, the nostrils shrunk and sharpened, the lips foaming, the tongue foul and motionless, the palate parched and dry, the languid head and panting breast, the hoarse murmur and sorrowful sigh, the evil smell of the whole body, the horror of seeing the face utterly unlike itself – all these things will come to mind and, so to speak, be ready to one's hand, if one recalls what one has seen in any close observation of some deathbed where it has fallen to our lot to attend. For things seen cling closer to our remembrance than things heard."

(Petrarch)

Seldom do we find a philosopher, artist, or person of accomplishment from the ancient world who doesn't at least mention death in their works. The remembrance of, and the reflection upon, one's own mortality was common practice in ancient Greece and Rome. And as Renaissance Humanists began to comb through rediscovered texts, this awareness of death was prevalent throughout the works that they read from the ancients. Not only was death a part of ancient culture, but it was still very much a part of life in the Renaissance years as well. In fact, a severe strain of the bubonic plague ravished Europe throughout the 1340s. It is estimated that about half and possibly even up to 70% of the population of Florence might have died during the worst of the outbreaks in 1348. The outbreak was so severe that society in Florence literally broke down: dead bodies lined the streets and people were too afraid to move them to be buried properly. Farmers released animals into the countryside, and peasants and aristocracy alike dropped dead in the streets. As death was so imminent for the populace, people literally began to live as if they would die any day. The poor begin to indulge in lavish meals and feasts that they couldn't afford. Men and women married with no regard to social status or class. The price of labor skyrocketed due to its scarcity, as people refused to work or succumbed to the plague. And people began to dress in expensive clothes that were well outside of their means – after all you can't take money with you. Writers like Boccaccio and Petrarch claimed that the devastation of the plague would have been beyond belief if they hadn't experienced it for themselves. And Agnolo di Tura said that the death was so widespread that everyone believed the world was ending.

If old philosophical texts, myths of ancient heroes, and the memory of the plague wasn't enough to remind one of death during the Renaissance years, then there was also the constant threat of war and assassination to draw your eyes back towards your inevitable end – or at least to consider the ever-present possibility of doom. Wars broke out constantly in neighboring cities and bands of mercenaries traveled through Italy and the rest of Europe selling their services of destruction to the highest bidder. Since the fall of Rome, there had been no centralized government to provide protection to its people. And so, the fractured rule of city states throughout the region was a source of constant anxiety for its populations.

The ancients and the people of the Renaissance didn't just look upon death and lose all hope though. In fact, their connection to their mortality often pushed them to do great things. Perhaps just one small part of the motivation that fueled the greats of Rome, Greece, and the Renaissance was the general awareness that life would end. This knowledge that life is limited makes our time on earth even more precious for those of us wise enough to be enlightened about it. Mortality, when truly understood, is not a depressing knowledge but a liberating one. We will die but perhaps through living our lives to the best of our abilities in some way we may live on even after death.

Paired with the newly revived ideas of human achievement and of the new Humanist movement, the Renaissance was a perfect environment to generate a powerful moment where humankind was reawakened from the slumber of the Middle Ages to reach new heights. This juxtaposition of the certainty of death against the full potential of human life was never more evident than the Renaissance years. The Renaissance was a new flourishing of a society aware of both their mortality and of their potential.

This remembrance of death, and the subsequent generation of motivation to live life to its fullest, is needed even more deeply in today's world. We've been lulled to sleep by the decreasing frequency of wars, and distracted by modern entertainment, but people are beginning to remember death again. The phrase *memento mori* has seen a bit of a resurgence in recent years as coins, rings, necklaces, and other trinkets are now readily available for purchase as reminders of our own personal mortality. *Memento mori* is a call to meditate on the fact that we *will* die, and that it is a matter of *when* not *if*. Perhaps the death and fear experienced due to the modern Covid-19 pandemic has also caused a shift in awareness towards our own mortality as well.

If the idea of acknowledging that you will someday die, and that it could be sooner than later, seems morbid to you, then it simply serves as a testament to a society and age where comfort and distraction have detached us from our own mortality. Today's world boasts endless adventures and distractions. We can now easily keep our minds busy from the moment that we wake up until the moment that we go to sleep. Sometimes we use superficial means to distract ourselves from our impending doom – TV, social media, drunken revelries, or shopping. At other times we use our internal drives for achievement to keep us focused and distracted – working intensely at a job, going to school, building a business, or even starting a family. These can work as powerful ways to better our lives and serve as positive outlets for our energies, but they can also be distractions preventing us from looking deeply at our own lives and realizing that we will someday pass on. The truth is this: we will pass one day from this earth, no future amount of time in life is guaranteed and, after we die, the world will continue to turn and function despite our passing.

Unfortunately, this knowledge that we will die can cause a temporary existential crisis in many people. We've seen a bit of this in our own age due to the COVID-19 pandemic, increasingly it seems that this outbreak has cause people to ask themselves deeper questions about life and about themselves. It isn't because something is wrong with us. It's because we live in a world where we have been programmed to live for the moment with no regard for tomorrow. It is possible in today's world to live a life so removed and insulated from death, so busy and full of stimulation, that one might never stop to ponder the fact that one might leave this life at any moment. Up until the point that some event (like a cancer diagnosis or death of a loved one) shocks us out of the trance of a busy life. The ancients made a practice of not only acknowledging that death comes for us all. They made a habit of meditating on it as a reminder, not of how meaningless life might be, but of how precious the moments that you have truly are.

Epicurus and his followers gave us some great wisdom on how to deal with death. They wore rings and had engravings on tombstones stating that death was nothing. In fact, Epicurus had a saying, "Non fui, fui, non sum, non curo" (I was not; I was; I am not; I do not care). The reasoning went something like this. The mind is attached to the body. The mind fears death. If the body ceases to exist then the mind ceases to exist. If the mind ceases to exist there is no mind to experience the non-existence that is death. We may have some valid concerns about the manner of our death, as the process of dying can be painful, but we should hold little opinion about death. After all death is nothingness; death is nothing to us.

Sometimes, though, the practice of remembering death can become a rallying call for those who wish to behave impulsively and seek immediate gratification. "YOLO" they say as they empty their checking account, "You can't take it with you anyway" they call out. Some use the knowledge of death to justify taking the easy way out or to justify doing what feels good *right now* instead of what is *right*. It is important to remember that when you are remembering death, while your life could end at any moment, it would still be prudent to live life in a way that won't leave you worse off whether you are around for five more minutes, five more days, or 50 more years (not to mention the fact that we should seek virtue in life, not pleasure). Unless your death is certainly just around the corner, then don't be like the peasants in Florence who spent their life savings on luxurious meals. The goal of life shouldn't be pleasure anyway; it should be virtue and *eudaimonia*. (More about this in the next chapter.)

We should let death serve as a reminder to practice the art of mindfulness, that is, being aware deeply of the moment that you exist in right now. In Seneca's words:

> "The greatest obstacle to living is expectancy, which hangs upon tomorrow and loses today. You are arranging what lies in Fortune's control, and

abandoning what lies in yours. What are you looking at? To what goal are you straining? The whole future lies in uncertainty: live immediately."

By reminding ourselves of the fact that we are mortal, that life is precious, and that nothing is guaranteed we become better attuned to the preciousness of life. Suddenly even seemingly banal activities like going for a walk with a loved one or spouse, doing our job, or even going home to a roof over our head take on new meaning and relevance. A human life is many small moments stitched together. Maybe if we are fortunate and lucky enough, there are some extravagant ones mixed into our movie reel as well. We don't know how long the movie will play, but we do know that eventually it will end.

So, remember death. Live and feel each moment deeply. Don't sweat the small stuff. Forgive others, love deeply, and appreciate what you have. Be prudent and make decisions that enrich your life for the long run and not just for a moment until the consequences kick in. Life is precious and this moment is the only one that is ever guaranteed. Only once you realize and embrace the idea that you will die, are you truly free to live.

Chapter 11

Seek *eudaimonia*, not happiness

The boulder on the hill

> "What is the happy life? It is peace of mind, and lasting tranquility. This will be yours if you possess greatness of soul; it will be yours if you possess the steadfastness that resolutely clings to a good judgement just reached. How does a man reach this condition? By gaining a complete view of truth, by maintaining, it all that he does, order, measure, fitness, and a will that is inoffensive and kindly, that is intent upon reason and never departs therefrom, that commands at the same time love and admiration. In short, to give you the principle in a brief compass, the wise man's soul ought to be such as would be proper for a god."
>
> (Seneca)

In Greek mythology there was a man named Sisyphus who got himself into a lot of trouble with the gods. How he came to earn the wrath of the gods varies depending on the telling of the story; in one version he tells on Zeus for kidnapping a young woman, and in another he uses his cunning to chain death up in hell so that no one on earth can die. Whatever way that Sisyphus may have come to his fate is irrelevant to us for this chapter, but what *is* important is the fact that Sisyphus was condemned to the ultimate torture of eternal banality: each day he is made to roll a boulder up a hill all the way to the top, only to watch it roll back down again, on and on forever.

What could such a depressing story have to do with happiness you ask? The myth of Sisyphus is a perfect example of life; in a way there is a bit of Sisyphus in all of us. We are born, live a life, die, and are eventually forgotten, and yet we *exist*. We all go through life at times pushing our metaphorical boulders up the hill. There may be no end in sight, and there may be no clear reason why we get out of bed at all in the morning. But in these moments, it is even more important that we embrace the process and create our own meaning – even if only for the moment.

In the words of Albert Camus (absurdist philosopher) "The struggle itself towards the heights is enough to fill a man's heart. One must imagine Sisyphus happy." What he means, in terms too simple to do justice to Camus' complex philosophy, is that through embracing the journey instead of the destination, we can find happiness and fulfillment in the process of what we are doing, no matter how mundane the task may seem to us. The myth of Sisyphus is a reminder that, as human beings, we are condemned to living (condemned to be free in the words of Sartre), and at times it might seem like a dreadful routine. But it is not where we end up that matters; it is the path we travel and who we become along the way, that matters most.

Happiness is a fleeting emotion that can come and go based on our current situation, our mindset, and upon fortunate or unfortunate circumstances. Happiness can wax and wane, and it is rarely found if it is directly looked for. Happiness is a thing that seems to become more elusive when sought out, because the act of looking for it causes a self-awareness of the unhappy state of looking for happiness in the first place. Looking for happiness is a losing battle; this is why many of the ancients recommended seeking *eudaimonia* and virtue over seeking happiness. The great thing about *eudaimonia* is that happiness is often the by-product of *eudaimonia* anyway.

Eudaimonia is a Greek word with no exact translation, but some suggest "flourishing" is the most accurate definition. Flourishing is what something does when it excels, when it grows, when it comes closer to being its best version of itself – to flourish is to thrive. But not even the philosophers of the ancient days were in total agreement about what *eudaimonia* is. Some felt *eudaimonia* was a state reached when we achieved our highest reason. Some believed it came when we achieved our highest form of virtue. Some felt it was a result of finding truth. However, it seems the consensus from all of them is that *eudaimonia* is an active pursuit; it comes from the pursuit of perfection, not from the attainment of a goal. Think of a plant that flourishes; it is growing and spreading out, growing deeper roots, absorbing light and sprouting new leaves. It is in its best form when it is in a state of growth. If we are not growing and becoming better then we have not reached the state of *eudaimonia*. *Eudaimonia* then is the pursuit of improvement and perfection, whatever that may mean to us as individuals.

When Sisyphus looks at the hill up which he must push the boulder for the rest of eternity, only to watch it roll back down again, it would be easy for him to fall into despair. It would be easy to focus on the misery and hopelessness of the situation. But in order to ever be able to find happiness again he must defiantly take control of the circumstances in which he now finds himself and he must become the maker of his own destiny. He musters up the courage to face his suffering with enthusiasm instead of hopelessness and he commits himself to the task of pushing the boulder more efficiently each time.

He alternates his pushing so that he can develop different muscles and become stronger. And he looks for ways to pass the time and better himself throughout the entire process repeatedly. Miraculously, through immersing himself in the process of making himself better, and instead of focusing on the situation at hand or on his current lack of happiness, he becomes lost in the moment and begins to improve. He becomes free of his woes and his hopelessness. And he begins to flourish. Even during endless toil, he finds *eudaimonia*. Flourishing comes not from *what we do,* but from *how we do it.*

Like Sisyphus, we too can flourish if we begin to focus our attention on the process of improving instead of focusing on the outcome of our efforts. By freeing ourselves from the need to be happy or of reaching a tangible goal, and instead focusing on ways to make ourselves thrive and flourish, we will find ourselves more immersed in the moment and less focused on our circumstances. When we become free from all the negativity and seek instead to grow and make the most of what we have, only then can we flourish as human beings. One can *always* find things that are wrong. One can always find reasons why a situation is not ideal. One can easily find a huge list of reasons why they shouldn't be happy. One can just as easily busy themselves with the process of becoming better or of creating something better.

We will never truly be happy until we learn to be content with what we have. One thing that we will always have is the ability to make the most of our situation and embrace the process. This focus on the process is the essence of *eudaimonia*. You can call it flow, *Dao,* loss of self, immersion, existence, or whatever else you want. But ultimately it is when we are free to live and work towards achieving our highest potential. Do not seek to be happy, but instead seek to thrive and flourish. Seek to be the best in all the ways you can. *Eudaimonia* will set you free, and *eudaimonia* is also the ultimate freedom: nothing else can compare. Though we can never reach perfection, just as Sisyphus will never end his journey with the boulder, we can and should embrace the process. When we do everything that we do to the best of our ability and immerse ourselves fully in the act of living, we flourish.

The Renaissance man, Universal man, or polymath

> "When I investigate and when I discover that the forces of the heavens and the planets are within ourselves, then truly I seem to be living among the gods."
>
> (Leon Battista Alberti)

As a final example of the concept of *eudaimonia* we will look at the fully realized and crystallized version of it that can be found abundantly in the Renaissance world – the Renaissance or Universal man. The idea of the Universal man was born in the mind of Leon Battista Alberti and he became a walking example of his belief that "a man can do all things if he will." In Alberti's opinion, the Renaissance man, placed in the center of the universe by God, was imbued with all the power and potential of his creator. Through cultivation human beings could attain the highest summits of knowledge and achieve personal greatness. Alberti himself was a gifted athlete, architect, painter, writer, philosopher, businessman, and mathematician. Alberti's belief in the potential of human beings (an integral part of the Humanist movement during the Renaissance) was also reflected in numerous other geniuses of the Renaissance – Leonardo Da Vinci, Michelangelo, Galileo Galilei, Michel de Montaigne, and Lorenzo de' Medici, to name just a few of the great polymaths of the Renaissance.

The icon of the Renaissance man is a hard one to define. Some polymaths exhibited proficiency in the arts and sciences. Others were great businessmen or political leaders. Some were great physical specimens. Others were purely intellectual giants. The Renaissance man is one thing for certain: he is an example of what happens when a human being seeks to: continuously grow and learn, to excel in life, and to make the most of each moment. The polymath is the crystallization of *eudaimonia*: it is what occurs when a human life is dedicated to flourishing and achieving their highest potential.

The Renaissance man is the complete manifestation of human achievement, and an example of what happens when we seek to flourish instead of simply seeking comfort or happiness. Just as the Stoics taught us that trials reveal a greater version of ourselves through hardship, the Renaissance men believed that, through continuous learning and through continuously pushing the limits of their minds and capabilities, they would be able to achieve greatness. As we go through our lives, we would do well to remember the Renaissance men. These people were not concerned so much with worldly achievement but believed that the personal growth and learning that they achieved was their everlasting legacy. When we seek to make ourselves better, *eudaimonia* is the outcome. This is the spirit of the Renaissance that we should choose to carry with us no matter where we go, the spirit of the Universal man. We too can choose to be a Renaissance man or woman when we place personal growth as one of our highest priorities. Together, we can bring in the new Renaissance as an army of Universal men and women, seeking above all else, to flourish as individuals.

Part III

Wisdom Reborn

"The only hope is that our civilization will collapse at a certain point, as always happens in history. Then, out of barbarity, a renaissance."

(Pierre Schaeffer)

Chapter 12

Applying ancient ideas to the modern day

The final chapter of this book is dedicated to quickly recapping the philosophical ideas and concepts in this book, and to giving guidance to you on how to practice and apply these ideas in your own life in the modern day. If you read through this book, put it down, and never practice applying its ideas to your life, you won'"t ever experience a personal Renaissance. This final section then should be seen as a guide on how to create a philosophy of life modeled directly on the ideas in this book and inspired by the Renaissance.

This book has five philosophical sections: Humanism, Platonism, Stoicism, remembrance of death, and *eudaimonia*. The Humanist movement promoted a belief in the individual, a focus on education and learning, and an emphasis on providing opportunity for even the less fortunate of society. The Platonist ideas discussed are being humble, questioning one's beliefs, and seeking to discover and better understand oneself. The ideas discussed in the chapter on Stoic philosophy are believing in providence, having courage, and being temperate. All these deal with the way in which we perceive life. Remembering death is a call for us to remember our mortality and try to always keep in mind how precious life really is. And, finally, *eudaimonia* deals with immersing ourselves in the process of living and focusing on personal growth rather than results. Someone that becomes capable of living their life based on all these philosophical ideas will have a firm foundation to build a happy and successful life.

The Humanist ideas presented in the book have much to do with our perceptions of the world and our attitude towards life, thus creating a positive self-image and positive mental make-up while also fostering the love of learning for ourselves and for others around us. The Platonist ideas deal heavily with epistemology and should foster a healthy skepticism of things that will encourage us to discover more about ourselves and our beliefs, to be humble and remain seekers of knowledge. The Stoic Ideas discussed deal with our inner world and give us powerful ammunition to shape our actions and our destiny through a practical and applicable philosophy. Remembering death can help ground us and give us a powerful motivation for living. And, finally, seeking *eudaimonia* helps us fully embrace living no matter what situation we find ourselves in. My hope is that shining a light on some of the virtues of ancient days might help the people of today, just as it helped people of yesterday.

I truly believe that violence, hatred, toxic culture and politics, and a slow dumbing-down and domestication of the masses due to consumerism and corporate greed have led the world, and especially America, to a tipping point. And yet, for all the world's problems; despite all of the suffering and oppression, and despite the seemingly hopeless place that we find ourselves in, there is *always* a chance for a new start. The new start begins with you, the individual. It does not begin in Washington DC or the United Nations. It doesn't begin with a book or a new political movement. It begins with individuals like you taking action to become better versions of yourselves. This book is not filled with new ideas; it is filled with the same ideas and concepts that sparked our first Renaissance and these same ideas possess the power to begin another rebirth. If you are ready to start your own rebirth, then let us not delay a moment longer. It all begins with you.

Humanist ideas (see chapter 7)

Believe in the individual

Many times, people start journeys of self-improvement without a clear confidence in themselves. Past traumas, failures, or setbacks have a way of scarring our psyche and paralyzing us with fear. If you don't already believe in the potential that lies deep within every human being on this planet, then it is important to first develop this belief as a starting point for your own personal journey. The key to self-belief is realizing that potential that exists within you; you may not be ready to do a thing today, but you must believe that if you put in the effort to improve, that you might be someday. If you don't believe in yourself already, start following successful people through interviews and biographies. Often you will find time and time again that most of the iconic names that you can imagine have pasts riddled with their own setbacks. It's important to realize that your idols, the most successful among us, are no different than you or me.

Everyone starts as a baby and grows up into an adult. Some people are born with a silver spoon in their mouths. Some people may be born in poverty. Some are born strong and healthy, others weak and sick. There are some limitations in your life based on where you are fortunate or unfortunate enough to begin, but those limitations are often more imagined than they are real. Say to yourself often, "if someone else can do it so can I". Your gifts and weaknesses might not allow you to be Usain Bolt or the next Steve Jobs, but everyone can find success somewhere.

If you believe that others could do it, then you must believe in yourself by extension.

A key tenet to success in anything in life is being able to believe in your own capacity to grow and learn. You might not have the skills or resources you need today, but you *must* believe that, through personal growth, hard work, and enough time, one day you could. The world that you live in is at least partially a product of your own making. Your own beliefs about limitations and the things stopping you from finding success and happiness become self-fulfilling prophecies. If you ever want to break out of the place you are currently in, then you must first be able to imagine yourself capable of doing so.

Learn to love learning

As just mentioned, a lifelong commitment to learning ensures that you become more capable with each day that passes. Learning makes people more successful, more effective, more efficient, wiser, and better prepared for adversity or opportunity. It can be easy to fall into the day-to-day grind of life, which is a trap all too common in the American dream. We go to primary school where a huge emphasis is placed on going to college and getting a good job. We study hard, get a degree, and soon find a well-paying entry-level job. And then we begin the day-to-day decay. We work long stressful hours and spend our free time coping by watching TV, scrolling through social media, or drinking away our stress. One day we look in the mirror and realize we are five years older and, despite looking worse for wear, we are in the exact same place as we were five years previously.

Lifelong learning brightens up our lives and breaks up the monotony. It gives our life meaning and creates flow states that set us free from troubles and stress. It is also invaluable in creating wisdom and knowledge that makes us better humans.

The decision to continue learning can take many forms. It can be a new hobby like chess or a casual or competitive sport. It could be blocking one hour per day to read novels or non-fiction, or to learn a new language or how to code. It could be finally enrolling in night classes to further your degree. It could be studying philosophy or volunteering/ apprenticing in an industry that interests you. It could be going to three workshops per year to further your career or learn job relevant skills. The unifying theme to all these ideas is that you must do things with the intention of learning and improving.

One area of learning that everyone should absolutely prioritize is reading. Reading is like exercise for your mind. As this book is a collection of wisdom gained from philosophy, I personally recommend at least 30 minutes of reading each day focused specifically on either expanding your mindset and or skills, or simply focusing on how to become a better human being. If you haven't read Plato, Aristotle, Seneca, Cicero, Epictetus, and Marcus Aurelius, then I would highly recommend starting there. These philosophers dedicated their lives to the search for truth, and the ideas in this book are directly based on some of the wisdom that they gained. There is endless wisdom to be gained from books. Therefore, reading must be a priority in your life. Just 30 minutes per day, even in a busy life, is enough to read one to three books per month (that's a lot of learning!)

Keep in mind, as you seek new learning, that doing is an action, and someone can "do" things repeatedly without ever learning a thing. *Learning*, however, requires intentional practice. I'll give you a personal example. I learned to play chess when I was around ten and played maybe 100 or so games throughout the next 20 years of my life and never got one bit better. One day I decided that I wanted to "learn" to play chess for real and started taking online lessons, watching videos, and dissecting my games to improve. Within a year, I had doubled my online rating. I probably wouldn't have gotten better if I had simply played 1000 more games though. My improvement was a product of the hours of "unsexy" and boring things that I did to get better: memorizing openings, solving thousands of chess puzzles, analyzing my games to look for mistakes, or studying master games to look for new ideas and concepts. I am not special; I was not and still am not naturally talented in chess. In fact, my starting rating was below average. But because I was dedicated to learning, I improved significantly as a player. Sure, there are limits; I'll likely never be a national or world champion. But I can certainly be a much better player next year than I am today with continued practice. The lesson is that learning requires intention and focus; just going through the motions will not produce real growth.

I encourage you to think about your goals in life or pick some areas you'd like to improve in. Think of a few hobbies that you can do for fun or, if you already have some things in mind, shift your focus to the act of learning and improving and away from just getting results. Make a commitment to read 30 minutes each day and, if you have more time, then aim for more! Focus on making sure that each day when you go to bed you know a little more about something than you did when you woke up. And, one day soon, you will be a force to be reckoned with in whatever areas you choose.

Help others achieve their potential

Success is rarely a zero-sum game. Aside from special areas like business competition or competitive sports, there is plenty of room for everyone to be successful in their own way. Businesses where employees work together and help each other are more successful long term than businesses where employee interactions are cutthroat. Helping others can make you feel better, it builds relationships, empowers others, and creates a bubble of positivity around you in your day-to-day life.

Encouraging others is easy to apply practically ... just don't be negative towards others or towards their goals and dreams. Avoid being a "hater". Give people genuine advice and help where you think you can help. And if you can't contribute to someone's success directly then just give someone a high five or tell them "Good job". Encouraging others can pay off directly, indirectly, or simply end up making the world a better place to live in.

Platonist ideas (see chapter 8)

Be humble

Humility can help keep us stay focused on learning instead of celebrating how much we know. Remember the story of Socrates visiting the successful men of Athens only to realize that their success in one area of life had given them the false belief that they were knowledgeable of things outside of their expertise? By focusing on our successes instead of what we can learn and how we can improve we can often end up developing a type of tunnel vision that warps creativity and creates a fear of failing that can paralyze us. Ego is not the friend of progress. In fact, the need to look good or curate an image of ourselves for others can hinder personal growth. When ego takes over, we become more concerned with how knowledgeable we look rather than how knowledgeable we are.

Practicing humility comes easy if you focus your attention on how much you don't know rather than what you do. A champion athlete or a successful businessperson who thinks they have nothing left to learn because they are currently #1 won't stay on top for long. It's through the continuous seeking of new knowledge that our skills stay sharp and relevant, and that we continue to adapt and grow as we develop new ones.

Make a habit of constantly looking for people more knowledgeable than yourself in areas that you are focusing on learning. And if you are fortunate to be good enough that someone better is hard to find, then you'll need to look even deeper introspectively at yourself to find areas that you can improve on your own. There is always something new to learn and it is important to remind oneself that past success is no guarantee of future success. Extreme pride almost always comes right before the fall. Always stay vigilant and stay focused on learning.

Question everything

Skepticism is often misconstrued as pessimism. But it is a key to being informed and realistic in your world views and beliefs. Through questioning things, especially our own beliefs, we can become better informed on topics that matter most to us. As humans we have a natural bias to follow the crowd, because if everyone else is doing it, it must be right...right? It takes discipline to question and refuse to go along with the crowd. But it isn't exactly complicated.

Try to make a mental habit of checking yourself on things you think or say. If you make a firm statement about a belief, try to ask why you believe what you do and where that belief came from. If you can't explain it to yourself in a well-formed and congruent way, chances are the belief is a house of cards.

When questioning your beliefs, it is important to not only examine self-affirming information that supports the belief that you already have, but to spend serious time examining the opposite argument as well. You can only begin to come close to impartiality and a balanced view on a subject if you can make an intelligent argument for both sides of an argument. Even our beliefs on the fundamentals of right and wrong are often erroneous and ambiguous if we are honest with ourselves.

A great way to foster healthy skepticism and develop the habit of questioning beliefs is to study and read philosophy. Even a very superficial study of philosophy through introductory books that summarize major philosophical ideas can be extremely potent at helping one to see how complicated the world truly is. Just Descartes' brain in a jar thought experiment or the trolley problem is enough to make one realize the lack of certainty that there truly is even in the fundamental beliefs that we hold (if you don't already know these philosophical thought experiments, look them up!). Questioning is just an extension of remaining humble and continuing to seek out new knowledge. And this will go far in transforming your worldview and helping you to grow.

Know thyself

Self-knowledge is fundamental to personal growth as a human being. Past scars, fears, strengths, and weaknesses can dictate our world view and therefore steer our course through life if we don't take action to take control of the reins ourselves. Self-knowledge is often only found through painful self-discovery and brutal honesty. We must be willing to accept that the place that we are in life is in our control; and realize what limiting beliefs and circumstances have placed us exactly where we are today.

Counseling, journaling, practicing philosophy, seeking out new challenges, defining personal values and trying to live by them, and doing things that we are afraid of can all help us discover more about who we are. The more in touch we become with who we are, the better prepared we are to shape ourselves into who we'd like to become. Living comfortably in a 9–5 job safe in our cubicle and spending our nights and weekends either in an alcohol-induced stupor or glued to the couch in front of a TV will not develop self-knowledge. Self-knowledge comes from living a fulfilling life, asking questions, challenging ourselves, learning new things, and not being afraid to fail. Practicing introspection, like journaling, counseling, or sharing more about ourselves with the people that we are close to, can all help reveal more about ourselves.

Stoic ideas (see chapter 9)

Believe in providence

As discussed previously, providence is traditionally associated with a faith in a governing intelligence (nature, destiny, the universe) or God. But even an atheist can find the benefits of providence through a strong belief in self. Providence in its essence is simply the faith that things will work out for the best. It doesn't matter if you believe that it's because God predestined everything to work out, or if you simply believe in your own capability to make the best of a situation and take control of your own "destiny".

Essentialism is the belief that something beyond mankind determines our meaning (destiny, fate, God, nature, etc), while existentialism is the belief that even if God exists there is no meaning attached to life until we create it through living. The most important idea to take from all of this is simple: you must have meaning in your life, and you must have faith in something. Believe in God, believe in destiny or the universe, or simply believe in your own power to create your own meaning. This faith in something is paramount to getting through tough times and adversity. It is easy to be positive and mentally tough when things are easy, and times are good. But when the world feels like it is crashing down on you, it's a belief in providence that will help you get through it all.

I can't tell you what religion to follow, if you should be an atheist or pantheist, or what the right belief is for sure. But I can tell you that belief is a powerful source of strength through adversity. Just like the myth of Sisyphus, if you don't have faith in destiny or in God's plan, then you need to find and create meaning in your own life before you fall prey to hopelessness.

How does one form a belief in providence? This one is *not* easy. It takes soul-searching and it requires you to ask yourself serious questions about existence and what your idea of meaning in life looks like.

The first step is to ask yourself whether you do or don't believe in God. If you do believe in God, then you need to figure out what version of God you believe in. God can take many forms. Pantheism preaches that the universe is God. Christianity preaches Jesus is the way. Islam tell us there is one God, but many prophets sent to guide us toward God. Judaism preaches one God. Paganism places nature at the head of things. And you could even worship multiple gods in Hinduism or the Norse or Greek gods. Once you've established what your version of God looks like, then you need to start studying the teachings of that God to find the universally shared truth that God has a plan and, whether or not intelligible to you, God must have a plan for you that is the best use of your life on earth. You need to find the faith to know that, even if you are going through troubles and trials, that it's necessary to cultivate you into the person you are destined to become for God's/destiny/the universe's plan.

If you can't bring yourself to believe in God/gods/destiny/or the universe, or if you are simply atheistic in your beliefs, then no faith in a higher being or power is required to find providence. If you believe in nothing, then this life is all that you have – there is only darkness at the end of life. Therefore, any meaning that your life might possess can only be relevant to the way it is lived or the impact that your life can have on the world. If there is no guidance from a higher power on how to live your life meaningfully, then you must commit the act of creation – become your own god and forge your own unique meaning.

I am not condoning atheism or belief in God or a religion. The benefits of providence can be had for believers and nonbelievers alike. The truth is that no matter what you may or may not believe, no one knows for sure what comes after death and, most likely, it will never be proved one way or another. The best we can do is take a leap of faith and believe in what makes the most sense to who we are. But a belief in providence of some sort is 100% required to ever find *eudaimonia*. We need to believe that either something greater than ourselves is in control of our fate, or that we are in control of our fate. Purpose and providence give us the power to persist, the energy to keep going, and fills in the areas of life that might be devoid of enjoyment.

Be courageous

Courage, for the purposes of this book, is the ability to be undaunted by adversity or difficulty. But it can be developed in several different ways. Courage is a state of mind. It is not the absence of fear or pain, but the ability to proceed despite them. It is the knowledge of the fact that our struggles do not deter us, they give us opportunities to unleash and discover our higher selves.

How does one foster the growth of courage? The best ways to hone your courage are to purposefully seek out difficulty and challenge, to practice daily discipline, and to remind yourself daily about your belief in providence.

Seeking out personal challenges not only helps us learn and grow, but it also builds our self-confidence so that we feel more prepared to face adversity and challenge in the future. By slowly pushing ourselves and our bodies through more, we begin to rewire our own brains. As impossible goals, tasks, and achievements get closer to us we begin to see that perhaps we are more capable than we ever could have imagined.

Another powerful way to build up our courage is to simply practice discipline. One doesn't have to climb a mountain or save a life to build courage. Simply forcing yourself to not talk badly about a coworker, studying when you don't feel like it, eating a healthy meal instead of a burger, or working out instead of watching reality TV can make you more courageous. In the same way that purposefully seeking out challenges makes us more resilient and better prepared to face adversity, simply living a disciplined life makes us tougher. As you achieve more and gain more mastery over your basic impulses to seek immediate gratification you will become more effective, more powerful, and wiser. Small victories over one's own desires will make you more prepared to face fear, adversity, and trials when they appear.

And, finally, remember that if times ever do get tough, that is when you must remember your belief in providence. During times like these you must tap into the meaning of your life and draw strength from this belief to persist. You must always believe in yourself, and you must believe it is a fact that you can make it through whatever is in your way. Remind yourself daily that even if things don't work out how you planned, you must find the strength to derive new meaning from the situation and proceed regardless. Remind yourself daily that you have been born to discover your potential. Whether it's God, destiny, the universe, or simply yourself, you must always remember and believe that you were made for this. This is courage: to be never deterred, to be never broken by the happenstance of life.

Be temperate

Courage is the power to persist through difficulty and challenge. But temperance is the ability to use reason to make us more resistant to the emotions and impulses that often dictate our lives. Temperance is the ability to feel an emotion or impulse and to then use a pause in time, so that we can use logic to determine the best course of action, instead of simply reacting to our initial emotion.

Temperance can be developed in many of the same ways that we can build our courage. Discipline and seeking out challenges can help us feel less intimidated and calmer in the middle of intense situations (thus decreasing our reactivity). But there are other ways for us to foster the growth of temperance as well.

Many times, the simple act of not deciding immediately can allow us to exercise better judgement and exhibit more temperance. Often, during the heat of the moment, we experience strong emotional responses that can lead us into reactionary spirals. Simply removing yourself from the situation and giving yourself 24 hours to think and decompress can help a hostile situation.

But, what about when a pause to think and reset isn't possible? Techniques like counting backward from ten or counting five items in the room and saying their names out loud "red chair", "black remote" etc. can be helpful to help us recenter and detach from our emotions. Or you may prefer the act of simply "observing" your feelings. When you feel a strong emotion or impulse, try to step outside of the emotion by identifying what you are feeling. Often just identifying that you are angry, scared, sad (any other emotion) can help you view the emotion objectively and find a more reasonable response instead of acting hastily in the heat of the moment.

Temperance, much like courage, is not the absence of emotion. It is simply taking a pause to identify your emotions so that you can make a more logical and reasonable decision rather than reacting simply on an impulse. Emotions can be powerful indicators of what is going on in our inner world; they can help us navigate the world better, and they can help us to understand others around us. Temperance is simply choosing to be the master of your impulses and emotions, rather than being a slave to them.

Remember your mortality (see chapter 10)

Death comes for us all. This single, undeniable, fact should give significance and urgency to our lives. As humans we often push the knowledge of our mortality to the back burner of our thoughts and proceed to "stay busy" rather than to consider the fact that, at any second, our life could end. Our imminent end should not be a depressing fact that we dwell on and lose sleep over. After all, it is a certainty. Instead, it should remind us that every single moment is precious and that we should be living with intention, always remaining grateful for our life and every moment in it.

There is one caveat when remembering death though. Be careful not to fall into the hedonist trap. Meditation on death isn't meant to give us license to spend recklessly, live fast, and die young. It is meant instead to center us and allow us to focus on making decisions that will contribute to our legacy and life. Just remember, when remembering death, not to use it as an excuse to live superficially. Instead to focus on living intentionally.

Remembering death is easy if you make it a habit. Reminding yourself first thing in the morning of your mortality, or before you go to bed, is an excellent way to keep death on your mind. All it takes is to keep in mind that life is precious, fleeting, and that the current moment is the only moment guaranteed. This knowledge alone is often enough to trigger a deep response inside of us and help us live with more vigor. Remembering that you will die is one of the best ways to remind yourself of how precious your time on earth is. Use it wisely.

Seek *eudamonia* (see chapter 11)

We can find lasting happiness as a by-product of the state of flourishing that comes through *eudaimonia*. *Eudaimonia* comes when we reach a state of personal growth that takes us closer to our potential as human beings. We can find *eudaimonia* from following all the ideas listed above and throughout this book. Believe in individuals, help others, continuously learn, be humble, question things, seek to understand yourself, be courageous, be temperate, have faith in providence or in the power of yourself, remember your mortality, and seek *eudaimonia* (growth) not immediate gratification.

When you begin to apply these ideas of wisdom to your life, you will begin to thrive and flourish. This is the wisdom of the ancients reduced to their simplest forms. I promise you that once you begin to flourish, life will take on a whole new form. Every day is brighter. Every interaction is more meaningful. Every second is more valuable. Life is short, and each moment is precious. We should seek to flourish in every moment that we exist.

Closing words

The goal of this book from the start has been to show the historically potent ideas and philosophies that transformed the Western world during the Renaissance era. I have always had an affinity towards and appreciation for practical philosophy; not the type of thought experiments intended to reveal paradoxes or create unsolvable cognitive dissonance (although that can be fun as well), but the type of philosophy that is meant to be a way of life that improves its practitioner. The Renaissance is unique and special in that it was an age of inspiration that came immediately after one of the darkest periods in human history. From the ashes of a war-torn and plague-ridden Europe came a new period of Western thought that inspired invention, critical thought, and a better society for all. People during the Renaissance began again to believe that, through practice and philosophy, we could better ourselves and unlock human potential. This powerful belief in the individual changed the world.

My hope is that you will use the principles in this book and focus on practicing and applying them in your own life. I believe very much in you and your ability to find *eudaimonia* and lasting happiness. You can achieve many great things in life, probably far more than you could ever imagine. As you go forward in life, remember the ideas inside these pages:

1. Believe in the individual
2. Learn to love learning

3. Help others achieve their potential
4. Be humble
5. Question everything
6. Know thyself
7. Believe in providence
8. Be courageous
9. Be temperate
10. Remember death
11. Seek *eudaimonia*, not happiness

This book is not intended to be a shortcut to success and happiness. It is not a collection of 11 simple tricks to hack your mindset or achieve fame. It is more of a blueprint to follow as you rebuild yourself and your beliefs and as you seek to flourish in new ways and endeavors.

The same wisdom that inspired the people of the Renaissance can inspire us still today. Perhaps, if enough of us truly commit to living lives that are imbued with these ideas, our many lives and voices can combine into a more positive voice of change. The new Renaissance will be like the old one; a new age of individuals like you and I, seeking to improve, learn, and grow, and then to finally pass on what we have learned in order to help others. The truth is that humans are in this together. We are far less in opposition than it often seems. And when one of us grows we all grow. We need more individuals, and the principles in this book are more than potent enough to create a new movement of fully awakened and fully liberated human beings. So, awaken the greatness within you and be reborn. You are the new Renaissance.

I could think of no better way to end the book than by an excerpt of a letter from Niccolo Machiavelli written to

Francesco Vettori during Machiavelli's time during exile. Machiavelli, an avid Humanist, was expelled from the city he loved (Florence) and longed to return to his home. In this letter Machiavelli exhibits the true spirit of the Renaissance. Though disheartened by the sorry state of his life during exile, he still has the potency of ancient wisdom to inspire him...

> "I am living on my farm, and since I had my last bad luck, I have not spent twenty days, putting them all together, in Florence. I have until now been snaring thrushes with my own hands. I got up before day, prepared birdlime, went out with a bundle of cages on my back, so that I looked like Geta when he was returning from the harbor with Amphitryon's books. I caught at least two thrushes and at most six. And so I did all September. Then this pastime, pitiful and strange as it is, gave out, to my displeasure. And of what sort my life is, I shall tell you...I get up in the morning with the sun and go into a grove I am having cut down, where I remain two hours to look over the work of the past day and kill some time with the cutters, who have always some bad-luck story ready, about either themselves or their neighbors."

> "Leaving the grove, I go to a spring, and thence to my aviary. I have a book in my pocket, either Dante or Petrarch, or one of the lesser poets, such as Tibullus, Ovid, and the like. I read of their tender passions and their loves, remember mine, enjoy myself a while in that sort of dreaming. Then I move along the road to the inn; I speak with those who pass, ask news of their villages, learn various things, and note the various tastes and different fancies of men. In the course of these things comes the hour for dinner, where with my family I eat such food as this poor farm of mine and my tiny property allow.

> Having eaten, I go back to the inn; there is the host, usually a butcher, a miller, two furnace tenders. With these I sink into vulgarity for the whole day, playing at cricca and at trich-trach, and then these games bring on a thousand disputes and countless insults with offensive words, and usually we are fighting over a penny, and nevertheless we are heard shouting as far as San Casciano. So, involved in these trifles, I keep my brain from growing moldy, and satisfy the malice of this fate of mine, being glad to have her drive me along this road, to see if she will be ashamed of it."

And finally, after telling us of the banality of his days, Machiavelli gives us a great gift in his letter, a reminder that, though we may go through our days under duress (stuck living out our days like Sisyphus on his hill), the warm embrace of wisdom is never far away, if only we will open the pages of the great minds that came before us...

> "On the coming of evening, I return to my house and enter my study; and at the door I take off the day's clothing, covered with mud and dust, and put on garments regal and courtly; and reclothed appropriately, I enter the ancient courts of ancient men, where, received by them with affection, I feed on that food which only is mine and which I was born for, where I am not ashamed to speak with them and to ask them the reason for their actions; and they in their kindness answer me; and for four hours of time I do not feel boredom, I forget every trouble, I do not dread poverty, I am not frightened by death; entirely I give myself over to them."

A message from the author

Hopefully you have enjoyed reading this book and learning more about the ancient wisdom that inspired the Renaissance! If you learned something, felt inspired, or just liked what you read I would greatly appreciate you taking a few moments to leave a quick review on the Amazon page for this book. Positive reviews not only help others learn about the book, but it encourages others to dive into the book as well. As a first time, and self published author I GREATLY appreciate the review as it helps me tremendously to spread this message, so thank you in advance.

Simply scan the QR code above with your camera app on your smart phone to visit the Renaissance Wisdom Linktree; where you can leave an Amazon review or follow Renaissance Wisdom on Instagram all with a single click.

Further reading and sources

While this book is not intended to be an academic one, I would like to acknowledge some of the books, articles, and sources that I used to study the Renaissance period and the ancient world that inspired it.

I've listed both reference books that I used to gain a better understanding of the Renaissance period and philosophical texts (both books and letters) from many of the people profiled in the book.

I encourage anyone interested in learning further about the period of the ideas of the Renaissance to look further into any of the works or sources listed below.

Articles

www.jstor.org/stable/475608?read-now=1&seq=1#page_scan_tab_contents

SITE: Oliver, Revilo P. "Salutati's Criticism of Petrarch." *Italica*, vol. 16, no. 2, 1939, pp. 49–57. *JSTOR*, www.jstor.org/stable/475608.

www.jstor.org/stable/2901833?read-now=1&refreqid=excelsior%3A99bebf064402bec2c1dc5f813d4e81c7&seq=7#page_scan_tab_contents

Jurdjevic, Mark. "Civic Humanism and the Rise of the Medici." *Renaissance Quarterly*, vol. 52, no. 4, 1999, pp. 994–1020. *JSTOR*

Audio courses

The Great Courses (*The Italian Renaissance*)

The Great Courses (Renaissance The Transformation of the West)

Reference Works

Renaissance Philosophy of Man (Phoenix Books)

The Renaissance Italy: A History (Kenneth Bartlett)

Renaissance Humanism: Anthology of sources (Margaret King)

Renaissance Philosophy: History of Western Philosophy (Brian Copenhaver)

Routledge handbook of Stoic Tradition (Various Authors)

The Medici (Paul Strathern)

The Renaissance:Cultural Rebirth of Europe (John D. Wright)

The Civilization of the Renaissance in Italy (Jacob Burckhardt)

The Origins of the Platonic Academy of Florence (*Arthur Field)*

The Cave and the Light (Arthur Herman)

Know thyself (Ingrid Rossellini)

Lives of eminent philosophers (Diogenes Laertius)

The Swerve (Stephen Greenblatt)

A History of Western Philosophy (Bertrand Russell)

Philosophers

Petrarch (Assorted works and letters)

Giovanni Boccaccio (*The Decameron*)

Cicero (Selected works)

Plato (*The Socratic Dialogues)*

Leonardo Bruni (*New Cicero* and *History of the Florentine people*)

Seneca (Assorted books and letters)

Epictetus (*Enchiridion* and *Discourses)*

Marcus Aurelius (*Meditations)*

Quintilian (*Institutio Oratoria)*

Pico Della Mirandola (*Oration on the Dignity of Man*, and assorted letters)

Poggio Bracciolini (*On Avarice,* and assorted letters)

Marsilio Ficino (Assorted works and letters)

Gionazzo Manetti (*On the Dignity and Excellence of Man*)

Leon Battista Alberti (Assorted Works)

Printed in Great Britain
by Amazon

85702650R00129

THE LAST TRAIN HOME

BOOKS BY MARION KUMMEROW

STANDALONE NOVELS

Not Without My Sister

The Orphan's Mother

The Last Safe Place

MARGARETE'S JOURNEY

A Light in the Window

From the Dark We Rise

The Girl in the Shadows

Daughter of the Dawn

GERMAN WIVES

The Berlin Wife

The Berlin Wife's Choice

The Berlin Wife's Resistance

The Berlin Wife's Vow

LOVE AND RESISTANCE TRILOGY

Unrelenting

Unyielding

Unwavering

WAR GIRLS SERIES

War Girl Ursula

War Girl Lotte

War Girl Anna

Reluctant Informer

Trouble Brewing

Fatal Encounter

Uncommon Sacrifice

Bitter Tears

Secrets Revealed

Together at Last

Endless Ordeal

WAR GIRLS ROMANCE SERIES

Second Chance at First Love

BERLIN FRACTURED SERIES

From the Ashes

On the Brink

In the Skies

Into the Unknown

Against the Odds

THE LAST TRAIN HOME

MARION KUMMEROW

bookouture

Published by Bookouture in 2026

An imprint of Storyfire Ltd.
Carmelite House
50 Victoria Embankment
London EC4Y 0DZ

www.bookouture.com

The authorised representative in the EEA is Hachette Ireland
8 Castlecourt Centre
Dublin 15 D15 XTP3
Ireland
(email: info@hbgi.ie)

ISBN: 978-1-80550-681-2
eBook ISBN: 978-1-80550-680-5

1

COLOGNE, DECEMBER 1938

Tibor and his cousin Roxy were feeding the horses when the sound of engines interrupted their morning routine. Tibor set down the bucket and turned around to find out who the unexpected visitor might be.

"Wait." Roxy put a hand on his arm. "It's the SS. It might be better if they don't see us."

"How do you know?" Tibor squinted at her, wanting to tell her they hadn't seen anyone and neither had they heard voices.

Roxy sighed the way his mother Gisela sometimes did when she was about to explain a very obvious fact to the clan's children. "Do we know anyone who owns a vehicle?"

"I guess not. Still, it could be anyone."

"It's just a hunch, feel free to ignore it." She patted Chavo's neck. The huge black gelding was her favorite horse.

Since his cousin's intuition was usually right, Tibor hesitated before curiosity won over caution and he walked toward the center of their campsite. Just as he was about to reach it, the engines fell silent. Car doors opened and slammed shut. Boot steps thumped and soon after came the unmistakable sound of heels clicking together.

Tibor's neck hairs stood on end as about half a dozen men in black uniforms appeared between the wagons. *Damnit*! He should have listened to Roxy and kept away. Intending to hide among the horses, he turned on his heel, when an imperious voice barked across the grounds, "Inspection! Everyone step up! No exceptions!"

Despite his intention to hide, his feet began to move toward the center of the campsite. Within seconds, he reached the place where some of the men had already gathered. Tibor's normally fearless mother Gisela was surprisingly pale as she joined the others, carrying her youngest grandchild on her hip and dragging another by the hand behind her.

It took less than five minutes for every family member to line up, waiting to hear what the SS had to announce—with the exception of Roxy. Tibor stood with a sullen expression next to his cousins Romeo and Christian, the latter wearing his favorite cap, frayed at the edges.

Secretly, he wished he'd listened to Roxy, who surely was watching the proceedings from a safe distance, perched high up in one of the surrounding trees. If only he possessed as much courage as she did. Because unlike her, he'd never dare to disobey an order from the authorities.

"Who's in charge?" asked one of the uniformed men.

Tibor's father Gottfried stepped forward. The tall, broad-shouldered man seemed small and insignificant compared to the SS men with their arrogant demeanor and rifles at the ready.

"I am the clan elder." Gottfried showed no sign of fear.

The SS-Scharführer eyed him with contempt. "Gypsies and Gypsy half-breeds over six years of age must report immediately to the police headquarters for racial hygiene registration. Anyone who resists will be arrested."

"My family has lived in Germany for generations, and each of us has German citizenship—" protested Gottfried.

"Shut up!" the Scharführer cut him off. "Your kin belong to

an inferior race, not worthy of being part of the German Volksgemeinschaft." After the Nuremberg Race Laws came into effect, not only the Jews, but also the tribes subsumed under the word Gypsy had lost their citizenship and had effectively become people without civil rights.

Gottfried's Adam's apple bobbed up and down several times, but he didn't rise to the bait.

The Scharführer spat at his feet. "Have you understood, you filthy swine!"

"Yes, Herr Scharführer." Gottfried's voice was eerily calm, the way it used to be just before he was about to explode. Instinctively, Tibor ducked his head.

"In one hour, your entire dirty clan will assemble in front of the police headquarters, or you'll all be taken into protective custody."

Gottfried pressed his jaws together so tightly that Tibor swore he could hear a grinding sound pierce the air. A few seconds later, he answered, "Understood, Herr Scharführer."

Tibor swallowed his rising anger. Why wasn't his father fighting back? He should have told the SS men to go to hell. He exchanged a glance with Romeo, standing next to him with clenched fists, apparently having similar thoughts.

"In one hour, not a minute later," threatened the Scharführer before turning to his men, who shouldered their rifles at his signal. "Move out. We're done here."

The half-dozen men turned on their heels and marched in unison to their vehicles. A shiver ran down Tibor's spine at the eerily impressive spectacle. The last boot steps faded, car doors banged, engines roared to life. The vehicles left a trail of dust as they sped off. As soon as they were out of sight, a murmur passed through the family.

"Go, get ready!" Gottfried's wife Gisela, a stately woman with a severe bun and an even more severe gaze, barked at the children gathered around her, her usually bold voice trembling.

"Put on your best clothes. Comb your hair. Wash your hands and face."

The gathering dispersed, everyone returning to their own wagon to prepare for departure. Tibor followed his mother, not wanting to be responsible for the family arriving late at the police headquarters.

In front of the wagon, Roxy appeared as if by magic. Tibor had long given up wondering how she pulled it off. This girl could appear and disappear at will without anyone noticing. Not that the adults paid much attention to any of the older children, which Tibor considered a good thing.

"Did you hear what the SS said?" he asked her.

"I did." She grabbed his shoulder, forcing him to turn toward her. "We need to tell your father not to go to that registration."

Her words intensified his unease. Roxy had an infallible instinct; if she didn't trust a situation there was definitely something wrong with it. But the fear of his father was stronger. "You know as well as I do that my father doesn't like his orders to be questioned."

Roxy's eyes bore deep into Tibor. "Regardless, we have to warn him. I can't explain it, but deep in my gut I know the registration means trouble."

Tibor sighed. "We can try, but I don't think my father will listen to us."

"Then we have at least tried. The Nazis want to brand us, just like they did with the Jews."

A chill raced down Tibor's spine. The Jews were harassed even more severely than the Roma. There had been cases of Jews being beaten to death by the Brownshirts in broad daylight, and none of the passersby had protested with a single word. "All right, let's try and warn my father."

Gottfried, though, wasn't willing to listen. He cut Roxy

short. "We can't simply ignore an SS order. The Sturmführer was clear that anyone who doesn't show up will be arrested."

"To do so, they have to find us first," Roxy pleaded with her uncle.

"Nonsense. We're law-abiding citizens, not some random vagrants who are on the run from the authorities. There's nothing to gain from skipping the registration."

"Are you sure?" Roxy stretched the words to show her uncle she thought he was naive.

Tibor observed the angry glint in his father's eyes and jumped to his cousin's rescue by nudging his elbow in her ribs, saying, "I'm sure there's nothing to worry about."

"Get yourselves ready, we must leave soon if we are to arrive punctually." Gottfried left them standing as he walked away.

"I have a very bad feeling about this," whispered Roxy.

2

Roxy stood in front of the brick building of the police headquarters, surrounded by her entire family. A nervous tension hung in the air. Other clans gathered in the large square, apparently having received the same summons.

Aunt Gisela had obliged her to exchange her worn-out pants for a clean dress. The coarse fabric scratched her skin and the long skirt dragged on the ground. It was incredibly impractical. Even worse, the unfamiliar shoes squeezed her feet, making it feel as if she had lead weights around her ankles. It was a mystery to Roxy why most people insisted on wearing shoes day in day out. Barefoot, one was so much more agile.

Suppressing a deep sigh, she observed with growing unease the faces of people leaving the building. Without exception, every single one of them looked deeply disturbed, as if a monster lived inside the brick walls. From everything she'd heard—and Roxy heard a lot when she went exploring the neighborhoods—the Nazis were worse than monsters. If they weren't parading around in goose step, they were cruel and rude, attacking passersby and beating up anyone whose nose they didn't like. Boiling anger burned through Roxy's veins. If she ever caught one of those lumps alone, she'd scratch out his eyes.

Another family left the building. The women held their children tight by the hand, their gazes lowered, as if they wanted to sink into the ground from shame. The men stared straight ahead with carefully schooled features, though they could hide neither their clenched fists nor their tightly pressed jaws. Terrible things must be happening inside, of that Roxy was certain.

"I treat my horse better than these pigs treat us," complained a man as he walked past her.

"It's an absolute outrage, what they're doing," grumbled another.

"They say I'm a Gypsy half-breed, what do they know! I'm a Sinto and a proud one."

"Why are they doing this to us?" lamented a girl.

"What does all this mean?" another wanted to know.

"Who knows," answered an old woman who was probably the girl's grandmother.

An icy chill ran down Roxy's spine. She could all too easily imagine what it meant. The reason for this summons was to brand her people like cattle for slaughter. The Nazis would enter them in their ubiquitous lists, write down their names, where they lived, and what occupations they pursued. It was easy to predict that the Nazis, who'd always despised the free-spirited lifestyle of the traveling folk, would use this information for more harassment.

Roxy had no intention of playing along with their game. Nobody had the right to inspect her like a piece of livestock.

A few meters away, Aunt Gisela stood with a stony expression next to the other women of the clan. For a moment their eyes met. Aunt Gisela pursed her lips, silently letting Roxy know that she was supposed to behave.

Her heart ratcheted up a notch, even as she mustered her

most innocent face. If her aunt as much as suspected what Roxy was up to, she could kiss her planned escape goodbye. Seemingly inconspicuously she turned her head to the side, and talked to her younger cousin Maria while surveying the surroundings with a practiced eye.

To her left lay a meadow. Roxy nibbled on her lower lip. The low grass offered no visual cover, and the distance to the next house was too far to cross unseen. If just one family member looked in that direction, she'd be done for. Besides, the meadow was visible from both the street and the gathering place in front of the police headquarters. There had to be a better way.

On the right side stood a wall about hip-high, behind which lay a large parking lot. There she could hide among the police cars and wait for an opportunity to sneak away. However, if she were discovered, she wouldn't have a credible excuse. Aunt Gisela's ire would be horrible. After her mother's death in childbed and her father dying when she was five, Gottfried and Gisela had taken her in and raised her like their own child.

The safest way would be to take the route across the meadow. She waited until Aunt Gisela was busy with one of the small children, then leaned toward Maria and whispered, "I need to go for little girls."

"Wait until we're inside," Maria whispered back.

"It's urgent, I'll be right back. Don't tell Aunt Gisela."

"I won't. But hurry up, it probably won't be long before it's our turn." Maria nodded with an earnest face.

"Sure." Roxy knew she could rely on the eight-year-old, as long as nobody asked her a direct question about Roxy's whereabouts. She strolled toward the corner of the building, where she intended to wait for a good opportunity to cross the meadow. After checking nobody was watching her, she disappeared around the corner with a quick leap.

Once out of sight, she immediately slipped out of the

uncomfortable shoes she'd been forced to wear. As if shoes would make any difference to the condescending manner the Nazis treated them. Her soles stood on the hard, cold ground. A few weeks ago it had snowed, though Roxy was glad it had melted now.

The temptation was strong to leave the clunky shoes behind, but sooner or later Aunt Gisela would miss them. That would result in a beating, which Roxy absolutely wanted to avoid. So she took a deep breath, tied the annoying things together by their laces and hung the bundle around her neck. Pressed tightly against the wall, she let her gaze wander over the grounds.

A few steps further stood a wall about three meters high, which probably enclosed the backyard of the police headquarters. The bricks offered sufficient hold for the hands and feet of an experienced climber. Roxy's heart jumped with joy. Climbing the wall was clearly the better alternative to crossing the meadow.

Once she reached the top, she'd get a better view of the surroundings and could search for an escape route. Adrenaline shot through her veins. She closed her eyes for several seconds, drawing the cold air in through her nose. It smelled of smoke from the coal stoves in the neighboring houses—and of adventure.

She gathered up her long skirt and tied it into a knot above her knees. It wasn't ideal because the thick bundle of fabric hung heavily against her thigh, still it was better than risking the hem getting tangled in the bricks or stepping on it while climbing.

One last glance over her shoulder and she walked to the wall. Her fingers and toes found the small protrusions between the bricks without effort. Elegant as a cat, she climbed upward. The ascent was child's play. Disappointment dampened her euphoric mood, since she'd looked forward to a greater challenge.

Just before she reached the top of the wall, loud noises drifted over. She froze, pressing herself flat against the wall, barely daring to breathe. From the gathering place in front of the police headquarters, she heard voices. One of them was Aunt Gisela's. Roxy briefly considered whether she should return. If Aunt Gisela demanded an answer about her whereabouts from Maria, the girl wouldn't dare to lie. It wasn't too late to show up as if she'd indeed stepped around the corner to relieve herself.

Roxy tilted her head to the side, peeking upward. She was so close. Just two, maybe three more moves and she'd reach the top. No, she wouldn't change her plan. As long as she was careful not to be discovered, it would turn out just fine. Aunt Gisela was much too preoccupied with the clan's dozen younger children to notice Roxy's absence.

The only person who'd realize she was missing was Tibor, and she could count on him to keep his mouth shut. They always had each other's back. She shoved the doubts away and focused on the task ahead. Concentrating, she climbed further until she pulled herself up in a fluid motion and lay flat on the narrow top of the wall.

On the other side wasn't the backyard she'd expected, but a flat shed. Her heart leapt with joy. This was even better. As far as she could tell, a street ran directly behind the shed. That was her escape route. A satisfied grin spread across her lips as she crawled along the wall until she slid over to the other side at the level of the shed.

Once more she peered in every direction before scurrying forward in a crouched position. Without a sound her feet landed on the tin roof warmed by the sun. Her heart hammered against her ribs, though not from fear. It was the blissful sensation of freedom.

Nobody would brand her. She was a proud Romani woman, and as such, she'd continue to live as she pleased. Nobody would change that. Not Aunt Gisela and Uncle Gottfried, who tried to make a soft-spoken young woman of her, and certainly not the Nazis.

Not even Tibor, who often tried to talk her out of her endeavors, because he still believed that in this country, one had to obey the laws. Laws that were made exclusively to harass people who didn't belong to the so-called master race. Roxy's face twisted into a grimace. Master race. Yeah, right. The Nazis were nothing but a miserable bunch of authority-worshipping fools who found strength only in numbers.

The Nazis didn't deserve for Roxy to adhere to their unjustified rules and laws. She had other ideas about her life. She'd never submit to these crooks, no matter how loud they clicked their heels, shouted Heil Hitler, or screamed hateful slogans.

As she peered down onto the street looking for passersby, she entertained the notion of disappearing for good and going her own way. But the idea of living entirely on her own without the support of her clan caused a wobbly feeling in her stomach. Her loyalty gained the upper hand, and she shook her head. Family stuck together. No matter what.

With an elegant jump, she landed on the street and returned to their campsite, where she waited for the rest of the family members to trickle in.

3

VIENNA, DECEMBER 1938

Marek paused to catch his breath before climbing the three wooden steps to his wagon. As soon as he opened the door, the smell of paprika and ripe tomatoes wafted toward him. His wife Rosa stood at the wood stove, while his son Stefan was doing his homework at the dining table next to it.

"Vati!" Stefan, who'd noticed him first, jumped up.

He shook his son's hand firmly. "How are you doing in school?"

"Fine," Stefan said.

"Remember, you need to be better than the other children to justify your right to attend school." Marek patted him on the shoulder, incredibly proud of his son, who was the first family member to attend a public school.

Marek himself had never enjoyed the benefit of a formal education. During his childhood, he'd traveled around the country with his family. He and his cousins had learned reading, writing, and counting from a childless aunt. It had taken him much effort and diligence to earn the modest prosperity they enjoyed these days.

Even his five daughters, all of whom had since married and

left the nest, hadn't been able to attend school due to their constant traveling. But his youngest should have better opportunities in life.

On Stefan's fifth birthday, Rosa and Marek had decided to stop traveling together so their son could attend school—a good education would open doors to any profession he wanted, especially since the boy had a talent for mathematics and technology.

Rosa dried her hands on her apron, greeting her husband with a kiss. "You were gone a long time. Did you do good business?"

Marek took off his jacket, hanging it on the hook next to the front door. "It was difficult, but eventually I sold three horses at an excellent price. The customer even placed an order for two more, which means I'll have to return to Silesia next month."

"That's good news. You look tired. Would you like some coffee?" As usual when he returned from a business trip, Rosa took loving care of him.

"Yes, please. The long journeys wear on my bones." He dropped onto the corner bench. "I'm getting too old for the constant traveling."

"You've been saying that for years, and you're not even fifty yet."

Under the table, Marek slipped off his shoes and wiggled his toes. "On days like today, I feel like an old man."

"Don't exaggerate. I'll heat some water for you to wash up, and you'll feel like new." Rosa understood what he needed to recover his energy.

"That would be wonderful. I feel dirty through and through. Even my mouth and nose are full of road dust."

Rosa put a pot of water on the stove while simultaneously cooking dinner.

"What's new at home? Have you heard from our daughters?" Marek asked.

"Dora is expecting her second child," Rosa beamed. "And Anna's little Josef has gotten his first tooth. On Sunday, they want to visit with their families, if that's alright with you."

"You know that they're welcome anytime. I see them rarely enough nowadays." Marek leaned back contentedly. He was very proud of his five daughters, each of them married and well-established in life.

Unfortunately, just Dora and Anna lived in Vienna. His other three daughters had married within the traveling folk and stopped by at most once a year. Whenever possible, Marek would detour on his business trips through Bohemia, Moravia and Silesia to visit one of them. Although it wasn't easy to find out where they camped at any given time.

He'd always wished his children would settle down and stay nearby, partly so Rosa would have company during his long absences. With a shrug, he pushed the thought aside. It wasn't his place to dictate where or how they should live their lives.

Rosa took the pot of boiling water from the stove and crossed the wagon to the other corner where a small wooden tub stood behind a curtain. She poured in the pot's contents, before testing the temperature with her hand. "The water's ready, Marek. By the time you've washed, I'll have your coffee and a good dinner prepared."

"Thank you, Rosa." Marek stroked her cheek, then disappeared behind the curtain, took off his dusty clothes and put them in the laundry basket. A warm feeling spread from his heart all through his limbs, as he discovered that Rosa had laid out fresh clothes next to the washtub.

His father had been right: Rosa was the best wife Marek could wish for. After nearly thirty years of marriage, he still loved her with all his heart. Giving a contented sigh, he dipped the washcloth in the tub, wrung it out and washed away the dust and dirt of the past few days from his body.

On the other side of the wagon, dishes clattered as Rosa set the table. As promised, food and coffee stood on the table once he emerged into the living area, clean and dressed in fresh clothes.

"Mmm. That smells delicious."

"I've been making your favorite dish for days now, expecting you home every evening," Rosa said with a laugh.

"It's true," Stefan chimed in with a grin. "We've been eating nothing but paprika goulash with bread dumplings."

Another warm shiver raced through Marek's veins at such caring love. During the meal, he reported on his journey, before he asked Stefan about his experiences at school.

Normally, his son would elaborate in detail what he'd learned in the various subjects, knowing how much his father valued a good education. Today though he was surprisingly terse.

"Why are you so quiet? Haven't you covered any new material in the last few weeks?" Marek asked.

"Yes, we have," Stefan hedged.

When his son offered no other explanation, Marek asked, "Has something happened?"

"Not really."

Marek gave him a stern look. "Don't lie to me."

Stefan lowered his gaze. "I'm sorry, Father."

"Well? What's going on? Have you been up to something?" As much as Marek loved his youngest, he wouldn't let him get away with foolishness. Unfortunately, Stefan was held to higher standards than the other students. Due to his Sinti heritage, he needed to behave impeccably at all times to overcome stubborn prejudices and earn the respect of his classmates and teachers.

"We have a new teacher, who doesn't like me."

Marek put down his spoon and was about to retort that this was nonsense. A teacher had to judge students by their performance, not by personal preferences. Then he thought better of it. "Did he say so?"

"Not directly." Stefan stared at his plate.

"So, how do you know he doesn't like you? You shouldn't put stock in others' rumors." Marek caught Rosa casting him a warning look just in time and swallowed the lecture that was on the tip of his tongue. "Well. Why doesn't your teacher like you?"

"The teacher put me in the last row."

"Have you been disrupting class?" Marek was on the verge of reprimanding his son.

"No." Stefan chewed on his lower lip before pushing it forward defiantly. "He said he doesn't want a Gypsy in his class because we're all thieves and cheaters. He also claimed we're dirty and smell bad. The other children laughed and called me names."

Rosa placed a calming hand on Marek's arm. He gave her a look meant to indicate that she needn't worry. Mainly thanks to her influence, he'd learned to keep his hot temper under control for many years.

He folded his hands and fixed his gaze on Stefan. "My son, unfortunately you will often encounter people like your new teacher who have prejudices. They fear what they don't know or understand. Therefore, it is all the more important for you to do well in class. That way you show him his prejudices are wrong."

"Why do I always have to be better than the others just to be accepted?" Stefan asked in a bitter tone.

"That's just how it is." Marek ran his hand through his short hair. "Most Austrians don't understand the lifestyle and culture of the traveling folk and thus are afraid of us. In ten or twenty years, that'll change."

"That long? I'll be ancient by then." The horror was evident on Stefan's face.

"Well. It's not that long, your father and I are even older than you'll be in twenty years." Rosa's intention to reassure

Stefan had the opposite effect on him. Aghast, he dropped his spoon onto his plate. The goulash sauce splattered onto the table.

Rosa stood up and wiped away the splatters with a damp cloth, albeit not without giving her son a disapproving frown.

"You need to be more careful, Stefan," Marek admonished. "Good table manners are just as important as a good education."

From Stefan's sullen expression, Marek could tell that he wasn't thrilled with the lesson. Regardless, he lectured him on the importance of good manners if one wanted to be accepted in Viennese bourgeois society.

Afterward, Marek picked up his own spoon again. Both Rosa and he were aware that their son wouldn't have an easy time. Still, they were determined to give him opportunities they themselves had never enjoyed.

4

COLOGNE, DECEMBER 1938

Family by family, the waiting people were led into the police building. When it was Tibor's clan's turn, they were called one by one into an office to provide their personal information. A bored official recorded the details in thick ledgers: name, date of birth, parents and siblings, place of residence.

Tibor breathed a sigh of relief. It hadn't been half as bad as he'd feared. He was about to turn and head back outside when the official pointed to a door on the other side. "That way for the racial hygiene examination."

"I beg your pardon?"

"Are you stupid or what? I said that way." The official looked as if he was to hand out a slap, so Tibor hurried to comply with the instruction, even though he didn't understand exactly what was expected of him.

Separated by gender, the family had to gather in front of two rooms. They waited for quite some time until the door opened and a Roma family he recognized walked out. The men stared straight ahead as they passed them without the usual friendly greetings. A shiver ran down Tibor's back. He tried to make eye contact with one of his friends, but even the normally outgoing boy directed his eyes to the ground.

Tibor would have liked nothing better than to flee, just as Roxy had done. He'd seen her sneak around the building's corner, and she hadn't returned. Knowing her, she was probably already on her way home to wait for the family as if nothing had happened.

She was a master escaper, a talent she'd perfected throughout the years, always seeming to vanish into thin air moments before one of the adults showed up to assign a task, usually an unpleasant one, to the youth of the clan.

Unfortunately for him it was too late to follow her example. Together with the other male members of the clan, he walked behind his father into a bare room furnished only with an enormous desk and a small table full of medical instruments.

Behind the desk sat three men in white coats, flanked on either side by a woman in a nurse's uniform. One of the men leafed through some papers. Eventually, he stopped to examine the assembled group. "What a pathetic bunch."

Tibor glared daggers at him.

The doctor picked up a form, reading in a monotonous voice, "Tibor Popa."

Tibor's stomach cramped. Why did he have to be the first one?

"Hurry up!"

Tibor stepped forward to the desk. The three doctors inspected him from head to toe as if they'd never seen a human being before. Uncertain of what to do, Tibor stood still, though his skin tingled as if a thousand ants were crawling over it.

After what seemed like an eternity, one of the doctors ordered, "Turn around."

Relief washing over him, Tibor followed the instruction. At least he didn't have to stare any longer into the impassive faces of the doctors, who observed him like an animal in a zoo. His father encouraged him with a wink, and some of Tibor's tension dissolved.

"Undress," barked the voice behind him.

Cheeks burning with shame, Tibor removed his clothes. A pencil scratched across the paper. From the corner of his eye, he noticed that the nurse was documenting his every movement.

"Take off everything, you idiot," she snapped. He'd kept on his underwear.

Tibor's entire body erupted in a hot blaze once he stood completely naked on display in the middle of the room.

The doctors seemed to have waited for this moment. They rose like lions circling their prey. Clasping their hands behind their backs, the three men positioned themselves in front of him. The second nurse fetched a caliper from the table. Head circumference, nose length, distance between eyes—everything was measured and noted.

Next, she clamped his head in a kind of vise. The cold metal tips of the instrument bore into his skin, causing a violent shudder. Tibor feared she was about to drill a hole in his skull. Thankfully the pressure ceased just as he thought his head would burst.

The nurse dictated, "Length-width index eighty-two, brachycephalic."

He didn't understand the medical jargon nor could he guess the purpose of this measurement. Though her dismissive tone was enough to make his stomach clench. One of the doctors stepped forward and palpated Tibor's face with ice-cold hands. "Clearly Asian characteristics."

"Arms up," came the order. The doctor examined Tibor's nipples under a magnifying glass, pressed painfully on his collarbone, pinched various muscles, and commented on everything with Latin terms Tibor had never heard before. Meanwhile, the second doctor photographed every part of his body with a camera. Frozen in place Tibor fixed his gaze on a spot on the wall, as embarrassment swept over him in a hot wave.

"Give me the color chart," the doctor ordered. The nurse handed him a piece of cardboard with beige and brown shades ranging from almost white to brownish-black.

"Skin color: Level six, minimal body hair."

"Ouch," Tibor hissed.

"Don't make such a fuss!" The doctor held out a tuft of hair he'd pulled from Tibor's armpit, handing it to the nurse. She compared the hair against a second color chart, scribbling the result in her file.

He desperately tried to think about something else—anything but his current situation. The attempt proved futile, because the doctor was stretching out his ice-cold hand again, abruptly tearing out a tuft of pubic hair. It hurt like hell. Tibor bit his lip just in time to avoid being scolded whining a second time.

Even horses at the market weren't examined this thoroughly.

Still, the ordeal wasn't over. The doctor proceeded with the same treatment to Tibor's head hair, after which the nurse neatly placed all three tufts of hair between two blank pages in Tibor's file, in which every detail was meticulously recorded.

Using yet another color chart, they determined his eye color and shape.

The third doctor grabbed a metallic device, holding it like a weapon as he walked across the room. "Open your mouth!"

Eyes wide with panic, Tibor somehow managed to keep the instrument in sight while he complied with the order—too slowly, according to the doctor.

"Hurry up!"

Tibor felt the urge to bite off the repulsive man's finger. His father's warning cough stopped him. The doctor who'd just rushed him now took his sweet time. He rummaged with his fingers in Tibor's mouth, tapping his teeth with the instrument and scratching at the gums. He commented on everything using Latin words, which the nurse recorded.

After a final examination of the spaces between his toes, Tibor was dismissed. Hastily, he grabbed his clothes. His hands were shaking so badly it took him two attempts to step into his underwear. Never in his life had he been so humiliated.

Meanwhile, the triumvirate had conferred and announced their conclusion. "Clearly a mixture of different Gypsy breeds."

After the degrading examination, that was the last straw. Tears of anger shot into Tibor's eyes. Since he didn't want to show weakness in front of his family, he swallowed hard until he finally regained control over himself.

"Next is Christian Wehlen."

A wave of relief washed over Tibor. His ordeal was over. He threw his cousin a sympathetic glance—perhaps it had been an advantage to be first one after all: those who followed already knew what to expect.

About an hour later, all family members had been measured, cataloged, and categorized. Tibor didn't even begin to understand the rules by which the result was reached. Some members were classified as first-degree Gypsy half-breeds, others as pure Gypsies. Afterward, they returned to the office next door, where they were handed their new papers. In Tibor's ID, the word "Gypsy half-breed" was stamped across the page as a permanent reminder of the embarrassing procedure he'd just undergone.

Once they finally left the police building, they joined his mother along with the female family members, waiting for them. As expected, Roxy was nowhere to be seen. He envied her for having had the correct instincts. If only he'd followed her advice!

His mother's lips were pressed firmly together, yet she couldn't hide a subtle trembling. She looked even more distraught than two years ago when one of her grandchildren had died of influenza. The shock of seeing his mother so upset took his breath away.

"What does all of this mean?" Tibor asked his father, who in a rare display of public affection had put his arm around Gisela's shoulders.

"Nobody can tell," his father answered in a rough voice. "Hopefully that is the last of it."

As the family arrived at the camp, Roxy sat on a log, carving a piece of wood. She turned her head in his direction before he'd even announced his presence.

Tibor walked over to her. "So this is where you are."

Without interrupting her carving, she answered, "Where else would I be?"

Tibor dropped down next to her on the log. His fingers drummed on his thigh. After a while, he commented, "You weren't there."

"Where wasn't I?"

"At the police headquarters. At the examination." He looked straight into her eyes. "You ran off."

Roxy shrugged and concentrated on her piece of wood. "What nonsense. Of course, I was there. I just finished faster than you."

Tibor snorted. "Don't lie to me, Roxy. I saw you sneak away."

She paused in her movement, looking up. "I had to relieve myself."

"You don't need to make excuses to me. You didn't come back."

"How would you know?"

"Because you warned me not to go there, remember?" Again, he wished he'd heeded her advice.

Roxy put aside the carving, hugging her knees to her chest.

"Alright, I ran away. I could sense the evil emanating from the building."

"I sensed it too, but..." He shrugged. It was pointless to tell her that he'd been afraid to act on his hunch. "I should have listened to you."

"You probably should have." She gave him an empathetic smile. "Was it that bad?"

"Even worse. They registered every single one of us. Even the little ones received identity cards."

"I don't need that kind of thing. Then I won't be missed if I ever need to disappear."

Tibor fell silent for a while, staring into the distance. The shame sat deep in his bones. As he spoke again, his voice sounded strangely hollow. "It was humiliating. They measured me like an animal. They even tore out my hair." He didn't mention that he'd been forced to strip naked in front of two women.

"Then I'm certainly glad I snuck away." Roxy wrinkled her nose.

Tibor sighed. As much as he loved his cousin, he feared that her constant solo actions would one day endanger the family, since she never seemed to consider the consequences of her actions. "Do you realize what will happen if the authorities find out you're not registered? The whole family will be punished because of you."

"They'll never find out. I'm much too clever for the Nazi scum."

Tibor shook his head. "You don't understand. They don't give up. They wrote down our names, took our fingerprints, and labeled us as Gypsies."

Goosebumps appeared on Roxy's arms. "That's nasty! They have no right to call us Gypsies. We are Roma."

"No one is stopping them, so they do it anyway." Tibor narrowed his eyes. "Did anyone see you?"

"No. Not even Aunt Gisela and she usually notices everything." She tilted her head. "You won't tell on me, will you?"

"What do you take me for?" Tibor would never rat her out to his parents. Besides, his mother would be angry with him for not immediately reporting Roxy's disappearance. In her current state of mind, he'd likely receive a beating alongside his cousin and he'd rather avoid that. "Listen, you need to be careful. Very careful. Times are getting harder, everyone says so."

"Exactly the reason why I don't want my name on any list." Roxy ran her finger over the bridge of her nose. "You should've run away too."

"Probably." He raised his chin. "Regardless, I want you to promise me one thing."

"What?" Roxy eyed him suspiciously.

"No more going off on your own. We need to stick together, you understand? We're family."

"Fine by me."

Tibor held out his hand. Hesitantly, Roxy took it. "Promise. The family sticks together."

The warmth of her palm made his anger vanish. Despite their differences, Roxy was his best friend.

"Always." Tibor squeezed her hand firmly. "Against the entire world, if necessary."

"Are you planning an uprising?" Their cousins Christian and Romeo had strolled toward them, overhearing his last words.

Roxy challenged them. "Wouldn't be the worst idea, now would it?"

"No need for that. The Nazis' barks are worse than their bites," Romeo said.

Tibor wasn't so sure about that. He remembered that during the Olympic Games in Berlin two years ago, everyone who couldn't prove a permanent residence had been arrested and locked up in a reception camp for weeks. Since he didn't want to argue with his hot-headed cousin, he kept his mouth shut.

Roxy though, didn't have the same qualms. "That would be a relief."

"Pah. Let them try," Christian chimed in, raising his clenched fists in the air like a boxer.

"You think they'll fight you?" Roxy mocked. "No, they'll put a bullet in your head. To them, we're nothing but vermin. An inferior race of foreign blood, only useful as slaves to the Aryan master race. Since the Nuremberg Laws, we don't even belong to the German Volksgemeinschaft."

"Listen to that," Romeo scoffed. "Where did you pick up all that high-flown nonsense, Roxy?"

"Here and there." Roxy always knew more than the others, which Tibor found alternately useful and frustrating.

"Well, then, it ain't true," Christian interjected. "You just want to make yourself important again."

"You know that Roxy has an unerring instinct and it usually pays off to heed her warnings," Tibor protested. She constantly learned things that remained hidden to others. Exactly how she managed this was a mystery to him.

She cast him a grateful glance.

"What do you suggest?" Romeo asked as he kicked a pebble in front of him.

"We need to unite and fight," Roxy said it as if it were the most obvious thing in the world.

"Mere seconds ago you claimed the opposite." Christian tapped his forehead with his index finger.

Roxy sighed theatrically. "Man, are you really that stupid? Our family alone isn't strong enough to stand up against the Nazis, but if we join forces with other Roma... with Sinti and Jews, with everyone who's being persecuted—"

Tibor interrupted her. "As much as I love your idea, it'll

never work. The clans are far too divided, and nobody wants anything to do with the kikes anyway."

"Which is exactly our problem. As long as we don't stick together, the Nazis can do whatever they want with us." Roxy shrugged her shoulders and turned her face away, as if none of this concerned her.

Tibor had a horrible feeling deep in his gut. Her gumption would one day get her into some serious trouble. He absolutely had to find out if she had a plan, but knew she wouldn't divulge anything in the presence of Christian and Romeo. He'd have to catch her alone to worm anything out of her.

5

A WEEK LATER

They were on the move again. Chickens ran around clucking. The women packed pots and blankets, rolled up tent tarps and stored everything in the wagons, while the men checked the wheels and made minor repairs before the big journey.

The clan's youths, including Roxy, had collected firewood for the trip the night before. As usual, they were left to their own devices, as long as they didn't get under the feet of an adult. Roxy enjoyed even more freedom than her cousins. After her father's death when she was five, she'd grown up as part of the extended family, where everyone looked after her, yet nobody felt exclusively responsible for her.

She quite liked the situation, since she much preferred to explore her surroundings than to sit in the wagon of an elderly aunt, who taught the girls cooking, sewing, knitting and other women's chores.

With nimble movements, she climbed onto her aunt's wagon, where Tibor was leaning over two crates, a long rope in his hand. Together they secured the crates rock-solid to the wagon's roof so they wouldn't fall off during the bumpy journey over rough terrain.

As they finished, they grinned at each other. Neither of them was particularly eager to heave more heavy crates up onto the wagon roof.

Tibor shrugged. "Let's harness the draft horses."

"Oh yes!" Enthusiastically, she jumped from the roof, landing smoothly on her bare feet in the trampled grass.

"Do you know where we're going next?" Tibor asked as they wandered to other side of the campgrounds, where the horses were tied to a tree.

"Your father said something about going up north." She squinted her eyes. "They noticed I was eavesdropping and shooed me away before they decided on a city."

"Too bad. Do you want me to ask him?"

"Better not." The adults never divulged information to the youths and Tibor would only risk his father's wrath by asking. "But thanks."

"It doesn't actually matter. Home is where our wagons stand." Tibor poked her in her ribs, causing her to smile. He knew her better than anyone else in the family.

"And where our animals are," Roxy added.

The horses sensed the atmosphere of departure and impatiently pawed the earth with their hooves. Just like Roxy, they loved moving on after staying a while in one place. Her favorite horse, a huge black gelding with powerful legs, snorted in greeting. His dark eyes gazed at her with longing as she stroked his broad nose bridge.

"Hello, Chavo." Roxy dug a shriveled apple from her jacket pocket. "I saved this for you."

The horse carefully took the apple from her flat palm. His soft lips tickled her hand. It reminded her of her father, who'd instilled the love for horses in her. Automatically she touched the wooden pendant hanging from a leather cord around her neck. It was a beautifully carved horse—the only memory of her father, who'd made it for her fifth birthday, shortly before he died after being hit by a car.

"Stop dawdling," Tibor told her off. "If we're caught doing nothing we'll be assigned to crate hauling again."

"Then we'd better get to work, so your father doesn't get any ideas."

"Or my mother," sighed Tibor.

With practiced movements, Roxy placed the collar around Chavo's neck. Then she waited for Tibor, who'd gone to fetch the heavy harness. She leaned against the horse, patting his neck. The animal turned his head toward her, seemingly saying, "Finally, we're moving on. We've eaten all the grass in the camp, and I could use some fresh food."

"I know, Beautiful." She planted a kiss on his nose.

Tibor was taking unusually long, giving her the leisure to observe the bustling activity. To the uninitiated, it resembled the busy chaos of an anthill. But the chaos that reigned before every departure to a new location had a system to it.

Each family member had a specific task. Aunt Teresa took down the freshly washed laundry from the line and distributed it among the wagons. Uncle Ewald checked the roadworthiness of the wagons. Romeo and Christian secured the firewood on a wagon roof. Only the smallest children played tag, having long since learned not to get in the adults' way to avoid being snapped at or deemed old enough for a chore. On the fire pit in the middle of the camp sat the large soup pot, guarded by Aunt Gisela.

"Anton! Leave your sister alone this instant!" Aunt Gisela's voice thundered across the campsite. Roxy often wondered how she managed to cook the food while simultaneously keeping track of all activities in the camp. Nothing escaped her eagle eyes. She seemed to have a sixth sense especially for when one of the many children in the clan stepped out of line. "And you, Maria, stop whining and help your mother pack!"

From a safe distance, Roxy observed how her aunt called the younger children to order with sweeping gestures. As the wife of family patriarch Gottfried, she ran a strict regime over all the children and youths in the wagon encampment. Like always before departing for a new location, Aunt Gisela was more irritable than usual and it was safest to make oneself scarce.

Roxy had made it a habit to know where Aunt Gisela was at all times, so she could disappear to the horses or roam the area, after completing the inevitable tasks, and return home just in time for dinner.

Just two days ago, she'd wandered into town and eavesdropped on two men in Wehrmacht uniform, mentioning the Munich Conference. They seemed to believe that it had been a huge mistake by Chamberlain—she made a mental note to find out who that was—to allow Hitler to annex the Sudetenland. The Sudetenland, she knew, was a region in Czechoslovakia where many people with German roots lived. Her family had once been there several years ago and she remembered the beautiful mountainous forests.

Once again, the excursion had proven to be useful. Every time she ventured out, she learned exciting and useful things about her surroundings, the people, as well as life itself. From doing so she gained a good understanding of events at the various locations where the clan stayed, even if she often didn't comprehend the meaning behind them.

"Hey, are you daydreaming, or what?" Tibor had showed up next to her.

"I was waiting for you, slowpoke," she said, anticipation bubbling in the pit of her stomach. "Do you know who Chamberlain is?"

"No idea. Where did you hear his name?"

"A few days ago in town. Two men were talking about the Munich Conference and the Sudetenland."

"I don't understand why you find this talk about politics so interesting." Tibor shook his head. "Let's get to work with the horses."

"No need to hurry. Your mother is handing out slaps left, right and center."

Tibor rubbed his cheek, making a face. As the youngest child of Gottfried and Gisela, he was well acquainted with the cooking spoon and the leather belt. He grinned. "We can absolutely dawdle. Sometimes harnessing just takes longer. It's the horses' fault, since they're particularly nervous today."

"I'm not interested in politics per se," Roxy returned to their earlier topic. "It's just all information is valuable, since you never know when it will come in handy."

"Right. You could ask Uncle Markus. He knows that kind of stuff." Tibor nodded toward the horses. "We do Chavo first?"

"Yes." Roxy backed Chavo up to the drawbar of the first wagon. As if to prove Tibor wrong, the powerful animal stood perfectly still while she and Tibor tightened the straps.

"Make sure the chains don't chafe," she cautioned as he fastened the harness.

Of all her cousins, she liked Tibor the best. The two of them had been inseparable for as long as she could remember.

Deliberately slow and thorough, Roxy checked each strap for a perfect fit before attending to the next animal. At last, she returned to Chavo, patting his muscular neck as she buried her nose in his mane. The familiar smell warmed her heart. No matter where they went, as long as she was with her clan and her four-legged friends, she was home.

Aunt Gisela's voice pierced through the air, "Come get your food! And wash your hands first!"

Children streamed toward the soup pot from every direction, but they had to be patient because the adults were served first. Roxy kept away from the crowd.

"Aren't you hungry?" asked Tibor, who was elbowing the younger children aside to secure one of the front spots in line.

"No," Roxy lied. In truth, she preferred to wait until just before the end. Almost always, Aunt Gisela forgot to stir the soup during the meal distribution, so that the heavy chunks of meat or potatoes gathered at the bottom of the pot.

Therefore, the best places in line were either right at the front—which was reserved for the adults—or at the very end. There was no need to worry about not getting her share, because Aunt Gisela might be strict, but she was fair. Seconds were only given after everyone had eaten.

With her bowl full of stew and a slice of bread, Roxy sat down on a log next to Tibor, who'd already emptied his plate.

"I'll see if there's anything left." He stood up.

"Go ahead." Roxy shrugged. One portion was enough for her, in contrast to Tibor who was constantly hungry. When he returned, there was a pitiful dollop in his bowl.

"That wasn't really worth getting up for," Roxy teased him.

"At least I know what we're having tomorrow." Tibor cast a hungry glance at her half-full plate. "If you give me some, I'll tell you."

"No, thanks, I don't need to know that badly." She knew he was bursting to brag about his findings and would tell her sooner or later anyway.

"It might be something you don't like," Tibor needled.

That was indeed possible. If Roxy knew beforehand, she'd organize some other food and wouldn't have to stand hungry next to the soup pot watching others eat. Because she'd rather starve than eat carrots.

"So? You sure you don't want to know?" Tibor asked, drawing out his words.

She scrunched up her nose. She hadn't seen carrots during packing, just plenty of potatoes. Furthermore, there was always a chicken that hadn't survived the journey in the cramped cages unscathed, which would be slaughtered at the new location. The risk was too small to give up the rest of her portion for. "No, thanks. I'll pass."

Disappointed, Tibor peered at the remainder of the stew in her bowl.

Roxy pitied him and said, "Try Maria, she almost never finishes her food."

Tibor's face brightened and he sauntered seemingly casually over to his eight-year-old cousin. However, Romeo and Christian, both the same age as Tibor and also perpetually hungry, had already positioned themselves next to her in waiting.

Roxy giggled. Should the boys fight over Maria's leftovers, she'd pick a few apples or pears from a tree along the way for herself. She always found something. She was good at improvising.

After the meal, Aunt Gisela clapped her hands. "As soon as the dishes are washed and everything is stowed away, we're going to depart."

As if by magic, each family member set into motion to complete their task. The women washed and packed the dishes, two men heaved the cast-iron soup pot into one of the wagons, and the youngest children searched the campsite for things that absolutely couldn't be left behind. Roxy and Tibor had to catch the dozen chickens, at which Roxy was particularly skilled.

"Hey, Roxy!" Tibor challenged her. "Want to bet I catch more chickens than you?"

"Keep dreaming. I'm much quicker than you."

The chickens hated the cramped travel cages. They sensed what awaited them and scattered in all directions, loudly clucking. With cat-like movements, Roxy crept up on a brown one, darted forward, and caught it by the legs, before she grabbed it under the wings and carried it to the cage. Then she set off to hunt the next one.

"Seven!" she called, while Tibor was chasing his fifth.

As they stowed the chickens in their cages, the women and children had already climbed into the wagons. The men led the horses, and the youths were more or less left to their own devices.

Roxy licked her lips as the convoy set into motion. One last look back at the abandoned campsite, and she turned forward. Her heart made a joyful leap.

She loved the traveling lifestyle of her folks and couldn't wait for the adventures awaiting her at the new location.

6

VIENNA, OCTOBER 1939

The official at the police office slammed his palm on the wooden table. "It's official. The detention decree is clear. Gypsies and people wandering about in a Gypsy-like manner may not leave their resident city or current location until further notice."

"But—"

"No buts. Find a permanent residence within seven days or we'll find one for you, and you won't like that one."

Marek stared at the document. The words blurred before his eyes, but their meaning was unmistakable: From now on, Sinti and Roma were forbidden to leave their hometown. His world was collapsing: his business, his independence, his entire life.

"I make my living trading horses. How am I supposed to feed my family if I can't travel anymore?" he asked, making an effort to keep his voice calm.

The official shrugged. "Find yourself a respectable job. You have one week to provide proof of a permanent residence. Otherwise, you and your family will be taken to a detention camp."

Dejected, Marek left the office. Outside on the street, Rosa and Stefan were waiting for him.

"What did they say?" asked Rosa, though he suspected she could read the answer from his facial expression.

"He won't give me an exemption. I'm not allowed to leave Vienna," Marek answered.

"And the horses?" asked Stefan.

Marek placed a hand on his son's shoulder. "We need to sell them quickly, my boy. There's no point in keeping animals we can no longer trade."

"What will become of us?" Rosa furrowed her forehead in fear.

Marek ran a hand through his hair. "One thing at a time. First, we need to find an apartment for ourselves, then I'll look for employment."

He spent the next few days searching for a solution. His two daughters Anna and Dora, who were in Vienna, lived in quarters too cramped to take them in. His other relatives were themselves searching for housing.

With each passing hour, Marek grew more desperate. Most landlords slammed the door in his face as soon as they saw Marek's new racial identification card with the inscription "Gypsy half-breed." Even the few who showed empathy for his situation fobbed him off with good wishes and an apologetic shrug. Nobody wanted anything to do with him. He felt like an outcast.

On the fifth day, when hope threatened to fade, Marek went through his customer list. He hated being a supplicant, but what choice did he have? He visited them one by one, knocked on every door. Again, everyone, even his best customers, turned him down more or less politely.

If he didn't find a residence, he'd have to send Stefan to live with Dora and quarter Rosa with Anna. He'd swallow the bitter pill of going to the detention camp until he found a place for his family.

In the evening, he was walking home with a lowered head when he passed a butcher shop. Years ago, he'd sold the butcher an injured horse for slaughter. Involuntarily, he hunched his shoulders at the memory. It had been a difficult decision because Marek cared more about the welfare of his animals than a businessman should.

He'd already walked past when he decided to turn around. Hesitantly he approached the shop. The butcher was a friendly man, though he probably wouldn't remember Marek. The whole endeavor was hopeless. Marek pulled himself together. He had nothing to lose, but everything to gain.

"How can I help you?" asked a young saleswoman.

"I'd like to speak to Herr Huber. My name is Marek Wesel. I sold him a lame mare some time ago."

The young woman gave him an uncertain gaze, before she disappeared into the back room. Shortly after, a corpulent man with reddened cheeks came through the door, wiping his hands on a blood-spattered apron.

"Marek. It's been a long time since you came here," Butcher Huber said. "Do you have another horse for slaughter? Just bring it in, horse meat may not be a delicacy, but people buy it anyway. Especially when it's cheap."

Due to the friendly greeting, the tension seeped out of Marek's body. "Herr Huber, I'm afraid I have nothing to sell. I've come to you to ask for help." In brief sentences, he reported on the detention decree and its consequences. The butcher listened without interrupting him, his forehead creased in thoughtful wrinkles.

"These damned bureaucrats," Huber finally growled. "And now you're looking for a place for your wagon?"

"Yes. If we don't have a regular address by the day after tomorrow, we face the detention camp."

"Those pigs. I have a good mind to hang them on a hook in the cold room." The butcher scratched his chin. "My backyard is big enough. There's only the old shed where I store the smoking wood. Next to it, there's more than enough room for your wagon. Bring it here and use my shop as your official residential address."

Marek's heart leapt for joy. "Thank you very much. That... that would be our salvation."

"Come with me," said Huber, pointing to the back door. "Look at the yard and tell me if the space suits you."

Marek wouldn't have needed to go with him. In his current predicament, he'd gladly accept any location that was big enough to fit his wagon, as long as he could give the authorities the address of a residential building as his domicile.

The backyard was surrounded by high walls and accessible through a narrow driveway, just wide enough to push the wagon through. They'd be well accommodated here. An additional advantage was that they were protected from curious glances from the street.

"What do I owe you for staying here?"

The butcher waved it off. "It's just an empty spot."

"It's so much more than that. You have no idea how much you've helped me."

On his way home, Marek had a buoyant spring in his step. The threat of deportation to a camp had been lifted from his shoulders.

As soon as they'd moved to the butcher's backyard, he'd start looking for employment. He'd be damned if he didn't find a job to feed his family.

The next evening, long after dark, when Vienna's streets were lonely and deserted, they hitched up their only remaining horse to pull the wagon into Huber's backyard.

"Don't you think the sound of hooves might wake someone?" Worry laced Rosa's voice.

"That's always a risk." Marek rubbed the bridge of his nose. "It's not forbidden to drive through the streets at night."

"No, it's not, but we don't want to attract attention," Rosa pointed out. "It would be unwise if someone observed us pushing the wagon into Herr Huber's backyard."

Marek sighed. As usual, Rosa was right. They'd chosen the protection of darkness to avoid being seen. However, if someone heard them, the disguise would be futile. On the other hand, the danger of a neighbor waking up from the clatter of hooves was minimal. "What do you suggest?"

Rosa bit her lip, searching for a solution.

"Vater, I have an idea," Stefan spoke up.

"Go ahead," he encouraged his son.

"We could wrap rags around the horse's hooves so they won't make a noise."

Marek smiled. "A great idea, that's how we'll do it."

After wrapping the animal's hooves with old rags, doubts crept in. Wouldn't that arouse suspicion if they encountered someone on the way? Marek swallowed his concern, he'd deal with that problem, if and when it actually happened.

Fortunately, they didn't meet a soul on the way. Marek was drenched in sweat as they arrived in the butcher's backyard. He unhitched the horse and maneuvered the wagon into the designated spot.

The next day, he took the animal to a buyer, while Rosa and Stefan disguised the wagon with boards and rubble stones so that for anyone catching a glimpse of it through the narrow driveway, it would look like an ordinary shed. The wheels disappeared under a wooden cladding, and on the roof, they draped corrugated metal the butcher lent them. Marek was endlessly grateful to Herr Huber for the help everyone else had refused out of fear of reprisals.

"So what do I do now?" asked Marek as he sat with his

family for dinner in the disguised wagon. "Besides horse trading, I haven't learned anything."

Rosa took his hand. "You're a smart man, Marek. You speak three languages and can calculate in your head. Something will turn up."

Stefan, who'd been sitting silently beside them, spoke up, "Vati, maybe you can still work with horses? You could ask the carters."

"I'm not allowed to leave my district anymore, so how can I work as a coachman?" Marek shook his head. Regardless, his son's idea stuck with him. There were many horse carriages in Vienna, even though automobiles were replacing them at an increasing pace.

In the following days, he approached carters, milk dealers with horse carts, and even the Spanish Riding School stables.

The answer was the same everywhere: "We don't hire Gypsies."

With each passing day, Marek grew more desperate. The modest savings they possessed were melting away. Rosa took up hours helping out in Huber's butcher shop and brought home scraps of meat every evening, so the family at least didn't go hungry. But that wasn't a permanent solution.

One evening in December, after he'd unsuccessfully knocked on countless doors, the family sat together for dinner. The damp cold hung heavily in the air. They used the stove exclusively for cooking due to the high cost of firewood.

"I'm going to the train station tomorrow," said Marek in the flickering light of the kerosene lamp.

Rosa looked up from her darning work.

"I've heard the railway is looking for workers. It's hard, physical work doing track construction, but better than nothing."

Stefan's face brightened. "You'll definitely get a job, Vater. You're strong and hardworking!"

Marek stroked his son's head with affection. He'd so desperately wanted Stefan to have a better life. Completing his education would have opened up so many possibilities to him, but Stefan had been expelled from school after severe hostility from teachers and classmates. There was no place to live for Sinti in the Nazis' world. It broke his heart to look at his son's hardened features. At barely twelve years old, he'd had to grow up much too fast.

By now, Marek was willing to do just about anything, if only he earned money to keep his family afloat. Stefan might think him strong, but Marek would turn fifty next year and had long since lost the strength and energy of a young lad.

"We'll manage somehow, Marek. You'll find a job, I'm sure of it." Rosa nestled against him.

He nodded, despite the worry gnawing at his soul. For the first time in his life, he wasn't the master of his own fate. The detention decree had taken more than just his freedom of movement, it had robbed him of his opportunities for development and his self-determination.

The next morning, Marek got up early. He put on his best suit, which he'd previously used for important business deals. This would show the railway employers that he wasn't an ordinary day laborer, but a man of education and decency.

In front of the mirror, he examined his face. It was gaunt and gray. Deep wrinkles had etched around his mouth. His eyes had lost their luster. It was an image of total brokenness.

Stefan stood next to him. "They'll surely hire you, Vater."

Marek forced himself to smile. "I think so too. We Sinti have endured many terrible things and we've always survived. We'll manage this time too. One day we'll be free again. Until then, we must persevere."

He embraced Stefan before leaving. At the door, he turned around once more. "Even though you're no longer in school, you must diligently study whenever you can. It'll be useful to you in the future."

On his way, he wondered if the advice he'd given his son was sound or if he was deceiving himself. Did he genuinely believe that one day they'd be able to return to their original way of life, without being harassed by the Nazis?

He wished for it so desperately.

As he stood at the entrance to the hiring department at the train station, he took a deep breath, encouraging himself, "For my family."

7

BERLIN, LATE 1939

Utterly exhausted Tibor dragged himself to the campsite. A few days ago, his father had informed the family that they'd be placed in an internment camp if they couldn't provide a permanent address. Subsequently, everyone old enough had scattered to search for accommodation for the approximately forty clan members. Without success.

He and Roxy had been out all day, being turned away everywhere. Time was running out.

"No Gypsies!" said the farmer on the outskirts of town.

"We don't want your kind here," explained the caretaker of an apartment building.

"Get off my property, you rabble!" another man shouted at them.

Eventually, the clan decided to split into smaller groups, hoping it'd be easier to find permanent housing for five or six people than for the entire family. Eva, one of Tibor's adult sisters, had succeeded; probably because she was heavily pregnant and the landlords had taken pity on her.

It had been a strange atmosphere: everyone had tried to look cheerful and happy, wishing Eva and her husband Harald a good time at their new place. But Roxy hadn't been fooled. She'd seen how Aunt Gisela had furtively wiped her watery eyes as she hugged her daughter goodbye.

For as long as Roxy could remember, nobody had ever left the clan to live on his own. The entire day Roxy wandered around aimlessly, not knowing why she felt so strange, until an overheard exchange between two of her aunts made her realize that the family wasn't complete anymore.

It reminded her of the time her father had died; and she feared the splitting up was only the beginning of more awful changes to come. Two days later, the rest of the clan was still without permanent housing. The sword of Damocles—being sent to an internment camp—hung lower over their heads with each passing day.

After dinner, Roxy and Tibor sat in a dejected mood on a fallen tree trunk at the edge of the campsite, where they could talk without being overheard by an adult.

"It's hopeless." Tibor fixed his gaze on his worn-out shoes. "The answer is the same everywhere. Nobody wants to take us in."

Roxy wiggled her toes while drawing patterns in the dry earth with a stick. "We're running into a wall."

He pointed to her dirty feet. "Did you see how the landlords stared at your bare feet? Maybe that's the reason we're turned away all the time."

"Do you really believe we'll be welcomed with open arms if I wear shoes tomorrow?" She rolled her eyes.

"It's worth a try."

"Fine," she drawled. "But you'll see, it won't make any difference, otherwise the others would've been successful already. After all, I'm the only one who doesn't wear shoes."

As much as he wanted to cling to the idea her bare feet were the problem, he couldn't refute her logic. The fear of being sent to an internment camp gnawed at his insides. They'd heard about these places from other Roma families—terrible stories of hunger, forced labor, even death.

Tibor gave a heartfelt sigh. "Father said the police won't extend our deadline."

"Of course they won't. Why would they?" Roxy snorted. "They don't want us living undetected among other citizens. They want to isolate us, just like they're doing with the Jews."

Fear snaked up Tibor's spine. Although he didn't understand why the Nazis despised everyone who wasn't Aryan, it had long been impossible to overlook the fact that they did.

"I've been thinking," Roxy said after a while. "What if we leave? Just you and me."

Tibor looked up in surprise. "Are you serious?"

"Well, like your sister Eva, we separate from the clan and try our luck on our own."

"You're crazy." Tibor shook his head. "My sister is an adult with a husband and will soon have a child of her own. But you and me, how would that work? What would we live on?"

Roxy lowered her voice. "We'll manage somehow. We can work. Or take things that nobody will miss."

"You mean stealing." Normally Tibor wasn't too particular about following the law to the letter. In their current situation though that was extremely dangerous, since the Nazis pursued even minor offenses with draconic punishments—if they were committed by a non-Aryan.

"It's not theft, it's survival. The Nazi laws are so unjust." Roxy looked at him with a pleading glint in her eyes. "Or do you have a better idea?"

Tibor was silent for a long time as thoughts raced through his mind. He occasionally played with the idea of running away, but the fear of being completely on his own out there always gained the upper hand. He simply didn't feel up to the challenge of life with a Gypsy identification card, without the clan to back him. Everywhere you went, people insulted you, sometimes even threatened to beat you.

However, he'd rather bite off his tongue than admit to Roxy that he was scared. "We can't just abandon the family. My parents need us."

Roxy examined him with her steel-blue eyes. "That's nonsense. You must realize that we can't help them. No one wants to take in a large family. But the two of us, we can find shelter." Her eyes bored deep into his soul. "Once we're settled, we can return to fetch them. What do you think?"

"You're dreaming." Bitter bile rose in Tibor's throat. "Who would offer housing to two youths like us? They'd most likely alert the authorities, and then we'd end up in a re-education camp." A shiver ran through his veins. He knew a boy who'd spent six months in a camp for troubled and delinquent youth. He had barely survived the treatment.

"We have to do something." Roxy's voice sounded unusually vulnerable. "The Nazis will never let up. They've registered and cataloged every Roma like... like those damn beetles they pin and put in display cases. Do you want to end up behind glass in a museum?"

"You're exaggerating." Tibor pulled his knees up, wrapping his arms around them. "We have to be realistic. If we run away, we have to take care of everything ourselves. We'll have neither a roof over our heads nor regular meals."

"Better than a camp," she growled.

"You don't know that. Maybe these camps aren't so bad?" Tibor stared into the dusk. The situation was tricky. If anyone could make it, it was Roxy, who had an unerring instinct for danger. However, she had no idea what she was getting into. Nobody was a match for the Nazis. Sooner or later, they'd catch them. "What happens if we get caught? The punishments for vagrants are harsh."

"We'll just say we're Italian. Italy is allied with Germany."

Tibor couldn't help but chuckle. Roxy was resourceful, she always came up with a solution, even if a harebrained one like pretending to be Italian. "That'll get busted as soon as they check my *Kennkarte*. Furthermore, we don't speak a single word of Italian."

"Neither will the guards."

"You don't know that."

"Perhaps you're right." A few seconds later a mischievous grin tilted up her lips. "Since I'm not registered, I'll just claim to be an Aryan."

"No one will believe that, with your black hair."

"At least I have blue eyes. Besides, many Aryan women have dark hair."

"Not curly hair like yours." Tibor leaned back. "It won't work. Your plan is absurd."

"Not if we're clever about it." Roxy slid closer to him. "Listen, I've thought it all through. In spring we'll help with planting fields, in autumn with the potato harvest. There's always work with farmers, and they don't ask for papers."

Tibor was silent. Thoughts whirled in his head. The idea of surviving alone both frightened and tempted him. Trading security for freedom...

"We have to tell my father," he finally said. "I can't just run away."

"He'll never allow it."

"Then we have to stay with the family. He's the patriarch, we mustn't defy him." Tibor hoped she understood what he didn't want to say out loud. He'd never oppose his father and leave the family, regardless of the consequences.

"We'll ask your father first thing tomorrow morning," she agreed. "Maybe he'll be glad to have two fewer mouths to feed."

"We'll do that. It's late, let's go to sleep." Tibor stood up and extended his hand to pull her up. He wanted so badly to be as brave as Roxy, but he wasn't. He admired her for her courage and independence, even if he'd never admit it to her.

As expected, his father outright refused the idea. And if Tibor was honest, he was glad about that outcome.

As the deadline set by the authorities expired, the family still hadn't found housing for most of the members. Tibor's father presented himself at the Office for Gypsy Affairs, which assigned them a place in the municipal Gypsy camp.

"Gross. It's located next to the sewage fields in Marzahn. It stinks terribly there," Roxy complained. She and Tibor pushed the wagon from behind, while Gottfried and Uncle Ewald pulled from the front of the drawbar. They'd had to sell the horses weeks ago, along with the goats. Since the family was no longer allowed to travel, they hardly had any income.

Tibor had seen the unshed tears in Roxy's eyes when the buyer had led her favorite horse away. He'd wanted to console her, but had been at a loss for words. The chickens were the only animals left. Tibor was sure they'd soon be slaughtered.

"Come on, I'm sure it won't be that bad." Tibor tried to cheer her up.

"Soon you'll smell it with your own nose."

The closer they got to the Gypsy camp, the queasier Tibor felt. Long before he saw anything, he smelled the acrid stench of waste and decay that almost took his breath away. Crows circled over the sewage fields next to the camp.

"We're supposed to live here?" Tibor's mother asked in a high-pitched voice.

Gottfried made a grim face. "Only until we find a better place."

From his father's expression, Tibor recognized that he didn't believe they'd be able to leave this stinking hole in the foreseeable future. His impression was confirmed once a barbed wire fence appeared in front of them, surrounding the camp as far as the eye could see. The only entrance was guarded by police officers.

Horrified, Tibor gazed at Roxy, who gave a shrug, which probably meant: *I told you we should have run away.*

"We might as well go straight to a concentration camp," grumbled Romeo, who was pulling a handcart loaded with chickens.

"Why should we be treated better than them?" Roxy nodded toward the cackling chickens in their tiny cages.

"Come on, now you're exaggerating. This is a collection camp, not a prison." Tibor tried to preserve a last bit of hope.

"If that's true, what is the barbed wire for?" Romeo asked.

"Surely just to protect us. We also build fences around our wagon camps."

"Yes. To keep our animals from escaping." Roxy narrowed her eyes. "The barbed wire serves to protect the Volksgemeinschaft from us. We are the pests, they want to lock *us* away."

Roxy wasn't clairvoyant. She simply moved through the world paying more attention than other people. She observed her surroundings carefully and usually drew the correct conclusions—moreover she didn't care whether anyone believed her or not.

A chill ran down Tibor's spine. He prayed that this time her predictions would turn out to be wrong.

Once they passed through the entrance gate, the family looked for a place to set up their wagons, which proved difficult because they weren't the only ones who'd been sent there. Behind them, a line of dozens of Roma and Sinti families formed, all of them looking for a suitable spot for their wagons in the muddy ground criss-crossed with tracks.

8

VIENNA, FEBRUARY 1940

"Next!" called the foreman. Marek stepped forward, shovel in hand. His application at the railway company had been successful, if you could call it that. He hadn't received a position as a track worker because the hiring manager didn't consider him strong enough, but instead as a simple station worker who shoveled coal into the tenders and cleaned the platforms. The work was hard, the pay meager. Combined with the food Rosa received from Butcher Huber, it was still barely enough to survive.

Marek wiped the sweat from his brow. This had been going on for almost three months now. During the day, he tried to think of nothing while mechanically performing his tasks. At night though, he was plagued by nightmares. In a recurring dream, Butcher Huber turned against them, throwing them out on the street in nothing but their underwear. Marek tried to beg and plead as he watched Stefan freeze to death, but the butcher who wore the black SS uniform merely sneered and turned away. Then he woke up lying in his own sweat, his heart racing as he tried to dispel the worrisome thought.

This morning the station was particularly crowded. A group of important-looking gentlemen in dark suits beneath long coats made their way through the masses. Marek, loaded down with a heavy coal sack, watched as a young lad approached the group, stole one man's wallet and disappeared.

While he was still watching the scene in disbelief, Marek felt a strong shove in his back, stumbled, and collided with the theft victim.

"Clumsy dog!" The man brushed the dust from his coat, making a disgusted face. "Watch where you're going!"

"I'm sorry, someone just..." Marek searched for the right words to explain what had happened, but it was too late.

The man reached into his coat pocket and his eyes widened. "My wallet is gone! You filthy thief!"

In a split second, the conversations around them fell silent. All eyes turned to Marek.

"I didn't take anything. It was the young lad back over there." Marek searched with his eyes for the real thief, who'd long since disappeared into the crowd.

"Search the thief. I want my wallet back!" the man ordered. As if from nowhere, two railway police officers rushed over and roughly grabbed Marek. Despite the body search yielding nothing, the accuser wouldn't back down. "He must have thrown it away. Arrest him!"

"Papers," one of the policemen ordered.

This was the moment Marek had dreaded. As soon as he showed his identification card with his classification as a Gypsy half-breed he would be done for. Everyone would consider him guilty without further questions. Anxiously, he fished out his papers and handed it to the policeman.

As Marek had foreseen, the officer's face twisted in disgust. "A Gypsy."

"That was obvious. Thieving rabble," said the theft victim.

"He must have had an accomplice, everyone knows this riff-raff always works in gangs," a second man chimed in.

"You should be ashamed of yourself! Stealing from honest citizens!" An older woman struck Marek with her handbag.

He didn't dare ward off the blows for fear of being shot as a violent criminal.

"Enough!" a deep voice suddenly thundered.

Just as Marek was about to breathe a sigh of relief, a man in an SS uniform strode through the crowd.

"What's going on here?" he asked the railway policeman.

"Herr Hauptscharführer. Heil Hitler!" There wasn't enough space for a proper salute, so the policeman settled for clicking his heels with effort. "This Gypsy was caught red-handed stealing a wallet."

"Where is the wallet?" The Hauptscharführer examined Marek with sharp eyes.

"I didn't steal it."

"He must have given it to his accomplice," said a bystander.

"It wasn't me. I saw a young lad steal from the gentleman," Marek tried to defend himself. "He had light brown hair and wore—"

"Lies, nothing but lies!" screeched the old woman with the handbag. The onlookers agreed with her.

"Please, ladies and gentlemen, calm down." The Hauptscharführer raised his hands in a placating gesture as he addressed the crowd. "I'll take over the situation. Please disperse now so that justice can be served."

The crowd followed his order grumbling. The Hauptscharführer turned to Marek. "You're under arrest."

"But I haven't done anything," Marek protested.

Shrugging, the SS officer replied, "That doesn't matter. If it wasn't this theft, then another one. You Gypsies never have a clean record."

After they'd loaded him into the police car, Marek pleaded,

"Please let me notify my family. My wife and son will worry about my whereabouts."

The policeman laughed. "You're never going to see them again. So why bother?"

What followed was worse than any nightmare: hours of interrogation, beatings, and sleep deprivation until he collapsed. At last Marek was crammed into an overcrowded cell. Even days later, the police refused to inform Rosa that her husband was in prison, no matter how much Marek begged the guards.

After a week, the inmates were taken to the train station, where they were loaded into cattle cars. No one told them where they were being sent to. The men were packed so tightly it was impossible to sit, let alone lie down. Throughout the entire journey, they received neither water nor food, just a bucket for bodily needs stood in one corner. It soon overflowed, spreading a bestial stench.

The journey lasted two full days. Each time the train stopped and the doors opened, the corpses of those who'd died during the last leg were thrown out, and new people were squeezed in. Gritting his teeth, Marek fought against despair. This hell ride had to end sometime. Once he'd arrived at their destination, he'd hopefully get a chance to send Rosa and Stefan a sign of life.

When the train doors opened at the next stop, Marek was so weakened he could barely stand. The blinding sun, the bitingly cold air—it seemed unreal after the darkness inside the wagon.

"Out, hurry up!" shouted the guards. Blows rained down on anyone who didn't jump quickly enough from the train.

Before them lay desolate land. There were no buildings or trees in sight. Nothing but steppe-like land as far as the eye could see. Was this supposed to be his home? Marek almost wished they'd continue the hellish journey.

It wasn't long before a man on horseback rode toward the group. The horse was a magnificent animal, its black coat shining. A fuzzy feeling warmed Marek's heart. A horse lover couldn't be a bad person. As the horse approached in a perfect step, the rider's polished boots glinted in the sun. Marek recognized the SS uniform.

The rider positioned himself in front of the exhausted people, his gaze sweeping over the ragged crowd. A smile played around his lips.

"I am Hauptsturmführer Goslar, and from now on, you are my prisoners," he explained in a voice sharp enough to cut through glass. "To teach you lousy criminals discipline, I will draw a line on the ground. Whoever crosses this line will be shot!"

Goslar used his riding crop to draw a line in the dirt in front of his feet.

"Form rows of five!" shouted one of the guards. Exhausted from the long journey, Marek staggered forward on stiff limbs to follow the instruction. He came to a stop next to a gaunt man whose coughing seemed to rattle his bones. In front of and behind them, along the line on the ground, the required rows of five formed. The Hauptsturmführer observed the proceedings from the back of his horse, his hand with the crop resting casually on his thigh.

"Faster, you lazy dog!" A guard shoved an old man with his rifle butt in the back.

The old man stumbled forward, directly toward Marek and his coughing neighbor. At the last moment, Marek dodged, clinging to another prisoner to avoid a fall. The coughing man though was caught by the old man's momentum. He stumbled and fell over the line, landing with his knees on the other side.

An eerie silence permeated the air. The coughing man froze as soon as he realized what had happened. Marek held his breath.

In a fluid movement, the commandant drew his pistol.

Without batting an eye, he aimed at the kneeling victim and pulled the trigger.

The shot echoed in Marek's ears. Eyes wide with horror, he watched how the man collapsed and fell to the side in seemingly slow motion. A dark pool of blood formed under his head.

"I never make empty threats," said Hauptsturmführer Goslar in a cool voice, returning the still-smoking pistol to its holster. "This line is the frontier between life and death. Remember that."

Marek swallowed the bile rising in his throat. The old man who'd unintentionally pushed the victim had turned chalk-white and was trembling all over. No one dared to speak or move.

Goslar seemed to enjoy the situation, letting his gaze wander across the crowd, before he said with a satisfied expression, "Welcome to your new home."

Then he turned his magnificent horse away. Marek's mouth hung agape as his gaze followed their departure. Never in his life would he have believed that a horse lover would be capable of doing such a despicable thing.

Shortly afterward, the guards distributed rusty shovels and blunt pickaxes until none were left. Marek went empty-handed, waiting alongside the other prisoners for instructions.

"To prevent anyone from escaping, you'll build a fence around the camp," ordered one of the guards.

Because Marek hadn't received a tool, he took a step to the side—away from the death line on the ground. The next second, a baton hit him in the back. "Do you think this doesn't apply to you, you lazy pig?"

"I didn't get a tool," Marek defended himself.

"Then dig with your hands! We don't like slackers here."

Another blow made him stagger and brought him dangerously close to the death line. Marek fell to his knees and began scratching with his bare hands at the hard, frosty ground.

Three full days they dug from early morning until late at night, always careful not to touch the death line. The first day was the worst. Marek's hands turned bloody and raw. His fingernails broke, tearing deep into the nail bed. In the evening he plummeted exhausted onto the bare ground.

Morning and evening, the prisoners received a meal consisting of a slice of hard bread and a bowl of soup. The lucky ones found a piece of potato, cabbage, or in rare cases, a bit of bacon in their soup. Hunger gnawed at Marek's insides with a vicious force he'd never experienced before. At night he couldn't sleep because he fantasized about delicious food. Or he dreamed of holding Rosa in his arms and stroking Stefan's head. He wondered if Anna had given birth to her child yet, and hoped that Dora's husband had been allowed to keep his job.

Despite his terrible situation, he worried constantly about his family. In the evenings, he prayed that Butcher Huber had taken Rosa and Stefan under his wing. During the day though, he forbade himself any thought of his loved ones. If he wanted to survive in this place of horror, he had to channel his energy solely into his work.

"Faster, you Gypsy filth!" A rifle butt hit Marek's back. He stumbled, gritted his teeth, and continued digging.

After the holes came the posts, made of heavy tree trunks, which the prisoners had to drag for kilometers into the camp. More than once, Marek believed he couldn't take another step.

Next to him, a prisoner collapsed under his load. Marek stopped, stretching out his hand to help the other man up. Out of nowhere a guard appeared at their side. Not showing the slightest trace of emotion on his face, he shot the man lying on the ground. Marek received a lash from a whip as punishment for wanting to help.

He continued working as if in a trance, hardly noticing what was happening around him anymore. He no longer helped anyone and cared solely about himself, always watching the guards out of the corner of his eye and keeping as far away from them as possible.

That was his survival strategy: avoid trouble, don't stand out, don't be remembered, and never be in the wrong place at the wrong time. He locked his empathy for the suffering of others deep in his soul. Compassion might mean death. And he had to try and make it home to Rosa and Stefan.

On the fourth day, they began with the barbed wire. It needed two men to carry the heavy rolls, unwind them, and stretch them between the posts. The wire tore Marek's already bleeding hands to shreds. Although he'd ripped strips from his shirt and wrapped them around his hands, after a few hours, the raw flesh peeked through the damaged skin. Every touch sent stabbing pains from his palms up the arm to the shoulder. All around him, men were becoming infected with tetanus and dying painful deaths.

The irony of the situation didn't escape him: The prisoners were doing their executioners' work by building their own cage. Once the fence was finished, they spent an entire week building primitive barracks where the wind whistled through the cracks in the brickwork.

"Nothing but straw on the floor!" growled one man. "We're being treated like cattle."

Marek didn't comment on the statement. He chose a sleeping place in the back corner, hoping to be somewhat safe from the guards' freely distributed blows. Night after night, he lay on the scratchy straw, staring at the ceiling and wishing to return to his beloved Rosa. What had he done to deserve this treatment?

He already knew the answer: No one, not even the shabbiest violent criminal, deserved the treatment the Nazis were inflicting on the people in this camp.

When he'd finally fallen asleep after endless hours of lying awake, it didn't take long until the command "Get up! Roll call!" was barked through the barracks.

Another new day had dawned, as horrible as the previous one. Marek's former life seemed so far away. He barely remembered the details; often it seemed to him as if it had been nothing but a dream. His hope withered to a small, flickering light that he no longer had the strength to protect.

If only he could let Rosa know where he was.

9

BERLIN, MAY 1940

The smell of decay hung over Camp Marzahn, mixed with the acrid stench from the sewage fields. Roxy sat on the step of the wagon where she lived with Tibor and other members of their clan, staring at the muddy ground, which had been trampled by countless feet.

For months, they'd been vegetating behind barbed wire. Their temporary quarters had turned into a permanent situation. Roxy hated every minute she was forced to spend in this dreadful place. The harsh winter was over, but the long-awaited spring hadn't improved their situation. On the contrary, with the first rays of sunshine, mosquitoes had sprung to life, devouring the residents alive, and on rainy days, enormous puddles transformed the ground into a muddy pool.

Only people with jobs were allowed to leave the camp during the day. Everything was rationed: water, firewood, food. Even the chickens suffered under the terrible conditions and hardly laid eggs anymore.

The only bright spots in Roxy's current situation were her secret excursions—sometimes with Tibor, sometimes alone—into the world beyond the barbed wire. She had found a spot where a slender person could slip through a hole in the fence. Just the long march through the sewage fields dampened the pleasure of her small escape.

During each trip beyond the fence, Roxy toyed with the idea of not returning. But she had promised Tibor not to go off on her own, and she always kept her promises. The family had to stick together. They only had each other left. Besides, the youngest cousins in particular depended on the food Roxy brought back from her excursions. Thus, she slipped back through the hole in the fence into her family's prison every single time, despite the heavy grief she felt for her lost freedom.

"I can't stand it anymore," Roxy grumbled as she drew patterns in the muddy ground with a stick. "I want to get out of here."

"We all do. This place is pure hell," answered Tibor, sitting next to her on the narrow steps. Over the months they'd been living in Marzahn, he had changed. The inadequate diet showed in his appearance, but the change went deeper: these days he was rarely in the mood for adventures and was quick to snap at anyone, constantly picking fights, if he wasn't sulking and staring into space.

Roxy missed the funny, alert and adventurous boy who was her friend. She wanted him back, but she had no idea how to do this. It was even worse that almost everyone in the family, except for the small children, had changed in the same way. As if an invisible curse hovered over Marzahn, slowly turning the inhabitants into old grumps.

"Let's get out of here." Roxy examined her drawing. Unconsciously, she'd traced in the dirt the outline of the camp including the barbed wire fence. She tapped on the spot with the hole in the fence. "We could simply not return from our next trip out."

"We'll never live to tell the tale. My father said yesterday we should be grateful they're not killing us." The bitterness in Tibor's voice was unmistakable.

"All the more reason to leave." Roxy hesitated to leave completely on her own, but with Tibor by her side, she'd be gone in an instant.

He shrugged. "We wouldn't survive two days out there. I'd rather stay with my family. And you should too."

"Why?" Roxy tilted her head. "We've been here for months now and the situation gets worse by the day. Even Aunt Gisela's meals seem to shrink and don't taste good anymore. Cabbage and potatoes are all we ever get."

"That's not true," Tibor protested weakly.

But Roxy knew better. She'd overheard Gisela and Gottfried talking about how Tibor and Roxy were old enough to ask for work at the camp headquarters so they could contribute to the family income. As if the food she smuggled in was worth less than the few Reichsmarks her uncles earned for hard labor.

Not wanting to argue with Tibor, she remained silent and instead decorated her drawing of the camp with trees, horses, chickens, and a campfire. Deeply absorbed in her activity, she startled when the sound of engines rumbled in the distance. Alarmed, she jumped up and rushed into the wagon. "Trucks are coming."

Aunt Gisela carried her youngest grandchild on her hip while stirring soup with her other hand. "That doesn't concern us. Make yourself useful and fetch the potatoes from the hiding place."

"I think it's the SS. They're coming with several large vehicles." Roxy's sharp hearing had detected about half a dozen different engines.

"Get going, will you?" Aunt Gisela swung the cooking spoon in Roxy's direction.

Just as Roxy had dragged the sack of potatoes to the wagon, a loudspeaker voice boomed through the camp. "The resettlement begins. You have thirty minutes to pack your belongings. Trucks are waiting at the entrance gate for transport." The brief announcement raised more questions than it answered.

Immediately, hectic activity broke out. The residents raced to their accommodation, gathering their possessions. Roxy knew from experience that the Nazis made short work. If someone hadn't packed, they'd be forced into the trucks without luggage, so she left the potato sack standing in front of the wagon and rushed inside to stuff her few belongings into a backpack.

Aunt Gisela stared at her in bewilderment. "What the hell are you doing?"

"Didn't you hear?" Roxy crawled under the large bed that served as sleeping quarters for her, Tibor, and three younger cousins, even as she explained, "We're being resettled. We leave in half an hour."

"If this is another one of your imaginations, you'll get a beating."

As Roxy had collected the bags and backpacks stored under the bed and was backing out, the door opened and Gottfried burst in. "Put the baby down and pack our things, Gisela. We're leaving."

"But..."

Gottfried was already gone. Gisela set her grandchild on the bed and began frantically filling bags and backpacks. "Don't just sit there doing nothing, help me," she snapped at Roxy.

One by one the other family members showed up. Less than half an hour later every single wagon was emptied. Every person had put on several layers of clothing. The rest of their belongings was carried in bundles on the backs of those who were old enough to walk.

A long line had formed in front of the camp exit. Aunt Gisela gazed back at the wagon they'd lived in for as long as Roxy could remember and sighed, "I wonder if we'll ever see it again?"

Roxy echoed her feelings. The wagon had been her home. Here she'd slept, eaten, played, learned, laughed and cried for so many years. It was the only home she knew. How could she leave it behind? Automatically her hand reached to the pendant around her neck. As soon as the wagon was no more, the wooden horse would be her only connection to her parents.

Just then Gottfried showed up by Gisela's side and placed his hand on her shoulder. "We're being resettled. They say we'll get a nice house in Poland. There's enough land, food, and work there. We're supposed to form our own village."

Gisela smiled. "Anything is better than this nightmare. I don't even remember what it's like not to breathe the stench of sewage."

Roxy wanted to be happy. After all, she'd dreamed of leaving the camp since the moment she'd first set foot into it. So why did the hair on the back of her neck stand up? She exchanged a glance with Tibor who stood several steps away. He seemed to sense her skepticism because he hissed, "Don't do anything stupid."

The line moved slowly toward the exit. An engine revved up. The first truck, presumably fully loaded, sped away. Roxy still had not been registered with the authorities. If she wanted to disappear, this would probably be her best chance. But she had promised Tibor not to go off alone.

Torn between the urge to avoid resettlement and the need to honor her promise, she squeezed through the crowd to sidle up with Tibor. After making sure his parents were out of earshot, she whispered, "You don't seriously believe they're taking us to a better place?"

"It can't be worse than here."

Roxy moved her head from side to side. Part of her clung to the hope that things would indeed get better and they would be taken to a place where they wouldn't have to live in filth. Still, she attempted one last try. "Come on, let's run away. I'm serious."

"Man, you're crazy." Tibor punched her in the side. "Just wait and see what the new place is like. If it's really that bad, you can still run away."

"Will you come with me then? I mean, if it's unbearable there?"

Fear gleamed in Tibor's eyes. Regardless, he nodded. "Sure. If it's as terrible as here, I'm all in."

"You won't change your mind again?"

Tibor squirmed. "Let's see what the new place is like first."

Roxy didn't miss the fact that her cousin didn't want to commit. A queasy feeling pooled in the pit of her stomach and, for a moment, she considered taking off right there and then. She knew her way around Berlin. She'd explored the area for months, knew where to organize food and where to find shelter for the night.

On the contrary, nobody knew where the SS was taking them. If they indeed ended up in Poland, there was a chance that nobody understood their language, which would make it harder to go into hiding. The smartest decision would be to leave in this instant, before the family boarded one of the trucks.

Something held her back. She didn't want to admit it even to herself, but she needed the support of family. Venturing out during the day was one thing. It was exciting. But it was something entirely different if she couldn't return to the safe embrace of family at night. In the evenings when Roxy came home with stolen food, she knew Aunt Gisela had cooked dinner and that she had a warm spot to sleep in inside the wagon.

She wished so much that Uncle Gottfried and Aunt Gisela would realize that fleeing was their only chance of survival. Or at least Tibor. By his side, she felt capable of facing all adversities... being two was so much easier than being alone. In the end she decided the benefit of having an ally was worth the delay.

Moreover, there was still a chance that the new place would be better than this rat hole in Marzahn.

So she nodded. "Alright. But if it's as bad as here, you'll run away with me. Promise?"

"Promise." Tibor shook her hand and then punched her in the side. "Don't always be so negative. I'll protect you when it's needed."

Every fiber of her being rebelled against his assumption that she needed protection. Shoving her fear aside, she vowed to run away on her own if necessary. She'd show Tibor that she didn't need his protection—even though she felt safer in his presence.

The crowd pushed them forward. As Roxy climbed onto the truck, she cast one last glance at the camp. As much as she'd hated living there, in this very moment she'd have preferred to stay, since she feared what lay ahead. Knowing the Nazis, this resettlement meant nothing good.

After several hours of driving, the truck stopped abruptly. Roxy clung to an iron rod to keep from falling. The tarp was pulled back and bright daylight blinded her.

"Out, out, out!" a voice shouted. "Hurry up!"

On stiff limbs, Roxy climbed down from the truck bed. Before her stretched an expansive area with warehouses and cranes. The smell of salt water and fish hung in the air.

"Where are we?" she asked Tibor, who'd landed next to her.

"At the Hamburg Harbor, I think. Remember?" During one of the clan's trips to northern Germany, they'd spent a few weeks near the Hamburg Harbor. Back then, she'd watched the large ships from the wagon, marveled at the huge cranes and perused fresh fish with Tibor in the market hall. The smell of the sea was still the same and even the cranes seemed not to have changed.

"Do you think we're taking a ship to Poland?" Tibor asked.

"Poland is on the Baltic Sea, whereas the Hamburg port is on the Elbe river, which flows into the North Sea." Roxy had never gone to school, but she eagerly absorbed any knowledge she could gather. One never knew when it might become useful.

"Sea is sea. Baltic or North, what's the difference?" In contrast to her Tibor wasn't interested in geography or the other subjects an elderly aunt had taught them. He didn't understand that good orientation was vital, not just in one's immediate surroundings, but far beyond.

"I'll have a look around." Roxy didn't wait for an answer, before she slipped away quietly from the crowd on bare soles. Behind them, more trucks drove onto the grounds. The squeak of the entrance gate closing behind them sent violent chills down Roxy's spine.

The crowd began to move, or rather, they were herded by SS men toward a warehouse which had a sign over the entrance that read "*Fruchtschuppen*."

Roxy followed her family at a safe distance. She'd observe events from afar. She had no intention of being trapped in the place that had been used as a fruit warehouse. Rather, she'd use the first opportunity to run away.

10

HAMBURG HARBOR, MAY 1940

Tibor was seething as he sullenly trudged behind his father into the *Fruchtschuppen*. As usual Roxy had vanished without a trace. Possessing an unerring sixth sense for uncomfortable or dicey situations, she'd made herself scarce just in time. It was the habit he'd come to despise about her: she came and went whenever and however she pleased, without anyone noticing. More than once, he'd searched everywhere for her without success, only to have her appear like a ghost out of nowhere, standing right beside him.

Nobody else seemed bothered by her disappearances, probably because no other family member truly cared whether Roxy was there or not. Since she'd been taken in by his parents at the age of five, she'd always done her own thing. Meanwhile everyone had grown accustomed to her sitting apart on a log for hours, carving—or simply being impossible to find.

Wavering between frustration and admiration, he wondered how long it'd take for the rest of the family to notice Roxy no longer lived with them if she actually carried out her plan to run away. He knew that one day she'd follow through with it. Like a cat, she always landed on her feet and wriggled out of every tight spot.

How often had he himself played with the thought of running away? Each time he'd lost his nerve and chosen the familiar surroundings in the bosom of his family. Roxy, however, was fearless. He didn't doubt for a second that one day she'd leave him behind in his misery, if he didn't muster up the courage to join her.

Although he'd told Roxy it was safer under the protection of the family, deep in his heart he realized this wasn't true. The former fruit shed certainly wasn't an improvement to the camp in Marzahn, aside from the lack of the sewage stink.

He vowed to himself that the next time Roxy asked him to flee with her, he'd grab the opportunity with both hands and agree.

The *Fruchtschuppen* was enormous—at least fifty meters long and thirty meters wide. Dozens of families camped on blankets or on the cold, dirty concrete floor.

"Line up for registration!" barked a uniformed man with a peaked cap.

Gisela, carrying her grandchild, gazed anxiously at Gottfried. "What's happening now?"

"I can't tell. We'll stay together," Tibor's father answered, split seconds before guards separated them into men and women.

The two lines inched forward at a snail's pace. His heart pounding viciously, Tibor stood wedged between his father and his cousin Romeo. Repeatedly, he peered over at the women's line. As he'd imagined, not even his mother had noticed Roxy's absence.

Men and women in police uniforms sat at tables at the front of the two lines. When Tibor's turn came, the man examined him with expressionless eyes. "Identity card?"

"Here." Tibor held out his *Kennkarte* to the policeman. The officer dictated to the woman next to him: "Tibor Popa, Gypsy half-breed, fifteen years old, from Berlin-Marzahn." Then he threw the *Kennkarte* into a box on the floor, where countless others already lay.

"I need that back," Tibor protested. A painful blow to his side silenced him.

"Should I have you arrested?" asked the policeman.

"No."

"Then shut up. You speak only when asked."

Tibor nodded. From the corner of his eye, he observed the policeman standing behind him shouldering his rifle again.

"Do you understand?"

"Yes, Herr Wachtmeister."

"Valuables?"

"I don't have any." Tibor's teeth were chattering so hard he could barely speak.

"No watches, rings, or other jewelry?"

"No."

"Cash?"

"No."

"Good, we'll see about that. Next."

Tibor was pushed along. Behind a curtain stood two tables with two men in white coats sitting at them.

"Strip naked," ordered a nurse.

Tibor had to swallow several times as memories of the humiliating racial examination surfaced. He clenched his fists, considering making a run for it. However, a single glance at the guards standing at attention with their rifles was enough to change his mind. He reluctantly pulled his shirt over his head.

Just as he was unbuttoning his pants, his five-year-old cousin next to him burst into tears. "I want my mommy."

"Do you know that child?" a doctor asked Tibor.

"Yes, that's my cousin Anton."

"Make sure he's quiet."

"I don't want to undress," whined Anton, who didn't grasp the seriousness of the situation.

"Undress the child, or you'll both regret it," threatened a guard.

His fingers trembling, Tibor undressed his little cousin while whispering reassuring words into his ears. Then he pushed the squirming, naked boy into the arms of the waiting nurse. Next, he removed the rest of his own clothing, his cheeks burning under the nurse's stern scrutiny. Scalding hot shame coursed through his veins.

"Hurry. Over there." A guard jabbed him in the side with a baton.

Tibor stumbled toward another nurse. In panic, he barely caught himself in time, before he accidentally bumped into her. It didn't bear thinking what the guards would do to him if that happened.

"Open your mouth," she commanded. Although he wasn't particularly tall, she had to stand on tiptoes as she poked her fingers around in his mouth. The taste of her rubber gloves made Tibor gag. At the thought of the beating he'd receive from the guards if he happened to vomit at her feet, he froze like a pillar of salt. The bile remained stuck in his throat. Frantically, he gasped for air. Black dots danced before his eyes. Finally, she finished her inspection. Her gloved fingers withdrew from his mouth; and he could breathe freely again, swallowing the bile seconds before he passed out.

The nurse didn't seem to have noticed his inner struggle. Unperturbed she picked up a strange-looking metal instrument, which she inserted deep into his ears and nostrils. Once more, panic shot through his veins. Although just one nostril was painfully blocked with the device, Tibor had the sensation that he couldn't breathe anymore. His knees wobbled.

"Hold still!" She pushed the instrument forcefully deeper into his nose until it seemed as if she was going to scrape out his brain. A disgusting pulling sensation spread all the way from his face through the back of his head throughout his entire body. Tibor prayed for the examination to finally stop. Once it did, he breathed a sigh of relief. The worst was over.

But the nurse wasn't finished with him yet. "Turn around and put your hands on the table."

"What are you doing?" His protest was silenced by her gloved finger in his ass. Humiliated to the core, he clenched his hands around the edge of the table, his jaws pressed together so hard it hurt, until she ended the degrading procedure and he was allowed to stand up straight again.

After this violation of his dignity, he barely cared that he was standing stark naked in front of the young woman. She didn't as much as glance at him as she turned to a policeman Tibor hadn't noticed before. "He's clean. No hidden valuables."

"Good, next one," replied the man.

Shaken to the bone, Tibor slipped into the wrong pant leg, needing several attempts before he managed to button up his pants. At last he staggered away, disoriented and with damp eyes, until someone called out to him: "Tibor. Over here."

He wiped the tears from his eyes and moved to the spot where a large part of his family was gathered. Roxy was sitting among them as if she'd never disappeared, chewing on an apple.

The shame turned into unbridled anger. He hissed at her: "You dodged it again."

She shrugged. As if to placate him, she held out her bitten apple. "Here, take my apple. It helps."

Reluctantly, he took the offered fruit and sank his teeth into the juicy flesh. As he tried to swallow the bite, the memory of the rubber glove in his mouth overwhelmed him and he gagged violently.

"They took my wedding ring," his mother complained.

"And my silver necklace," added an aunt.

"They even took my pocketknife," said Tibor's oldest brother.

Tibor sank to the floor next to Romeo and Christian. "What's going to happen to us now?"

"No idea," came the unanimous answer.

That night, Tibor barely slept. Squeezed between his cousins on the hard floor, he stared at the high ceiling of the *Fruchtschuppen.* The embarrassment burned deep in his soul. In the current situation, the camp in Marzahn seemed like paradise compared to this new hell.

He hoped it wouldn't get worse.

11

BELZEC, MAY 1940

Almost daily, new arrivals flooded the camp in Belzec. The barracks Marek and the other prisoners had built were so overcrowded that by evening, not a patch of floor remained visible. Those who arrived late had to squeeze in between people already lying down, who were reluctant to give up part of their space, or crouch along the narrow path on the long side of the barracks. The lucky ones found at least a spot against the wall and could lean their backs against it to sleep.

Even the camp administration had realized that conditions were unbearable and condemned the prisoners to build more barracks.

"Watch out, that post is damn heavy," one of the veteran prisoners said to Marek.

Grateful for the warning, Marek bent his knees to grip the post from below. In that moment, a stabbing pain shot through his thigh. He groaned, lost his grip and the heavy beam landed on his right foot.

It took him quite the effort to suppress a scream. Black dots danced before his eyes as he tried to breathe through the pain.

As if through a wall of fog, he heard a guard's mocking laughter. "Look at that, our Gypsy isn't dancing anymore!"

The next morning he woke to his foot burning like fire. Marek couldn't remember how he'd made it through the rest of his shift the previous day. He recalled neither the so-called dinner, which consisted of a thin soup and a cup of coffee that tasted like dishwater, nor the walk back to the barracks.

His foot had swollen to twice its normal size, so he couldn't lace up his shoe. Every step was hellish agony. Nonetheless, he dragged himself to roll call with superhuman effort. His bunk neighbor supported him under the arms for about half the way but ran off as soon as a guard approached.

Marek watched him disappear. He wouldn't have done anything different if he'd been in his place. Nobody wanted to risk being late for roll call or being punished for helping another prisoner.

Jaws tightly clenched, Marek limped to the assembly area at the last second. Since he didn't stand at his usual spot, a guard barked at him, "What's wrong with you, lazy pig?"

"My ankle. I can't walk."

The guard looked down at Marek's foot, which sat bare in the unlaced shoe. The skin around the swollen ankle glowed in purple and green hues.

"Well, that's what happens when you don't pay attention." The guard played with his whip. "Name and barracks?"

Marek was sweating blood as he provided the requested information. If the guard was in the mood for playing a sadistic game like "rabbit hunt," he'd be done for.

Handing him a slip of paper, the guard said, "To the infirmary with you. Report back for work in three days."

"Thank you." Relieved, Marek limped away. It seemed he'd dodged death once again.

The infirmary was a low building with barred windows. The smell of carbolic acid hit Marek as soon as he limped inside. Men with feverish eyes or gaping wounds lay on the beds. Half of them looked like grotesque clowns, their jaws contorted beneath sunken cheeks. Marek turned away. Few people survived tetanus; at this stage, there was no hope left.

"Out of the way." An older nurse pushed him aside to help a man with a head bandage onto a cot.

Undecided, Marek stood at a distance. She didn't seem unfriendly, though she appeared to be under severe time pressure. Her movements were economical and efficient, dark shadows hung under her eyes, and her once-white coat was stained in multiple places.

"You're still here, what do you want?" she asked after covering her patient.

"My foot." Marek showed her his swollen ankle.

The nurse pointed to a bench along the wall where two ragged figures sat. "Sit down there and wait. I'll take a look as soon as I can."

He sank gratefully onto the bench, keeping his eyes on the floor so he wouldn't have to look in the faces of the men marked for death around him. The nurse seemed solely responsible for the care of several dozen patients. She hurried constantly through the barracks, distributing water, dressing wounds, speaking encouraging words.

Minutes dragged by, yet she didn't return. She must have forgotten about him. Eventually, Marek leaned his head against the wall and closed his eyes. The rhythmic throbbing in his ankle was like the beat of a drum. Suddenly he was back in Vienna, many years in the past, when he'd taken Rosa to a concert by the Vienna Philharmonic. They were in the standing area all the way up on the balcony, because he couldn't afford the expensive seats in the orchestra section. Nevertheless, it had been a feast for the ears.

Someone nudged his shoulder. "Let's have a look at that foot."

He started, confused by the face leaning over him. "Who are you?"

"Helga. You came to the infirmary because your foot is swollen." Despite her obvious exhaustion, she radiated kindness.

It took a few seconds for him to blink the sleep from his eyes and extend his leg toward Helga. He explained, "One of the wooden posts fell on my foot during work."

"Do you have confirmation from the guard about the accident?"

Marek shook his head not quite understanding why she'd need this information. "I didn't know something like that exists."

"I'm not allowed to treat anyone who was punished by a guard."

His foggy brain cleared up and he reached for the slip of paper the guard had given him. "Is this what you're looking for?"

"Exactly." She pocketed the paper and bent down to examine his ankle with practiced fingers.

"I stumbled and the post slipped out of my hands." Marek suppressed a groan as she rotated his foot in all directions.

"You've been lucky. Nothing seems to be broken or torn, just a severe bruise." Her fingers moved gently over his swollen skin. "When did this happen?"

"Yesterday, just before the end of my shift."

"Why didn't you come earlier?"

"I tried to tough it out. This morning at roll call, the guard told me to go to the infirmary and report back for work in three days."

"Then you're very lucky indeed. Every day I have to turn away men whose lives hang by a thread. I'm not allowed to ease the wounds from a whipping or other punishments." She looked up from his ankle, a wistful expression in her eyes. "It's deliberate. They call it deterrence." Her voice dropped to a barely audible whisper. "In reality, it's brutality. These sadists revel in the suffering of their prisoners."

Marek felt a deep connection with this woman, whose eyes expressed how much she suffered under the conditions. Instinctively, he knew she was a good person. "Thank you, for understanding."

"I'll make you a cold compress, that's all I can do for you. Lie down and come back tomorrow, so I can take another look."

While she wrapped a wonderfully cold, wet cloth around his ankle, Marek asked in a whisper, "Are you a prisoner too?"

The woman hesitated briefly. "That's none of your business."

"Please. I have a wife and son in Vienna. They don't know where I am."

Helga paused, her gaze hardening. "Forget about them. You'll never see them again."

His heart contracted painfully, yet he dared one last attempt. "Please. Couldn't you forward a letter..."

"Be quiet!" she hissed. "If someone overhears you, it'll cost us both our lives."

After she'd applied the bandage, she said curtly, "Wait here."

Then she disappeared behind a locked door at the end of the hallway, which Marek assumed was the nurse's room. He wrestled with himself over whether to leave or wait as she had ordered, and came to the conclusion that he was a fool if he didn't stay. If she was calling camp management to report him, running away would only get him into deeper trouble.

No matter how he looked at it, he had to stay put and wait for his fate. After several minutes she finally reappeared, her lips pressed into a thin line.

She walked up to Marek, saying in a loud voice, "Don't put weight on the foot and return tomorrow morning." At the same time, she pressed a piece of paper and a pencil stub into his hand, whispering, "For the letter."

After Marek had limped to his barracks, he took advantage of the absence of the other inmates to write to Rosa and Stefan.

My beloved wife, my good son,

I am alive and think of you every day. I am in a camp, deep in eastern Poland. Send my greetings to Kate Mundaren. Stay where you are as long as you can. Don't try to find me. I love you and hope to return to you one day.

Your Grast

His oldest daughter had always called horses "grast" because an acquaintance who was Lovara-Romani had taught her this word from his language. He hoped Rosa would remember and identify Marek as the sender of the letter.

He thought for a long while about who to address the letter to. He didn't want to get anyone in trouble. For lack of a better idea, he decided to give Helga the address of Butcher Huber. The next day he gave her the letter during his visit to the infirmary.

Helga inconspicuously slipped it into her bag. Neither she nor Marek spoke another word about the matter, nor did they talk while she examined his ankle and applied a new bandage.

"Whenever you can, cool your ankle. It'll be as good as new in two to three weeks."

Marek's heart ached at her advice. Water was scarce—unless it had rained and huge puddles had formed on the ground. Moreover, he was supposed to report back to work the day after tomorrow. How would he endure the exhausting shifts with his injured foot?

Two days later, he was pulled from his sleep in the middle

of the night. Two SS men dragged him to a concrete bunker on the edge of the camp. In a bare room, Kommandant Goslar sat at a table. Marek's letter lay before him.

"Is this letter from you?" Goslar asked with deceptively genuine friendliness.

Marek swallowed. Denial was probably the best option. "No."

"Don't lie to me!" Goslar's fist slammed onto the table. "The nurse has confessed that she was supposed to smuggle the letter out for you. Who was she supposed to give it to? Who is your contact outside the camp?"

So Helga had either been caught or had betrayed him.

"No one. She was supposed to put it in the mail," stammered Marek. "I just wanted to tell my wife that I'm still alive."

"Now she'll never know." A cold smile appeared on Goslar's face. "Who knows if it still would've been true by the time the letter reached Vienna."

"I'm... sorry." Desperation constricted Marek's throat so that he could barely breathe. With a racing heart, he stared at the pistol in Goslar's holster, hoping the commandant didn't intend to shoot him on the spot.

"Who is Kate Mundaren? Why are you sending her greetings?"

"She's a good friend."

Just as Marek was sure his final hour had come, help arrived from an unexpected quarter. The door flew open and a low-ranking SS man rushed in, stopping before the commandant and clicking his heels. "Heil Hitler!"

"You dare to interrupt me during an interrogation, Schumacher?" Frantic red splotches gleamed on the commandant's cheeks.

"I beg your forgiveness, Hauptsturmführer Goslar." If Marek hadn't been in such a precarious situation, he'd have laughed at the man's submissive posture. "The office of Reichsführer Himmler is demanding to speak to you on the telephone."

The commandant's face fell. He rose abruptly and stormed out. At the door, he turned once more, ordering, "The prisoner receives one week in solitary confinement."

Marek bit his tongue to keep from shouting aloud with relief. The incident could have ended much worse.

When he returned to his barracks a week later, he learned from a fellow prisoner that the nurse had been transferred to another camp. No one knew why or where to. Marek never saw her again.

The letter never reached its destination either. And yet Marek had won a tiny victory. The commandant hadn't deciphered the hidden message.

"Kate Mundaren"—in the Sinti language meant: "They're killing people here." It had been an attempt to warn those at home. Sadly, the message hadn't reached them.

12

HAMBURG HARBOR, MAY 1940

For three days, Roxy had been living with her family in the *Fruchtschuppen* at Hamburg Harbor. Indescribable chaos reigned. Nearly a thousand people were crammed into the warehouse, more arriving every hour.

At some point, each family had been assigned a square space barely larger than a matrimonial bed. Aunt Gisela and the other women had tried to create a homey atmosphere with the blankets and pillows they'd brought along, yet everyone's nerves were stretched to breaking point.

They had to sleep in shifts since there wasn't nearly enough space for all family members to stretch out. The small children remained constantly with Gisela in their assigned corner, whereas the older children were too fidgety and wandered around among the seated people.

Roxy slithered through the huge warehouse. She inspected every detail with utmost attention: the only exit was always guarded by SS men, the narrow windows high up under the ceiling, and there were only a few water taps where prisoners formed endless lines day and night.

During the day, the large entrance gate was opened to let in air and light. Every few hours, more trucks roared up and spat out hordes of desperate newcomers who were herded into the *Fruchtschuppen* by SS men.

By now, not a spot of floor space could be seen in the enormous hall, and Roxy wondered how all the new people would fit inside. The outdoor area was off-limits to the imprisoned Sinti and Roma families, despite it being enclosed by a high wall.

Roxy didn't care about the rules. She was determined to explore and find an escape route. For several minutes, she'd been observing the entrance gate, waiting for an opportunity to slip through.

Just as a new load of people was being herded in, she used the cover of the crowd to stride in the opposite direction. Shortly before reaching the gate, she collided with a girl who suddenly stepped out of the stream of people.

The girl was about Roxy's age, wearing a light-blue dress that was remarkably clean despite the circumstances. She had braided her long blonde hair into two plaits winding in a crown around her head.

"Watch where you're going!" groused the girl.

"You're the one who stepped out of the crowd, not me." Roxy glared at her.

"But you're walking in the wrong direction." Recognition flashed in her eyes. "Where do you want to go anyway?"

"Wanted." Roxy turned and trudged alongside the girl. She had missed her opportunity. The guards had formed a chain again, making it impossible for anyone to get past them.

"What do you mean you wanted?" The girl gazed at Roxy in confusion.

"No one's allowed to leave this place." Roxy pointed to the guards. "They make sure we all stay inside."

"Never to leave again?" The girl gasped for air.

Roxy ran her hand through her curly hair until it got stuck

in a knot. "I don't know. In the three days since I've been here, people have only come in, and no one has ever been allowed to leave the hall again."

"We were told we'd be resettled to Poland. They said there's plenty of land there, proper houses, and work."

"You were lied to." Roxy had no idea where they'd be taken to, but one thing she knew for certain: not a single word of the Nazis' promises should be believed. "You seem nice, what's your name?"

"Livia. And yours?"

"Roxy." They'd now reached the tables where newcomers were registered. It was high time for Roxy to disappear. "When you're done, we can talk. My family is sitting over there." Roxy pointed to the spot where Aunt Gisela was changing her grandson's diaper, before quickly making herself scarce.

Roxy was still slightly annoyed that Livia's sudden veering from the crowd had prevented her from exploring the outdoor area. On the other hand, Livia seemed smart and it couldn't hurt to have a friend. An escape would be easier to pull off with two people and by now she had serious doubts that Tibor would ever muster the courage to join her.

From a safe distance, she observed Livia until she disappeared behind the curtain. Sometime later, Livia returned with a rigid expression. Roxy tapped her on the shoulder. "Come with me."

On the first day of her stay, Roxy had spotted the perfect hiding place behind a loading device. A skinny person like either her or Livia could squeeze through a gap into the surprisingly spacious area behind it. "Welcome to my kingdom."

Livia raised an eyebrow. "It's quite dirty."

Roxy couldn't believe her ears. Who worried about cleanliness in this situation? Since she wanted to be friendly to Livia, who'd just endured the horrible body search for valuables, she explained, "The SS doesn't come in here and nobody else either. We're alone and can't be overheard."

"Thank you." Livia looked at her, unshed tears making her eyes shine. "These guards are so rough, even the nurse handled me like a criminal. I'm not used to being treated this way."

"Didn't you live in a camp before they brought you here?" Roxy examined the delicate, pretty girl who, featuring blonde hair and fair skin, didn't resemble the rest of her family.

"No. My father is a violinist. He's one of Germany's best musicians." Livia's eyes gleamed with pride. "He was allowed to continue playing in the state orchestra undisturbed until... well, until a few days ago. The SS stormed our apartment at dawn and forced us to gather our most important belongings, before they squeezed us into an overcrowded truck." Livia pinched her nose. "I can't stand the stench. I haven't been able to wash for four days."

"You won't be able to wash here either." Roxy wrinkled her nose. Even worse than dirt and sweat on her skin was her hair, which hung matted and sticky around her head. As soon as she got her hands on a pair of scissors, she'd cut off her curly mane.

That'll upset Aunt Gisela, said a voice in her head. Roxy snorted. Since making the acquaintance of the SS, Aunt Gisela no longer frightened her.

"How long do you think we'll have to stay here?" Livia asked in a thin voice.

"Nobody knows. The SS never gives explanations. Whenever they feel like it, they'll stand at the gate, yelling at us to grab our things and hurry into a truck."

"Do you honestly believe they'll take us to a better place soon?"

Roxy opened her mouth to say no, but looking at Livia's hopeful face, she didn't want to discourage her new friend. "Could be. But I wouldn't bet on it."

Livia's gaze wandered to the leather cord around Roxy's

neck. Hanging from it was the small pendant in the shape of a horse her father had carved for her. It was her most precious possession; the one thing connecting her to her deceased parents.

"That's beautiful," said Livia, pointing to the pendant. "How did you save it from the search?"

"It's just wood," Roxy explained curtly. Nobody except Tibor knew she'd dodged the registration and body search, and she wanted to keep it that way.

A brief silence settled between them, before Livia spoke up, "Do you want to see what I have?" Without waiting for an answer, she pulled a worn hand mirror from the pocket of her dress. "I managed to hide it in the sole of my boot in time."

Roxy's gaze automatically traveled to Livia's knee-high boots, which were much too warm for the season, and from there to her own bare feet. She wrinkled her forehead trying to remember what had happened to her own shoes. Until this moment, she hadn't even missed them. They probably still stood in the wagon in Marzahn, if they hadn't been stolen by now.

Livia seemed to notice nothing of Roxy's mulling, since she kept chattering. "It's important to look neat, no matter the circumstance. My mother always says that."

Roxy suppressed a chuckle. The idea of worrying about her appearance in their current situation was absurd. Still, Livia's seriousness about the topic touched her.

"Here." Livia held out the mirror to Roxy. "Do you want to take a look?"

"Not necessary." Roxy had never cared much about her appearance.

"Yes, it is. Look at your reflection. When you know how you look, you can change something about it." For a youth, Livia was full of wise sayings.

Hesitantly, Roxy took the mirror in her hand. Since their hasty departure nearly a week ago, she hadn't washed or even combed her hair. A dirty face stared back at her, surrounded by tangled, matted curls. She absolutely had to cut her hair. She returned the mirror. "Do you happen to have scissors too?"

"What do you need those for?" Livia closed the hand mirror and tucked it away.

"To cut my hair."

"You can't do that!" Livia clapped her hand over her mouth.

"And why, pray tell, not?" Roxy examined her new friend thoroughly. Had she been mistaken, and Livia was nothing more than a spoiled brat?

"It's not ladylike."

"I don't give a damn about being ladylike. Short hair is so much more practical. Especially since the SS didn't give me a hairbrush."

Livia shook her head with pursed lips. "Oh, Roxy, especially in our current situation, it's important to look presentable. You never know what it might be useful for."

Roxy nibbled on her lower lip. "What do you mean?"

"People are more willing to help someone who looks pretty and clean than someone whose appearance makes them wrinkle their nose. Even some SS men have soft hearts."

"That's disgusting." Roxy's stomach clenched at the mere thought of smiling at one of the black-uniformed guards.

"Yes, it is." Livia didn't even flinch. "But not half as disgusting as being locked up in this warehouse, surrounded by dirt and stench. Believe me, I'd do anything if it would buy me my freedom."

Roxy hadn't been mistaken after all, Livia was a fighter. She was a kindred spirit who, just like Roxy, didn't accept the mistreatment by the Nazis. Their methods might differ, but Roxy knew they'd get along splendidly. If Tibor was too much of a coward, she'd escape with Livia.

After chatting about this and that, Livia said, "I need to get back to my parents, they're probably worried about me."

"Shall we meet again later?" Roxy asked.

"Absolutely. I can hardly wait to explore the hall." Livia gave Roxy a small smile.

On Roxy's fifth day at the *Fruchtschuppen*, a sudden unrest swept through the crowd. Guards shouted orders, and the families had to once again hastily pack their meagre belongings.

"What's going on this time?" Roxy asked Tibor, who'd squeezed in behind the storage unit to join her and Livia.

"We're being relocated," he answered in a hushed voice. "To the train station, they say."

Roxy's heart raced. Over the past few days, she'd ventured several times into the outer grounds to scout possible escape routes. Unfortunately, none had proven feasible. The guards were too numerous, the exit too well guarded. She was counting on the chaos during the walk to the train station to make her escape.

"Come on, pack your stuff," Tibor urged. "We don't want to get separated from the rest of the family."

"Just a second. I'll be right there." Roxy grabbed Livia's arm as she was about to leave. "I'm going to escape when I get the chance. Are you coming with me?"

Livia bit her lower lip. Excitement flashed in her eyes at the suggestion, before the light faded. "I'd love to, really. But I can't. I can't leave my parents alone."

"This might be your only chance to make it through this hell in one piece," Roxy tried to convince her.

"I... I know... and believe me, I'd join you in a heartbeat... but... no... I can't." Livia looked at her with tears shining in her eyes. "I don't expect you to understand, but I love my parents very much. The three of us have always been a tight-knit unit, sticking together. I can't abandon them now. We only have each other left."

"Even if that decision might mean your death?"

Livia nodded with a serious face. "Even then. My mother isn't feeling well. I want to stay with her and do everything I can to make things a little easier for her."

"Alright. That's your choice, but I'm getting out of here." Roxy couldn't begin to understand her friend. She didn't love anyone enough to sacrifice herself for them. Not Tibor, and certainly not the rest of the family.

"I wish you good luck." As Livia hugged her a wave of longing washed over Roxy. "Don't worry, I won't tell anyone."

Roxy quickly looked away as her eyes grew moist. Despite not believing her own words, she reassured her friend. "I'm sure wherever they're taking you it'll be better than here."

One after another, they squeezed past the storage unit into the hall. Roxy stood around somewhat lost, watching Livia as she walked toward her parents. When her mother embraced her tightly, Roxy felt a stabbing pain deep in her soul.

In that moment, she missed her parents terribly. If they were still alive, she'd have gone with them too. In her clan nobody would miss her. Aunt Gisela was far too busy with the younger children. Even her best friend Tibor had lately been hanging out mostly with Romeo and Christian. Roxy was seldom allowed to play with them, despite her being much better than her cousins at almost anything. She climbed faster, held her breath longer, and always found the best hiding places. Still, they claimed their games were not for girls. It made her so sad, because she didn't have close friends among her female cousins, who were more interested in cooking, knitting and cuddling babies than in adventures.

At her family's space, chaos reigned. Everyone stuffed belongings into bags, adults snapped at each other, children wailed, while youths pretended not to be affected by the situation.

Roxy hadn't unpacked her belongings after arriving at the

Fruchtschuppen, wanting to be ready for an escape at any time. So she simply grabbed her backpack. From a few steps away, she observed the commotion, realizing it'd take days before one of the adults noticed her absence. By then, she'd be far, far away.

"Finally, we're moving on," Aunt Gisela said to her eldest daughter Claudia. "The sooner we leave this terrible place, the better."

"I'll be so glad when we arrive in Poland," Claudia replied.

"Once we're settled, we can send a note to Eva and her husband to join us."

"She was lucky to find a home where she can give birth, but she's better off with the family."

Roxy shook her head. Eva would be wise to stay where she was, sheltered by an Aryan couple who'd taken in the heavily pregnant woman and her husband.

The SS ushered everyone out of the *Fruchtschuppen*. The sun shone bright from the sky, though the air was still cold. Roxy took several deep breaths. The air smelled of salt and freedom. She'd explored the outdoor area several times, but the high walls were topped with barbed wire, and heavily guarded. An insurmountable obstacle. There was one single spot from which escape might be possible: a loading dock at the pier. The opposite shore was tantalizingly close. Nonetheless, she'd abandoned that plan because she'd never learned to swim.

Today might be her last opportunity to slip away unnoticed. She absolutely had to try her luck during the march to the train station. It was a disadvantage that she hadn't been able to explore the surroundings there, so she'd have to improvise. She wasn't too worried though, since she'd find a way. She always did.

Her nerves stretched to breaking point as her gaze swept across the grounds. She stood with tense muscles, ready to dart away instantly should an opportunity to escape present itself.

Suddenly, a bone-chilling screech filled the air. Roxy spun around. The large gate leading to the harbor area opened in a slow movement. Her eyes widened in horror, as she watched a train rolling in, pulled by a black locomotive belching black smoke clouds into the air like a fire-breathing dragon.

"Damn it," Roxy cursed. She'd noticed the grass-covered tracks on the ground but hadn't given them much importance. This oversight was now coming back to haunt her. Instead of a path to freedom a trap was revealed. The train rattled on, soon it'd stop to absorb its human cargo.

Her escape plan melted away like snow in the spring sun—and with it, her composure. Frantically, she looked in all directions. As usual, nobody was paying attention to her. Even Tibor was busy arguing with Romeo and Christian instead of observing his surroundings.

Around her, a murmur went through the crowd. Some people waved with their hands, pointing at the train. Others shrank back from the hissing monster. The smallest children reached out their tiny hands in excited delight toward the locomotive.

Desperation threatened to overwhelm Roxy. She stood frozen, staring at the gate through which the train was rolling in. Once the SS pushed her into one of the wagons, her chances of freedom would drop to zero. She had little time to act. She absolutely had to slip through the gate before it closed. Her heart pounding against her ribs, she trained her eyes on the guards who'd positioned themselves in front of the gate with their rifles at the ready. She slowly but deliberately moved in their direction.

"What are you up to?" As if he'd sensed her intentions, Tibor showed up next to her.

"Nothing." She pulled her most innocent face.

"You're lying. I know that look." He grabbed her arm. "Don't do it, Roxy, please. They'll shoot you."

She shook off his hand. "Let me go. I'm not getting on that train."

The last wagon was chugging through the opening in the wall. The waiting people were ordered to line up. The train stopped. The first wagon doors were opened. Roxy used the moment of general confusion and slipped through the crowd toward the exit, keeping the gate and its guards in focus. She absolutely had to escape. It might be her last chance.

As she reached the edge of the crowd, there were about twenty meters left to the gate. She leapt out of the protection of the gathered people and sprinted. The gate began to close. Her bare feet flew over the asphalt of the harbor grounds. She'd make it. Freedom was just a few arm's lengths away.

Nobody was following her. Nobody screamed. The waiting people were too preoccupied with themselves, whereas the guards had begun herding them into the open maws of the wagons.

Just two more steps until Roxy reached the rapidly closing opening. At the exact moment her fingers touched the metal, two strong hands grabbed her by the scruff of her neck. Furiously kicking and striking out, she realized that an SS man held her firmly in his grip, his fingers digging painfully into her shoulder.

Tears of disappointment pooled in her eyes, as she observed the closing gate. As the sliding door shut, a heavy smack vibrated deep in her bone marrow. Her escape was over before it had even begun.

"Where do you think you're going, Gypsy brat?" the guard hissed in her ear.

Roxy bit her tongue to keep from telling him her exact thoughts about the Nazis, since she feared the retaliation he was capable of if she angered him. He didn't bother to put her down, and instead carried her to the last wagon, where he shoved her inside.

"Special treatment for runaways," he growled, swinging his rifle butt after her.

Roxy ducked just in time, before it would have hit her head. However, the butt painfully struck her upper arm. To avoid further beatings, she crawled on all fours into the farthest corner of the wagon, where she stood up and pressed her nose against a tiny gap in the wall.

Behind her, more and more people squeezed into the half-darkness of the wagon. She turned around, searching for a familiar face. In vain. Even though Tibor certainly was angry with her, she wished he was standing next to her for comfort. Feeling utterly alone, she touched the wooden horse pendant, which was the closest thing to a human connection she had.

After two days and two nights, the train finally stopped and the doors were torn open. Bright sunlight blinded Roxy. She stumbled out of the wagon on stiff limbs, propelled forward by uniformed men with rifles.

Before her stretched a vast compound filled with barracks, surrounded by barbed wire and watchtowers. No sign of the promised fertile lands. No solid houses. There probably wouldn't be abundant food either.

The only promise the Nazis always kept was plenty of work.

She had no intention of participating in that.

13

Tibor had imagined the journey very differently. He'd believed the Nazis' promises, had assumed they'd travel in passenger trains, complete with seats and windows that could be opened. The reality had seen them pressed into a cattle car in the dark.

"Out, quickly!" shouts rang as the doors were torn open. Bright sunlight blinded Tibor. Around him, people stumbled toward the open door. His joints were stiff from standing for such a long time in one place. Casting a quick glance around, he made sure his family was nearby before jumping down from the wagon.

Since the train hadn't stopped at a station, the huge height difference between the wagon and the ground surprised him and he all but fell to his knees. His father stood on the ground, handed a child by his mother before she climbed out herself and took the child back into her arms. Gottfried helped the smaller children, while the rest jumped from the wagon without assistance. As usual, Roxy was nowhere to be seen.

After she'd broken loose from him at the Hamburg Harbor, Tibor had caught just one more glimpse of her: when a guard had manhandled her into the last wagon, beating her in the process. She really should have heeded his warning. He needed to assure himself that she wasn't seriously injured.

Frantic with worry, he scanned the crowd. Anger morphed into fear that she hadn't survived the journey, or might be in mortal danger. He absolutely had to find her. No matter how stubborn and rebellious Roxy was, she was his best friend and he needed to protect her.

Alone, she stood no chance of survival—neither out in freedom nor in this dreadful place that didn't match any of the promises the Nazis had made. But before Tibor could embark on a search for her, the crowd pushed him forward. As far as he could see, there was nothing but trampled earth, fenced in by barbed wire, guarded by SS men wielding machine guns.

A uniformed SS man on horseback barked orders while the guards on foot generously distributed blows with their rifle butts, as they ordered the newcomers to form proper rows. "Line up by family. Move, fast!"

Tibor stood next to his parents. Gradually, the other family members, who'd all been in the same wagon joined them.

"Have you seen Roxy?" Tibor asked his father.

Gottfried shrugged. "Not since we left Hamburg. Don't worry about her, she'll show up eventually. At the latest for dinner."

Tibor was beginning to doubt they'd actually receive a meal in this place. He peered over at the train, from which people were still pouring out. It was unimaginable that so many had fit into it.

An SS man with a list in his hand stepped forward. "Name?"

"Popa family." As the head of the family, Gottfried spoke for everyone.

"Barracks Seven. Over there." The guard pointed his chin toward a wooden barracks at the other end of the grounds.

When Gottfried didn't move immediately, he snapped at him, "What are you waiting for, Gypsy? Get moving."

The rude address sent a punch to Tibor's gut. There was nothing worthwhile or inviting about this place. On the contrary, this camp exuded a desolation much worse than Berlin-Marzahn. As they marched across the dusty place, Romeo and Christian joined him.

"This place is absolute hell," Christian complained and pulled his cap deeper onto his forehead.

"With each relocation, it gets worse." Romeo ran a hand through his much-too-long hair.

"Have you seen Roxy?" asked Tibor.

Romeo shook his head. "You know her, she'll show up eventually. She always does."

"I saw one of the guards at the Hamburg Harbor beating her."

"Serves her right," Romeo smirked. "What did she do this time?"

"Probably tried to escape." Christian bent down to pick up a small piece of wood.

"What do you want with that?" Tibor didn't want to elaborate on Roxy's intentions.

"Looking at this place, anything will come in handy at some point." Christian slipped the piece of wood into his pants pocket.

"Halt!" a command barked, just before they reached their assigned barracks.

The group stopped so abruptly Tibor bumped into the person in front of him.

"What's going on?" whispered Romeo.

"I don't know."

A guard explained an endless list of rules about what was forbidden in the camp and what had to be observed at all costs.

Tibor pricked up his ears, but it was hopeless to remember everything.

Finally, the guard pointed at a ditch just in front of a barbed wire fence, which was about two big steps wide. "See that ditch over there. Anyone who sets foot in it will die."

Tibor tapped his forehead. "He must be loony." Regardless, he decided not to test his theory. In that moment he was glad Roxy wasn't with them, since she never passed up an opportunity to see how far she could go.

"What would we want at the fence anyway? There's nothing but dirt and dust. Just like here," complained Romeo.

A second later, the guard came to a stand directly in front of Romeo. "Did you say something?"

"N-n-no," stuttered Romeo.

"Lousy Gypsy scum! Just wait and see. You'll learn discipline soon enough." The guard walked away.

Christian whispered, "Bigmouth."

Tibor clapped his hand over his mouth as the guard turned around in a deliberately slow movement. He pointed at Christian. "Did you just call me a bigmouth?"

Before Christian could answer, the guard knocked the cap off his head with a flick of his hand. It sailed in a high arc through the air and got stuck in the fence on the other side of the ditch.

"Don't you want to get your cap, you piece of filth?" A threatening undertone resonated in the guard's voice.

"No. I... I don't need it."

"When I say you get it, you do, understood?"

"Yes." Christian's knees were shaking.

"But always remember: don't cross the ditch." A nasty grin spread across the guard's face.

"But how am I supposed to...?"

A wave of nausea washed over Tibor as he looked at his cousin. The poor lad faced an almost impossible task. If no miracle happened, the sadistic guard would... Tibor pushed the thought aside.

Christian trembled visibly as he approached the ditch. There he knelt down and stretched his arm toward the cap. He was about a hand's length short of being able to touch it. Tibor was drenched in sweat just from watching. Everyone in the family, even the smallest of the children, was completely silent as Christian stretched one leg backward to provide counterbal ance. Next, he leaned his upper body further forward until he managed to grasp the cap with his fingers.

Tibor exhaled in relief.

The next second, Christian lost his balance and braced himself with one hand in the ditch to keep from falling. A collective gasp went through the clan, followed by a ghostly silence.

Nothing happened.

Encouraged by the lack of punishment, Christian took his cap, put it on his head, and scrambled back up until he was standing on both feet in the ditch.

A shot cracked.

Christian staggered, his face a grimace of disbelieving horror. Seconds later he collapsed, a dark pool of blood spreading beneath him.

"Christian!" Tibor rushed forward, falling to his knees next to his cousin—carefully avoiding to step into the ditch.

Christian was gasping as he pressed his hands against the wound in his upper body.

The guard raised his rifle a second time. "Back! Now!"

"He needs help," Tibor pleaded.

"Please. He's still alive. May we take him to the barracks?" asked Gottfried in a surprisingly calm voice. Only his chalk-white face betrayed the fear he must be feeling.

The guard seemed to consider. Then he spat on the ground.

"Take him away. If he survives, he's lucky. If not..." He shrugged. "One lousy Gypsy less."

Tibor and Romeo grabbed Christian under the shoulders, pulling him away from the death trap. His eyes glazing over, their cousin groaned in pain.

"Hang in there. You can't die now," Tibor encouraged Christian as they carried him to the barracks. Blood seeped through Christian's shirt, dripping onto the dusty ground, leaving a horrid trail.

Another nasty surprise awaited them in the barracks. There were no beds, nothing but a layer of straw scattered on the floor. An older man from another family approached them and examined Christian's wound.

"The bullet is still inside," he stated. "Without medical help, he won't make it."

"Is there a doctor in the camp?" Romeo pleaded.

The old man revealed two broken front teeth as he answered. "A German doctor dirtying his hands on one of us? Keep dreaming, boy."

Christian's mother knelt next to her son, her face a grimace of pure pain, stroking his sweaty face and murmuring comforting words. Tibor stood beside them wringing his hands in despair. Uncontrollable rage ravaged his guts. The Nazis didn't have the right to treat his people this way.

He barely noticed as the barracks filled up with people, while he sat down in the dirty straw next to his cousin. A bug jumped onto his pants. He ignored it. Absentmindedly he scratched himself and stared anxiously at Christian's chest moving irregularly in tune to his shallow breathing. If only he could help his cousin.

"Water," Christian rasped a while later.

"I'll get you some." Tibor looked around. He hadn't seen water anywhere in the camp.

Before he'd managed to get up, Roxy bent down to him,

holding a tin cup filled to the brim with water. He stared at her, wondering if she was an apparition. The matted hair, a bruise on her cheek, and filthy with dirt, she looked worse for wear, though the familiar defiance sparkled in her eyes.

And it was definitely her voice that said, "Here. Use it sparingly. Water is only distributed once a day."

"Where did you get that?" In the turmoil with Christian, his worry about Roxy had completely faded into the background.

"From a tank truck, like the ones farmers use for field irrigation. You have to get in line to receive your share. Once the tank is empty, it's taken away and doesn't return until the next day."

He didn't ask how she'd gathered this information or how she'd managed to organize the water while everyone else was barely getting settled in. In that instant, he was simply relieved she was alive and well.

"Thank you, Roxy." He took the cup from her hand. "I was worried about you."

"You know what they say: weeds don't die," she replied with a crooked grin.

"We'll talk later." Sitting cross-legged next to Christian, Tibor carefully lifted his cousin's head and brought the cup to his lips. "Drink slowly. Just take small sips."

Despite some of the liquid running down Christian's chin, he managed to swallow most of it. Tibor was relieved to see signs of life returning to his pale face. After a while he looked at Roxy, just to find his confidence melting away. In her eyes flashed fear—an emotion he'd never seen in her before.

"Do you think he'll make it?" she asked in a strangely husky voice.

"Of course he'll make it. He's a fighter." Tibor desperately wanted to believe his own words. Christian simply mustn't die while he sat next to him, unable to help.

"There's an infirmary," Roxy offered.

"Why didn't you say so right away?"

She grimaced. "Because they only treat patients who were injured at work or are sick, not those punished by the SS."

"That cannot be true!" Tibor cast her a pleading look, willing her to say her words had been a bad joke.

"I'm afraid not. Believe me. I want Christian to survive as much as you do. I'll see if I can get medicine for him." She turned away.

"Wait. Stop." Deep down, he believed her, even though he refused to accept the truth. "If we take Christian to the infirmary, they might have mercy on him."

"The Nazis and mercy? Man, Tibor, what dream world are you living in?"

"What harm will it do to try?" Tibor was grasping at every straw to save his cousin's life.

"If we drag him to the infirmary in his condition, he won't survive," Christian's father interjected.

Christian's mother wailed with such force Tibor was tempted to cover his ears. Roxy touched his arm, gesturing for him to follow her. Though reluctant to leave his cousin, he wanted to know the plan she must be hatching. Casting one more glance at Christian's parents huddled around their son, he stood up and followed Roxy outside.

"What do you have in mind?" he asked once they were out of earshot.

"I'm going to sneak into the infirmary to steal sulphur and bandages," she offered.

Tibor wanted to stop her because the punishment would be draconian if she got caught. But without medicine, Christian would die, so he nodded. "I'll come with you."

"I'll be less conspicuous alone." She inspected him from head to toe. "You can keep watch."

"When are we going to do it?"

"Right now."

Just as they walked away, Romeo called out to them, "You

need to come inside. Uncle Gottfried wants to say something." Every time they arrived at a new location, Gottfried addressed the family, explaining the situation, assigning roles, and lately, repeating the Nazis' rules. In short, he listed everything they needed to know about their new location.

Roxy rolled her eyes and hissed, "We're going to do it tonight then."

"Alright. As soon as everyone's asleep," Tibor agreed.

As if they hadn't just planned a criminal act, Roxy placed a hand on his shoulder, squeezing it briefly. It was a rare gesture of affection from her that said more than a thousand words.

Later, as they lay down side by side on the scratchy straw, Roxy winked at him, put her head on her backpack and fell asleep immediately.

Tibor admired her coolness. In contrast, he lay awake for a long time while people around him searched for a place to sleep, until everyone had found a spot on the floor. It never became truly silent, though. A constant snoring, wheezing, sneezing, and coughing filled the air, combined with the noise of people tossing from one side to the other, pursuing the sleep that didn't want to come. The noise level kept Tibor awake. The barracks had a ghostly quality in the pale moonlight. At some point, he turned to Roxy and nudged her. "It's time."

As if she'd been waiting for this, Roxy opened her eyes instantly. She rose without saying a word and signaled for him to follow her. One after another, they stepped over closely packed bodies, careful not to wake anyone. Roxy moved silent and fluid in the darkness like a cat. Tibor mimicked her movements, even though he wasn't half as graceful as she was.

Upon reaching the barracks door, Roxy grabbed the handle, pressing it down gently. Nothing happened. She pressed harder. Next, she softly jiggled it. The wood creaked.

"Damn it. Those bastards locked us in," she whispered.

Tibor's tongue stuck to his palate. "What shall we do now?"

After taking a full turn, she stopped and pointed to a small window in the side wall of the barracks. It was located just below the ceiling and was large enough for a slender person to squeeze through. Giving each other a leg-up, they'd be able to reach it. She moved toward the window without waiting for Tibor's answer.

Once they stood beneath the window, Roxy knelt down, forming a stirrup with her hands. "I'll help you up, then you reach down for me."

Tibor hesitated. "Shouldn't you..."

"You're stronger. You can pull me up."

He couldn't argue with her logic and placed one foot in her interlaced hands. Supported by a powerful boost, he swung upward, grabbed the window frame, and pulled himself up. The window could indeed be opened. Relieved, he pushed it outward and looked outside. No guard in sight.

His heart hammering against his ribs, he turned around and stretched his hand downward to pull Roxy up. In that moment, he lost his balance. He desperately tried to regain control, but his feet slipped away and his hands didn't find grip on the smooth frame. He fell in a slow motion. During his fall, he tucked and rolled to avoid hitting his head on the ground.

What he hadn't accounted for was the metal bucket standing a few meters away. He hit it with his feet, causing a terrible clatter. Roxy jumped to grab the bucket before its entire contents of human excrement spilled onto the straw-covered floor.

Tibor's heart skipped several beats. Lying on the floor, his eyes wandered through the barracks. It didn't take long before a figure rose and walked toward him. Tibor's mouth went bone dry as he recognized his father.

If there was anyone Tibor feared even more than the SS, it was his father. Gottfried grabbed him by the ear and pulled him up, glared furiously at his son. Tibor knew this expression, which usually promised a beating.

"What the hell are you two doing?" Gottfried hissed.

Tibor swallowed hard. His mind raced. "We... I just wanted to..."

"We wanted to go to the infirmary and get medicine for Christian," Roxy admitted.

Gottfried audibly sucked in air. From experience, Tibor knew his father was about to explode. "Is that true?"

His knees trembling, Tibor nodded, even as one of his ears was still in his father's painful grip. "It was Roxy's idea. I tried to stop her."

Out of the corner of his eye, Tibor noticed how Roxy winced. A moment later, the pressure on his ear eased. Gottfried's hand shot forward, delivering a resounding slap to Roxy's cheek.

Gottfried snapped at her. "Do you know what the SS does to people who sneak around at night? Do you want to be shot?"

"No, Uncle Gottfried." Roxy stared at him, her lips pressed into a defiant line, while a red handprint was forming on her cheek.

"I'm sick of your shenanigans. You're not only endangering yourself with your reckless behavior, but also the entire family."

"I'm sorry, Uncle Gottfried. I just wanted to..." Tibor nudged her in the side so she wouldn't dig herself deeper into trouble. By now, she should've learned that his father tolerated no contradiction.

"No buts. You must learn to obey." Gottfried's Adam's apple bobbed frantically up and down.

A stubborn expression, which Tibor knew all too well, appeared on Roxy's face. "I just wanted to help. Christian will die if he doesn't get medicine."

A second smack landed on Roxy's cheek. People stirred. Someone shouted, "Quiet over there. We're trying to sleep."

Trembling all over, Tibor watched the scene unfold. In a desperate attempt to make Roxy relent, he nudged her a second time, hoping she understood the hint and would keep her mouth shut.

Gottfried glared at his niece with barely concealed fury while saying in a calm voice, "I'm fed up with your antics. Tomorrow morning you'll receive a beating you won't forget for the rest of your life. Now get back to sleep."

"Yes, Uncle Gottfried." Roxy cast a look laced with resentment to Tibor before slinking off to her sleeping spot with her head down. He stood frozen, unable to meet her eyes.

"And you, my son, should know better than to help Roxy with her escapades," Gottfried said to him. "We'll talk tomorrow."

"Yes, Father." Relieved by the relatively mild outcome and simultaneously ashamed of his cowardice, Tibor trudged away. As he lay down in the straw next to Roxy, guilt burned like fire through his limbs.

"I'm sorry," he whispered.

She didn't respond. Her back was turned to him, her shoulders tense. He knew she wasn't asleep, and that she wouldn't answer him. Perhaps never again.

That night, Tibor lay awake while the barracks once more sank into dull snoring and coughing. Apart from the worry about Christian, guilt gnawed at him. Putting the entire blame on her had been a shameful act of cowardice. He'd hung out his best friend to dry, because he'd been scared of the punishment his father would dole out. He vowed to make amends in the morning.

14

The smell of freshly dug earth hung heavy in the air. Marek wiped the sweat from his forehead as he leaned on his shovel. His injured ankle hurt with every step he took. For two weeks now, he'd been assigned to the construction detail tasked with digging a fifty-kilometer-long anti-tank trench between Belzec and Dzików Stary. The guards drove the prisoners to a pace even strong, well-nourished men couldn't maintain for long.

Marek snorted. None of the people in this camp were strong or well-nourished—except the guards, who used their energy to harass the emaciated prisoners. Irrespective of exhaustion or illness, they were mercilessly harassed until the weakest literally fell by the wayside. Anyone who collapsed couldn't expect leniency: if they didn't manage to get up on their own, they remained lying in the dirt until the end of the shift, when their comrades had to carry them back to the camp—dead or alive.

"Move on!" One of the guards had seen Marek leaning on the shovel and cracked his whip in warning.

Marek gritted his teeth, thrusting the shovel into the hard earth. His back ached, his hands were covered in blisters. Every thrust of the shovel sent excruciating pain from his fingers up to his shoulders.

Next to him in the trench worked two newcomers who'd arrived the day before with a transport from Hamburg. The older one, a big man with thinning, gray hair, worked methodically, efficiently conserving his energy. The younger one, no older than fifteen years, sinewy and gaunt, was more impetuous. He tried to accomplish too much at once and quickly exhausted himself.

Neither of them featured the dull, resigned look of long-term prisoners, nor the creeping movements. Out of the corner of his eye, Marek watched as the two tried to adjust to the brutal work routine.

"Dig deeper, you lazy dog!" a guard shouted at the boy, while striking him with the butt of his rifle.

The boy staggered and nearly fell, catching himself at the last second. His eyes flashed with anger. But he turned away and continued digging without uttering a word.

Smart boy, Marek thought with approval. Anyone who wanted to survive in this hellhole must learn quickly to keep his mouth shut and his head down. The slightest whiff of resistance was punished.

After several hours of working in the scorching sun, the guard finally shouted into the trench, "Thirty minutes lunch break!"

The men lined up in front of the field kitchen. A female prisoner, whose blonde hair stuck out among the others, distributed soup. One ladle per person, plus a cup of coffee. Marek had long since stopped wondering why one thing was called soup and the other coffee, when both tasted equally like disgusting dishwater. The only notable difference were the unidentifiable chunks floating in the soup.

Marek sat with his portion at a distance from the rest of the group in the shadow behind a mound of earth piled up that morning. He greedily spooned the soup from his dirty tin bowl. The two newcomers sat down next to him, listlessly stirring their watery soup. The boy poked around with his spoon until he found a chunk and put it in his mouth, followed by a disgusted grimace.

"Eat," Marek urged him. "You'll need the strength."

"This is supposed to be soup?" the boy complained. "It looks like dirty water and tastes like shit."

"You'll get used to it." A lump formed in Marek's throat as he observed the defiant expression in the boy's eyes. Stefan used to pull the same face when something displeased him. The thought of his beloved son sent a stab through his heart. Would he ever see him again?

"I'm Gottfried, by the way," the older man introduced himself. "And this is my son Tibor."

Marek shrugged. He'd forget their names in the next minute. Names were dangerous because they created bonds. And bonds were something you couldn't afford in here. They made a person vulnerable. Moreover, it was easier to ignore a stranger when he begged for help, which Marek had learned to do. After receiving a whipping, he'd never again reach out to pull up a fallen man.

Gottfried nodded to Marek. "Have you been here for long?"

"Almost three months." Marek brushed aside the memory of his previous life. Nostalgic feelings were even more dangerous than friendships, because they weakened the resolve to stay alive no matter the cost.

"Is it always this bad?" asked Gottfried.

"Yes." Marek bit his lip. He'd already talked too much with them. But Tibor's horrified expression reminded him of Stefan once more and so he made an effort to be kind. "Listen. If you want to survive, follow a few rules. I'll only say this once, what you make of it is your business."

"Of course, and thank you very much." Gottfried seemed to be a sensible man.

"Always keep your head down. Don't make eye contact with the guards. And, for heaven's sake, never contradict them. Work as slowly as possible, but never stop moving. Don't take breaks, even if you're exhausted. And above all—don't help anyone."

"But if someone collapses—" Tibor protested.

"Then you walk past," Marek interrupted him. "Otherwise you'll be punished. The guards are just waiting for an excuse to play their sadistic games."

Tibor stared at him in disbelief. His youthful features reminded Marek so much of his son that he had to turn his head away. Would Stefan even recognize him if they saw each other again?

"Thirty minutes are up!" a guard shouted. "Back to work, you lazy scum!"

Marek struggled to his feet. Slowly he put weight on his injured ankle, which always protested particularly strongly after a rest. "Remember my words," he said, before limping back to his spot in the trench.

Several days later, Marek peeled himself out of the thin blanket after the wake-up call. Although the cloudless blue sky promised wonderful weather, a queasy feeling pooled in his stomach. He ignored it. It was a day like any other day in this hell on earth.

On the way to the assembly square, he was intercepted by the kapo of his construction unit. "Hey, Marek. You need to find yourself another work detail."

"Why?" Marek froze instantly. Whoever didn't work, didn't get food.

"We're being relocated. With your gimpy foot, you won't be able to march the distance to our new location fast enough. So do yourself and me a favor and find something else. I've already got a replacement for you." The kapo walked on without another glance in Marek's direction.

The kapo wasn't a bad man, he simply did what needed to be done. He removed the weakest link so the others had a chance. If someone didn't manage the distance or was too slow, the others had to pay for it by taking on part of his tasks or, in the worst case, having to carry him. In his position, Marek would've done the same. It hurt to be the weakest link.

So close to roll call, it was too late to apply for one of the more coveted work details. If he asked the barracks elder, he'd certainly assign him to the murderous work in the quarry, where numerous men died every day. Marek had no desire for that.

Rosa's face appeared before his mind's eye. He desperately wanted to see her again. Her, Stefan, his daughters, his grandchildren. His gaze swept over the prisoners assembled on the *Appellplatz,* while he racked his brain for a way to find a work detail that offered better chances of survival than the quarry.

In spite of himself, he slowed his steps as he passed the spot where the bodies of those who'd died during the night were laid out. Since the arrival of the newcomers from Hamburg, sadly the dead were mostly children.

In the face of one of the children, he recognized his son Stefan. Although he knew better, he stopped and crouched down. The face became alien to him. It hadn't been Stefan, because his son wasn't here—hopefully neither he nor his daughters would ever have to experience this most terrible place on earth.

As he stood up, he nearly bumped into a bull-necked, surprisingly well-fed prisoner.

"Hey you. You need work, don't you?"

Marek nodded.

"I'm looking for volunteers for the Sonderkommando."

Marek's throat constricted as he frantically tried to swallow the rising bile. Among other things, the Sonderkommando handled the transport of bodies to the mass graves near the edge of the camp.

"No, thank you." Marek was going to move on, but the other man put a huge paw on his shoulder.

"It's not as bad as people say." He exposed black, half-rotten teeth. "Better than the quarry anyway. Plus you get extra rations."

Marek became suspicious. "Why me? What's in it for you?"

"You keep your mouth shut. Have no friends. Plus you can pull your weight. I like that."

Marek lowered his head as he wrestled with himself over whether or not to accept the offer. The Sonderkommando wasn't physically demanding, but psychologically hard to bear—if a man had feelings. Marek however had become numb to human suffering. He peered over at the crew gathering for their march to the quarry. The sight of these figures, looking like walking dead, even worse than the pitiful rest of the inmates, eased his decision. "Alright."

"Good. I'll notify the camp administration."

After roll call, Marek joined his new colleagues in the Sonderkommando. Every fiber in his body rebelled against what lay ahead. But it was too late. If he backed out now, he would soon be lying on the pile by the side of the camp road. He clenched his jaw, murmuring to himself, "I'll get through this. For Rosa. For Stefan. For my daughters."

Working in pairs, the prisoners in the Sonderkommando picked up a lifeless body—rigor mortis had already set in—and carried it the few steps to the cart. With each new corpse, the pile on the cart grew higher. Some of the children had faces contorted with pain, others looked strangely peaceful.

As he set about his work, Marek silently wondered if there was a life after death. Would he finally see his beloved Rosa again in the next life? Marek pushed the thoughts away. Sentiments were out of place. Only those who faced the harsh reality survived.

Several stops later they found a boy kneeling over a lifeless body, sobbing, "Christian."

"Keep quiet," Marek snapped at him, recognizing Tibor, while he inconspicuously looked out for a guard. Fortunately, none was in the immediate vicinity. "Pull yourself together. If the SS sees you, you'll be punished."

"This is my cousin Christian. The Nazi bastards shot him for no reason at all on the day we arrived." Tibor's forehead wrinkled in angry folds. "And then they wouldn't give us medicine for him."

Marek got the impression there was more to this story. He inwardly shrugged. It wasn't his problem. Curiosity could prove fatal. He had to continue with his work, if he didn't want to get into trouble. "Go away so I can move your cousin, or we'll both end up in the mass grave next to him."

"Please, may I?" Tibor looked up, his wounded soul reflecting in his eyes. It struck a chord deep down in Marek's heart, thus he nodded and waited until Tibor had closed Christian's eyes and said a prayer. Then Marek grabbed Christian's feet, while a colleague took the shoulders, and together they lifted the body onto the cart. Once the cart was full, they pushed it to the pit, which another group of the Sonderkommando had freshly dug.

In the meantime, the sun had climbed high into the sky, shining bright and clear, casting its warming rays across the land. Birds were chirping in the distance, as if there was no horror in the world. Marek wished he could be like them, open up his wings and fly away.

Arriving at the pit, they threw the bodies inside. One by one they fell onto the hard ground. Each time, another piece of humanity died within Marek. He doubted he'd ever be able to live in a normal environment again. The camp was destroying his very soul.

The last two bodies were holding hands. They were a boy and a girl, neither of them could be older than six. As Marek lifted the girl, he sensed a weak vibration under his fingertips and froze mid-movement.

"What's the matter?" Out of nowhere, a guard appeared by his side.

"Nothing," Marek answered quickly.

The kapo had noticed it too. "Herr Aufseher, this girl... she's still moving!"

The SS man stepped closer and bent over the child. Now it was clearly visible how the girl's chest was rising and falling in irregular intervals. "Throw her in the pit."

"But she's alive!" protested Marek. "We can't just—"

The butt of the rifle hit him hard in the stomach. Gasping in pain, he doubled over.

"When I say she's dead, she's dead," the guard said, without batting an eyelid.

The kapo took the girl with a stone-faced expression, placing her mechanically next to the others in the pit.

"Fill it in." The guard pressed a shovel into Marek's hand.

"I, please..."

"Fill it in, or I'll push you into the pit right now."

Marek's eyes filled with tears as he threw shovelful after shovelful of earth into the mass grave. As the soil trickled onto the little girl's emaciated body, the unthinkable happened: her legs moved reflexively, as if she wanted to run away.

"Keep going," growled the SS man, jabbing his rifle barrel into Marek's back.

When it was over, Marek fought against the violent sobbing that threatened to overwhelm him. He'd experienced many atrocities and, until a few minutes ago, had believed that he was numb to emotions. But at this moment, it felt as if his heart had been torn from his chest. Nothing but an empty shell remained of the man he'd once been.

"Back to work," ordered the guard.

On the way back to collect more bodies, Marek wasn't the only one staggering like a sleepwalker. Nobody spoke. There were no words for what they'd done. There wasn't even an excuse. They'd have to bury the guilty act for the rest of their lives.

"How can you bear it?" he asked the kapo.

"You don't bear it," the kapo answered. "You survive it. That's all we can do. Survive so that one day we can tell the world about it."

Marek didn't believe there was any hope of survival left. Not after what he'd just experienced. His gaze wandered to the sky, where the sun shone radiantly down on the world.

15

To say Roxy was furious at Tibor would be an understatement. The morning after, he'd come to apologize, squirming under her stare. But she wasn't ready to forgive him, even after her rage had subsided, because beneath it she was devastated. So many years of being friends and the coward put the blame on her, because he feared his father's scorn.

She vowed never to trust him again, no matter how often he apologized for his betrayal. Moreover, if not even her best friend had her back, how could she hope to trust anyone else in the future? It seemed she was utterly, truly and completely alone.

Observing the barracks door with eagle eyes, she waited for it to be unlocked from outside. Then she slipped out under the cover of the crowd to disappear toward the latrine, where she was going to hide until roll call ended. Nobody must notice there was an unregistered person in the camp.

The Nazis had a terrible fear of escape attempts, and they counted the prisoners—dead or alive—twice a day, checking them against their lists. Roxy had no desire to be discovered by an overzealous guard, be registered, and condemned to forced labor.

She darted nimbly between barracks, always careful to avoid the watchful eyes of the guards. The closer she got to the latrine, the more unbearable the stench became. She swallowed her revulsion, since it was the only place where she was safe from discovery because the guards despised the foul smell just as much and never ventured near the latrines.

As she crouched among the excrement, holding her nose, her thoughts wandered to Uncle Gottfried. He outright refused to accept the notion that they were doomed if they didn't unite and rebel against the Nazis and always implored the family that only abiding by the law would keep them safe. On her own Roxy wouldn't accomplish anything, thus she contented herself with silent protest by not letting the Nazis use her labor for their means.

During the past few days, she'd systematically explored the camp. The facility at Belzec was more extensive than the one at Marzahn and much better guarded. Watchtowers with heavily armed SS men stood at regular intervals along the double barbed-wire fence. Behind it stretched a wide strip of plowed earth—a death zone where an escapee would immediately be spotted. An escape was all but impossible.

Roxy wasn't one to give up easily, though. There had to be a way out of this camp, especially since she officially didn't exist. She needed to explore the area close to the entrance, where they'd arrived a few days ago.

A sharp whistle announced the end of roll call and those fit for work shuffled off to their assignments. Roxy used the commotion to blend into the stream of people heading toward the kitchen barracks. Directly behind the kitchen was the section cordoned off for the guards.

The area bustled with activity. Men hauled wood, women peeled potatoes. The aroma of soup wafted through the air. Roxy's stomach growled louder than a vicious dog. At each new location, the food had gotten worse. In Marzahn, Aunt Gisela had managed to cook sparse, but at least tasty, meals. Even in the *Fruchtschuppen* the family had eaten like royalty compared to Belzec. Here the meager, disgusting food—coffee and soup with rotten vegetables or meat—was never enough to satisfy her hunger, merely dampening the worst stomach pains.

Roxy was so hungry she'd eat carrots if she could find them. As she was about to peek around the corner of the kitchen barracks she nearly collided with a guard. At the last moment, she pulled back, pressing herself flat against the wall.

"Hey you!"

Startled, she sucked in her breath. Her fingers clawed at the small projections in the wall, pulling herself up, her bare toes feeling for a foothold to swing herself onto the roof of the barracks.

"Keep working!"

The command hadn't been meant for her, but for a man who apparently was working too slow. Flat as a flounder, she lay against the roof shingles. Almost ten feet below, not far from where she'd just been standing, a whip cracked through the air, followed by a blood-curdling scream of pain.

Roxy crawled to the back end of the roof, where she was less exposed. She'd have to find another way past the kitchen. Jumping down at the rear end with catlike agility she crept on until she came upon a shed and slipped inside. It served as storage for work tools, a fact which might come in handy.

Through a narrow gap between the boards, she observed a group of prisoners marching past a cart carrying large kettles, heading toward the exit. Two SS men accompanied the group, apparently on its way to a work detail outside the camp.

Thoughts whirled in Roxy's brain. If she could join an outside work detail without anyone noticing... A groan interrupted her thoughts. Her heart skipped a beat.

Moments later, a blonde girl with two buckets in her hands passed the shed. Her blonde braids were arranged in a neat wreath around her head, forming a strange contrast to her tattered dress.

Roxy smiled with delight and stepped out of the shed, whispering, "Livia!"

"Roxy!" Livia put down the buckets and embraced her. "I had lost hope of ever seeing you again."

"Careful," Roxy warned, pulling her behind the shed. "Are you alone?"

"Yes. But I don't have much time, I need to carry water to the kitchen." Livia pointed to the buckets. "I work there. The cook chose me because I... well, because I look neat."

"Good for you," Roxy said without a trace of envy. "Working in the kitchen must be a lot less exhausting than digging tank trenches."

"You're right. Plus, I can occasionally pocket a handful of potato peels or some breadcrumbs." Livia cast her a curious gaze. "What about you? What detail are you in?"

"Some clean-up crew," Roxy hedged. Her aching backside was a constant reminder that her best friend had betrayed her to save his own skin. She didn't want to risk that happening a second time.

A loud call rang through the air. "Where's that water, Livia?"

"I have to go," Livia said hastily. "Meet me behind the kitchen after lunch distribution. Then we can talk." She grabbed the buckets and hurried away before Roxy could agree.

Watching Livia walk away, a warm feeling filled Roxy's chest. She'd missed talking to a friend—so much so that she'd actually considered forgiving Tibor despite the deep-rooted pain in her soul over his actions.

The sun hung high in the sky when Roxy approached the meeting place. She still hadn't discovered a promising escape route, but at least she'd internalized the rhythm of the camp—when the guard changed, when the supervisors took breaks, where they sat to drink coffee. She memorized every tiny detail, since one never knew when it might become useful.

Livia was waiting in the shade of the barracks with a tin bowl of soup standing next to her on the ground. Roxy stared hungrily at the food. "Aren't you going to eat that?"

Livia laughed. "No. Kitchen staff always eat before the others."

"Then this is for me?" Roxy's stomach growled so loudly that both girls gazed over their shoulders in alarm.

"Yes. The cook has a good heart. She allowed me to take a second portion."

"You didn't tell her about me, did you?" Roxy pricked her ears for approaching footsteps.

"Of course not. The cook thinks I'm too skinny." Livia pointed at her legs, which were nothing but skin and bone. "Do you think I'm ugly?"

"No." It took great resolve for Roxy to set down the bowl she'd just raised to her lips. "Sure, you've grown thin, but you're definitely the prettiest girl in the entire camp."

"Thank you." A radiant smile spread across Livia's face.

It'd been worth waiting to eat the soup to see her friend smile. A warm feeling spreading through her limbs, Roxy brought the bowl to her lips a second time. Two medium-sized potato pieces floated in it. The stuff was lukewarm and tasted awful, yet she gulped it down to the last drop. Once she finished, she proceeded to lick the bowl clean.

This was by far the most substantial meal she'd eaten since arriving at the camp. Wiping her mouth with her hand, she asked, "How are your parents?"

Livia's eyes filled with tears. "My father was sent to another camp two days after we arrived. My mother is in the infirmary barracks with typhus."

"I'm so sorry." Roxy put a hand on Livia's shoulder. Since

she knew how close Livia and her parents had been, she offered, "If there's anything I can do for you, just tell me."

"Thank you. Except for a miracle, I don't need anything right now."

"We could all use one."

Livia furtively wiped the tears from her eyes. "The cook needs more helpers. If I put in a good word for you, I'm sure she'll take you. Wouldn't that be fabulous?"

Roxy hesitated. The prospect of working at the source of food was tempting. However, she'd have to be registered with the camp administration, which would make her planned escape more difficult. "Thanks, but I don't think that's possible."

Livia frowned. "The cook is on good terms with the SS, she can get you transferred from your current work detail."

Roxy bit her lip. She didn't want to tell Livia the truth. Tibor was the only person who knew her secret and she wanted to keep it that way. But she had to give her friend a compelling reason for turning down the generous offer. After fighting with herself, she lowered her voice. "I'm going to escape soon."

Livia's eyelids twitched several times, while she scanned the surroundings for eavesdroppers. "That's insane. They shoot anyone who tries."

"Not if you're smart enough about it," Roxy insisted. "There are work details leaving the camp."

Livia nodded. "They usually leave the camp before breakfast. There's one kitchen helper standing near the entrance gate, handing them a piece of bread for the walk."

"They don't even receive the miserable soup the rest of us get?" Roxy was shocked on their behalf.

"They get food at their place of work; some have sympathetic employers and get the same as the Polish civilians." Livia squinted her eyes at Roxy. "You're planning to join an outside detail, aren't you?"

Roxy didn't exactly want to join it, however she agreed. "It has crossed my mind, yes. One guard for twenty prisoners. I'd just have to wait for the right opportunity to get away."

"You wouldn't be the first one to try, but nobody has succeeded so far." Livia grimaced. "Furthermore, the entire detail gets punished for an escape attempt. I've seen men torn to shreds by whipping."

"Well, that... can be worked around."

"In any case, you won't get far without papers," Livia warned.

"How do you know...?" *that I don't have papers*, Roxy wanted to say, until she remembered that the Nazis had taken everyone's *Kennkarte* during the registration in the *Fruchtschuppen*. "Shoot. I'd completely forgotten about that detail."

"Moreover, you don't speak Polish. If the local population is suspicious, they'll hand you right back. There are big rewards for catching escaped prisoners."

"How do you know all this? Are you planning to escape as well?"

"Me? No." Livia waved off the notion. "It's not possible. You know, in the kitchen, we pick up plenty of information that doesn't circulate in the rest of the camp. The Nazis have put a chain of controls in place that makes it virtually impossible for an escapee to stay in freedom longer than a few days."

Roxy gazed at her friend. "Nothing is impossible, it's just very, very hard." She hesitated, wanting to ask Livia to come with her, because truth be told, she'd feel more comfortable with a companion by her side. But then she pushed the thought away. Livia was registered and would be missed during the next roll call. Then the Nazis would inevitably send a search party after her.

No, taking Livia with her would complicate things too much.

Livia opened her mouth to say something, but closed it

again, because an older woman with a stern face peeked around the corner.

"My break is over." Livia pulled a crust of bread from her apron pocket and pressed it into Roxy's hand. "For later. Be careful."

"Thanks." The bread disappeared into Roxy's pocket in a flash. "Shall we meet again tomorrow? Same time, same place?"

Livia nodded and slipped away. Roxy watched her with admiration. In appearance and in character, she was the complete opposite to Roxy, yet they both possessed the survival instinct that was so crucial in their situation.

Her stomach full and her energy renewed, Roxy continued her exploration. The outside work details offered the most promising chance to escape. But how could she join such a detail without being noticed? Deep in thought she almost missed the group of newcomers crossing her path. Curiously, she followed them, hoping to gather vital information about the situation beyond the fence.

After the usual demonstration of power by Kommandant Goslar, the group was dispersed and ordered into different barracks. That was the moment Roxy had been waiting for. She'd mingle with one of the group, striking up a conversation.

She fell in step with two young women, asking, "Where are you from?"

Even before they had a chance to answer, the woman in front of them turned around, her eyes wide. "Is that really you, Roxy?"

It took a few seconds for Roxy to recognize the dirty, emaciated woman as Tibor's adult sister. "Eva! You are here? But I thought... I mean, you found a place to live."

"I did." Furrows were etched deep around Eva's mouth and eyes, making the formerly beautiful woman resemble an old hag.

Roxy's eyes roamed across the group, coming up empty. "Where's your husband?"

A visible tremble wrecked Eva's body from head to toe. "Harald is dead. They shot him."

"I'm sorry." Roxy had always liked the quiet young man who'd had such a kind soul. She almost didn't dare to ask after the baby Eva had been due to deliver shortly after separating from the clan in Berlin. But curiosity won over. "And the baby?"

A deep sigh escaped Eva's throat, followed by a smile. "It's a girl. Natalie. I gave her to my landlords when the SS came to fetch us. They promised to raise her like their own. She'll be safe under their protection."

"That is good news." Roxy wasn't sure whether that was true, but it didn't hurt to pretend the little one would have a good life. Eva would most certainly never find out anyway; judging by her looks, she wouldn't survive the harsh conditions that awaited her in the camp. "Come with me, Aunt Gisela will be so pleased to see you."

A scared expression entered Eva's eyes. "But... won't I get into trouble? The Kommandant said..."

"I'm sure Uncle Gottfried can have you assigned to our barracks. You must know he's someone in the camp hierarchy."

"It's so awful here." Eva's voice broke. "They told us we'd be sent to Poland where we could settle and live in our own communities."

"They lied." For lack of anything encouraging to say, she added, "Let's bring you to the family. They'll be so pleased."

16

A FEW DAYS LATER

The queue at the food distribution moved forward in an agonizingly slow pace. Tibor stood with his father and the rest of the family, each of them holding an empty tin bowl. Hunger gnawed at his insides. Since their arrival at the camp, they'd received the same disgusting soup every day.

"Where's that girl got to this time?" Gottfried swept his gaze across the family.

Tibor shrugged. He hadn't seen Roxy since waking up. The guilt for putting the blame on her still weighed heavily on his soul. Roxy continued to give him the cold shoulder and didn't make him privy to her explorations around the camp. He missed their friendship and was determined to win back her trust, so he lied, "Probably still working."

"Which work detail is she in anyway?" Gottfried pressed.

"I... I don't know." Tibor avoided his father's gaze.

"You don't know?" Gottfried's tone promised trouble. "Or you don't want to tell me?"

"I swear, I don't know, Vater." That technically wasn't a lie, since Roxy wasn't part of any work detail.

Gottfried eyed him suspiciously. "Why are you covering for

her escapades? Don't you understand that her behavior is dangerous? If Roxy gets caught red-handed, the entire family will pay for it."

"Uncle Gottfried," Romeo, who was standing behind them, chimed in. "I saw Roxy at the kitchen barracks this afternoon. With that blonde girl who sometimes serves the food."

Tibor wondered if the blonde girl was Livia and if Roxy had found a way to secure additional food. He certainly wouldn't put it past her.

"She's working in the kitchen and hasn't told anyone?" Gottfried growled.

By the time, they approached the soup pot, Roxy showed up next to them, effectively jumping the queue. Standing in line wasn't her thing. Her feet were caked in mud, but her equally dirty face couldn't hide a spark of satisfaction.

"Where did you come from?" Gottfried demanded to know.

"From work." She joined her family seemingly unperturbed.

"Which detail are you assigned to?"

Roxy hesitated a moment too long, which told Tibor she was searching for a plausible answer. "Look, it's our turn."

Indeed, Gottfried had just reached the soup pot as the first in their family. Tibor glanced into the half-empty pot.

"Don't think you'll get off that easily. We'll continue this conversation later," Gisela interjected.

Roxy put a hand on Tibor's arm. "Wait a bit, the last third contains most of the chunks," she whispered in his ear and paused before she added, "This doesn't change the fact that I'm mad at you."

One by one, the family members got their portion of soup until it was Tibor's turn. Much to his surprise she'd been right and he noticed at least two pieces of potato swimming in his bowl.

"How did you know?" he asked, while the next person was served.

"Figured it out years ago. Aunt Gisela kept forgetting to stir the soup as she served. It is the same here."

A stab cut through his stomach, because she'd known this detail for years and had waited to tell him until now? Remembering his intention to win her back, he swallowed down the hurt. "Thank you, I truly appreciate it."

Next it was Roxy's turn. Instead of wordlessly holding out her bowl to the older woman swinging the ladle like everyone else, she said, "Thank you so much for giving us food."

The corners of the woman's mouth twitched upward. "Well, look at you. No one's ever thanked me for this foul-smelling brew before."

Tibor's jaw dropped as Roxy replied, "I for one am grateful for every drop of this soup. Especially when there's a piece of meat in it."

"Well then, let's dig for something good for you." The woman stirred deep into the pot with her ladle. Tibor's eyes nearly popped out of his head as he watched her dump several pieces of potato and meat into Roxy's bowl.

"Thanks again. I really appreciate it." Roxy attempted an awkward curtsy before strutting away, carrying her bowl in both hands like a treasure.

Unfortunately for her, Gottfried hadn't forgotten about her work detail and joined them. "Romeo saw you at the kitchen barracks. What were you doing there?"

"Working." Roxy lifted the bowl to her mouth, slurping it half empty before putting it down again.

Gottfried frowned. "Where's your apron? Kitchen helpers get clean aprons."

"I don't work directly in the kitchen, just unloading deliveries."

"Show me your hands," Gottfried ordered.

Reluctantly, Roxy stretched out her hands covered in clay and something that looked like rust.

"You're lying," Gottfried said with cutting sharpness. "Where are you truly working?"

"I was unloading deliveries, like I said." Roxy defiantly lifted her chin.

A guard walked past them. Gottfried instantly fell silent. As soon as the man was out of earshot, he grumbled, "There's nothing but trouble with you. If my brother hadn't begged me on his deathbed to take care of you, I'd have marooned you long ago."

Roxy squinted her eyes. Too late. Tibor had seen the tears there, revealing how much his father's remark had hurt her. Yet she remained silent, which was probably a wise decision. From experience Tibor knew it was better not to contradict his father.

"Oh, Roxy." Gottfried sighed, his outburst apparently forgotten. "I know you mean well, but your behavior puts the whole family in danger. If the SS finds out you're not obeying their rules, they'll shoot us all. Don't you understand that?"

"They'll shoot us anyway, if they feel like it," Roxy said, so quietly only Tibor heard it.

Gottfried walked away, while Tibor emptied his bowl of watery broth and was staring with a growling stomach at the meat pieces in Roxy's soup. She always managed to get something extra. Until recently, she'd shared fairly with him. It drove the thorn of their damaged friendship deeper into his side.

She must have noticed his greedy gaze, because she picked up the meat with two fingers, held it in front of Tibor's nose for a moment, then pushed it slowly into her mouth. Chewing with pleasure, she closed her eyes and murmured, "Delicious."

Tibor clenched his jaws. This was her way of showing him that she was still angry. He inched closer to her. "How many times do I have to tell you that I'm sorry?"

"You were a coward. And mean. I was only trying to help."

"Please, Roxy, it'll never happen again. I made a mistake." If necessary, he'd lick her dirty feet clean just for her to gift him a piece of meat.

"Alright." She cast him an expectant gaze. "If you promise to escape with me once I've found a way."

"Absolutely." He didn't believe she could pull it off, so his promise carried no risk.

"Alright, you can have the rest." Generously, she handed him her bowl, before she pulled something from her pants pocket and stuffed it into her mouth.

"What was that?"

"A crust of bread. Livia gave it to me."

Gottfried had watched the exchange with narrowed eyes. Once they finished eating, he beckoned Roxy over. Tibor followed her at a distance.

"Tell me the truth," Gottfried demanded. "Where do you roam during the day?"

Roxy stayed silent for several seconds, before a jolt went through her body. "I explore the camp looking for weaknesses."

"Weaknesses?" Gottfried's eyes widened. "For heaven's sake, what does that mean? Do you want to get us all killed?"

"On the contrary, I want to get us out of here," she retorted with vehemence. "Do you truly believe we have a chance of survival in this camp? Have you already forgotten what happened to Christian? That they shot him like a mangy dog."

The mention of Christian's name hit Tibor like a punch to the stomach. His father also flinched.

"Roxy, you're still a child. No matter how good your intentions are, you can't save us."

"I know more about this camp than all of you combined. And whether you believe it or not, I'll find a way to escape." Roxy jutted out her chin, seemingly ready to take on the entire world—or at least the SS.

Tibor wanted so badly to possess the same confidence,

though he couldn't help but agree with his father's assessment. Their only hope was to keep their heads down and not provoke the guards' anger.

"Roxy," Gottfried said with a tired voice, "I understand your desire to help. I really do. But you need to get these silly ideas out of your head. Our best chance of survival is to make ourselves indispensable to the Nazis. As long as they need our labor, they won't do us harm."

"On the contrary, they won't stop harassing us until the last Roma is dead."

A depressing silence followed her words. Tibor fervently hoped that Roxy was wrong. Although she rarely was.

17

BELZEC, JUNE 1940

Roxy opened her eyes at dawn way before the wake-up call. Lying motionless on the scratchy straw, she listened to the breathing of the people asleep around her. Today she planned to join an outside work detail that was harvesting potatoes at a farm. She'd figured out a sure-fire way to escape: fall in line with the group as they readied themselves to leave the camp, march through the gate, and disappear at the first opportunity. Since she wasn't registered, the camp administration wouldn't miss her and send a search party for her, which made her escape so much easier.

She peered at Tibor, lying next to her. Despite his promise to join her next escape attempt, he'd reacted negatively to her vague hints at her plan, claiming it was too dangerous. He might have a point there, because he was registered, which meant the SS would search for him after the evening roll call. His odds to get away were so much lower than hers. His presence would only endanger her, because if he was found, Roxy would be found as well.

She bit her lip. She couldn't wait forever. It was probably for the best if she risked it alone. In a smooth movement she stood up, gliding silently between the sleeping people toward the door of the barracks, until a strong hand grabbed her ankle.

"Where are you going so early in the morning?" asked Uncle Gottfried.

Roxy startled. "I need to pee."

"The bucket is on the other side." He stood up and his other hand grabbed her arm, as if he feared she'd make a run for it.

"I'd rather use the latrine, the bucket is disgusting."

Uncle Gottfried blocked her path. "The door is locked."

"It won't be much longer, I already heard the guards' footsteps." Roxy liked to position herself near the door so she was among the first group to leave the barracks.

"Don't take me for a fool, Roxy. Where do you disappear to every morning?"

"I told you, the latrine. I have diarrhea." She held her stomach with her free hand. "Let me go."

"No. You're coming with me." Gottfried pulled her along. "Since we arrived at this camp, you've been wandering around during the day. Nobody knows where you work, or what you do."

"Because it's none of your business," she hissed. Panic crept up her spine. She absolutely had to shake off her uncle before the door was opened.

"Everything that concerns you is my business. I'm your uncle and the head of the family. Therefore, I'm going to find out right now which work detail you're assigned to."

"How are you going to do that?" An icy shiver ran through her veins. Livia had said the farm detail was the first to leave the camp—even before morning roll call.

"We're going to the camp elder." Gottfried dragged her toward the door, which would be unlocked any minute.

Roxy's mouth went dry as dust. If Gottfried brought her to the camp elder, he'd surely find out that she wasn't registered. "Wait, I can explain."

"You will. Not to me though, but to the camp elder."

Outside, dawn was breaking. The barracks lay silent, just a few prisoners hurried to early work details. Gottfried pulled Roxy to a barracks at the edge of the grounds, which was larger and more robust than the rest. There he knocked on the door.

An old man with hollow cheeks opened, growling, "What do you want?"

"Good morning. This is my niece. She won't tell me which work detail she's assigned to."

The camp elder examined Roxy with a sharp gaze. "What's your name?"

"Roxy," she answered through gritted teeth.

"Your full name."

"Roxana Popa," Gottfried answered in her place.

"In which barracks do you live?"

Her refusal to answer didn't help. Gottfried willingly provided the information. "Our entire family is in Number Seven."

The camp elder flipped through a list lying on a rickety table. His eyebrows drew together. "I don't have any Roxana Popa here."

"Perhaps in another barracks?" Gottfried suggested.

"Where do you sleep?" The camp elder squinted his eyes at Roxy.

"With the others." She raised her head. The next moment, a slap landed on her cheek. Resisting the urge to rub the spot, she glared at him with barely concealed fury. Why didn't he just leave her alone? She'd soon be gone for good by the end of the day, and he could focus on more important matters.

"Hasn't anyone taught you to obey?" asked the camp elder.

Gottfried felt compelled to excuse his niece's bad manners, "Since we left the Berlin-Marzahn camp, she's been as stubborn as a mule. Even beatings haven't helped. Just before the transport from Hamburg, we lost sight of her in the commotion and thought she was dead, until she recently showed up in our barracks."

Roxy stared straight ahead, her lips pursed. She saw through Uncle Gottfried's intentions. He didn't care what happened to her, if he could just save his own skin.

"How did you get here, girl?"

"By train from Hamburg, like everyone else," Roxy answered, not wanting to earn a second slap.

"And where do you work?"

"I suspect she doesn't work at all. Somehow she's managed to dodge the assignment," her uncle answered for her.

Roxy pressed her lips harder together. She hated her uncle. Why did he have to do this? Without his interference, she'd already be on her way to the farm.

"This is a case for the commandant." The camp elder scratched his head. "Since she's not on my list, I can't assign her to a work detail. But you'd better think of an explanation why you didn't bring the brat to me earlier."

"As I said, we thought she was dead. I just found her this morning and came straight to you," Gottfried lied without blinking.

Roxy clenched her hands into fists, helpless rage coursing through her veins. *Such a nasty traitor! What does he even care whether I work or not?*

On the way to the commandant's office, images of medieval peasants on their way to the scaffold crept into her mind. Fear and anger in equal measure threatened to explode her chest. She was furious at Gottfried, and at herself for being stupid enough to seek out her family after her arrival at the camp. If she'd instead joined Livia and her parents, she wouldn't be in this predicament. What hurt the most was the realization that the family didn't stand together after all, and that she would be better off on her own.

Kommandant Goslar, a sadistic man with cold eyes, liked to

ride around on horseback playing cruel jokes on the prisoners. He listened impassively to the camp elder's explanations.

"So you slipped through the net, little Gypsy. Did you genuinely believe you could hide in my camp?"

Roxy stared at the ground.

"Answer, brat!" Goslar cracked his riding crop.

Although fear nearly robbed her of her senses, Roxy met his gaze. "No, Herr Kommandant, I didn't think that. I wanted to escape before anyone noticed I was here. Unfortunately, my uncle ruined my plans." She threw an angry side glance at Gottfried.

"Normally, this would be a case for special measures." The commandant tapped his fingers on the table. A wave of dizziness caused Roxy to sway. Blood-curdling screams could regularly be heard from the bunker behind the commandant's office. "But I like you."

A glimmer of hope let her breathe easier.

"It takes a lot of gumption to sneak into a Gypsy camp." The commandant drew flourishes in the air with his crop. "However, it also testifies to a lot of stupidity, and stupidity must be punished."

The blood in Roxy's veins froze to ice. She cast a pleading gaze at Uncle Gottfried, who merely shrugged. "Don't look at me like that. I told you that we have to follow the rules."

"Pretty pendant." Goslar pointed to Roxy's neck.

"Thank you." She wanted to slap herself for not removing the necklace and hiding it in her pocket. But how could she have surmised this morning that Uncle Gottfried would drag her to the camp commandant?

"Let me see it." Goslar stretched out his hand, palm up.

Roxy wasn't fooled by his friendly tone, though she had no choice but to obey. Everything in her resisted as she untied the knot of the leather cord and placed the necklace with her beloved wooden horse pendant in his hand.

"Very pretty indeed." He took the pendant, turning it in every direction. "Who carved this?"

Roxy clenched her teeth. She wouldn't allow Goslar to tarnish her father's memento.

"The pendant has no material value. Roxy's deceased father carved it for her many years ago."

She was tempted to scratch out her uncle's eyes. Hadn't he caused enough trouble for one day?

"It must have great sentimental value for you, right?" A cruel undertone accompanied Goslar's kind words.

Roxy would've liked nothing better than to run away, but she had to look this sadistic monster in the eye. Not batting an eyelash, she lied. "The pendant meant a lot to me when I was little. Now it's just pretty jewelry."

"I don't believe you." Her answer seemed to amuse Goslar. A satisfied grin lifting the corners of his mouth, he dropped her necklace into his pocket. "But that's completely irrelevant, because you'll never see this pendant again."

It took all of Roxy's self-control not to pound on him with her fists, demanding to return her beloved necklace. She swallowed the rising tears and schooled her features into an indifferent expression.

The commandant paid no further attention to the issue. "Where were we? Ah yes, your punishment. Since you were so eager to be in my camp, you shall get what you deserve. Let's see how you like the Sonderkommando."

Goslar turned to Gottfried. "You did well to report your niece. I'm going to reward you for your loyalty."

Gottfried's eyes widened.

"I hereby make you the barracks elder," announced the commandant.

"Thank you, Herr Kommandant." Gottfried bowed slightly.

Roxy couldn't believe the scene unfolding before her eyes.

Her uncle had betrayed her, and as a reward, he received a private room at the head of the barracks as well as extra food.

Ten minutes later, Roxy joined the rest of the family on the *Appellplatz*. Tibor sidled up to her. "What happened?"

"Your father sold me out."

"I'm sorry, I had no idea."

"Save your sympathy for someone who wants to hear it. As far as I'm concerned, the family is dead," she hissed, before she walked away to join the Sonderkommando.

"So you're the new one. Normally they don't send us women, and certainly not children." The man standing next to Roxy was older than Uncle Gottfried but significantly stronger. His emaciated features couldn't hide the fact he'd once been well-fed.

Roxy ignored him, removing the shoes from a dead person.

"Tie the laces in a bow knot so they stay together as a pair," explained the man.

"I know what I'm doing," Roxy snapped back.

"Sure, little peewee. That's why you ended up in the Sonderkommando." The man chuckled. "What did you do anyway to deserve this punishment?"

Roxy glared at him. She'd learned her lesson and would never trust anyone again. "Leave me alone."

Instead of being offended, the man grinned. "Wise attitude. Trust no one, especially not me." He lowered his voice. "Not even your own family. They're capable of selling you out for an extra slice of bread."

The words hit Roxy like a whiplash. That's exactly what Uncle Gottfried had done—betrayed her for some privileges. Not acknowledging how deeply she'd been hurt by her family's actions, she stared at the man with defiance. "What do you know anyway?"

"Not much, it seems." After a pause he added, "I'm Marek, by the way. Did you check the mouth?"

"Why should I?"

"So you don't know everything after all." He stood beside her and pressed his thumbs against the man's jaws, forcing the mouth open. "We have to break out the gold teeth."

Roxy gagged violently several times. To distract herself from the gruesome scene, she said, "I'm Roxy."

"Nice to meet you. Pass me the pliers."

With the tips of her fingers, she picked up the tool and handed it to him. Then she watched, horrified yet fascinated, as he broke out the gold tooth and handed it to the SS man standing guard to make sure they didn't steal the valuables.

The horrible sound echoed in her ears as she desperately swallowed down the rising bile. Marek seemed to have noticed her rapid gagging motions, for he said in a calm voice, "Focus on that building over there. If you throw up at the SS man's feet, you'll regret it for the rest of your life—if you even get the chance."

His statement hit her like a cold shower. She wanted neither to die nor to be mutilated. So she pulled herself together and diverted her thoughts to her favorite horse, wondering if he'd found a good home after being sold. Once she regained control, she asked, "How can you be so indifferent?"

"Get used to it or die. It's that simple."

"How long have you been doing this?" she asked.

"This job? Three weeks. The camp? Almost six months." He grabbed the man under the shoulders. "You take the feet, then we'll swing him onto the cart."

As they pulled the full cart, Marek said, "I want to give you some advice."

"I don't need advice," Roxy snapped.

"Pride dies first," he replied, unimpressed by her rebelliousness, "next is hope, and finally your soul."

"Oh, what kind of stupid advice is that?" Roxy kicked a pebble with the wooden clogs she'd been forced to wear.

"Listen, peewee, if you want to survive, you need to learn a few rules. First: Don't stand out. Second: Take what you can get —food, medicine, clothing. Third: Help no one but yourself."

"I'll help whoever I want," Roxy dared him.

"Then you won't last long." Marek pulled the cart around a bend. "The Nazis want us to fight each other like rats. And that's exactly what we do. Hunger turns us into animals."

"Not me," Roxy protested.

"I wouldn't put much stock in such vows." Marek looked her straight in the eyes. "In my first week here, I helped a comrade who'd fallen to the ground. Do you know what happened? The guard shot him, and as a reward for my help, I got a few lashes. It's a miracle I'm still alive."

"I don't believe in miracles." Roxy wrinkled her nose.

"Now would be a good time to start. Because only a miracle can save you." Marek shrugged. "Use my advice or don't, I don't care. I stick to my rules and I'm still alive. Most of those who arrived with me are buried in the dirt."

Roxy glared at him, wanting to despise him for the cynical advice, but she couldn't help but feel a warmth in her heart. This stranger had cared enough to give her advice—which was a lot more than her family had done.

18

Marek's own scream tore him from his nightmare. For several nights, the same scene had been haunting him: Rosa and Stefan stood in front of their wagon, reaching out their hands to him. But his legs seemed to be made of lead; no matter how hard he tried, he couldn't move an inch, until they eventually turned their backs in disappointment and walked away. Desperately, he called out to stop them from leaving, but they didn't hear him.

Darkness surrounded him, mirroring the state of his soul. All around, people wheezed, grunted, coughed, and panted. His heart pounding, he lay on his back trying to shake off the nightmare. But again and again, Rosa's fearful face pushed into his mind. This time she was surrounded by his adult daughters, who'd transformed into hollow-eyed skeletons. They stared at him accusingly until they pulled Stefan into their midst.

"Where are you? Why aren't you there for us when we need you most? Why did you leave Mother and our little brother? Why did you abandon them without an explanation?"

The accusation weighed heavily on his chest until he fought

for breath. It'd be so much easier to give up the fight. To stop breathing. To stop suffering.

The man lying next to him whimpered. He probably wouldn't live to see the coming morning. Marek turned his head away. Compassion was out of place, the other man should consider himself lucky to soon be done with the hellish torment of this camp.

When the wake-up call trumpeted through the barracks, Marek was still dazed from his nightmare. Mechanically, he stretched his aching limbs, struggling to his feet. His injured ankle protested with every step. It was getting worse each day because he couldn't give it the required rest. For a fleeting moment the nurse Helga appeared in his mind, until he pushed the image away. Guilt gnawed at his soul. One more action he'd have to make amends for before the final judgment.

During breakfast, he heard the news: the previous evening a transport with prisoners from Vienna had arrived. Most were in a pitiful condition, half-starved and infested with vermin.

A flicker of hope warmed him from within as he heard the name of his hometown. The next moment, he smothered the flame under a distraught indifference. It didn't matter where the newcomers came from; they meant nothing to him. Nobody meant anything to him, except for his family.

A heavy burden threatened to crush him, as he feared that one of them might be among the new prisoners. That was the sole reason he visited the barracks of the Viennese group when the opportunity arose. Half hoping, half fearing to actually meet Rosa, Stefan, or one of his daughters in this terrible place, he wandered back and forth, looking into each person's face.

He breathed a sigh of relief when he recognized no resemblance, only to nearly succumb to his longing for a loved one in the next minute. It was a situation with no winner, and Marek scolded himself a fool for trying to locate his family members.

Utterly desolate, he was about to return to his barracks when an emaciated middle-aged man addressed him, "Hey, aren't you Marek, the horse dealer?"

"I once was," Marek replied brusquely. He didn't want to burden himself with additional suffering, and above all, he didn't want to be reminded of his former life in freedom. It was hard enough to fight death anew each day.

"I'm Oskar. My cousin, the tailor Blumenthal, bought two horses from you."

A faint memory of better times flickered up. "Could be. I sold horses to many customers."

Oskar persisted. "You'll definitely remember him, he was often at Butcher Huber's place. He made the wedding dress for Huber's daughter."

Marek didn't care who had tailored a wedding dress for whom, but at the name Huber, he perked up. "The butcher Huber from Holzgasse?"

"That's the one, your family used to live in the courtyard."

Now Marek was all ears. "Lived? Don't they still?"

"No." Oskar stared at the ground, clearly reluctant to continue. "I'm so sorry. But I think you should know. Someone denounced Huber. The Gestapo forced him to put Rosa and the child out on the street. Two days later, they were arrested by the Gestapo for loitering and later shot."

A wave of nausea swept over Marek. He swayed under the onslaught of emotions. Once he regained his composure, he asked, "Are you sure?"

"One hundred percent. My cousin told me. He was in jail with them. A guard recognized him and spared him from the execution. That's him." Oskar pointed to a shriveled man leaning crouched against the wall a few meters away. "Not that it did him much good."

"I'm sorry," Marek stammered, as the world blurred around

him. As if through thick cotton, he heard Oskar relating details. Details Marek neither absorbed nor cared about. The thin thread of hope, which had kept him alive all these months, had snapped for good.

The urge to vomit became overwhelming, but Marek knew better than to throw up on the ground. Only beginners made that mistake. Many paid for it with their lives. Without uttering another word, he turned away and marched to his work detail. His soul was destroyed and as a result his heart turned cold. Deprived of his beloved Rosa and the son who needed him, there was no reason to continue his life.

He spent the rest of the day in a trance. Angrily, he dug the shovel into the hard earth; observing with sadness how the mass grave became deeper, longer, and wider. Tomorrow morning, he'd fill it again with numerous, nameless people. People who'd had families, hopes, expectations—a life.

Mechanically, he obeyed the guards' orders, even though his mind was far away. Images of Stefan and Rosa flickered through his mind—their laughter, their faces, the meals they shared together. Silenced. Forever.

What did he have to lose? Why should he continue to suffer when no one was waiting for him? His adult daughters had long since moved out of the home and started their own families. They no longer needed him—if they were even still alive.

A wave of deep sorrow seized him. After each shovelful, he sank deeper into depression until he saw only one way out: He'd follow his beloved Rosa to the other side. Finally, he'd find the courage to end his suffering forever. Let the Nazis rejoice in having destroyed another Sinto, he no longer cared. He looked forward to the peace that would follow.

The perfect opportunity came sooner than expected. A cart loaded with bricks rumbled along the path. Four prisoners pushed against the vehicle to prevent it from rolling uncontrolled down the shallow slope.

His work detail was marching straight toward the cart. He quickened his pace, his eyes fixed on the vehicle. He was already within a few steps of it. His co-workers slowed down to cross behind the cart. It was so simple. A few steps to salvation.

Marek waited for the right moment, stepped out of line, and threw himself in front of the wheels. He closed his eyes. And waited. Images of Rosa, Stefan, and his daughters flashed before him. Soon he'd be with them. The expected impact came. Surprisingly gentle. His body turned.

As Marek opened his eyes once more, he caught a glimpse of the cart thundering past him. A shocked cry went through the line of prisoners. Bitterly, he rammed his fist into the ground.

"What was that about? You nearly got run over." On the ground next to him lay the little rebel Roxy, genuine worry on her face.

"That was exactly my plan," Marek growled, regretting he'd ever talked to her. "And you messed it up. Didn't I tell you not to help anyone?"

Her blue eyes flashed at him with fury. "Stick your rules. I'll help whoever I want."

The stubborn expression on her face reminded him of Stefan. A terrible stab threatened to slice his gut. Despite his determination never again to care for another human, he couldn't help but feel a warm spark melting his heart.

A guard came running, holding a raised whip in his hand. "What's going on here?"

"Nothing, Herr Aufseher," Roxy assured him. "This man stumbled, and I fell over him."

The SS man looked at her with suspicion, then struck them with the whip. Marek welcomed the burning pain on his shoulder, since it drowned out the anguish in his soul that was a thousand times worse.

"Get up and keep working!" ordered the guard.

As they walked back to their work detail, Marek snapped at Roxy, "Who asked you to interfere?"

"Nobody. But I can't stand by and watch you kill yourself." Her gaze was reproachful and affectionate in equal measure. "Life here is atrocious, I get it, but you mustn't give up. There's still a way out."

"There is no way out." Bitter bile rose in his throat.

"There's always a way out," she contradicted him. "We just have to find it."

Marek shook his head. What a foolish notion. Roxy was young and inexperienced, which is why she believed in goodness in this world despite all evidence to the contrary. He regretted ever having spoken to her. He'd felt sorry for her and so had given her survival tips on her first day in the Sonderkommando, with the result that she'd felt obliged to save his life. What a perfidious irony of fate!

"Listen, Roxy. I appreciate that you wanted to help me, but it's not worth it. Stay away from me. And for heaven's sake, don't interfere in things that don't concern you. You're better off alone."

Her eyes glared daggers at him. "You think you're so terribly clever! But you're not! You mustn't let the Nazis win. If you kill yourself, Kommandant Goslar will rub his hands in glee because there's one less Sinto he has to exterminate. Is that what you want? Do you truly want to hand over your power to those stupid Nazis?"

Speechless, he endured her outburst. It was the first time in his life that he'd received such a dressing down, and by a young girl no less. In different circumstances he would have liked her, might even have considered her a suitable girlfriend to his son. But in Belzec, friendships could kill and he most certainly didn't need the complications of looking out for anyone but himself, least of all an adolescent girl.

"If you really want to kill yourself, find a way that doesn't harm someone else." Roxy stomped her foot. "It's all well and good not to trust anyone. But if you make others pay for your actions, you're no better than the Nazis."

"No one will pay for it if I'm dead," he protested lamely.

"Oh, really? Then you're even more stupid than I thought." She put on an important face. "Those men would've been punished because their cart ran you over. Do you want them to be tortured just because you're too much of a coward to keep fighting?"

Unfortunately, she had a point, which infuriated him. He'd thought only about his own suffering. Anger clouded Marek's vision. "I'm a coward? You have no idea, peewee. For almost six months, I've been fighting every minute of every day just to take another breath."

There was a brief silence between them before she quietly asked, "So, why do you want to give up right now?"

"There's no point anymore. I've lost everything. My wife, my son... they're both dead. There's nothing left worth fighting for." The words sent surges of pain through his body.

Roxy's face contorted into a grimace, even as she put her small hand on his arm. "I'm sorry."

He looked at her in surprise. No platitudes, no false consolation. Just that simple "I'm sorry," which radiated more sincerity than all the phrases he'd heard in recent months.

"Thank you," he muttered despite himself.

They'd reached the location of their work detail. Marek continued to be far away in his thoughts, but his intention to kill himself faded into the background. Roxy's lecture had ignited a spark in him—not hope, it was too late for that. Perhaps... curiosity, since she genuinely seemed to believe there existed a way out of this hellhole?

Unexpectedly another emotion snuck up on him. A warmth

in his heart that he'd felt each time Rosa had born him another child. He shook himself. Roxy wasn't his child, and she sure as hell couldn't fill the hole in his heart Stefan's death had left. He had no business letting her believe that he actually cared about her.

19

Three days later, the Sonderkommando entered an area separated from the rest of the camp by a fence. Among other things, food was stored there before being processed in the kitchen. The guard led the group into a flat concrete building.

Upon entering, Marek's breath caught. In the middle of the room stood a row of tables, along the walls piles of bags, suitcases, backpacks, and bundles of clothes accumulated. He even discovered a pram among the things.

"What does this mean?" asked Roxy, showing up out of nowhere.

He flinched, snapping at her, "Stop that!"

"Stop what?"

"Sneaking up on me like a ghost."

"Sorry. Old habit." Her alert eyes inspected the room.

"Quiet!" boomed a guard's order. "Your task is to sort this stuff. Usable clothing goes over there, sorted by type, neatly folded and stacked." He pointed to a flat platform at the head of the room. "Food goes in the box next to it. Valuables go in the bowl on the table. Understood?"

"Yes, Herr Aufseher!" echoed the answer in the room.

"These are the belongings of the new arrivals," whispered Roxy with a trembling voice. She'd been following him like a puppy ever since she'd thwarted his suicide attempt.

As much as he wanted to keep her at arm's length, he still found her presence comforting. Seeing her so distraught hit him deep in the guts. Somehow Roxy managed to be assigned a place next to him, her nose pointed and pale in her otherwise tanned face.

The guard dumped the contents of the first suitcase onto the sorting table. Marek felt the blood drain from his head. After all the terrible things he'd been forced to do in the Sonderkommando, he wondered why the—comparatively harmless—sorting of objects moved him so deeply inside. Apparently, the others felt the same way, because no hands moved.

"What are you slackers waiting for? Get to work!" To emphasize his words, the guard cracked his whip through the air.

Quickly, Marek reached for the nearest piece of clothing. It was a colorfully patterned dress with ruffles at the neckline. The memory of Rosa hit him unexpectedly and he pulled back his hand as if he'd been bitten by a poisonous snake.

Roxy pulled the dress to her station before the guard noticed and instead pushed a dark gray pair of suit pants toward him. This incorrigible peewee noticed details nobody else did. She could read people. Once again, she had rescued him.

His first instinct was to scold her for it. She had as little business to care for him than he had to care for her. They weren't family, and owed each other nothing. Despite his intention, he whispered beneath his breath, "Thank you."

"Don't even mention it. I did it only because I was afraid the guard would hit me too."

Out of the corner of his eye he glanced at her, inwardly shaking his head. Her entire posture belied her words. There was no time to reiterate his lecture about not trusting anyone, especially not him, because the contents of one piece of luggage after another were poured onto the sorting tables.

The members of the Sonderkommando got to work and soon, impressive stacks of clothing accumulated at the head of the room. It was amazing how resourceful people were in hiding valuables. Banknotes in skirt hems, golden chains under loose shoe soles, gemstones in well-hidden false pocket linings.

The food box continued to fill up, too: hip flasks containing liquor, bread, canned goods, and medicine. Often Marek was tempted to slip a cookie between his teeth when the guard was looking the other way. He never dared.

Next to him, Roxy searched a woman's handbag with nimble fingers. Once she finished, she placed a gold coin in the bowl on the table and tossed the handbag onto a pile. Marek spotted something glittering in her hand.

"What are you doing?" he hissed, after making sure no guard was within earshot.

She flinched, replying with fake innocence, "I'm searching for valuables, just as we were ordered to do."

Marek raised a skeptical eyebrow. He knew this supposedly innocent look—both Stefan and his daughters had used it when they'd done something wrong. "Don't lie to me. You're holding something in your hand, so show me."

"I can't. I don't want to get caught."

"You're stealing valuables?" he asked so quietly that he wasn't sure if she'd heard him.

Her face turned crimson red before she replied, "Better me than the Nazis."

Under normal circumstances he'd have scolded her, demanding she return the stolen goods and apologize. For obvious reasons, this wasn't an option in the camp. As much as he despised thievery, he admired her brazenness. Her theft demonstrated a will to survive that impressed him—a sentiment immediately replaced by utter horror. If she were caught, she'd probably not survive the punishment. "Do you know what they'll do to you if they catch you?"

"They won't catch me." Roxy had recovered from her shock and slipped the glittering ring into her pants pocket. Afterward she grabbed the next piece of clothing as if nothing had happened.

"We'll be searched on the way out." Although Marek had sworn never again to feel pity for anyone, or to have any emotions for that matter, he couldn't help but like the little rebel and didn't want to watch her run headfirst into disaster.

"I promise no one will find it where I'm going to hide it." Her eyes flashed conspiratorially. "I'll swallow it."

Marek shook his head in awe. The peewee apparently had an answer for everything. Sensing movement behind him, he got up to carry a stack of folded pants to the other side of the room, since he didn't want to give the guard a reason for dissatisfaction. The sight of the neatly arranged belongings of people suffering under the Nazi yoke in this camp landed like an uppercut on his jaw.

Black dots danced before his eyes. He quickly turned his head. Was it indeed morally reprehensible for Roxy to steal from the Nazis' plunder? Didn't she have more right to the things than the oppressors of her people?

Until lunch break he didn't speak another word to her, but the incident wouldn't let his mind rest. When the bell finally rang, he took his soup bowl and walked over to Roxy, who was sitting outside the barracks, lifting her face toward the sun.

"Doesn't the sunshine make everything so much friendlier?" she asked, smiling at him.

"Friendly isn't exactly what would have occurred to me to describe this place." Marek couldn't help but return the smile.

"You have to see the positive. Even here." After they'd greedily drunk their disgusting soup, Roxy pulled two unwrapped candies from her pocket. "Would you like one?"

Marek's eyes all but bulged. "Did you steal those too?"

"Well, let's just say I didn't want the Nazis getting too fat." When he didn't take the offered food, she nudged him in the side, "Go on, eat it. Or aren't you hungry?"

Of course he was hungry. The thin broth filled the stomach, but was never able to drive away the gnawing hunger in his gut.

"Thank you." Marek put the caramel candy in his mouth. The sweetness exploded on his tongue, overwhelming his senses, and he closed his eyes to savor the rare sensation.

"Delicious, isn't it?" Roxy sighed deeply. "Aunt Gisela used to make caramel candies for every birthday. We children loved them."

He opened his eyes. "My daughters used to love them too, and Stefan..." A deep sadness enveloped him, shrouding the short-lived happiness at the taste of caramel.

A small hand touched his arm. "I didn't want to make you sad."

"It's not your fault, it's just I loved him so much, I can't fathom that I'll never see him again." Tears pooled in Marek's eyes as he fought for composure.

"You'll get used to it." A serious expression on her face, Roxy touched her chest, just above the heart, before she gave a deep sigh. "The pain keeps getting lighter, until one day it's not there anymore, leaving only fond memories."

Amazed he raised an eyebrow. She seemed quite young for such wise words. "How do you know?"

"I lost my father at a very young age." She blinked furiously, apparently fighting to keep the tears away.

"I'm sorry." Marek squeezed her hand for a few seconds, before he drew it away, reminding himself that friendships made a person vulnerable. He shouldn't have asked her. She might misunderstand his moment of weakness for genuine caring—which he'd sworn never to do again. He'd lost his son, he certainly didn't need to burden himself with a surrogate daughter instead.

Roxy seemed to share his opinion, because she pursed her lips as she said, "Don't think I still miss him. I'm perfectly fine all by myself. Family means nothing to me. And neither do friends."

To steer their conversation back on safe ground, he asked, "Why are you taking this risk? What do you want with the ring?"

Her eyes turned dark and serious. "I don't intend to stay here much longer. For a successful escape, I need money."

Marek gave a bitter laugh. "Keep dreaming, peewee. Nobody gets out of here, not even feet first."

"There's always a way. I've scouted the entire camp. The guard changes the patrol patterns. We just have to wait for the right moment. I had the perfect opportunity to escape on the day my uncle dragged me to the Kommandant and betrayed me." She bit her lip. "It hasn't become impossible, just more difficult."

He tilted his head, studying her. She seemed very certain of herself. "Why has it become more difficult?"

"Because they're going to search for me. Breaking out of the camp is the easy part, afterward you have to keep hiding until you're far enough away." Her expression filled with profound sadness. "You know, I wasn't registered. Nobody would've noticed my absence. But now... now they'll search for me."

"You're positively insane." He said it with admiration. It took special guts to slip through the cracks. Maybe she had a chance; he wished her all the luck in the world. "Let's say you manage to break out. You'd need papers, clean clothes, and a convincing story."

"All that can be obtained with money." Roxy said it so casually, as if she were talking about buying bread at the bakery.

"Do you even speak Polish?"

She grimaced. "No, but—"

"Then you'll inevitably stand out. The local population will turn you over to the Nazis, since they'll do just about anything for a pound of butter or a bag of flour."

Roxy furrowed her brow in deep thought. After a while, she said, "You speak Polish."

"How would you know that?"

"I know many things," she hedged, moving closer to him. "Think about it. Together we can make it."

A suspicion dawned on him, as he replayed their conversation. "Is that the reason you shared your candies with me?"

"You are clever." She smiled at him. "Consider it a prepayment. Now you're in my debt. Plus, you know I can organize food, so you'll come with me once I make my move to escape."

"Wouldn't it be easier for you to run away on your own?" Marek had resigned himself to the fact that, unlike the other prisoners, she wouldn't be deterred by his cynical behavior.

"Sure would. Without an old man like you, I'd be faster and less noticeable. Unfortunately, I need you." She jutted her chin upward. "We need each other. Without me, you'll conk out digging graves. Without you, I'll get caught on the run because I don't speak Polish."

She apparently had thought it all through. Still, he made one more attempt to scare her away. "Aren't you afraid I might betray you?"

"That's a possibility. You yourself advised me not to trust anyone, so I've taken precautions. If you rat me out, you'll go down with me." Roxy smirked. "In your position, I'd prefer escape—or at least to keep quiet about our conversation."

While she spoke, she stood up and vanished like a ghost that had never existed. Where she'd been sitting seconds ago, a gold coin gleamed in the dust. If a guard saw it, he'd accuse Marek of theft. A week in the standing cell would be his punishment. Just like everyone before him who'd suffered the cruel treatment, he'd go mad in there and babble senseless sputter once they let him out again.

Marek grabbed the coin, put it in his mouth and swallowed it. For the first time in weeks, something other than dull despair stirred within him.

It was fear of the hope this strange young girl wanted to awaken in him.

20

"Why are you always hanging around with that old man?" Tibor had been watching Roxy and Marek with growing anxiety. They were spending a lot of time together. She thought nobody noticed, but he'd been following her. Every day after dinner, the unlikely pair met at changing locations, whispering to each other.

He couldn't find out what they were talking about. They were too careful and whispered too quietly. The whole affair was a thorn in his side. Tibor used to be Roxy's best friend; she'd confided in him, included him in all her plans. How often had they sneaked away together, to be with the horses, or to venture into town when they weren't supposed to? When growing up, he and Roxy had been the ones having secrets, whispering, always planning their newest adventure.

But lately she'd avoided him like the plague. And it was the fault of this man who was old enough to be her father. He'd wedged himself between Tibor and Roxy, destroying their friendship.

Roxy pretended not to hear him. Perfectly composed she squatted on the dusty ground in front of their barracks, rubbing the worst of the dirt from her feet. Since she didn't possess shoes, the camp administration had issued her with wooden clogs. Roxy hated the stiff things and wore them only during her work in the Sonderkommando in order not to be punished. Immediately after roll call, she took the clogs off, hanging them around her neck on a string so nobody could steal them.

"You two are plotting something." Suppressed fear bubbled up in Tibor's gut. It was obvious that she was hiding something from him.

She looked up at him. Her eyes had that certain gleam they always got when she was hatching a plan. "Nothing that concerns you."

Tibor peered around to see if anyone was within earshot. Then he placed his arm on her shoulders. "Don't get involved with Marek. He only helps himself."

"How would you know?" Roxy shook off his arm. "You don't even know him."

"I don't need to know him to realize that. He makes no secret of his disinterest in others. You can't trust him." Jealousy boiled in Tibor's veins. For weeks, he'd been trying to mend the old camaraderie with Roxy, instead she seemed to slip away more each day.

"You mean the way I can't trust you?" The ice-cold sparkle in her eyes made him shiver. "At least he doesn't pretend that he's my best friend. He says exactly what he thinks."

"What do you mean by that?"

"You know exactly what I mean." Roxy snorted. "You always talk of loyalty, but at the first opportunity, you ratted me out."

Despite knowing she was right, the accusation drove a deep stab into Tibor's gut. "That's unfair! I was afraid of my father."

"Marek says fear is no excuse for betrayal."

"Marek says this, Marek says that," Tibor mocked. "What does he know? Do you believe the old man actually likes you?

He's just using you. He's a worse egoist than everyone else combined."

Roxy shook her head. "You just don't get it. I don't care if he likes me or not. He helps me because I help him. It's a business arrangement, nothing more. We're not friends, nor do we trust each other."

"What are you planning?" Tibor's eyelid twitched nervously. He knew Roxy well enough to surmise that she'd never give up on her plan to break out of the camp. If her plan worked against all odds, he absolutely wanted to be part of it. And he didn't want to be left behind, being punished for his complicity. Even if the SS believed he knew nothing, his father would never believe him.

"Do you really think I'm going to tell you? So you can run straight to your father and spill the beans?"

"We used to be best friends, Roxy. Why can't we be that again?" he pleaded with her.

"True friends don't stab each other in the back. What guarantees do I have that you won't rat me out again the next chance you get?"

Tibor lowered his gaze in shame. "I've apologized a thousand times already. It'll never happen again. Big promise."

"Christian is dead because we didn't organize medicine for him." Roxy folded her arms. "Your father killed him just as much as the SS man who shot him."

"That's a terrible thing to say!" Tibor clenched his hands into fists. "My father wants to protect our family. He says if we adapt, we'll survive."

"Adapt?" Roxy laughed bitterly. "Your father is deluded if he actually believes the Nazis will ever accept us. He can't protect us, and worse, I can never trust him again. Don't you always say we are family, and family has to stick together?"

"Yes," he answered lamely.

"Then why would he rat me out to Goslar? He betrayed me."

"He did it for the greater good. He has to keep the needs of all family members in his mind." Tibor had ambivalent feelings about his father's actions. On the one hand, he had to look out for the entire family, but did that mean he should hurt one person in the process. Honestly, he didn't know what he would have done in his stead.

She stomped her foot. "Whatever his reasons were for ratting me out, I can never trust him again. There's no way I can go back to being a part of this family."

Tibor's stomach tightened. "You still want to escape?"

"You can bet on it." She crouched before him, her eyes flashing with anger. "Thanks to you, I'm now registered, and just escaping isn't enough anymore."

"That wasn't my fault," he defended himself lamely. "Romeo told my father—"

Roxy waved his objection away. "Whatever. As soon as I've scouted out a way, I'm gone, and none of you will ever see me again."

"Please, let me come with you."

"Why?" She eyed him coldly.

"I can help you."

"With what?"

"We make a good team, you and I..." He broke off, realizing that Roxy had always been the driving force behind their undertakings. She didn't need him to escape. He, on the other hand, would perish in this dreadful camp without her help. If he was honest with himself, he didn't believe his father's optimistic statements either.

"Do you speak Polish? Do you have money? Valuables to trade? False papers? Do you know a guard who'll help us? Or have you figured out a weakness in the surveillance?"

With each of her questions, he slumped deeper. Her planning seemed to be in quite the advanced state. He, on the other hand, had nothing, absolutely nothing, to offer. Except one thing... he returned her gaze with defiance. "If you don't take me with you, I'll tell my father."

Horrified, Roxy backed away. "Get lost, you snake in the grass."

As soon as he realized that threats wouldn't change her mind, he resorted to begging. "Please, Roxy, that was stupid of me. I didn't mean it. I genuinely want to escape with you. I don't want to die in here."

The corners of her mouth twitched, as she apparently mulled over his plea.

"Roxy, please. We used to be best friends. I made a mistake once, it won't happen again."

At last she said, "Fine. But you do what I say. I don't have a definite plan yet. Until then, you can make yourself useful and find out if there are civilian workers we can bribe to help us."

He bit his tongue to hold the anger bubbling up at bay. The little brat had outmaneuvered him with a cold smile, putting him to the test. If he backed out now, she'd never again give him another chance. He growled, "You want me to approach civilian workers and ask if they'll help us escape? That's suicide!"

"Not if you're clever about it." Roxy smirked, stood up, and disappeared without another word.

Tibor was sure she'd lied to him. She definitely had a plan ready and didn't want to tell him about it. His mood soured, he stood up as well and went in search of Livia, hoping she'd tell him about Roxy's plans.

He found Livia in front of her barracks, sitting in the evening sun combing her hair with her fingers. It was a mystery to him how the two girls got along so well. Livia was the complete opposite of Roxy, who didn't care one bit about her appearance. Shortly after their arrival at the camp, Roxy had cut off her long curls, wearing a boy's haircut ever since. That action had caused a dressing down by his mother Gisela, which Roxy had countered with the brief statement that her new hairstyle was much more practical, and that it was too late to get upset about it anyway.

In moments like these, he envied his cousin for her chutzpah. The day after, she'd appeared in the barracks wearing baggy work pants, which she'd traded for her tattered dress. Gisela had thrown her hands up over her head and lectured Roxy that pants weren't adequate clothing for a girl.

Roxy had interrupted her in the middle of her sermon, saying "It's also not proper for a girl to pull gold teeth from the dead, and yet I have to do that every day." It was the first time Tibor had seen his mother completely speechless.

He approached Livia, greeting her. "Hello, Livia."

Not interrupting the combing of her hair, she looked up briefly. "Oh, hello, Tibor."

"Have you seen Roxy?" he asked as innocently as possible.

"No, not for a while." Livia finished combing and divided her blonde hair into three thick strands, which she braided into a plait.

Tibor sat down next to her, trying to sound casual. "I thought you two were inseparable."

"You and she were once too." Livia cast him a meaningful look.

The blow struck home and Tibor winced. "Roxy is so stubborn. I worry about her. She's going to get herself into trouble."

"Roxy can take care of herself," Livia replied, tying the end of her braid with a piece of string.

"If she keeps stepping out of line, she'll end up like Christian," Tibor insisted.

A dark shadow flitted across Livia's face. "She isn't stupid."

"I always tell her to be careful, but she just won't listen." He sighed theatrically. "She's planning something, isn't she? Is it dangerous?"

Livia wrapped her braid around her head and peered directly at him. "Why are you asking me? Why don't you ask her yourself?"

"I did. She won't tell me anything."

"Well, I can't help you either. She hasn't confided in me about her plans." Livia took a hair clip from the pocket of her surprisingly clean skirt and pinned her braid to her head.

"I'm afraid she's planning to escape. That would put everyone in danger. An escape attempt will have consequences."

"Like I said, Tibor, I don't know a thing." Livia stood up, brushing the dust off her clothes. "I have to go, it's almost curfew."

"Will you please let me know if you find out anything?"

Livia cast him a mocking gaze. "Sure thing. If Roxy entrusts me with her secret, I'll gossip it to you right away."

With these words, she left him standing. Tibor remained more frustrated than ever. Livia definitely knew more than she was admitting.

In the days that followed, he observed how Roxy and Marek put their heads together and how Livia provided them with bread or other food when no one was looking. It was obvious that they were up to something. And he wasn't included in it.

The thought of being left behind while Roxy, Livia, and the old man fled was unbearable. He missed his cousin. He had to do something before it was too late.

21

Marek waited in the shadows behind the kitchen barracks. If Jakub didn't show up soon, he'd have to leave without having achieved anything. Roxy could cover for him only so long before one of the guards noticed his absence.

Finally, a blonde braid peeked around the corner, a small hand giving the agreed signal. Marek hurried toward Livia, his lips twitching up into a smile. It was a mystery to him how this girl managed to look pretty, wearing a tattered dress and high boots with holes so huge, her toes stuck through.

It must be her blonde hair, in which she took great pride, finger-combing it each morning and evening, before she fixed it in a crown-like braid around her head.

She and Roxy were more similar than anyone guessed. Both refused to give up hope and dignity, even in this hellish place. Their methods might differ, the result remained the same. Their ravenous will to live had even infected an old cynic like him. And now he was stuck in the middle of planning an escape attempt that might actually work.

"He's here?" The whispered question was met with a short nod. Livia had made the arrangements to meet the Polish civilian who entered the camp twice a week to deliver potatoes and cabbage in his truck.

Marek's stomach churned at the prospect of what would happen if Jakub wasn't as trustworthy, or rather corrupt, as the cook claimed. Apparently, Jakub was a reliable envoy to smuggle messages out of the camp, and food, tobacco or soap inside—for those who had the necessary cash to afford his services.

"Are you sure he'll agree?" he whispered to Livia, who only shrugged and put a finger to her lips, signaling him to be quiet.

The sound of boots on gravel made them both freeze. Seconds later, Marek relaxed when the boots stopped next to a gray van. The long legs emerging from them in gray-blue overalls and not the feared black uniform.

"That's him." Livia pointed at the man in his thirties with dark-brown short hair and hollow cheeks that spoke of wartime rationing, despite his role as supplier of produce to the camp. The Poles didn't suffer the same gnawing hunger of the camp inmates, yet they didn't get enough to eat either.

Most of the harvest was whisked away to Germany, to keep the population replete and their enthusiasm for the war high.

"Let's go." Marek nudged Livia. They'd argued the best approach endlessly, weighing the pros and cons. In the end they'd decided that Marek would do the talking, because he spoke Polish and such a delicate matter shouldn't be discussed in a language Livia only mangled.

Livia was there for the emotional impact. A pretty young girl, batting her eyelashes at a young red-blooded man would help them to convince Jakub that he was doing a good deed, which warranted the risk.

"You have a delivery for me?" Jakub's German was thick with a Polish accent that made him hard to understand.

"A bit unusual, but yes," Marek said, stepping slightly forward while keeping to the shadows.

Jakub glanced nervously toward the SS men guarding the entrance. "What do you want? I can't stay long."

Livia moved closer, giving the Pole a measured smile. "We need help to leave this place."

Jakub's face went pale, his left eyelid twitching nervously. For a moment Marek feared, he'd cry out and alert the guards, but then the fear left his face, leaving no trace of emotion. "I'm sorry, that's not possible."

He turned to leave, but Livia stepped in his way. "You've helped others before."

"Not in this way." He shook his head.

"You'll be rewarded handsomely." Marek switched to Polish, carefully observing Jakub's expression. A flicker lit up his face, followed by fear, then an effort to school his features. Clearly, the man was hooked. Whatever the reason why he smuggled messages and goods in and out of the camp, he just needed another nudge to agree to this more dangerous undertaking. "We pay in gold."

The air between them hummed as if electrified. Jakub's eyes widened, then narrowed with suspicion. "Where would you get gold?"

"Does it matter?" Marek asked. "What matters is that it's real, and it's yours if you help us. Think of all the things you could buy with it. Food, medicine, coal for your stove." He seemed to have guessed correctly what Jakub's biggest worries were. The man hung on his words, his features relaxing.

"How much do you have?"

Marek reached into his shirt and withdrew a gold tooth, holding it against the sun. Fascinated by the gleam, Jakub stretched out his hand, but Marek quickly removed it out of his reach. "Not so fast. There's three of us. You'll get one for each."

His inner struggle evident on his gaunt face, Jakub kept silent for a while, before he said, "Alright. What do you want me to do?"

"Your truck." Marek gazed at Livia, who'd been doing the reconnaissance. "We know your routine. You deliver vegetables twice a week. You park behind the kitchen, unload, spend perhaps ten minutes inside with the cook."

"You want to hide in my truck?" Jakub was quick to comprehend.

"With your help." Marek took over. "We need a safe space, perhaps an empty crate, large enough for a person to crouch inside."

"It's impossible," Jakub said, but his tone suggested he was considering the possibility. "The guards search the vehicles. Not thoroughly, but they look."

"You'll have to cover us with other empty crates, or a blanket of some kind," Marek said.

Jakub ran his hands through his hair. "Even if I wanted to help, the crates are small. I could maybe hide one person, certainly not more."

"We're three," Marek said.

"I'll come back another day."

Marek shook his head. "We must leave together. Once a prisoner goes missing, the security measures will be increased. There won't be a second chance—not in a long while."

"Three people," Jakub mused, a sly grin tugging at the corners of his mouth. "It would be cramped, a lot more dangerous than just one person." He left his statement hanging in the air, waiting.

Marek knew exactly what Jakub wanted. A game he'd played many times selling his horses. Back then, he'd enjoyed bargaining for a good price. Today, he simply wanted out, no matter how much it cost. But he knew better than to show his counterpart. Hence, he furrowed his brows, apparently thinking. "Three gold teeth is already generous, but I'm willing to offer two rings in addition..." He waited until he saw the reaction in Jakub's eyes. The other man apparently made the calculations in his head, coming to the conclusion it was a small fortune, certainly enough to feed his family for an entire year. Just when he noticed the feeling of richness settling in Jakub's mind, he added, "...if you drive us to the next town with a train station."

"What?" Jakub asked.

"We need to get far away from this camp before they notice we're missing." Marek held the other man's gaze. "Two golden rings. Just for driving us to the next town. In addition to the three gold teeth."

"I can't do that, I have a family to feed." The discomfort visible in the way his Adam's apple bopped up and down, Jakub needed a few inhales before he squared his shoulders. "When?"

Livia understood the word, because she entered the discussion, "During your next delivery."

Jakub effortlessly switched to German. "That's too early. I need time to organize everything."

"Then next week."

Jakub nodded. "That'll work. How will you get to the truck undetected?"

"Leave that to us." Marek wasn't going to spill the details, just in case. Dangling the gold in front of Jakub's nose he added, "Ensure the hiding space is prepared, and that you have a reason to delay your departure if needed."

Jakub nodded slowly, his decision made. "I'll leave a crate positioned in the door so you can slip into the truck while I'm in the kitchen. But you'll need to be quick—I can't idle long without raising suspicion."

"We'll be quick," Livia assured him.

Marek handed him the gold tooth. "Remember, you'll receive more once we're out of here."

"A lot more." Jakub's hand closed around the gold in a split-second.

"If you tell the Germans, you're going to hang alongside

with us," Marek threatened for good measure. It wasn't an empty threat either, since those harboring refuges from the camp received harsh punishments. Moments later they watched Jakub enter his truck, driving away.

Livia turned around as well. "I need to report for work."

"Me too. We'll talk tonight." Marek slunk away, arriving at his work barracks, everyone else already seated, the guards strutting about counting the workers. Just as one of them stopped at the empty space next to Roxy, Marek, thinking on his feet, grabbed a suitcase and carried it over to the table. He willed the tremble from his hands, as he poured the contents onto the table, under the watchful eyes of the guard.

"What do you think you are doing?" he barked at him. "Nobody moves before the counting is done."

"I'm so sorry. I... I... thought it was done. I wanted to start the work." It didn't need much acting for Marek to make a frightened impression.

"Stupid Gypsy!" The guard slapped him on the shoulder. "Sit and wait until the signal is given."

For the next thirty minutes Marek's hands worked sorting the belongings of other people, his eyes staring straight forward, not daring to move his head or whisper a word, always feeling the guard's stare boring into his back.

Finally, the guard seemed to get tired of supervision and moved, sitting down by the door, lighting a cigarette. Only then did Marek dare to murmur in Roxy's direction, "All settled."

She was clever enough not to respond or ask for details, since this wasn't the place for conversations. They could discuss the long list of things to prepare after dinner in the short free time before curfew. Sitting together like a family, a father and his two adolescent girls.

22

SEVERAL DAYS LATER

In the brief span between dinner and curfew, Roxy strolled across the *Appellplatz* after shaking off Tibor, who'd been sticking to her like wet tar. Cautiously, she peered one last time in all directions. Assured that the coast was clear, she slipped silently between the barracks to the agreed meeting spot with Livia and Marek.

"You're late," Marek growled.

"Sorry. Tibor was on my tail," Roxy replied tersely.

"He's turning into a real problem." Marek pulled a grumpy face.

"He even asked me what you're up to," Livia said.

A horrified expression showed up on Roxy's face. "Did you tell him?"

"What do you take me for?" Livia shook her head, her braids swinging. "I told him that you weren't planning anything."

"Which he apparently didn't believe." A deep furrow appeared on Marek's forehead. "We can't risk him interfering with our plan."

"Maybe we should let him in on it before he figures it out himself?" Livia looked from Roxy to Marek.

Roxy shook her head. "Absolutely not. I don't trust him. He's betrayed me before."

Marek moved his head back and forth. "He could be useful once we're in hiding, he's very skilled with his hands. If we can rely on him one hundred percent."

"Which we can't." Roxy raised her hands. "If he's in, I'm out."

Livia rolled her eyes. "Calm down. We always decide unanimously."

"Sorry," Roxy mumbled. The upcoming escape was straining her nerves.

As if he hadn't listened to their exchange, Marek added, "It wouldn't work. Jakub expects three persons, not four. No, it's too late to make changes."

Since Livia's and Marek's conversation with Jakub, they'd meticulously planned the escape. Livia had talked to him briefly during his last delivery, and received the confirmation that everything was ready from his side. He'd even enlisted the help of someone working at the train station in Zamość, obviously for an extra charge.

The plan was perfect—if everything went smoothly, they'd soon leave this horrible camp forever. Roxy almost smelled the intoxicating scent of freedom.

"The day after tomorrow Jakub delivers the potatoes, then we go," Livia declared. "Do you have the gold?"

Roxy nodded. She had stolen enough valuables during the past week to pay Jakub and keep something to pay their way out of the country.

"Let's go through every detail one more time." Marek had taken on the leadership role of the trio. "Jakub will provide us with clothes and drive us to the station in Zamość, where we'll hide by the tracks. According to his friend Pavel there are always pallets full of materials, which will provide us cover."

Roxy nodded. She wished she could have scouted the area beforehand to look for a suitable hiding spot. As it stood, they had to rely on Jakub's friend—and improvise.

"Pavel will signal us once a freight train heading west is ready, and he'll open one of the wagons for us." This was probably the most critical part, because even Pavel didn't know how long it'd take for a freight train to arrive, as the war had made all schedules meaningless.

Livia coughed, pressing her hand against her chest.

"Are you sick?" Roxy inspected the unusually pale complexion of her friend. Her cheekbones protruded even more sharply than usual beneath her skin.

"Just a scratch in my throat," Livia dismissed. "Nothing serious."

"We can't afford any illness. Not now." Roxy was seriously concerned about her friend. Despite all odds Livia had become the person she trusted most—effectively taking Tibor's role, who'd been her confidant throughout most of her life.

"It's nothing," Livia insisted. "I'm just tired."

Despite knowing she couldn't actually help, Roxy offered, "If there's anything you need?"

"A miracle maybe?" Livia smiled until another cough shook her bony shoulders.

"What about an escape instead?" Roxy tried to cheer her up, noticing how exhausted her friend looked. "We're all tired. Go to sleep early, do the least possible at work and before you know it, we're gone."

A dreamy expression showed up on Livia's face. "I can't wait."

Marek raised his voice to run over the plan again. "The day after tomorrow, we leave. Wake-up call is at five in the morning. Between wake-up and roll call, we have about fifteen minutes.

Livia goes to work as usual and opens the side door of the kitchen barracks." Behind the kitchen was a fenced area, which only the kitchen staff were allowed to enter. That's where Jakub's delivery truck would be parked. "Roxy slips through the kitchen first. I'll follow three minutes later.

"Livia makes sure she's standing next to the delivery truck when it's being unloaded. At Jakub's signal, she crawls into an empty crate. As soon as she's disappeared, Roxy follows, then I do the same. We have very little time until Jakub closes up the back of his truck. If anyone doesn't make it in time, the others leave without him."

"But..." Roxy protested. Marek had handled most of the negotiations with Jakub, since he was the only one of them who spoke Polish. Now he was assigning himself the riskiest part, as he'd be the last to climb into the truck. If anyone didn't make it, it would be him. That wasn't fair.

"No buts." He gave her a stern gaze. "This is our only chance. Any questions?"

Roxy and Livia shook their heads.

"See you the day after tomorrow." Roxy said goodbye seconds later with a queasy feeling in her stomach. To keep the risk as small as possible, they wouldn't meet again before the breakout attempt.

Roxy slipped into her barracks just in time before curfew.

"Where have you been?" Tibor asked.

She bit her tongue to stop herself from snapping at him to keep his nose out of her business, since that would only make him suspicious. "Exchanging the latest camp gossip with Livia."

"Anything significant?" Tibor perked up his ears. The kitchen helpers were usually better informed than the rest of the inmates.

"A load of turnips came in today. You'll find them in your soup tomorrow."

Tibor grimaced. He hated turnips.

"Oh, and one of the cooks cut off the tip of his finger." Roxy smiled maliciously. "If you find a meaty bit, thank the generous donor."

"Gross. You're disgusting."

"You're probably right." For a change, she was honest. Since being imprisoned in Belzec, she'd done things she couldn't have imagined a year ago. She'd become a perfect fit for the Nazi stereotype of a lying, stealing, and cheating Gypsy. And she hated herself a little for it.

During roll call the next morning, news spread like wildfire that one of the kitchen helpers had collapsed with a high fever. Rumors circulated that the entire kitchen brigade had been taken to the infirmary for isolation due to suspected typhus.

Roxy's hands grew sweaty. Her heart hammering against her ribs with fear, she raced to the infirmary. The sharp smell of carbolic acid hit her as she opened the door. At the other end of the long hallway, in a separate room, was the isolation chamber. She'd almost reached it when a nurse stepped out of the door, wearing a cloth over her mouth and nose. The nurse snapped at her, "What are you doing here? Get away!"

"I'm supposed to bring water to the patients," Roxy lied.

"No, you're not. Get out. Or do you want to catch the disease?" The nurse shooed Roxy ahead of her toward the exit. Glancing at the clock above the entrance, Roxy realized she had only a few minutes until she needed to show up at her work detail. Still, she crept around the outside of the infirmary barracks. After making sure the nurse wasn't in the isolation room, she climbed through the grilled window. Even six months ago, she probably wouldn't have fit through the bars. It seemed even the terrible hunger had served a purpose.

Mindful of the nurse's warning, she pulled up her blouse to cover her mouth and nose. On one of the cots, she discovered Livia, her face flushed with fever, her eyes half-closed.

"Livia?" she whispered.

Livia stared at her with glassy eyes. "Roxy? Why are you here? Go away, or you'll catch it too." Her voice was barely louder than a breath of wind.

"How are you feeling?"

"Bad." A shudder racked Livia's body. "The plan... you have to do it without me."

"No," Roxy protested. "You'll get better and then—"

"I'm dying, Roxy." Livia grabbed her hand. The touch was burning hot. "I can feel it. Use your chance. At least one of us shall survive."

Tears burned in Roxy's eyes. She was better than this. She'd never abandon a friend. "I'll take you with me, somehow. As soon as we're free, I'll bring you to a doctor and nurse you back to health."

"No." Livia's fingers clutched Roxy's hand, her grip faint. "Promise me you'll do it without me. That you'll survive and tell everyone. What they... did to us."

Just as Roxy was about to answer, footsteps approached in the hallway. If the nurse discovered her, she was done for.

"I'll come back," Roxy promised before slipping out the window as gracefully as a cat, split seconds before at least two people stopped in front of the isolation room door.

"Lock the door. No one goes in or out," ordered a deep male voice.

"But what about the patients?" the nurse objected.

"They'll die anyway."

The impact of his words took Roxy's breath away. He'd just delivered Livia's death sentence. And there was nothing she could do. There wasn't even enough time to grieve; she needed to hurry if she were to arrive at her work detail on time. Otherwise, she'd follow her friend to the other side all too soon.

Literally at the last second, she joined the group whose first task of the workday was to collect the dead of the previous night. Marek gave her a questioning look, to which she merely put a finger to her lips.

Her entire body tingling with impatience, she forced herself to wait for an opportunity to give him the bad news. The chance came when they stood side by side shoveling dirt.

"Livia has typhus," she reported.

"Damn," he grumbled with a stony expression.

"She begged me to do it without her."

"That won't work. She needs to leave the back door to the kitchen open so we can get in."

"Crap." Roxy hadn't thought of that detail and racked her brain for a solution. "We'll have to go through the front entrance."

"Too dangerous."

"Hey, stop dawdling!" a guard shouted, causing Roxy to shovel with more vigor.

Without moving her lips, she murmured, "I'll climb in through a window and open the door for you."

"They're barred."

The shovel nearly slipped from Roxy's fingers, along with her hope for freedom. The kitchen barracks was a tempting target for potential thieves and therefore well secured, the space between the bars about half the size as in the infirmary. Lacking help from inside, it was next to impossible to enter unseen during the short time Jakub's delivery truck was being unloaded in the cordoned-off yard.

Though Roxy wasn't ready to give up yet. "Someone has to let us inside."

Marek grunted. "Just how do we find this person by tomorrow morning?"

"We'll think of something." Deep down, Roxy didn't believe it herself, but she was too stubborn to admit defeat. She'd come up with something. She always did.

That evening, Roxy sneaked to the infirmary because she wanted to visit Livia. Sadly, one look through the window showed her the futility of her plan: Livia's cot was empty. Feeling as if someone had torn a hole in her chest, Roxy trudged away, tears running freely down her cheeks. Normally she didn't allow herself to indulge in emotions, because crying was a luxury one couldn't afford in this terrible place. Today, however, she was on the verge of throwing herself on the ground and never getting up again.

How could the world be so unfair? What had Livia done wrong? Why did she have to die?

Eventually, she bumped into Tibor.

"Where have you been?" he asked, a steep furrow on his forehead.

"Livia is dead." She wiped the telltale traces of her grief from her cheeks.

"I'm sorry."

"You never liked her."

"That's not true. We weren't best friends like you two, but I certainly didn't want her to die. Honestly." He took Roxy by the arm.

She resisted the impulse to push him away. Desolate beyond measure, she leaned against his shoulder, a horrific dread squashing her soul. She hadn't felt this hopeless, since... since her father's death. Deep grief bubbled up in her, diffusing throughout her body, until it filled every one of her cells. In a grave voice she said, "Soon we'll all be dead."

"Don't be so pessimistic." Tibor's voice had an artificially cheerful tone. "I think it's time we made plans for a breakout."

Shocked, Roxy broke away from his embrace. Surely he didn't suspect that she, Livia and Marek had planned exactly that for the next day. A brilliant idea occurred to her about how they might still be able to escape. "That's suicide. We're better off securing a higher place in the camp hierarchy. There are several positions open in the kitchen right now."

Tibor narrowed his eyes. "What's gotten into you? Haven't you always dreamed of escape?"

She sighed theatrically. "I have. But now I know it was stupid. No one gets out of here alive."

23

A shrill whistle tore through the night's silence. Disoriented, Marek opened his eyes. It was too early for wake-up call. Absolute darkness reigned outside. Doors slammed. Boots stomped.

"Everyone out! Now! Fall in at the *Appellplatz*!" echoed the orders through the barracks.

Around him, sleep-drunk men rose, slipping into their shoes while half-asleep and searching for their caps at once. Marek's blood froze to ice. Nighttime roll calls never meant anything good.

"What's going on?" someone asked.

"Hurry up! Everyone out." A guard stormed through the barracks, generously distributing blows to anyone who didn't get out of the way in time.

Marek slipped into the shoes he'd placed next to his head the night before and followed the stream of prisoners. A light-blue streak appeared in the eastern sky. People were herded to the *Appellplatz* from all barracks. The entire camp seemed to be on its feet.

Children cried, parents called out. The sound of whips cracked through the air. Whatever was happening must be important. Cursing, Marek allowed himself to be pushed forward by the crowd.

The SS couldn't have chosen a worse time for this action, because it was the day he and Roxy had planned their escape.

Frantically, he scanned the crowd, hoping to spot her. It was futile. Roxy was too small and delicate, effectively disappearing amidst the masses. He might have found Livia since her blonde hair had been easy to recognize, but Livia was dead.

His hands sweaty, Marek followed the other inmates to the *Appellplatz* waiting for an opportunity to slip away unseen. With or without Roxy, he'd try to reach the kitchen barracks. Perhaps the general chaos would compensate for the lack of inside help, and he'd be able to sneak unnoticed into the loading area. Jakub would arrive in the morning. After all, the Pole didn't know that Livia had died.

Several times Marek attempted to separate himself from the crowd. Each time, a guard stepped in front of him, baton raised. Frantically searching for a way out, he glanced at the fenced area behind the kitchen where Jakub's delivery truck was entering just now.

Marek's stomach cramped. It might be his sole chance to leave this hellhole behind. His eyes darted back and forth, searching for a gap between two guards while he was mercilessly pushed toward the main gate.

"They say we're being relocated. They need our labor more urgently elsewhere," mentioned an older prisoner beside him.

"I heard they're afraid of a typhus outbreak. They'll probably kill us all," whispered another.

Streams of sweat ran down Marek's back. The rumors might be true or not, he certainly had no desire to find out. Jakub's delivery truck stood less than fifty meters away in the fenced area. This was his chance. Another quick glance to make sure the guard was distracted.

Marek stepped sideways out of the line and moved slowly

backward, as if looking for something on the ground. Then he turned on his heel. His head lowered, he marched toward the fence with determined steps. His heart hammered in his chest as he approached the barrier. In his head, he repeated the command to himself: *Don't run. Don't attract attention. Walk normally.*

Less than ten meters left to the fence, behind which the delivery truck stood. Was Roxy waiting for him there? Had she managed to sneak into the kitchen? He wouldn't know until he crawled into one of the crates. Hesitating for a moment, he let his gaze wander across the masses once more, hoping to spot her somewhere. Nothing.

For a split second he toyed with the idea of staying to find her, then he shrugged the thought away. He couldn't wait for her, or do anything for her. He had to get himself out.

"Hey, you! This way!" Marek froze. A young guard stepped in front of him, his chin jutting forward, his baton raised.

"I... need to use the latrine," Marek stammered.

"Back in line!" The guard jabbed the baton into his ribs. "Move it!"

Marek wanted to protest, wanted to explain that he had to go urgently, but the man's unyielding glare silenced him. One last wistful glance at the delivery truck, before he rejoined the column marching toward the main gate.

Jakub would leave without Marek. Every spark of hope seeped from his bones until he staggered against his neighbor.

"Hey, watch where you're stepping!"

There was but one glimmer of hope keeping him upright: the wish that at least Roxy had made it. She was small and nimble like a cat. Hopefully she was already lying in one of the crates in Jakub's truck by now. She must have made it. At least her.

Without meaning to, she had crept into his heart. So much so that the thought of her escaping brought a smile to his lips.

"I'm keeping my fingers crossed for you, little peewee," he mumbled so softly no one could hear.

They reached the entrance gate. He was shoved into an overcrowded truck. An SS man rammed the butt of his rifle into Marek's back because he didn't climb over the tailgate quick enough. The inmates stood packed tightly in the cargo area as the tarp was lowered and tied. The engine roared to life and the vehicle lurched into motion.

"Where are they taking us this time?" someone asked in the darkness.

Nobody answered.

Marek feared the next location would be even worse than the camp they'd just left. Since Austria's annexation to the German Reich, things had gotten steadily worse with each new decree or transport. Although he couldn't imagine anything crueler than Belzec, he feared the Nazis' perfidy might still have unimaginable horrors in store.

At the next pothole, someone bumped into Marek. He shifted his weight to his other leg and suppressed a cry of pain as a violent stab shot through his bad ankle. No sooner had he regained his balance than the vehicle bounced over the next uneven patch. The journey dragged on endlessly.

Gritting his teeth Marek clung to the certainty that it must eventually end. At some point, he must have passed out. He stared confused into the darkness when the truck came to a halt after heavy braking. Blinking, he tried to remember where he was and why. He needed several seconds to recall the events of the morning.

The tarp was ripped open and bright sunlight blinded him.

"Out! Everyone out!" the uniformed men shouted.

Marek squinted as he stumbled stiff-legged from the cargo bed. Before him stretched a desolate moorland as far as the eye could see. Here and there, stunted trees jutted from the damp ground. The air was saturated with moisture and filled with a putrid smell. In the distance, he spotted primitive wooden barracks, their outlines blurring in the shimmering heat.

"Welcome to Krychow," said an SS man with a mocking grin. "This is your new home. You lazy slackers will drain the moor to create fertile farmland for the Thousand-Year Reich."

A collective groan went through the ranks of prisoners. Work in the moor—that meant wading through brackish water up to their hips in scorching heat while mosquitoes feasted on them.

The barracks in Krychow were just as dilapidated and dirty as those in Belzec. The only improvement was three-tiered bunks instead of straw on the floor.

Marek mulled over which level might be the best choice: Should he fight for a place at the bottom, which wouldn't require climbing after a hard day's work? Or the top, where nobody could urinate on his head? The middle had the disadvantages of both without any real advantage. After brief consideration, he decided on a top spot and elbowed his way to the back of the barracks, where there was the least chance of being singled out by guards for special work duties.

"Damn them," he groaned as soon as he noticed that there were no mattresses on the bunks and they had to sleep on the rough wooden planks. At least each man received a thin blanket. In the muggy August heat, he could use the blanket as padding to protect his skin from wood splinters.

That same day, they were driven into the moor, where a guard distributed rusty spades.

"You'll dig drainage ditches," he ordered. "Three meters per man per day. Anyone who doesn't meet his quota gets nothing to eat."

Marek swung the spade over his shoulder and trudged with the others into the moor. After a few steps, he sank up to his knees in the muddy water. His injured foot protested painfully. Regardless, he was grateful to have escaped the Sonderkommando. It was a choice he'd regretted every single day, because the limited extra benefits hadn't been worth it. Every night the sound of extracting a gold tooth with pliers haunted him into his dreams.

After several hours of toil in the moor, though, he considered whether the Sonderkommando might have been the more pleasant alternative after all. The soil consisted of a mixture of mud, roots, and rotting plant parts. Each shovelful was a struggle, as water immediately seeped back into the excavated ditches. The mosquitoes had caught the scent of fresh sweat and descended in swarms upon the prisoners. Within minutes, every inch of exposed skin was covered in itchy bites.

As the midday sun beat down upon them without mercy, Marek's neighbor collapsed to the ground. Marek stepped around the fallen figure without interrupting his work. For a fleeting moment, he sensed a deep regret that caring for a fellow worker had become a hazard. Some men, however, set their spades aside to help the victim up.

"Who gave you permission to stop working, you dirty slackers! Get back to it!" barked the SS guard.

Marek peered enviously at the guard's knee-high rubber boots. In these waders, he could stand in the muddy water up to his thighs without getting his feet wet, while Marek's own soaked shoes squeaked at every step, rubbing against his swollen skin.

Eventually, just as Marek was about to plunge headfirst into the muddy water to end his suffering, the longed-for whistle sounded, marking the end of the shift. Exhausted to the bone Marek dragged himself back to the camp, where he received a bowl of watery broth alongside a slice of hard bread. A few cabbage leaves swam in the soup.

Done with himself and the world, he sat apart on the trampled ground so nobody would venture to have a conversation with him.

"Room for an old friend?"

Marek groaned. Standing before him was Roxy, exhausted but alive. Her face and arms were covered in mosquito bites, her short curls sweaty and sticking to her head. Yet her blue eyes radiated with their unique indomitable gleam.

"Sure." Marek made a welcoming gesture.

She flopped down next to him in a swift movement, while somehow managing not to spill a single drop of her soup. Peering into his bowl she asked, "Would you like to swap the cabbage for a piece of carrot?"

"Well, sure. Why not." Marek was too taken aback to refuse her request and watched how she fished for two big pieces of carrot, depositing it into his bowl, before taking out the thin cabbage leaves.

"That was a rather bad deal for you, don't you think?" he said once he'd regained his faculty of speech.

"Objectively, yes, but I hate carrots." Roxy shoved the cabbage into her mouth closing her eyes as if she were eating a delicacy.

"After how many months in Belzec and you still afford the luxury not to eat the food you don't like?" He shook his head at her foolishness.

"Only when I can swap. I'm not that dumb." She grinned. "Also, I know where they store the provisions."

Her answer filled him with pride. "You never give up, do you?"

"Not until I've avenged everyone murdered by the Nazis."

"You'll be busy with that for a long time."

"I swear to you, one day I'll find Commander Goslar, and he'll pay for everything he did to my people. He'll wish he'd never been born."

"An excellent idea." Despite not believing this would happen, her plan kindled his confidence. Someone had to survive, after all; the Nazis couldn't eradicate every single Sinti and Roma. Even if nobody but the young girl survived and passed on testimony of their suffering to posterity.

The warmth of his pride about her vanished at the reminder of their precarious situation, leaving a bone-deep chill behind. "I had so hoped you'd managed to escape."

"I was close. But Jakub got cold feet and backed out."

"The bastard!" Righteous anger on Roxy's behalf streamed through his veins.

She didn't seem overly saddened by the setback. On the contrary, her eyes sparkled. "Hence I still have the gold we promised him as payment." She glanced over her shoulder in all directions. "This camp is practically unsecured. We just need to find a way through the moor."

Marek couldn't help but smile. Her indestructibility was balm for his wounded soul. She reminded him so much of his own daughters that he all but reached out to press her against him. At the last second, he stopped himself.

"You look exhausted." Roxy rummaged in her pants pocket and produced a small piece of bread. "Here, take this."

"Thank you." Marek took the food, surprised by her gesture. "Why are you doing this?"

She tilted her head. "Because I like you. You're not like the other adults."

He liked her too. Something about her reminded him of his son Stefan and his daughters when they were still children. Deep in his heart, he felt the desire to protect Roxy and shield her from the suffering the Nazis had in store for her.

"It's dangerous to like someone," he warned her. "In case an opportunity to escape presents itself, you don't want to be held back out of loyalty for someone you like."

"I do like you, but rest assured that I wouldn't sacrifice my life or my freedom for you." Roxy pushed out her lower lip. "That should make you feel better."

It didn't. Despite what he'd just said, he very much wanted

her to care about him. "A very wise decision. So why give me your bread?"

The defiant-sad expression on her face disappeared and she grinned with a carefreeness as if she wasn't sitting in a Nazi labor camp. "Nothing has changed, just because our first attempt failed. I still need you for a successful escape."

So that was which way the wind was blowing. For a moment, disappointment bubbled up in him, because she was using him for her own purposes. Seconds later he chided himself for being foolish. Hadn't he been the one who'd drummed into her countless times to behave exactly this way?

"It's a deal?" Roxy held out her hand.

"What?"

"That we'll make another attempt to escape. We'll stay together until we're back in Germany. Once there I can manage on my own and so can you."

"Agreed." He shook her hand. "I admire your optimism."

24

KRYCHOW, LATE OCTOBER 1940

The biting frost crept through Tibor's thin clothing, making him shiver. In the past two months the weather had gradually changed: gone were the scorching hot and humid days, replaced by freezing nights and fog so thick it clouded out the sun. The primitive barracks offered little protection against the icy winds sweeping across the moor. They slept pressed tightly against each other to avoid freezing to death.

Tibor rubbed his numb hands, blowing warm air into them while observing Roxy and Marek. They stood on the other side of the square, talking quietly, as they had been doing since their arrival. In recent days, they'd become more cautious, meeting less frequently and barely speaking to each other during the day. But Tibor hadn't missed Roxy's frequent glances toward the camp fence. She was up to something, he knew, without a shadow of doubt. And it would happen soon.

The security measures in this inhospitable area were a joke. The fence was more symbolic than a real deterrent; any reasonably agile person could squeeze between the wires or jump over with a running start. It had taken Tibor a while to understand the reason for the lax measures. Once the first prisoner had attempted an escape, the realization hit him like a bolt of lightning.

His work detail had discovered the unfortunate fugitive by chance the next morning. He'd strayed from the solid path after just a few hundred meters and was stuck up to his hips in the moor, unable to free himself.

Even weeks later, Tibor gagged at the thought. The guards hadn't allowed anyone to help him—by evening the man had gone mad from thirst, and the next morning nothing but his mud-smeared cap floated on the surface of the moor.

Even if he'd made it by some miracle to the nearest village, the local population would've promptly handed him over to the Nazis, who promised substantial rewards to the starving Poles for captured prisoners.

Which was probably the reason why Roxy and Marek hadn't staged their escape yet. But as sure as he stood here, they were plotting something, and he'd be damned if he wasn't going to be a part of it.

"Why are you spying on Roxy again?" asked Romeo, sidling up to him.

"She's planning to escape with Marek," Tibor growled.

Romeo gave a dry laugh. "Good luck with that. It's winter. Even if they make it through the moor, they'll freeze to death the first night."

Tibor shook his head. "You underestimate Roxy. She's smarter than all of us combined."

The next morning, Tibor woke up before the wake-up call sounded. He lay on his bunk, his eyes open, staring at the ceiling. It was dawn already. The fact instantly sent waves of panic through his body. For several weeks now, they'd had to get up before sunrise.

Outside, nothing stirred. A peculiar silence hung over the camp.

Tibor sat up on the bunk he shared with Romeo, listening

hard. No whistles, no shouting, no boot stomping. To his left and right, other prisoners woke up, looking around in confusion.

"What's going on today?" someone asked.

"Why isn't there a wake-up call?" wondered another.

"Be happy and go back to sleep," someone chimed in.

For months, Tibor had wished not to be woken in the early hours of the morning just once, yet he instinctively knew the absence of the wake-up call was nothing to be happy about.

His father swung off his bunk and marched to the door. He rattled the handle. Nothing moved.

"I'll have a look through the window." Roxy pulled herself up to the windowsill. "I can't see anyone. I think the guards are gone," she announced.

An excited murmur went through the barracks. Someone shrieked, "They're going to set us on fire!"

People scrambled up, throwing themselves in panic against the door.

"The door," they yelled. "We need to break down the door!"

A man with shoulders the size of a prize boxer tore a board from one of the bunks and rammed it against the door. On the third thrust, the wood splintered. The door swung open, revealing a deserted camp.

For so many months, Tibor had feared the guards. Now their absence choked the air from his lungs. What could it mean? Were they gone for good, or was this a ruse to shoot the inmates in the back during an alleged escape?

Tibor shook off the emerging panic. Hesitantly, he followed the others outside. Apparently overnight every single guard had abandoned the camp. More prisoners streamed from the other barracks, cautiously exploring the common grounds.

"They're indeed gone," Romeo confirmed.

"We need to flee right now," Tibor told his father, standing in a group with Gisela and the other adults. Roxy sidled up with him.

Gottfried shook his head. "That's a momentous decision we shouldn't rush into. It might be a trap. Or they might return."

"That's exactly why we need to leave immediately. This is our chance." Adrenaline prickled all the way down to his toes.

"You're making it sound much simpler than it is," Gottfried said.

"Your father is right," his mother chimed in. "Where shall we go? We don't know the area and don't speak the language."

"Moreover, winter is approaching fast," said an aunt. "Where will we get food? Or warm clothing?"

"We'll find work." Tibor wasn't ready to give up yet.

Roxy raised her eyebrows in appreciation of his resistance.

"The Poles don't like our kind, they won't give us work," his father pointed out. "Apart from the fact that every family member is weakened, Hans and Maria wouldn't survive an escape."

Tibor swallowed hard. Except for Hans and Maria, every other young child in the clan had died.

"If we stay here, none of us will survive. We have better chances on the run," Roxy countered.

"I agree with Roxy." Tibor took a demonstrative step to stand next to her.

His father examined him with a stern face. "Such an unreasonable suggestion was to be expected from Roxy, but from you? You're old enough to understand this isn't just about you. We're staying together, and will wait to see what happens. Period." With that, Gottfried turned to his wife. "You, Teresa, and Rosina rush to the camp kitchen right now. Take all the food you can find."

Tibor glanced at Roxy. She hadn't waited for his father to finish talking but was already halfway to the kitchen barracks. Panic took Tibor's breath away. He absolutely couldn't dawdle. Hastening his steps, he rushed across the camp grounds. In the kitchen, several prisoners were already at work, rummaging through sacks of potatoes and flour.

Roxy stood next to Marek. Both of them were stuffing bread, potatoes, turnips, and everything else they could get their hands on, into a cloth bag that suspiciously looked like an apron.

"I'm coming with you," Tibor declared without preamble.

Roxy and Marek exchanged a glance. "We only have enough food for the two of us." Marek's voice was cool.

"I'll bring my own bundle," Tibor replied. "I won't be a burden, I just don't want to flee alone. Together we have a better chance."

Roxy examined him. "You want to come along, even though Uncle Gottfried forbade it?"

"Yes. I'm determined to leave. My father wants to stay because he thinks it's too strenuous for the little ones."

Roxy nodded. "It is indeed. Escaping won't be a walk in the park."

"So may I join you, please?" Tibor waited with baited breath for the answer.

"If you carry your own supplies and don't slow us down. Also, you do exactly as I say," Marek stipulated.

Tibor's blood boiled. Who, exactly, had made Marek the leader? Before he could respond, Romeo joined them. "If Tibor's escaping, I'm coming too. I don't want to stay behind and conk out in misery."

Marek pressed his lips together, whereupon Roxy placed a reassuring hand on his arm. "Eight eyes see more than four. They can come with us as far as I'm concerned."

"Alright," said Marek.

Roxy tied her full bundle together. "Collect everything you want to take, especially provisions. We leave in ten minutes."

Anger snaked up Tibor's spine. It was bad enough that Marek was giving orders, now even his younger cousin was acting like she was in charge. A nudge in his side made him flinch.

"Let's go." Romeo pulled him to the sacks of food, which were already heavily looted. With each passing second, more prisoners crowded into the kitchen barracks. If they didn't hurry, nothing would be left to take.

Since Tibor and Romeo didn't have bags, they stuffed bread, potatoes, and even the hated turnips into their pockets before leaving the kitchen.

A few meters away, Roxy and Marek were bent over a piece of cardboard. As he neared them, Tibor recognized a sketched map of the camp.

"Starting here, we'll walk north around the moor. Somewhere over there"—Marek pointed at the map—"must be a train station."

"We'll hide near the train station and wait for a freight train heading west in which we can stow away," Roxy explained.

It annoyed Tibor no end that the two seemed to have thought of everything. To justify his value for the venture, he pointed out, "I thought we wanted to get away from the Nazis. So why aren't we going east to the Russians?"

"Believe me, they aren't one bit better than the Germans." Marek's mouth twitched. "Besides, none of us speaks Russian. We wouldn't blend in with the people there."

"But we can in Germany? That's worked out really well so far." Romeo's voice dripped with sarcasm.

Roxy gave him a pitiful look. "Oh, Romeo. So far we haven't tried to hide. We've done what the Nazis ordered, hoping nothing bad would happen to us as long as we follow the laws. We've experienced firsthand where that led to. I, for my part, will never follow any of their stupid rules again."

Tibor agreed with her. "What Roxy says is true. We can't expect anything from the Nazis except lies and deceit. They'll never accept us Roma—"

"And Sinti," Roxy interrupted him with a nod in Marek's direction.

"One more reason to go underground as soon as we arrive in Germany. Roxy can get forged papers identifying her as an Aryan to live a free life in the Reich." Marek folded the cardboard and tucked it into his waistband.

"Why not us?" asked Romeo.

Marek pursed his lips. "Because you're almost of military age. Every patrol will inspect your papers very thoroughly. Even if they don't get suspicious, you'll end up as flak helpers faster than you can dash off."

Tibor bit his lip. Another threat he hadn't considered. Perhaps his father was right after all and it was better to stay with the family in the camp. But then he clenched his jaw. Anything was better than life in the camp, for he had no doubt that those staying behind would soon be transported to another location. Given their track record, that every new location was considerably worse than the one before, he absolutely wanted to avoid that.

Marek raised his voice. "But that's future talk. First, we need to cross Poland. Remember, we can't trust anyone. The local population dislikes Roma and Sinti just as much as the Nazis do. Moreover, high rewards are offered for escaped prisoners. Betrayal lurks behind every friendly face."

Was Tibor imagining it, or did Roxy stare in his direction? A shiver ran down his back. She still hadn't fully forgiven him for ratting her out.

"Back to the freight trains. What do we do if they don't stop at the station?" Romeo scratched his head.

"If they don't stop, they at least have to slow down while passing through the station. Then we jump on." Roxy seemed confident in her solution.

"You're loony." Tibor shook his head. Once more he mulled whether joining the escape party was indeed a wise decision.

Roxy seemed to have read his thoughts. "Nobody's forcing you to tag along."

"First, we need to find a train station. Then we'll see what's next," Marek intervened in an attempt to calm the waters.

Tibor exchanged a glance with Romeo, who winked at him. "Let's get going."

The four of them set off. His stomach tied in knots, Tibor marched up to the camp's entrance gate. As soon as they walked through, they'd officially be fugitive prisoners and could be shot without warning.

Romeo seemed to have the same thought, as he gave him an uncertain side glance.

"Better to be shot in the back while escaping than starving in this hellhole," Tibor said, to encourage himself even more than his cousin. It had the desired effect. Considering the alternative, the venture no longer seemed so outrageous. If they took their fate into their own hands, they had a fighting chance of survival. In the abandoned camp with winter approaching, not so much.

As he walked through the gate, the knot in his gut loosened and a deep relief spread through him: *Freedom, here I come!*

After about two hours steady marching, they left the moor behind, making faster progress. Another hour later, they reached the shelter of a pine forest. Tibor longed for a break, but Marek mercilessly drove the small group forward.

This time of year offered few hours of daylight, and they needed to put as much distance as possible between themselves and the camp before darkness fell. Nobody knew when the guards would return, but Tibor had the distinct feeling it wouldn't take long.

25

WARSAW, TWO WEEKS LATER

The streets of Warsaw bubbled with life despite war and destruction. Locals went about their business with downcast heads, while German patrols marched by at regular intervals. Her stomach growling viciously, Roxy pressed herself against the wall of a building. They'd arrived in the Polish capital three days ago, hiding in the basement of an abandoned bombed-out ruin that Romeo had scouted out.

The escape from the camp in Krychow had been easier than she'd expected. After an uncomfortable, cold night in the woods, they'd indeed found a train station the next morning. The guards didn't seem to have returned to the camp, since nobody had pursued them or alerted the railway police. At least there was no sign of commotion in the quiet town.

At the station, they'd waited a few hours until a freight train stopped to reload coal for the locomotive. Roxy and her companions had used the brief halt to hide in an empty wagon. In Warsaw, the initial euphoria of their quick success had rapidly evaporated. Reality had caught up with them—they were constantly hungry, exhausted, and under extreme tension.

This morning, Roxy and Tibor had set out to organize something to eat, while Marek, the only one among them who spoke Polish, was once again trying to pawn two of the gold rings Roxy had stolen in the Belzec camp. Romeo had stayed behind in the basement to guard their belongings.

She'd have preferred to go to the market with money to buy food, as every theft carried the risk of getting caught. But after three days going without eating, hunger gnawed unbearably at her insides, and who knew when they'd finally be able to turn the rings into money. So far, Marek hadn't had any luck. The jewelers and even the pawnbrokers were suspicious of strangers and wanted to see papers before doing business.

"Marek looks as ragged as a vagrant. He needs a decent suit, then the shop owners will do business with him," Tibor said.

"No money, no suit. No suit, no money." Roxy chewed on her lip. "I swear, as soon as I've eaten my fill, I'll steal a suit for Marek and decent pants for myself."

"A dress would be more fitting," Tibor answered.

"A dress is totally impractical." Roxy shook her hair, which had grown back into a curly men's haircut.

"A woman is less conspicuous, they hardly ever get checked."

"I'm inconspicuous as it is. But," she smirked, "you can wear a dress if you feel safer in it."

Tibor opened his mouth to reply just as they saw movement in the bakery across the street. The baker was unlocking the door. It didn't take long before the first customer entered the shop. The scent of freshly baked bread wafted over to them. Roxy's mouth watered.

"This is our chance," she whispered, moving closer to Tibor. "We'll walk over and as soon as the woman comes out, you bump into her while I grab a loaf."

"That's too dangerous," Tibor hissed back. "What shall we do if she notices what's happening?"

"Then we run." Adrenaline rushed through Roxy's veins.

She brushed aside her guilty conscience. They hadn't had a bite to eat for three days, hence drastic measures were excusable. "Do you have a better idea? Preferably before we starve to death."

Tibor cast a longing gaze at the loaves in the shop window. "Alright. As soon as you grab the bread, you disappear into the side alley and I'll follow."

"We'll meet two intersections down, where the cobbler is."

"Let's go."

During their discussion, the customer had left the shop and was walking down the street. They remained lurking in position. Roxy's heart pounded wildly against her ribs, and the adrenaline in her veins made her wide awake. Her senses sharpened, she watched the other side of the street with eagle eyes. It didn't take long before another customer entered the bakery.

Chatting, Roxy and Tibor crossed the street, positioning themselves near the bakery. As soon as the door opened, Tibor set in motion and bumped into the woman who was just stepping out.

"*Przepraszam, proszę,*" he apologized, using the few bits of Polish Marek had taught them. Roxy used the moment of confusion to pilfer a loaf of bread along with something wrapped up from the woman's basket. Once she held the bread in her hands, Roxy's stomach growled so loudly she feared the woman might hear it. She resisted the temptation to bite into the loaf, concealed the stolen goods under her shirt and walked away on her bare feet.

At the street corner, she turned her head. Frozen with fright, she witnessed how the woman struck Tibor. Apparently, she'd noticed that she'd been robbed and correctly guessed that he and Roxy were working together.

Her first impulse was to rush to his aid, but that would only have made the situation worse by putting herself in danger too. She couldn't and shouldn't help him. As much as it pained her, she had to move on, while Tibor got out of the predicament on his own. Her gaze fixed straight ahead, she hurried down the side alley, climbed over a wall, stowed the bread and the wrapped bun in her backpack, before she strolled leisurely to the designated meeting point.

Tibor wasn't there.

Since she didn't want to draw attention to herself, she walked to an advertising column, pretending to read the posters, while in reality observing the area. After an endless period of time, Tibor limped up. Roxy swallowed the cry of horror once she saw his blood-soaked, tattered pants.

She looked in all directions, to make sure Tibor wasn't being followed, before she walked toward him. "That looks pretty bad. What happened?"

"The woman suspected I was in cahoots with you and screamed bloody murder. I took to my heels, but she and a passerby chased me." Beads of sweat formed on Tibor's forehead. "I turned into the wrong side alley and ended up facing a wall."

"Ouch." From her exploratory tours, Roxy knew which wall he was talking about. The height wasn't a problem, since it offered plenty of handholds between the bricks for easy climbing. But on top of the wall, glass shards were embedded. She peered at his hands, which showed a few abrasions. "But why the leg?"

"I knew about the glass shards up there and was careful. However, in my hurry I forgot about the nails on the other side and got caught on one of them when I jumped down." Tibor's nose jutted sharply from his face.

"We need to return to the hideout instantly. Can you walk?"

"I'll manage." He clenched his jaw, trying to appear brave. However, Roxy knew him too well to be fooled by his show. His grimace revealed the huge pain he was feeling.

"Come and lean on me." She gripped around his waist and dragged him as quickly as possible to their hideout, her ears pricked as she suspected a pursuer in every passerby. The fear that someone might expose them as the bread thieves and set the patrolling soldiers on their tail accelerated her steps. Poor Tibor hung like a flour sack by her side, and with each step his weight bore down heavier on Roxy.

Now and then she glanced at the ever-growing bloodstain on his pants. Panic constricted her throat. She stopped and turned around to squint her eyes at the path they'd walked.

"What are you doing?" Tibor leaned against her, panting.

"I'm checking whether we've left blood trails. We can't risk leading a pursuer to our hideout."

"Oh my God." Tibor collapsed and Roxy had difficulty standing upright under his weight. She too was at the end of her strength. Fortunately, it wasn't far to their hideout.

"Stay here for a minute." Roxy leaned him against a wall before walking a dozen meters in the direction they'd come from. Once she was assured there wasn't a drop of blood on the pavement, she breathed a sigh of relief and returned to her cousin. "I didn't find anything. We can continue."

Tibor shook his head. "I won't make it. You go ahead and return with Romeo to get me."

"Absolutely not. If I leave you here, you'll surely be picked up. In your condition, you can't even run if a patrol appears." Roxy squinted her eyes at her cousin, who'd macerated to nothing but skin and bones in the camps. Although she herself was battered from the exertion, she wouldn't leave him in his desperate situation. "I'll carry you piggyback."

"I'm far too heavy for you." Beads of sweat stood on his ghostly pale forehead.

"No way am I leaving you behind. That'll be your certain death." He didn't need to know she had an ulterior motive for her selfless act: she feared Tibor might reveal the existence of the others under torture. If the authorities knew whom they were looking for, their chances of going underground would shrink considerably. "Come on now."

Roxy went down on her knees so he was able to climb onto her back. Swaying, she struggled to regain a secure stance. He was a lot heavier than he looked. But giving up was not an option. Conjuring up almost superhuman power, she carried Tibor two blocks to their hideout, where she fell to her knees at the entrance to the stairs, gasping heavily.

Romeo must have heard them arrive, because his dark hair appeared mere seconds later in the staircase. Once he assessed their awful condition, he asked in alarm, "What happened?"

"We had to run. Tibor tore his leg on a rusty nail," Roxy explained.

"Come on, let's carry him into the basement." Romeo grabbed Tibor's shoulders, Roxy his feet. Combined they lifted him almost effortlessly and carried him down the stairs. Just as they laid their cousin down more or less comfortably, Marek showed up, beaming with joy.

"Look, I got potatoes. We just need firewood, then we'll cook ourselves a real meal."

Roxy swallowed, unable to give a sensible answer.

It took a few seconds for Marek's eyes to adjust to the dim light and grasp the situation. "Good Lord! What happened to you?"

Marek knelt next to the injured boy, carefully removing the tattered pants. Tibor gave a heart-rending groan as he examined the wound. Marek's face darkened. "His wound needs stitches."

"We can't see a doctor," Tibor protested in a weak voice.

"Yes, we can," Roxy objected. "Marek speaks Polish. We're going to find a doctor and convince him to help us."

"Convince? How exactly do you intend to do that?" Marek was skeptical.

"We'll tell him about our predicament. There are sympathizers, people who don't collaborate with the Nazis." Fear for her cousin snaked up Roxy's spine. She had just started to forgive him, she absolutely couldn't lose him again. He and Romeo might well be the last survivors of her entire family.

"I doubt it. In general the locals, regardless of their political opinion, like neither Jews nor Sinti and Roma." Marek shook his head.

"Then we'll force him to help." Romeo pulled a folding knife from his pocket. "With this."

"Are you insane?" Marek hissed. "Put that away right now before you get any stupid ideas. If we're caught, the SS will shoot us on the spot."

"If we do nothing, Tibor could die," Roxy said. She went down on her knees next to Marek, grabbing his hands. Tibor might have betrayed her, but he was still her cousin. She'd do everything to save his life. "Please."

Marek peered at her for an endless time, before he nodded with a sigh. "How did this happen anyway?"

"We stole bread." Roxy pulled the loaf and the bun from her bag and gave it to Romeo. "Cut us four slices, will you?"

"That doesn't explain Tibor's injury." Marek's voice was stern. She half expected a lecture that stealing was wrong, but he kept silent and turned again toward Tibor, who lay motionless on the ground, his eyes closed.

The sight choked Roxy's throat. "Is he dead?"

Marek placed his hand on Tibor's chest, the rising and falling was barely visible. "No. But he's very weak. Did you see how he got injured?" he asked Roxy.

"No." Roxy wrinkled her nose. "The woman must have noticed that I stole from her. She suspected Tibor was my accomplice and started hitting him with her handbag. Then he ran away. When he showed up at our meeting point, he told me his leg caught on a rusty nail while climbing over a wall."

"You've gotten us into quite a mess." Marek ran his hand through his hair. "The police are probably looking for him."

"I walked back in our footsteps to check if he'd left blood drops that could give us away." Roxy was very proud of her clever action.

"That only helps so much. If the police send out search parties combing the area, they'll find us either way. We need to leave this place instantly."

"Tibor can't walk," Romeo objected.

"Then he stays here. Better just him getting caught than all four of us." Marek didn't even blink as he spoke these words.

"We're stronger together. Please," Roxy begged. "Help Tibor. You're the only one who can speak to a Polish doctor."

After some hesitation, Marek nodded. They bandaged Tibor's leg with a strip of cloth torn from his shirt. After nightfall they set out to find a doctor, leaving Romeo behind to guard their belongings.

In a quiet side street they found a small practice that was still open. Marek knocked on the door. An older man opened and said something in Polish. Roxy didn't understand what they were discussing, however she got the distinct impression that the doctor wasn't pleased.

As Marek pointed to Tibor, who was hanging onto Roxy like a wet sack, the doctor shook his head slamming the door in their faces. But Roxy was too quick for him and managed to stick her foot in the door just in time.

"Please," she said. "Our friend urgently needs help."

"He needs to go to a hospital," the man replied in surprisingly good German.

"That's not possible, he doesn't have papers." Roxy received a scolding look from Marek for her statement.

The doctor backed away as if she were holding a venomous snake, even as his eyes implored her. "Please, I can't do anything for him. If you value your life, leave and never return."

While Roxy was still thinking about how to persuade the doctor to help her cousin, Marek pulled a knife from his pocket, holding it to the man's throat. "I'm sorry, but that's not an option. The boy will die if you don't treat his wound."

"Come in," the doctor croaked. Without further ado, he backed up through the hallway, his gaze fixed on the knife in Marek's hand. As he reached the examination room, his trembling hand pointed to a cot. Tibor detached himself from Roxy and limped toward it, collapsing onto it with a heart-rending groan.

Fascinated, Roxy watched as the doctor cleaned and stitched Tibor's wound, until a clicking sound caught her attention. She crept on tiptoe to a door she hadn't noticed before and peeked into the adjacent room. Behind the desk sat a nurse, whispering into the telephone. Roxy wanted to slap herself for not checking whether other people apart from the doctor were in the practice. She rushed to the woman, yanked the receiver from her hand and slammed it onto the cradle.

"The assistant called the police! We need to leave right now," Roxy shouted, leaving the frightened woman sitting at the desk as she raced to the treatment room.

Marek cursed, grabbing the doctor by the collar, who dropped in shock the flat-nose pliers he'd been using to treat Tibor's wound. Marek spoke to him in Polish, the old man nodded, hastily stuck a large bandage on Tibor's leg and pointed to the hallway.

Before leaving, Roxy bent down for the pliers and pocketed them. One never knew when a tool might come in handy. She and Marek took Tibor between them, as they hurried through the hallway and out the back door. It wasn't long before she heard screeching brakes, loud voices, and heavy boots on the pavement. Panting with fear and exertion in equal measure, they hurried onward as fast as Tibor's condition allowed.

They were too slow. The footsteps closed in and would reach them within a few seconds.

In that moment Roxy spotted a fire escape. "We have to split up! I'll take the route over the rooftops!"

"Roxy, no!" Tibor called out, but she was already climbing onto the roof, where she lay flat on her stomach and peered down. Marek and Tibor did the only sensible thing and separated from each other; one turned right at the corner, the other left. Regardless, it didn't help, because four policemen took up their pursuit. Neither Marek nor Tibor had a chance.

Frozen with fear Roxy witnessed how her friends were thrown to the ground and led away in handcuffs. In a crouched position, she followed them across the rooftops, hoping to find out where they were being taken. At the other end of the alley, Marek and Tibor were shoved into the waiting police car. Shortly after, it sped away at breakneck speed. Any further pursuit was pointless.

Shaken to the core, Roxy continued jumping from roof to roof until she eventually found a way down. Back on the street, she trudged with slumped shoulders toward their hideout.

At the sight of her, Romeo backed away. "What happened? Where are the others?"

"Caught by the police. I couldn't do anything."

"Damn it all!" he burst out.

"We need to leave," Roxy whispered.

They both knew it: under torture, their friends wouldn't hold out for long until they revealed the hideout.

"And where should we go?"

"Anywhere, just away from here." Roxy gathered her belongings. "Once we're far enough from Warsaw, we'll organize decent clothes so we don't stand out."

"We can't just leave them behind."

Roxy paused and stared at Romeo. "The police arrested them. By now they're probably in the Pawiak Prison. We can't do anything for them. We can only save ourselves." Her own words tore Roxy's heart apart. Losing Tibor was bad enough, but Marek… it felt almost the same way it did after her father's death, when she had stared into space for weeks because the pain had threatened to crush her.

Since Romeo made no move to get going, she asked, "Are you coming with me or do I have to go alone?"

He shook himself. "I'm coming."

26

The handcuffs cut into Marek's wrists as he was manhandled toward the police car. Next to him, Tibor's face contorted in pain from limping the short distance.

"Where's your accomplice?" asked the older policeman in broken Polish.

Marek bit his tongue. He'd seen Roxy climbing onto the roof and hoped with all his might that she'd managed to escape.

"We know there were three of you. Where is he?"

Marek mulled over the decision whether he should answer in Polish or in German. Both alternatives had advantages. Perhaps speaking German might give him a bit of goodwill with the policeman, since the Nazis considered Poles an inferior race. Thinking on his feet, he decided to go with German. In his thickest Viennese accent he answered, "I have no idea what you're talking about."

The policeman's eyes narrowed. "You speak German? That makes things easier. So, where is the third man?"

"There's just two of us."

A blow with the rifle butt struck Marek on the chin. The

metallic taste of blood filled his mouth, yet he remained silent. He'd endured far worse.

"Don't worry, you'll talk soon enough." The policeman smirked. "The Gestapo knows how to handle the stubborn ones like you."

They'd reached the police car and Marek and Tibor were manhandled inside. The vehicle bumped through the city at a breakneck speed. Marek cast a worried side glance at Tibor, whose jaw clenched tighter at every turn or pothole. Beads of sweat glistened on his face and his eyes took on a glassy expression. Marek feared the boy might pass out at any moment.

After a short drive, the car stopped in front of a gloomy building featuring barred windows. One of the policemen opened the door and dragged them out of the vehicle and into the building, while the other one kept his weapon trained on them. This must be the infamous Pawiak Prison.

Tibor swayed on wobbly knees, so much that Marek put an arm around his waist. At the end of a long corridor, they were shoved into an empty cell. As the door slammed shut behind them, despair curdled Marek's insides. He dreaded the thought that they'd never again leave this place that reeked of urine, sweat, and naked fear. Once Marek calmed himself down, he inspected the cell. Bare stone walls etched with scratches; in the corner stood a bucket. Nothing else.

Suppressed whimpering reached his ear from the neighboring cells. Marek had had enough experience with Kommandant Goslar's sadistic punishments in the camp to not have any illusions about why his cell neighbors were moaning so pitifully —and what awaited Tibor and him.

The next morning, a guard came and asked for papers.

"I'm sorry, our papers were stolen," Marek answered for both of them, since Tibor dozed in a feverish half-sleep.

The guard made a skeptical grimace. "Everyone claims the same. Name, residence, date of birth." He pulled out a notepad.

Marek cast a worried glance at Tibor. "Please, this boy urgently needs a doctor."

"He looks fine to me," replied the guard. "What's your friend's name?"

"Tibor."

The guard frowned. "An unusual name. Where's he from?"

Marek could have slapped himself for letting the name slip out. "From Berlin, as far as I know."

"I see, and how did he get to Warsaw?"

"I'm sorry, I don't know. We just met a few days ago." Marek was on guard, he wouldn't provide any more incriminating information.

"Your name?"

"Mark Huber, butcher from Vienna." Again, he put on his thickest Austrian accent to emphasize his words.

"Vienna? Really? You don't look like an Austrian. Are you sure you're not an escaped Jew?"

Marek feigned indignation. "Listen! I'm certainly not a Jew."

"We'll find out. If you're lying..." The guard left the threat hanging unspoken in the room. Regardless, it was enough to freeze the blood in Marek's veins.

"Where are your papers?"

"As I said, they were stolen. We were ambushed from behind. There were three or four men, they took everything from us: money, papers, even our coats."

"Very convenient." The guard jotted something down.

Marek breathed slowly in and out to fight the rising panic. He needed to keep a clear head if he wanted to have the slightest chance of getting through this situation unharmed.

"Why did you go to the doctor?"

"My acquaintance was injured during the attack. A rusty nail ripped open his leg." Marek pointed to Tibor's bandaged leg. "The doctor wouldn't treat us because we didn't have papers."

"Is that why you held a knife to his throat?"

Marek lowered his gaze, feigning remorse. "I'm sorry, I made a mistake. It was a rash decision. I was desperate and couldn't think clearly. You must believe me, I never intended to hurt the doctor, I just wanted to scare him a little."

"Why didn't you go to the police?"

Because you dirty pigs would've locked us up immediately. "I was afraid the boy would die, so I planned to report to the police once his wound was stitched."

The guard snorted in disbelief. "Lies, nothing but lies. I'll tell you what happened: The attack is a fabrication. You and your little friend don't have papers because you're dirty Jews."

"We're not Jews," Marek insisted. That was true, however being a Sinto or a Roma was no better in the Nazis' book.

"Then you're asocials, criminals, or some other scum. Only people who have something to hide travel without identity cards. But,"—the guard pursed his lips—"the Gestapo always finds out the truth. Sometimes it just takes a little bit longer. If you want to shorten the process, you'd better come clean right away. It'll save you plenty of trouble."

Marek sensed an opportunity and pleaded, "Please, my friend urgently needs medical care. You can see what a pitiful state he's in."

The guard cast a scrutinizing look at the feverish Tibor. "I'll see what I can do."

With that, he left the cell. Marek sank to the cold floor next to Tibor, placing a hand on his scorching hot forehead. Despite the fever burning up his body, the boy was shivering. Due to the rough treatment during the escape and subsequent arrest, the fresh suture had burst open and the gaping wound on his leg was oozing.

"Hang in there, boy," Marek implored Tibor.

Tibor half-opened his eyes with difficulty. "What... what did you tell him?"

"I'm Mark Huber, butcher from Vienna, and you're Tibor from Berlin," whispered Marek. "If they ask you anything, pretend you can't remember. Just tell them your name, nothing else. And don't ever admit that you're a Roma."

Tibor nodded. "Got it." Then his eyes closed again. He fell into a restless sleep, interrupted by groaning and whimpering.

The day dragged on and nothing happened. Food was pushed through a hatch in the door. Although it smelled disgusting, Marek devoured it at lightning speed. Since his arrest, he hadn't eaten anything.

Once he finished his portion, he propped Tibor up against the wall and poured small sips of the awful soup into him. "Eat, so you can regain your strength."

The hours passed in paralyzing boredom. At irregular intervals, neighboring cell doors were opened and closed. Sometimes he heard tormented groaning when a prisoner was brought back from an interrogation. Fear of what awaited him gnawed through Marek's insides.

Gathering the last ounce of his willpower, he pushed aside the gloomy thoughts, forcing his mind to wander. It didn't take long until he thought of Roxy. He hoped, prayed, begged that she'd successfully escaped. The police apparently knew of her existence, or they wouldn't have asked about the accomplice. However, they seemed to believe the third member of the group was a man, which increased her chances of remaining undetected.

If anyone could hide from the police, it was her. In the next moment, fear choked the air from his lungs, because he knew this much about himself: once the Gestapo tortured him, he wouldn't remain silent for long. He'd talk like a waterfall and betray everyone he knew—including the girl he'd come to love like a daughter.

His only comfort was that she'd taken his warning seriously and trusted nobody—especially not him. By the time the Gestapo found the hideout, she'd be long gone.

A dull pain pulsed through his body. After receiving news of Rosa's and Stefan's deaths, he'd fallen into a hollow. He'd never wanted to care for another person again. And then he'd met Roxy. The peewee had crept into his heart a little more each day. At first he'd fought his emotions, until he realized that he was powerless and his heart had adopted her as a daughter. He'd never admit it to her, since she was skittish and independent; and he didn't know how she'd react.

The light falling through the barred window high up on the wall grew paler, until Marek wasn't able to make out more than shadowy outlines in the cell. But even without seeing anything, it was clear that Tibor's condition was deteriorating. His breathing became irregular with a wheezing sound, as if it caused him great effort. Marek reached for the boy's forehead, which alternated between burning hot and ice-cold.

Mentally, he steeled himself for the possibility that the boy wouldn't survive the night. Tibor was just another loss plastering Marek's path, the way so many had done during the past year. Yet he failed to establish the desired inner distance. He cursed for allowing himself to care again. The moment he'd given Roxy the advice on how to stay alive in the camp had forever changed him.

At some point, footsteps sounded in the corridor. They stopped directly in front of the cell. A key jangled, the door opened, and bright light shone in. Marek held a hand over his eyes against the sudden glare. A man in a white coat entered, followed by an SS man.

"Where's the injured one?" asked the SS man, as if it wasn't obvious.

"There." His gaze lowered, Marek pointed to Tibor lying on the cold floor.

The doctor bent down, feeling his carotid artery. "He's still alive. Irregular pulse, weak breathing. He needs to go to the infirmary."

"Well then." The SS man kicked Tibor in the side. "Get up."

With Marek's help, Tibor struggled to his feet and staggered toward the door. Just before he reached it, he wobbled and bumped into the doctor. After steadying him, the doctor ordered the SS man, "Brace him, the prisoner won't make it on his own."

"Do I look like I want to touch this piece of filth?" growled the SS man, before he turned to Marek. "You, help the prisoner."

"Yes, sir." Marek slung Tibor's arm around his shoulders, grasping his waist. The boy stumbled along on wobbly knees.

Every time Tibor faltered, the SS man jabbed his rifle butt into Marek's back. Boiling anger crept up his throat. He yearned to smash the guard's face with an uppercut. Unfortunately, that wasn't an option. Instead, his anger turned against Tibor, who'd gotten him into this situation in the first place.

Inwardly cursing, Marek walked through the corridor. At each step, Tibor became limper, until most of his weight hung on Marek, his feet dragging across the floor more than he actually walked. Despite being pulled down by Tibor, Marek somehow managed to keep his head up, studying his surroundings.

Cell doors lined the walls to the left and right until they passed a staircase. The memories of the night when they'd been brought here were blurry, yet Marek's heart sped up as he recognized the stairs down to the entrance hall. He filed that knowledge away, wanting to be prepared, if an opportunity to escape presented itself. In any case he preferred to be shot in the back rather than being tortured by the Gestapo.

"I'm dying," Tibor suddenly whispered. "You must find Roxy. Promise me you won't abandon her."

"Hey! No talking!" hissed the SS man and hit Tibor on the back of the head with his flat palm.

"Forgive us," Marek intervened. "The boy is babbling nonsense in his fever delirium."

A few meters further, Tibor leaned heavily against Marek, gasping. "I'll create a distraction so you can escape," he whispered barely audible. "Be ready."

Marek doubted that Tibor was able to plan a distraction in his current state, let alone carry it out. Nonetheless, he squeezed the boy's elbow as a sign that he'd understood.

At the end of the corridor lay the infirmary—a large room with about a dozen beds, most of them occupied. Two nurses stood gossiping in a corner, enveloped in a halo of cigarette smoke clouds. Their patients' heart-wrenching whimpering didn't seem to bother them. A white doctor's coat hung on the coat rack next to the door. On a table lay bandages, tablets and a stethoscope.

"Hurry up, bring him over there." The doctor who'd accompanied them pointed to an empty bed, just as a door opened at the other side of the room.

Another man in a white coat entered, grimacing. "God, it stinks in here." At his beckoning a nurse opened a window. Fresh air instantly wafted inside.

Marek sensed an opportunity to escape. But his hope was shattered as soon as he spotted the bars in the window frame. Just before they reached the empty bed, Tibor groaned loudly. In the next second, his arms were flailing through the air, while his legs kicked wildly. Marek brought himself out of the danger zone through a decisive jump backward.

"He's having a seizure!" someone shouted.

The nurses put their cigarettes in the ashtray and cautiously approached the convulsing boy. His back arched, his arms and legs twitched uncontrollably.

"Come on, subdue him!" the doctor ordered the SS man, who walked toward Tibor a disgusted grimace on his face. All eyes were fixed on the collapsing boy. Nobody was paying attention to Marek.

Whether Tibor was indeed dying or was staging the seizure, Marek didn't know. Neither did he care. Either way he couldn't do anything for Tibor, except save himself and find Roxy as promised. His eyes scanned the scene swiftly. The infirmary had two exits: the door through which the second doctor had entered and the door into the long corridor that led past the staircase into the cell block.

In a split second, Marek decided on the long corridor, because he had no idea what lay behind the side door. In two strides he reached the coat rack and grabbed the white coat. From the corner of his eye, he witnessed how Tibor's body went limp and his eyes rolled back. A theatrical rattle escaped his throat. It was the end.

Marek didn't waste time to mourn. He slipped on the coat, grabbed the stethoscope and hung it around his neck.

"He's dead," one of the nurses said.

"Check it," ordered a harsh voice.

Marek didn't hear the confirmation, because he left the infirmary in measured steps. His nerves stretched to a breaking point, he waited for someone to sound the alarm. But everything remained quiet. In the empty corridor Marek turned left toward the street and hurried down the steps to the ground floor.

He vaguely remembered the huge foyer. At its end was a door, which must be the exit from the building. A guard sat behind a wooden table reading a newspaper.

Marek forced himself to stay calm. Squaring his shoulders, he strode toward the exit with the self-confidence of a legitimate doctor. His throat constricted with anxiety, he approached the guard, greeting him with a brief nod. The guard mechanically returned the greeting, his eyes never deviating from his newspaper.

Seconds later, Marek stood on the street. A bus puttered by. Pedestrians walked in both directions. The siren of a police car blared. It was high time to disappear. He mingled with the crowd and marched down the street, radiating arrogance in his white coat on his way home after the end of his shift.

Two intersections later, he slipped out of the doctor's coat and stuffed it, along with the stethoscope, beneath the rubble of a bombed-out ruin. A triumphant smile played around the corners of his mouth. He was free again.

The relief quickly gave way to grief for Tibor and concern for Roxy. He'd promised to find her, so he pushed aside all caution and decided to visit their hiding place.

27

Roxy sat on a stack of logs, her knees pulled up to her chin. The shock of Tibor's and Marek's arrest had transformed into a dull despair. On top of that, Romeo was grating on her nerves. He questioned every suggestion she made, always wanting to do the exact opposite.

For twenty-four hours, they'd been constantly on the move until they'd settled in a timber company's storage yard. At least until the next morning they should be safe here.

"We need to free Tibor," Romeo suddenly suggested.

"We don't even know where he is."

"Then we'll search for him." Romeo planted himself in front of her, arms crossed, legs spread wide.

"Let's assume we find him. What are you planning to do next? March into the prison and order the police to release him?" Roxy looked up.

"It's worth a try. We'll tell them Tibor hasn't done anything wrong."

"Meanwhile they must have found out he's a Roma, which means they'll arrest us too." Roxy brushed a curl from her forehead. Her hair had reached the annoying length— long enough to fall into her eyes but too short to tuck behind her ears.

"You don't know that." Romeo took his pocketknife into his hand, playing with the blade.

"On the contrary, I know exactly." She stood up, positioned herself next to him. "Listen, Romeo. I'm sad too, but we can't do anything for Tibor and Marek. We can only save ourselves."

Romeo shook his head violently. "What kind of cold-hearted beast are you?"

The words hit her like a slap across the face. "That's unfair. I dragged Tibor halfway across the city searching for a doctor while you sat on your behind in the hideout."

"You abandoned him the moment the police showed up."

"What should I have done? Get arrested with them?" Boiling anger bubbled inside her body. "Then all three of us would be in a cell. I could help even less from inside the prison."

"Who says you're helping? I don't see you lifting a single finger!" Romeo stepped closer, his eyes flashing with rage. "You always think only about yourself. Uncle Gottfried was right; your selfish behavior puts the whole clan in danger."

The fury clouded her mind, the words bursting out before she could bite her tongue. "At least I don't betray my closest relatives."

"Excuse me? What kind of accusation is that? When have I ever betrayed you?"

"In Belzec. You told Uncle Gottfried that you saw me with Livia at the kitchen barracks," Roxy snarled. "And Tibor ratted me out when I tried to steal medicine for Christian. So much for family solidarity."

Romeo stared at her in disbelief. "You're still holding that against us?"

"Because of you, I was forced to work in the Sonderkommando. Do you think that was a walk in the park?" In her mind's eye, she relived the scene when Kommandant Goslar had stolen her horse pendant. Unbridled hatred for the Nazis boiled in her veins.

"Why do you always assume you're exempt from the rules? We all broke our backs working."

"Oh really? Because Uncle Gottfried had nothing more urgent to do than rat me out to the camp administration, I had to dig mass graves for months." The memory of the terrible things she'd been forced to do emerged from deep inside her soul until she fought hard against the urge to gag. But she wouldn't give Romeo the satisfaction of throwing up in front of him.

He didn't seem to notice her emotional turmoil and stared at her with cold glinting eyes. "Is that the reason you don't want to free Tibor? Then you're even more selfish than I thought."

"That's not true." Tears of rage burned in her eyes. "I always wanted us to escape together. Didn't I beg him a hundred times to run away with me? But he wouldn't. He preferred to stay with the family, even after Uncle Gottfried sold me out for a position in the camp hierarchy!"

"Uncle Gottfried is the family patriarch. He just tried to protect us. All of us."

"Oh yes? By trading me for a private partition in the barracks?" Roxy gave a bitter laugh.

Romeo snorted. "You don't understand anything. Sometimes you have to make sacrifices for the family. But you don't care about anyone, you just think about your own advantage. Aunt Gisela and Uncle Gottfried should've dropped you off in an orphanage back then, instead of taking you in. None of this would've happened without you."

His words struck Roxy like a knife to the heart. She stumbled backward. For a few seconds there was dead silence. Only their gasping breaths could be heard. Her insides burnt like fire. "So now I'm to blame for the Nazis putting us in a camp?"

"That's not what I meant," Romeo protested lamely.

"Save your apology." The fury evaporating, leaving behind a huge hollow in her heart, she grabbed the bundle lying by her side and stood up.

"What are you doing?" A hint of insecurity resonated in his voice.

"What do you think? I'm doing you a favor and disappearing from your life," she snarled, taking the remains of the loaf of bread and breaking it in half. "Don't worry, I'm not as cold-hearted as you believe. I'm going to let you have half the provisions."

"Don't be ridiculous, Roxy. You can't just up and leave."

"Actually, I can. As you so nicely put it, I've been nothing but a burden all these years." She tossed him the bread and shouldered her bag. "An orphan taken in because it was the right thing to do. From now on, you're rid of me. Congratulations." She climbed over the wooden beams.

Romeo followed her. "It's not safe for you alone on the streets."

"It isn't safe with you either." She flashed him a contemptuous look.

"Where are you going?" The pitiful expression in his eyes indicated that he was afraid of being left alone.

"That's none of your business." Without looking back, she set off. She didn't care whether Romeo followed her or not. If necessary, she'd shake him off eventually.

As she walked, her anger subsided. For a moment, she doubted whether she'd made the correct decision. Four eyes saw more than two. Then she shook her head vigorously. No. Marek had been right. She was better off on her own.

She'd take his advice to heart and never trust another person again for as long as she lived. A tug in her chest made her wince. Although she'd only known Marek for a short time, she missed him more than she cared to admit. Instead of her biological uncle, she'd have preferred Marek as a surrogate father. No matter how much he pretended not to care about the suffering of the people around him, she'd always felt shepherded in his presence. And respected. He didn't treat her in the condescending way most adults did; on the contrary, he listened and valued her opinion.

Her eyes grew moist. Defiantly, she wiped away the emerging tears and squared her shoulders. Now wasn't the time to be sentimental. She didn't have a family anymore—and since Marek's arrest, no friends either. From now on, she was on her own. It was for the best.

It was late in the evening when Roxy reached the freight train station. For hours, she'd crept through the streets of Warsaw, always careful to avoid German patrols, since she had no papers and certainly didn't want to be detained. Exhausted to the bone, she settled behind a stack of wooden crates. From there, she had a good view of the tracks while being protected from curious glances.

Despite ravenous hunger rumbling in her stomach, she didn't touch the bread. It was unclear when she'd be able to organize something edible again, thus she wanted to be frugal with her supplies.

The hours passed. A nasty sleet soaked her to the skin, still she didn't move from her vantage spot, as she patiently waited. A freight train pulled in, workers unloaded crates, before it moved empty onto the siding. Disappointment, combined with the cold sleet, made Roxy shiver. Still, she waited.

Another train stopped but remained closed while guards patrolled around it. Roxy's eyelids grew heavy. She'd hardly slept since the momentous visit to the doctor. Shivering, she leaned against a wooden crate. Eventually, her head fell back and she drifted into a restless sleep.

Metallic squeaking tore her from her dreams. She sat up and blinked several times to dispel the disorientation. In the east, a bright-blue stripe was drawing up the sky. Pale light announced another foggy-gray winter day. On the tracks, a long freight train rattled forward until it came to a stop right in front of her.

Her heart pounding louder than the rattling locomotive, she crept along the track in a crouched position until she discovered a wagon with an open door. She waited until the workers walked away to fetch new crates, before she peered inside—the wagon was approximately half-full, offering enough space to hide. Casting a glance over her shoulder, she reassured herself that no one was watching. Then she prepared to jump.

"I wouldn't do that," a voice hissed behind her.

Ready to flee, Roxy whirled around, freezing mid-movement once she recognized the figure standing a few steps away from her.

28

"And why not?" she whispered, defiantly pushing out her lower lip. Despite her decision never to trust another person again, she was glad to see him.

Marek put a finger to his lips and pulled her away from the train behind a pile of coal. "This train goes to Russia. You don't want to go there."

Roxy shook her head. "How would you know that?"

"That the train goes to Russia or that you don't want to go there?" he asked with a chuckle.

"The former," Roxy growled.

"Because I read the freight papers. A train to Berlin will be passing through in an hour."

"I don't need your help," Roxy protested, although she couldn't suppress a happy grin from spreading from ear to ear. "I can manage on my own."

"Sure you can. But I could do with your help."

Roxy bit her lip. She knew he was lying to spare her pride. It was eerie how well he knew her. Better than anyone in her family, perhaps even better than Tibor. A sense of foreboding tickled her skin. So, she asked, "How did you escape?"

"I'll tell you later. We'll have plenty of time to talk on the train to Berlin. First, we need to take care of a few things, including organizing provisions for the journey." He made it sound as if they could simply stroll to the nearest shop to buy food.

"I have some bread with me," Roxy replied, not wanting him to believe she'd skipped over crucial preparations.

"More is better. We might be on the road for several days."

Roxy's eyes widened. She'd calculated that the train would need about eight hours from Warsaw to Berlin.

Marek continued, "Over there is the cafeteria for the railway workers. The produce just arrived on the train you were about to jump onto."

She followed him to a flat building where crates of vegetables, bread and meat stood in the yard. Roxy wanted to pounce on the meat, but Marek held her back. "Better leave that alone. First, we can't cook it, and second, the dogs will smell it immediately."

"Do you think they're going to search for us with dogs?"

"Probably not, but you can never rule it out. More likely, a dog might smell the meat by chance and start barking. We don't want to take such a risk."

Her stomach protesting, Roxy left the meat behind and instead stuffed her bag full with other food until it was bursting at the seams. Once they were done, they hid between large wooden crates and waited for the train to Berlin.

It wasn't long before it announced itself with a long whistle, rolling slowly into the freight yard. They waited until the unloading was finished before choosing a wagon into which workers were loading furniture. As soon as the workers turned their backs, Roxy and Marek climbed into the wagon, hiding behind a huge wardrobe.

A few minutes later, the loading was complete. The workers left, slammed the doors shut and bolted them from the outside.

It went dark in the wagon, only a few rays of sunlight streaming through the cracks in the wooden walls. Roxy fought the urge to rush to the door and pound it with her fists to be let out.

It didn't take long for her eyes to adjust to the dim light. As she crawled out from behind the wardrobe, her panic dissipated. A broad grin appeared on her face. "Incredible," she whispered. "There's an entire living room in here."

A loud whistle rang out, chilling her to the bone. A moment later the train jerked forward. Roxy exhaled slowly, she absolutely needed to get her nerves under control. If she continued acting like a frightened rabbit, this journey wouldn't end well. At least for now, they were safe in the wagon.

The locomotive accelerated; the wagon bumped and swayed. Roxy stumbled. At the last second, she managed to grab hold of a table to avoid being thrown against the wardrobe. Her fingers cramped around the edge, she wondered how long she'd have to endure the wild jolting, while her eyes searched for a more comfortable place. After a few minutes, the ride became smoother, giving Roxy the chance to explore the wagon. Next to the wardrobe, there was a table, a dresser, stacked chairs, various boxes, and a sofa. She chuckled. "It's quite cozy in here."

"At least we're traveling in style." Marek flopped onto the sofa. "Now let's have something to eat."

They lounged on the sofa, feet on a box under the table, devouring their plundered provisions. Roxy alternated between bread and vegetables until, munching, she asked, "Where did they take you after the arrest? And where's Tibor?"

"To Pawiak Prison."

Goosebumps covered Roxy's skin, since she'd heard many terrible rumors about the notorious Gestapo prison for political prisoners. The methods the Nazis used to treat the Polish resistance were even more gruesome than what they did to the inmates in the labor camps. Not many survived the brutal torture.

"Tibor's condition worsened while we were stuck in the cell. I begged the guards several times for a doctor. This morning one finally looked at him and ordered him to be transferred to the infirmary."

Roxy's inner tension eased a little. Her cousin was being cared for and relatively safe, at least for the time being. The next moment, guilt shot through her like a lightning strike. If she'd stayed in Warsaw, as Romeo had suggested, they might have had a chance to free Tibor.

She nibbled on a piece of carrot. "And how did you escape?"

"Tibor couldn't walk on his own, so the guard ordered me to carry him to the infirmary. On the way, Tibor whispered in my ear that he'd create a distraction so I could escape."

"Clever boy." Roxy was damn proud of her cousin. So much so that she forgave him for ratting her out. One day, after the war, they'd hopefully meet up. Then they'd properly reconcile and become best friends again.

"He had a seizure and collapsed. I used the opportunity to throw on a doctor's coat and simply marched out of the building."

"Well done," Roxy praised him. Marek possessed an admirable presence of mind. He definitely was a fighter. "What about Tibor? Do you think he'll be punished for his act?"

Marek stayed silent far too long. Goosebumps crept across the skin of her arms. She was about to repeat her question when he finally said, "He's dead, Roxy."

"Dead? No, he created a distraction so you could escape." She stared at him. "That's what you said. I heard it clearly."

"I'm so sorry. That's what I thought at first too." Marek paused, seemingly searching for words. "The seizure wasn't fake, it was real. Just as I walked out the door, one of the nurses said, 'He's dead.'"

"Dead? But he was only sixteen." The idea that her best

friend was gone for good didn't register in her brain. They'd just been lying in wait together to steal bread, and now he was supposed to be gone—forever?

Roxy shook her head. "That's not possible. He wouldn't just die from a stupid scratch on his leg. Not after everything he went through."

"I'm sorry, but it's true. He got very ill in prison. On the way to the infirmary, he told me he was going to die. I didn't take his words seriously, thinking it was the fever speaking. But he knew."

Roxy braced herself for the impact of grief. But it didn't come. She felt nothing. There was just a huge black hollow in her soul. No emotions, except for relief that Tibor hadn't told anyone that she and Romeo were hiding somewhere in Warsaw. To drown out the terrible emptiness in her chest, she said, "He was lucky they didn't torture him."

Marek's voice sounded concerned. "You're taking the news surprisingly calmly."

"What do you expect me to do? Bawling won't bring him back." Her words were sharper than she'd intended. She despised herself for not grieving. The Nazis had turned her into an unfeeling chump, numb to human misery. So many of her friends and family members had died in the past year. Christian, Livia, five of the little children, Gisela's elderly mother, several cousins, aunts and uncles hadn't survived the camp in Belzec, and more relatives had died in Krychow.

Tibor was just another death in an endless chain of loss. She shrugged. More than ever, she was on her own. Completely and utterly alone. If she wanted to survive, she had to stay cool. Feelings clouded the mind and diminished her chances of survival.

"He's your cousin, it's completely normal to be sad."

"Family are those who don't abandon you." Roxy pressed her lips together. "Not those you happen to be related to."

Marek was silent. Once again, she wished he'd been her surrogate father, not Uncle Gottfried. Marek was the only adult who'd taken her seriously, instead of putting obstacles in her way any time he could.

Her full stomach and the sensation of being able to breathe freely again caused her to sink against the back of the sofa. Her eyelids grew heavy. After a while the steady rattling lulled Roxy to sleep. At some point, she startled awake. A ray of sunlight, piercing through the roof of the wagon, tickled her nose.

"Sleep well?" asked Marek.

Indignantly, she pursed her lips. "I wasn't sleeping, I was wide awake and just resting my eyes."

He chuckled. "Of course you were. You didn't miss much. The train stopped a few times, but as far as I could tell, nothing was loaded or unloaded." He ran his hand over his head. "It's nice, for a change, not to be on the run."

"I'm thirsty." She changed the subject, since she didn't want to think about their escape or Tibor's death. She rummaged in her bag for the water bottle.

"Listen," Marek said after a while. "Even when we arrive in Berlin, we are still far from safe. We don't have proper papers, so we'll have to go into hiding."

"Believe me, I know that," Roxy growled, the terrible loss of her entire family fresh in her mind.

"Today we're escaping together. But tomorrow? Or the day after? Each of us is better off alone, less conspicuous. Besides,"—he paused for effect and looked at her seriously—"if the Gestapo catches me, I don't want to know where you are, then I can't betray you."

It was the nicest thing anyone had said to her in a long time. A soothing warmth filled her heart and spread from there to the tips of her toes. Roxy studied his furrowed face in the dim light streaming through the cracks in the wood. There was no falseness in it, just deep resignation. He wasn't promising her a better world. He wasn't lying to her with empty pledges. Instinctively, she knew that he'd do anything to protect her—even if he didn't admit it. He was truly a special man. "What should we do once we're in Germany?"

"We'll separate," Marek answered. "On our own each of us has a better chance to go underground than the two of us together."

"Exactly my opinion." She'd never admit that deep in her soul she wished they could stay together, like father and daughter. Or at least like friends, because she yearned with every fiber of her body for a well-meaning human soul by her side. Someone who understood her situation and didn't raise a moralizing eyebrow when she stole food or clothing.

After a while, she added, "Thank you."

"For what? I haven't done anything."

"You've done so much for me, even more than my own family. Tibor..." She paused to examine her feelings. After all, Tibor had been her best friend for years. But in her soul reigned an eerie emptiness. "It doesn't matter anyway. He's dead."

The train rattled through the landscape while Roxy and Marek stretched out on the sofa and slept. Day turned into night, forests and fields rushed by and with every minute that they moved away from the horrible camps, Roxy's heart felt lighter.

Once she returned to her familiar surroundings, she'd be fine.

29

The train's rattling changed its rhythm, causing Marek to open his eyes. A ray of light fell through a crack in the wagon wall, traveling across Roxy's sleeping face. She'd curled up like a cat, her head resting on her worn bag. Her short black hair stuck out in all directions, making her look even younger than she was. A warm feeling spread through his chest, because she reminded him so much of his youngest.

The warmth evaporated, replaced by leaden sadness. Every single day he missed Stefan and Rosa. Every day he wondered why he kept fighting. Until he told himself that his five daughters—if they were still alive—though already grown and independent, still needed him.

Marek sat up, listening. The train was slowing down. It was possible they'd already reached Berlin. He wanted to be prepared if an opportunity to disembark presented itself.

He touched Roxy's shoulder. "Wake up. We'll be there soon."

She was instantly wide awake, a trait he admired in her. In the camps, he'd witnessed adolescents her age gradually lose their vitality. The youths and children, except for the youngest who didn't fully comprehend what was happening around them, suffered even more than adults under the terrible conditions.

Roxy, however, had never let herself be defeated. Determination flashed in her blue eyes. She possessed an impressive resilience, which would help her overcome every obstacle fate placed in her path.

"I need to pee," Roxy announced, as she stretched her limbs.

"Find a corner."

She disappeared to the other end of the wagon. As she returned, she looked at him with an adventurous spark in her eyes. "What's our plan?"

"Our?" He raised an eyebrow. As much as he wished to protect her, he knew she'd be better off without him. One person, especially someone like Roxy, attracted less attention than two.

The familiar defiant expression appeared on her face. "I mean, how do we sneak out of the wagon unnoticed? The train station will be swarming with workers and guards. After that, we'll go our separate ways."

Marek gave a deep sigh. "I'm afraid we'll have to improvise."

"Great. I'm good at that." She grinned.

"Then let's get ready." He stuffed his things into his bag, searching the sofa and the floor for crumbs.

"What are you doing?" Roxy had already shouldered her bundle.

"I don't want to leave any traces. If nobody suspects uninvited guests were in here, they won't be searching for us."

She looked at him skeptically. "If they're not completely stupid, they'll smell it."

"Right." He hadn't thought about the nature's call they'd left behind. "Still. The fewer clues, the better." Marek pondered the best way to exit the wagon undetected. "We'll get out the same way we got in."

"That's too dangerous. From inside, we can't see if the train is guarded or where the workers are."

"Do you have a better idea?" Marek frowned.

A smug expression on her face Roxy pointed to the ceiling. "As a matter of fact, I do. We'll abscond through the roof."

Upon closer inspection, he discovered the hatch she was pointing at. If they stood on a crate, they could reach it. No sooner said than done. Roxy climbed up and unlocked the mechanism before pushing her shoulder against the hatch. Nothing moved.

"Let me try," said Marek after a while. In the dim light, he felt around the frame until he found what he was looking for. "There's a security wire. We need to open it somehow."

Marek pulled and tugged, but the wire didn't give a millimeter. As the train lurched around a curve, Marek lost his balance and cut his finger on the wire end. "Damn it!"

"What happened?" Roxy stood directly beneath him, holding his legs so he wouldn't slip off the crate.

"I cut myself." Discouraged, he slid to the floor. "I can't get the wire open."

"Try these." She held out flat-nosed pliers about the size of a palm.

"Where did you get these?" he asked, even though he suspected she'd pilfered the pliers from the doctor's office in Warsaw.

"Found them," Roxy answered without further explanation.

Now wasn't the right time for a conversation about morality, thus he took the tool and cut through the wire. As soon as he opened the hatch a crack, ice-cold air blew into the wagon.

"What do you see?" Roxy asked impatiently.

"Nothing yet. I need to climb higher." He hoisted himself up and tilted his head to peer through the narrow gap.

"Be careful that nobody sees you," Roxy warned.

"Why do you think I'm not opening the hatch all the way? So it's not noticeable from outside." Their nerves were stretched to breaking point. They couldn't afford to make mistakes if the entire escape wasn't to be in vain.

"I'm sorry." Roxy sounded genuinely contrite. "I don't want anything to go wrong at the last minute."

"Don't beat yourself up over it." To the right and left of their train lay tracks. "We seem to be entering a marshaling yard. There are wagons and locomotives everywhere. Railway workers are walking along the tracks."

"We need to be up on the roof before the train stops."

"Are you sure?" Marek had his doubts about whether this was a good idea.

"As long as the train is moving, the workers won't pay attention to it. Once it stops, we might not have enough time to climb onto the roof. I'd rather try my luck while the train is in motion."

"It's worth a try." He pushed the hatch further open until it stood vertically. The train had slowed to a walking pace. It could come to a complete stop any minute. "Hurry up."

Marek climbed onto the roof, where he pressed himself onto the surface as flat as a flounder, while Roxy handed him the two bags. By the time he'd stored them safely and was about to extend his hand to help her up, she was already lying next to him, closing the hatch.

"We should put the bags on our backs in case we need to move quickly," whispered Roxy.

"Then we'll be less nimble," Marek pointed out.

"We just need to get off the roof and slip away. We don't need to be particularly nimble for that, just fast. Every second counts if we want to avoid being discovered."

Marek got the impression Roxy was speaking from experience, which she'd gained way before her stay in the camp.

Under different circumstances he'd have scolded her for the forbidden activities, in their current situation though, it gave him a sense of security. At least he didn't have to worry about her. She had all the traits needed to survive living rough.

As soon as the train stopped, he crawled to the side of the roof away from the station facilities and slid down the wagon wall. Finally, he jumped. A sharp pain shot through his damaged ankle as he landed on the gravel. He lost his balance and fell to his knees. "Damn!"

From the corner of his eyes, he watched how Roxy leaped cat-like from the wagon roof and landed next to him. Ignoring the pain, he tried to stand up. But as soon as he put weight on his foot, his ankle gave way.

Roxy bent over him. "Are you hurt?"

"My bad ankle didn't like the jump at all. Come on, we need to hide." Contorting his face in pain, he limped off. Roxy slung his arm around her shoulders.

"What are you doing?" he snapped at her.

"Helping you, of course. The way you're limping, you won't get far."

"Don't be stupid. Get yourself to safety. I'll be fine." He glared at her, intent on scaring her away.

"I'm not leaving you behind." Roxy continued pulling him along.

"We agreed to separate as soon as we reached Berlin." Every step sent hellish pain from his foot up to his thigh.

She didn't dignify him with an answer. "There's a bush up ahead. We can hide there and assess the situation."

Her stubbornness drove him to fury. "Damn it, get out of here! Think about yourself!"

"Shut up and lean on me," she replied, unimpressed by his outburst.

Railway workers were approaching, and with them grew the danger of being heard. Since it wouldn't do any good to argue with the headstrong girl, he allowed her to help him. Gritting his teeth and leaning heavily on her, he limped the roughly twenty meters to the embankment, where they squeezed into a dense thicket.

As he peered through the branches, he involuntarily held his breath: two railway workers were circling the train, approaching the space he and Roxy had been just seconds earlier. Sweat trickled down his brow into his eyes, but he didn't dare wipe it off. Every movement could give their location away. Fortunately, the workers paid no attention to their surroundings since they seemed to be checking the wheels of the wagons.

Marek closed his eyes. Taking shallow breaths, he waited until the throbbing pain in his ankle subsided. As soon as the railway workers were out of sight, they'd need to find a better hiding place. He whispered, "You should've gone without me."

"Stop telling me what to do." Roxy examined him through narrowed eyes. "I won't leave you behind while you're unable to fend for yourself."

In that moment, she reminded him so much of Stefan that it pierced his heart. His son had shown the same stubbornness, the same carefree attitude, the same will to do right by his fellow humans. He shook off the sad memory. Stefan and Rosa were dead. Murdered by the Nazis.

He'd sworn himself to avenge them one day. When this madness was over, when Hitler and his henchmen were brought to justice, his time would come. For that, he needed to survive.

"Thank you," he said reluctantly.

"No worries." They fell silent until Roxy whispered, "I'll have a look around, you stay here."

He didn't protest. On the one hand, she wouldn't listen to him anyway, on the other hand, he wasn't able to stand up and go with her anyway. "Please be careful."

"I always am." The next second, she silently glided over the embankment and vanished from sight.

A mixture of pride and fear invading his heart, he stared in the direction she'd disappeared. If she were clever, she'd be gone for good, rather than tie a lame chump like him to her leg. But no matter how often he'd tried to drum the opposite into her, she was deeply loyal at heart.

Roxy would never leave him to his fate as long as he was trapped by his damaged ankle. If he was honest with himself, the thought reassured him. And made him smile.

30

Roxy climbed up the embankment to lie in wait. On the other side, she discovered something that made her heart beat faster. As she patiently waited until the coast was clear, she thought about Marek, sat in the bushes with his injured ankle and unable to walk properly. He'd impressed upon her dozens of times that she had to look out for herself first and that she should leave him behind for her own safety.

That had been her plan. It really had been. A common enemy had bonded them together. But until the day he'd led her and her cousins from the Krychow marshes to Warsaw, she wouldn't have wasted a second thought on him.

Since their escape together, he'd grown closer to her heart than she wanted to admit. She liked him more than all the other adults who'd been entrusted with her care. More than Aunt Gisela, more than Uncle Gottfried, and perhaps even a tiny bit more than her father, whose memory faded with each passing year, so that lately she often had difficulty recalling his face.

Automatically, she reached for the horse pendant around her neck. Its usual spot was empty. Wild ire ravaged her body and she clenched her hands into fists, swearing that Kommandant Goslar would one day pay for what he'd inflicted on her and so many others.

Almost unnoticed, Marek had taken up her father's place in her heart. Roxy shook her head. Nobody could take her father's place. Simply because she hadn't needed a guardian in a long time. She could very well take care of herself. If she were clever, she'd disappear this very instant.

Yet everything in her resisted abandoning Marek. Livia and Tibor were dead. Romeo had shown his true colors: he despised her. Practically her entire clan was dead or had betrayed her. Marek was the only person in the world who'd helped her without asking for anything in return. She owed it to him to get him to safety.

As soon as there were no pedestrians in sight on either side of the road, she climbed over the embankment and headed straight for a bicycle leaning against a fence. This was their ticket to freedom. Even with his injured ankle, Marek should be able to cover long distances using the bicycle. Getting closer, she noticed that the bicycle was secured with a wheel lock.

A grin spread across her face. The wheel lock could be broken off with just a little force.

Before walking the last few steps, she cast a gaze over her shoulder in all directions. Still nobody in sight. Seconds later, she was crouching next to the bicycle, giving the bracket of the wheel lock a forceful tug.

A barely audible crack made her heart leap with joy. She needed four more yanks before the lock hung limply downward and the back wheel rotated freely again. A triumphant smile flashing from ear to ear, she swung herself onto the much too large men's bicycle and rode away, sitting on the crossbar rather than the saddle.

Lacking a better plan, she deposited it at the embankment, hoping the owner wouldn't return during the short time she needed to fetch Marek.

He was massaging his ankle, which had swollen to almost twice its original size. "That was quick."

"Guess what I found?" She couldn't help giving a smug grin.

"A bag of gold?"

"Not quite, but almost. A bicycle."

Marek's eyes widened. "You stole a bicycle?"

"Borrowed," Roxy corrected him. "I'll return it as soon as we don't need it anymore. Now hurry up, we need to get going before someone discovers you."

Marek cast her a piercing gaze. She knew that look—he was about to order her to leave without him.

Before he could open his mouth, she tugged at his sleeve and said, "Stop it already. I'm not leaving you, so save the moral lecture. The bicycle is on the other side of the embankment, and the longer we wait, the greater the probability that the owner will miss it."

Gritting his teeth, Marek pulled himself up. He leaned much of his weight on Roxy until they reached the embankment, where they lay down and crawled up on their stomachs. Roxy peered over the edge onto the street. Everything was quiet. The bicycle stood exactly where she'd left it.

"See? There it is." She nudged Marek in the side. "It's not far. You can manage those few steps."

"I don't feel good about this." He rubbed his chin. "If I ride the bicycle, what will you do?"

"I'll walk alongside you."

"That's too conspicuous," he objected.

Roxy shrugged. "Then I'll sit on the luggage rack."

"That's even more conspicuous."

"Nonsense. People are always taking someone on their luggage rack. It's completely normal."

"I'm not sure about that..." It was obvious that Marek didn't like the idea of riding the bicycle.

"Do you have a better solution?"

"Unfortunately not."

"Come on then, it'll be fine. In any case, we can't stay here."

"If we must." Marek pulled himself up and limped with Roxy's help to the bicycle, where he awkwardly swung his injured foot over the saddle and sat down. As he drove off, the bicycle wobbled dangerously.

"Can you even ride a bicycle?" Looking at the serpentine lines he was making Roxy got the impression this was the real reason why he'd been so opposed to her idea.

"Of course I can. It's just been a while," he growled. His uncertain movements suggested that it must have been decades since he had last sat on this kind of saddle. Like a drunk, he swerved across the street and would soon attract the police's attention if his riding style didn't improve.

Hoping to stabilize the ride, Roxy jumped onto the luggage rack. It had the opposite effect: the bicycle threatened to tip over. Marek planted his good foot on the ground to avoid falling.

"You're too heavy," he gasped. "My ankle can't handle pedaling that hard."

Roxy jumped off. "I'll walk beside you."

She matched her pace to his slow ride, always careful to keep a proper distance so she could jump away in case he fell down. Fortunately, Marek became more confident with each turn of the pedals. At the next intersection, they crossed into a narrow side street.

"Where to?" Marek gasped between two labored breaths.

"Just away," Roxy decided on a whim. "Later we can rest and figure out what to do next."

"Hey! That's my bicycle!" shouted a worker.

The call was so unexpected that Marek all but fell over. Roxy whirled around. A man in blue overalls stormed down the street, his fist raised.

"Quick! Go faster!" Roxy gave the bicycle a push.

"Stop the thief!" the man bellowed at the top of his lungs.

Out of nowhere, two policemen appeared on the street.

"These damn Nazis, they have their people everywhere," Roxy cursed to herself.

"Stop! Now!" shouted the two police officers while racing toward the faltering bicycle.

For a fraction of a second, Roxy froze. She and Marek looked at each other.

"Run," he ordered. "Now!"

"But—"

"Do as I say, Roxy. I'm beyond saving. At least you should be free!" With a quick movement, he pushed her away. "Run! Go!"

She still hesitated. The police officers had almost reached them. Only a few more steps. In that moment, Marek let himself fall, along with the bicycle, directly at the feet of the policemen.

His gaze met hers once more. It was a desperate plea for her to survive. He'd created the distraction she needed to get away. She just needed to grab it with both hands.

"Thank you," she whispered, even as her legs began to move on their own account. Her heart pounding and her feet flying, she raced down the alley until she turned a corner.

Behind the cover of a two-story townhouse she caught her breath for a moment, listening for footsteps. The police hadn't taken up pursuit. Quickly, she climbed up the façade using the drainpipe. Upon reaching the roof, she pressed herself flat against the tiles and crawled upward until she reached the ridge, where she crouched behind the chimney.

From her position, she could peer down onto the street without being seen herself. With baited breath she observed what was happening, hoping with all her might that Marek would find a way to talk himself out of his predicament.

He stood with his hands raised next to one of the two

policemen. The second officer was checking the papers of the worker, who, panting from the fast run, held his bicycle in hand. The officer jotted something down and waved him away.

Then he joined his colleague. Roxy couldn't understand what was being said. Marek shook his head. They'd probably asked for his identification card. In the Third Reich, being without papers was a crime in itself. However, possessing a *Kennkarte* wouldn't have helped Marek: the stamped Z for *Zigeuner* (Gypsy) marked him as a subhuman without civil rights.

The police officers were discussing something, while Marek must be explaining his situation. They didn't seem to believe anything he said. The words "Jew" and "deserter" drifted up to her. Marek shook his head and lowered one hand, pointing to his ankle.

Marek's gesture sent the policemen into a panic, they barked loud commands while simultaneously reaching for their revolvers. Marek seemed just as startled as they were; he lost his balance, put weight on his injured ankle, and buckled.

Two shots cracked through the street.

Roxy pressed her hand to her mouth to keep from screaming out loud. Before her eyes, Marek collapsed. A dull thud signaled his body had fallen onto the asphalt. Slowly, a red stain spread near his chest.

Tears streamed unchecked down Roxy's face. Rigid as a statue, she crouched on the uncomfortable ridge, never taking her eyes off Marek. Down there lay the sole person she still cared for in this cruel world. Shot by two police officers.

During the last minutes of his life, his actions had belied his cynicism. He'd sacrificed himself so she could escape. He deserved her mourning. He also deserved for her to take this chance and run with it, yet she couldn't tear her gaze away from his body.

Only when one of the policemen gazed in all directions

searching for her did she overcome the paralysis and creep across the rooftops on nimble, bare feet, until she slid down a drainpipe at the end of the block.

The tears dried on her cheeks as she marched through the streets of Berlin, determined to survive against all odds. At each step, her heart grew a little colder. Her father, Christian, Livia, Tibor, Marek—every single person she'd liked was dead. Nobody was left but her.

She swore never to let anyone get close to her. Never again would she make the mistake of trusting another person or even liking them. A leaden emptiness filled her soul until the small flame of revenge began to spread through her veins, slow at first, then faster. Soon, all-consuming hatred for the Nazis set her entire being ablaze.

Roxy swore that she would survive. And one day, when Hitler's rule was over, she'd avenge herself, her friends, her family, as well as every single Roma and Sinti who'd suffered the Nazis' harassment.

Driven by her newfound mission, Roxy straightened her shoulders and disappeared into the maw of Germany's capital.

EPILOGUE

TWO YEARS LATER, BERLIN, SUMMER 1942

Sultry heat hung leaden over the city. Despite the late evening hour, the air shimmered over the asphalt. Roxy wiped the sweat from her forehead. On days like this one, the temptation to sleep beneath the open sky was great. But staying overnight in a park or on a flat roof was too risky.

The police were everywhere and loitering individuals were regularly apprehended. Since Roxy didn't have papers, she'd be arrested on the spot and would soon be on her way back to one of the camps.

That was her greatest fear. Never again did she want to return to the places where she'd spent the most horrific months of her life. Never again did she want to throw emaciated people into a mass grave. Never again did she want to endure the humiliations of the guards.

Faced with this notion, she'd rather bear the oppressive heat in an enclosed hiding place. During recent weeks, she'd spent the nights in a garden shed in an allotment colony. There she'd felt relatively safe because due to the danger of bombing the owners were forbidden to stay in the colony after dark.

Thanks to the oppressive heat, some owners weren't

following this rule anymore. In addition, some well-meaning people were allowing Jews to hide in their sheds. In principle, there was nothing wrong with that, after all, the Jews were in a similar predicament as Roxy herself.

But the more illegal occupants hiding in the garden colony, the greater the risk of discovery—especially since not every secret inhabitant behaved responsibly and stayed quiet. Thus, she'd made it a habit to change her location every two to three weeks. No matter how careful she was, someone always noticed something, even if it was just missing vegetables in the garden.

The heat had made her complacent, and she'd postponed the time when she'd need to find a new location. Last night though, she'd been disturbed by loud laughter. That had been the last straw. Alarmed, Roxy had packed her belongings into a scavenged backpack that very minute and left the garden colony.

Tips about safe and not-so-safe overnight accommodations constantly circulated among those living underground. For several reasons Roxy considered it too risky to sleep in the apartments of sympathetic Aryans, but when someone mentioned empty railway carriages standing for repair on the grounds of a locomotive workshop, her ears perked up.

The following afternoon, she scouted the area. The expansive grounds bordered the marshaling yard and were secured only by a wire fence. Roxy crouched in a bush, patiently observing the activity on the grounds.

Within the fenced area stood countless locomotives and wagons, as well as various metal sheds. As far as she could tell, spare parts were stored in huge piles. One of the passenger wagons would offer the perfect shelter for a night.

At the other end of the grounds, the huge workshop hall rose up with a glass roof gleaming in the sun. A smile played around her lips. The glass roof was perfect—it meant that due to blackout regulations, work was restricted during night. Thus, no workers should be found roaming the workshop after dark.

Word of mouth claimed that no guards patrolled the grounds, a fact she wanted to verify for herself before slipping inside. For several hours, Roxy remained patiently in her hiding place until calm settled over the locomotive workshop. Long after the last worker had left, she watched with eagle eyes for any movement on the premises.

Once she was assured that no one was around anymore, she slipped through a hole in the fence, heading straight for the parked wagons. The third one had an unlocked door. A feeling of euphoric happiness shot through Roxy's veins. She debated whether to bolt the door to avoid being surprised. However, that would trap her inside.

So she left the door unlocked for now and explored the interior of the passenger wagon. From the corridor, she glanced into the first compartment. The low-hanging sun blinded her and she raised her hand to shield her eyes.

At the second compartment, she paused. Under the bench stood a bottle of water, beside it lay something wrapped in brown paper that strongly resembled a sandwich. Instantly, the hair on the back of her neck stood up. It was unmistakable that someone had deliberately placed these items here. The question was, who had done it, and why, or rather, for whom?

Was it a sympathizer of illegal people, offering them a place for the night by leaving the railway cars unlocked and edibles in the compartment? Or had the food come from the Gestapo, who'd set a trap?

Roxy listened, her heart beating loudly in her chest. Nothing stirred. Cautiously, she entered the compartment and opened the window. In case of trouble, this would be her escape route. She looked toward the fence through which she'd slipped onto the premises, over to the sidings in the marshaling yard.

There was an almost ghostly silence. Not a soul was in sight, either inside or outside the fence.

She locked the entrance door, before she examined the wagon compartment by compartment. Except for one, the others were empty, and the door at the other end was firmly locked. Somewhat reassured, she returned and eyed the items under the bench seat.

Water wasn't the problem, it could always be found. But food was far too precious to ignore. Her stomach rumbled audibly as she looked at the brown wrapping paper. It didn't take long before she reached for it and unwrapped it. Inside was a thick slice of bread, lovingly topped with cheese.

Her mouth watered and moments later her self-control was gone. She bit into the sandwich heartily—after two weeks of living exclusively on pilfered garden vegetables, bread and cheese were a true blessing. A shiver of delight ran through her body. Chewing with joy, she devoured the sandwich down to the last crumb.

Once she had finished eating, she closed the window and walked two compartments further on, where she unlocked the window and made herself comfortable on the bench using her backpack as a pillow. Her fingers felt for the crumpled piece of paper that she'd carried around for almost two years. Shortly after Marek's death, she'd found it in her bag and had curiously unfolded it.

She could see the situation as if it had happened yesterday:

In Marek's handwriting it said: "Nobody does anything for free. If you don't have to pay, you are the payment. Trust usually gets you killed."

Filled with anger, she'd crumpled the note and thrown it onto the street. *What an ass!* Even in death, he wanted to give her instructions. Roxy had walked on, just to turn back a few steps later and fish the note out of the gutter. Almost tenderly, she'd smoothed it while her thoughts drifted to Marek, who had sacrificed himself for her.

Since then, she'd kept the note as a reminder of the good person Marek had been—and as a constant warning not to trust anyone.

Lost in thought, she took the crumpled paper from the outer pocket of her backpack. Defying the wave of sadness washing over her, she swallowed the lump in her throat. Sometimes she missed her family and friends so much that it physically hurt. Not just Marek, but also Tibor, Livia, and Christian. Even Romeo, Aunt Gisela, and the rest of the clan. Yes, even Uncle Gottfried, who'd betrayed her to Kommandant Goslar.

In the evenings, before falling asleep, loneliness often gnawed at her soul and she wished for someone to talk to or to laugh with. Or simply a person she could lean on.

She'd survived alone for two years, always on the move, never staying long in the same place. She'd become a master of climbing façades, stealing food and clothes without getting caught, washing herself in the bathrooms of strangers when they weren't home. In short, she lived like a ghost in the big city of Berlin—visible only to herself and the sporadic strangers with whom she traded things or gathered information.

Roxy yearned to lead a normal life again. She wanted to have a home, family, friends, and regular meals. This train carriage reminded her so much of the wagons of her childhood. Everything she'd lost pressed into her thoughts until tears ran down her cheeks. Eventually, she drifted into a light sleep, ready to flee at any sound, like a wild hare out in the fields.

The next morning, the sentimental emotions had vanished. She couldn't afford feelings. She must never become weak, never trust anyone, must always be on her guard, because one wrong decision could mean death.

She packed her things, erased the traces of her presence and left the carriage before dawn to survive another day. Until someday Hitler's rule would be over and she'd be allowed to be part of the German people again.

Then she would take revenge.

A LETTER FROM MARION

Dear Reader,

Thank you for reading *The Last Train Home*. If you did enjoy it, I'd very much appreciate it if you would review the book on the retailer of your choice. If want to keep up to date with all my latest releases, just sign up at the following link. Your email address will never be shared and you can unsubscribe at any time.

www.bookouture.com/marion-kummerow

If you've read the German Wives series, you're already familiar with Roxy and know that she'll soon meet David in one of the railway wagons and fall in love with him. If you haven't read the series yet, it's best to start with Book One, *The Berlin Wife*.

The independent, unconventional young woman has grown dear not only to me but to many readers as well. I've received numerous messages asking about her life before meeting David, as well as after the war.

As happens for many of my books, the idea for this one came unexpectedly. A few years ago, I visited the very impressive exhibition "Topography of Terror" at the site of the former Gestapo headquarters on Prinz-Albrecht-Strasse in Berlin. In the exhibition catalog, there is a chapter about the persecution of Roma and Sinti. After reading it, Roxy appeared in my mind out of nowhere.

As usual, the historical events in this book actually happened, but the characters are entirely fictional. After the "*Festsetzungserlass*" in October 1939, which prohibited the Roma and Sinti from leaving their current residence, a large number of them were crammed into various camps. The largest of these so-called Gypsy camps was in Berlin-Marzahn, where terrible conditions prevailed.

Similar to the Jews, the Roma and Sinti along with other "Gypsy-like traveling" groups of the population were led to believe they'd be relocated to a better place. By the time nearly three thousand people gathered in the *Fruchtschuppen* warehouse at the Hamburg Harbor, most of them suspected that this promise had been a lie. Why else would they have their valuables and even their identity cards taken away?

From Hamburg Harbor, the journey continued to Belzec, close to the border with the part of Poland that the Soviet Union had annexed at the beginning of the war in September 1939. There the camp inmates were forced to build an anti-tank ditch to secure the German-Soviet border, among other tasks. This work was never completed because Hitler's invasion of the Soviet Union, Operation Barbarossa, made the bulwark unnecessary.

In Belzec many of the inmates, mainly children, died due to the inhumane living conditions. I didn't make up the anecdotes about the sadistic Kommandant Goslar, they come from the eyewitness account of Gottfried Weiss, a Sinti from Hamburg-Harburg.

The real commandant was SS-Sturmbannführer Hermann Dolp, who initially served in the concentration camps at Dachau and Sachsenhausen. In 1939, he was transferred to Kalisch in Poland. He ended up in Belzec due to a punitive transfer: he'd raped a young Polish woman, which was considered racial defilement and was severely punished.

In the fall of 1940, the few surviving inmates of Belzec were transferred to Krychow, presumably to make room in Belzec for newly deported Jews. There are contradictory statements about Krychow. Some sources claim that all prisoners had to perform forced labor, draining the moor.

However, other Polish eyewitness accounts state that this only applied to Jews. According to these accounts, the Roma and Sinti in Krychow were neither guarded nor forced to work. On the contrary, they were allegedly able to move about freely and leave the camp any time they wanted.

What is certain is that in the fall/winter of 1940, the guards abandoned the Krychow camp from one day to the next. The reason remains unknown to this day. Of the previously incarcerated Roma and Sinti, some hid in various Polish cities such as Warsaw or Lublin, while others made their way back to Germany. Most of them were recaptured, deported to other ghettos and camps, until they were eventually murdered. I couldn't find any information about those who remained in the Krychow camp. They were probably also deported to another concentration camp once the guards returned.

In December 1942, the Auschwitz Decree ordered the deportation of "Gypsy half-breeds, Roma Gypsies, and non-German-blooded members of Gypsy clans of Balkan origin" to Auschwitz.

Only a few survived.

Marion Kummerow

KEEP IN TOUCH WITH MARION

www.kummerow.info

facebook.com/AutorinKummerow

x.com/MarionKummerow

instagram.com/MarionKummerow

goodreads.com/MarionKummerow

PUBLISHING TEAM

Turning a manuscript into a book requires the efforts of many people. The publishing team at Bookouture would like to acknowledge everyone who contributed to this publication.

Audio
Alba Proko

Contracts
Peta Nightingale

Commercial
Lauren Morrissette
Hannah Richmond
Imogen Allport

Cover design
Emma Graves

Data and analysis
Mark Alder
Mohamed Bussuri

Editorial
Kelsie Marsden
Nadia Michael

Copyeditor
Jane Eastgate

Proofreader
Liz Hurst

Marketing
Alex Crow
Melanie Price
Occy Carr
Cíara Rosney
Martyna Młynarska

Operations and distribution
Marina Valles
Joe Morris

Production
Hannah Snetsinger
Mandy Kullar
Nadia Michael
Charlotte Hegley

Publicity
Kim Nash
Noelle Holten
Jess Readett
Sarah Hardy

RAISING READERS

Books Build Bright Futures

Dear Reader,

We'd love your attention for one more page to tell you about the crisis in children's reading, and what we can all do.

Studies have shown that reading for fun is the **single biggest predictor of a child's future life chances** – more than family circumstance, parents' educational background or income. It improves academic results, mental health, wealth, communication skills, ambition and happiness.

The number of children reading for fun is in rapid decline. Young people have a lot of competition for their time, and a worryingly high number do not have a single book at home.

Hachette works extensively with schools, libraries and literacy charities, but here are some ways we can all raise more readers:

- Reading to children for just 10 minutes a day makes a difference
- Don't give up if children aren't regular readers – there will be books for them!

- Visit bookshops and libraries to get recommendations
- Encourage them to listen to audiobooks
- Support school libraries
- Give books as gifts

There's a lot more information about how to encourage children to read on our websites: **www.RaisingReaders.co.uk** and **www.JoinRaisingReaders.com**.

Thank you for reading.

Printed in Dunstable, United Kingdom

80576442R00150